Conflict and Commerce on the Rio Grande

Number Twelve: Canseco-Keck History Series
Jerry Thompson, General Editor

Conflict & Commerce on the Rio Grande

Laredo, 1755–1955

John A. Adams, Jr.

Texas A&M University Press
College Station

Texas A&M University Press
College Station

Manufactured in the United States of America

First edition
This paper meets the requirements of ANSI/NISO Z39.48-1992
(Permanence of Paper).
Binding materials have been chosen for durability.
♾♻

Library of Congress Cataloging-in-Publication Data

Adams, John A., 1951–
Conflict and commerce on the Rio Grande : Laredo, 1755–1955 / John A. Adams, Jr. — 1st ed.
p. cm. — (Canseco-Keck history series ; no. 12)
Includes bibliographical references and index.
ISBN-13: 978-1-60344-042-4 (cloth : alk. paper)
ISBN-10: 1-60344-042-9 (cloth : alk. paper)
1. Laredo (Tex.)—Economic conditions. 2. Laredo (Tex.)—History. 3. Commerce—Texas—Laredo. 4. Commerce—Mexican-American Border Region. 5. Mexican-American Border Region—Economic conditions. 6. Rio Grande Valley—History.
I. Title. II. Series.
HC108.L25A33 2008
381.09764'462—dc22

2008012827

To Sherry, John, Calvin, and Mark
who made this possible

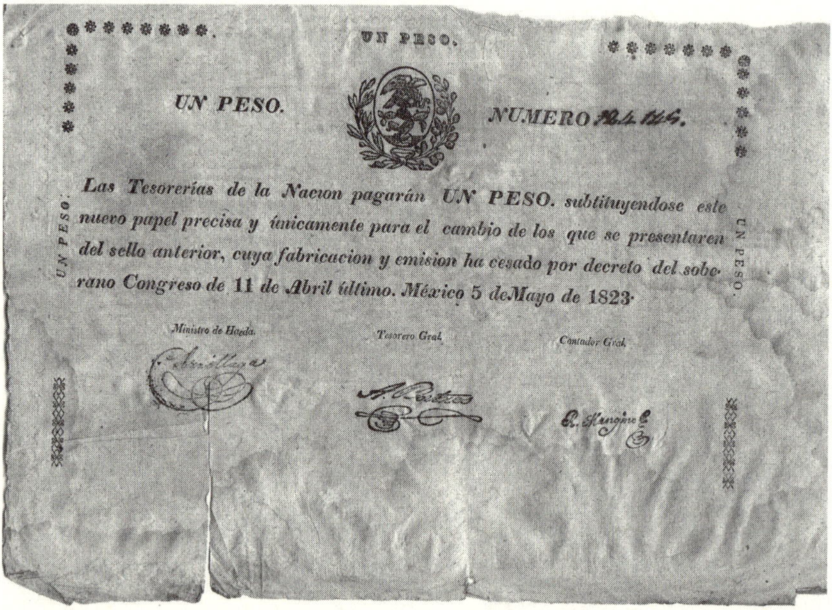

Mexican peso note, ca. 1823. The specie in circulation on the border was primarily silver or gold coin until the 1860s, with the exception of the peso-denominated paper currency first introduced around 1823. In spite of the extensive production of silver in Mexico, these notes were intended to augment a shortage of money in circulation at the time. This Mexico peso note measured 6 × 9 inches and was legal tender for all debts, public and private, throughout Mexico, Texas, and the border region. Source: author's collection

Table of Contents

List of Tables

LIST OF MAPS

LIST OF FIGURES

PREFACE

The vitality and measure of a community are the sum of its evolution and past history, and the legacy of Laredo is the result of this passage of time. Founded and located on the north side, or left bank, of the Río Bravo–Rio Grande in May, 1755, Laredo has been at the crossroads of regional trade since its formative years, and during the past century it has been the primary hub of north-south commerce between the Americas. The history of Laredo is both colorful and distinctive. The formative years on the raw northern frontier of New Spain, followed by development between two nations and numerous efforts at intrigue, honed the city and region into a unique area. Conquistadors, settlers, Indians, soldiers, cattle barons, merchants, coal miners, wildcatters, and bandits, along with border wars, land claim, oil and gas, as well as an environment of consistent drought accented by periods of tumultuous floods all contributed to a dynamic regional culture of nations and languages astride the great river.

The north-south crossing of the Rio Grande at the future site of Laredo had been in use for centuries before the first Spanish exploration in the mid-1500s by the local Indian tribes. The first documented use of the Paso de los Indios, or El Paso de Jacinto, in the bend of the river behind Fort McIntosh was by traders as early as the mid-1740s. Thus, the earliest identification of Laredo was as a major river ford that facilitated north-south trade. The families that settled the high bluff overlooking the river were there for the purpose of forging a new life and gaining access to a vast land in which to raise their families and prosper. Villa de Laredo became the second permanent chartered town settlement in what is now the state of Texas. It was one of the first fledgling settlements within the present border of Texas—including Laredo, San Antonio, La Bahía (Goliad), El Paso, and Nacogdoches—to survive and prosper following the three-hundred-year Spanish colonial period.

The rivalry and drive for globalized commercial markets and territory was in full swing by the late 1700s. National pride did much in the name of commerce to create conflict. Although distances for travel, transport of goods, and communications were long and the routes undeveloped, the intensity of trade in this early period was no less competitive than today's era of globalization marked by instantaneous communications, just-in-time logistics, and near unlimited access to virtually anywhere in the world. And the Rio Grande frontier would emerge as one of pivotal crossroads in the evolution of global commerce.

Throughout history, commerce and trade has held a preeminent role among factors that shape the foundation of communities. In the case of Laredo, the key to growth was at its origin (and continues to be today) the evolving nature of the international business and trade sector. Founded at the prime river ford to cross livestock, one thread of Laredo's history that has run constant over the past 250 years is the ranching industry that was the mainstay of the Laredo economy during its first century. As the strategic town grew, so too did the commercial activities. As a key crossing from New Spain into Texas, the site became one of the leading markets of goods—some for cash and some for barter—with a thriving open-air market along the bank of the river. Ferry service, costing two *reales* per trip, makeshift warehousing, and the movement of goods via pack mules and carts soon followed. By the mid-1800s, the Port of Laredo emerged as a prime shipping point for cotton, tobacco, and imported European-manufactured goods. The arrival of the Texas–Mexican Railway from Corpus Christi to Laredo, followed by industrial tycoon Jay Gould's International and Great Northern Railroad in late 1881 connecting to a line from Mexico City and a rail hub to Dallas, Kansas City, and St. Louis via San Antonio, was hailed across the graphic masthead of the *Laredo Morning Times:* "The Future Great Railroad Centre, and Grand Gateway of International Commerce." The announcement came complete with a visionary drawing of locomotives, trains, and a bridge across the Rio Grande.

By the turn of the twentieth century, Laredo was a booming port of trade, commerce, and financial intermediation as well as the principal facilitator of import-export services on the southern border of the United States—a position maintained to the current day. The growth of downtown Laredo amazed even the local residents, who expressed concern about the incredible growth, with a population in 1900 numbering 13,500. Also, in the early 1900s, the economic landscape dramatically changed with the discovery and exploration of coal, oil, and gas in Webb and Zapata counties. At last, the massive ranches that formed a near-interlocking maze across the region now had a secondary source of income from oil and gas royalties. These monies pumped jobs, new businesses, and investments into the local economy of both the city and state. As years passed, ranching and the oil and gas industry remained a steady underpinning and foundation of the local economy as Laredo emerged from World War II as the leading inland port on the southern border. By the 1980s, Laredo's image was due in large part to the globalization of commerce and the growth of the *maquiladora* or twine plant manufacturing sector in Mexico, driven by consumer demand in both the U.S. and Mexico. As the North American Free Trade Agreement (NAFTA) and World Trade Organization (WTO) of open markets and globalization unfolded, *Los Dos Laredos*—the sister cities of Laredo, Texas, and Nuevo Laredo, Mexico—further expanded to become by 2006 a well-synchronized inland port and merchandise distribution hub with a significant regional commercial financial sector, facilitating cross border growth in South Texas and Mexico.

A number of excellent works about Laredo chronicle the years prior to 1900: Robert D. Wood's *Life in Laredo* (2004) reviews the documents of New Spain from the first one hundred years of the Laredo Archives, and Kathleen Da Camara, in *Laredo on the Rio Grande* (1949), authored a thesis-turned-book. J. B. Wilkinson's *Laredo and the Rio Grande Frontier* (1975) provides a general overview of Laredo from the founding to 1900 and the Mexican Revolution; Gilbert M. Hinojosa, in *A Borderlands Town in Transition: Laredo, 1755–1879* (1983), offers a quantitative analysis of nineteenth-century demographics and social-class relations; and Laredo author Jerry D. Thompson's *Warm Weather and Bad Whiskey: The 1886 Laredo Election Riot* (1991) is a period piece on the political dynamics of Laredo in the late 1800s. This volume is the first comprehensive review to place emphasis on the rise of the commercial underpinnings from the city's founding through the dramatic nineteenth century; it is also a look at the emergence and importance of Laredo as the leading hemispheric cross-border trade center during the twentieth-century. Religious, social-cultural issues, and genealogy aspects, while vital and important, are included only as they pertain to the overall theme of the book.

Given the fact that terminology and language are constantly changing, I have endeavored where possible to preserve the vocabulary of the period in which the terms and spirit of the meaning were used. The language of the period was plain and to the point, which has caused some in our era to somehow transpose current terms and meanings back as if justified to align modern sociopolitical viewpoints. Examples abound with older forms of *frontera* and *margen* referring to the line of *villas*—settlements and towns—along the Rio Grande. Nuevo Laredo was originally Monterrey-Laredo, or Laredo, Mexico, and it was customary to call what became San Antonio by its original moniker, Béxar. It gets a bit more confusing with any clear reference to those who settled the region. Anglo immigrants and settlers were known in historical context as *Americans* or *Europeans,* without regard to color or national origin; while today, *American* has been redefined to include anyone from the North Pole to Tierra del Fuego. Names are also a concern. In Madrid, upon reviewing primary documents actually signed by the Viceroy, his name is two words: Revilla Gigedo, not Revillagigedo as is published in a number of present-day sources. In another example, *Texian* and *Texan,* or Mexican Texans, and the use of the word *Norteños,* confound and confuse researchers and readers as the boundaries and national prerogatives shifted. Thus, to allow the minimum use of [*sic*], all terms and quotations are preserved in the context of their original usage from the period in which they appeared.

As the diversified economies of the region, state, and two bordering nations grew, so too did the fortunes of Laredo. Destined to be under the governance of seven flags, Laredo, through periods of commercial expansion and periods of armed conflict, would etch its own destiny as a truly dynamic community. And little would its founders have guessed that by the third millennium, Laredo would be one of the fastest growing cities in Texas and the nation, as well as one of the world's premier international financial centers and inland commercial ports.

Telling the story of the ranching, commercial activities, urban and industrial growth, and international trade of Laredo from 1755 to 1955, as well as those individuals who made it possible, is the purpose of this work.

Acknowledgments

The history of the Rio Grande borderlands is one of the most fascinating sagas in modern times. Few regions are more dynamic, complex, and packed with personalities and drama than the urban and commercial center of Laredo, Texas. Researching its founding for the specific purpose of cross-border trade, I found myself casting a broad net to explore a vast array of primary and secondary sources. In this pursuit the researcher/author is forever thankful for those individuals and institutions that gave of their time and assistance while compiling the facts for this book.

Laredo has a wealth of knowledgeable devotees to the history of the city and region. First and foremost, Joe Moreno at the Special Collection at the Laredo Public Library provided assistance from the earliest days of my search and proved a valuable sounding board at each turn, as did the staff of the Republic of the Rio Grande Museum on the main plaza in downtown Laredo. The publications, research, and advice of border scholars Jerry Thompson and Stan Green at Texas A&M International University were timely, as well as was the assistance of bibliophile John H. Keck, whose extensive collection of Texana and border documents is a researcher's dream.

Margarita Araiza at the Webb County Historical Foundation provided valuable insight, as did Sam Johnson, Betsy Johnson, Guadalupe Martínez, Joyce L. Keck, Mercurio Martínez Jr., Bill Green, Carlos Villarreal, and Odie Arámbula, editor of the *Laredo Morning Times*. David L. Cardwell, formerly of CPL, Webb County ranchers Jim Winch and Joe Finley, Ivan Rodríguez of the Union Pacific, Laredo Mayor Betty Flores and City Manager Larry Dovalina, Carlos Mejía, David Killam, and Ray Covey also were insightful. The small but valuable special collections at the Texas A&M International University and documents at Laredo Community College were a most helpful surprise find.

In the survey of government documents, I was assisted by Gustavo Guevara, City Secretary of Laredo, and the staff of the Webb County Records Department, which generated a wealth of insight into the public-private dynamics that shaped the emergence of Laredo as the number one commercial trade center on the U.S.-Mexico border.

In Austin, materials identified with the help of Adán Benavides at the Benton Latin America Collection; by Evan Hocker at the Center for American History, formerly named the Barker Texas History Center; and the assistances of Bill Simmons with the primary documents at the Lorenzo de Zavala Texas State Archives in Austin, were enormously helpful. In an especially rare moment, I was able to hold and closely examine both sides of the Travis letter, "To the People of Texas," penned at the Alamo on February 24, 1836. The back side of the letter contained notes and delivery comments, which few historians have even seen, as the letter passed from the Alamo to Sam Houston.

Over an extended period of time, a number of archivists—David L. Chapman and Bill Page of the Texas A&M University Library in College Station; Karen Anson at the Franklin D. Roosevelt Library in Hyde Park, New York; Monte Monroe at the Southwest Collection at Texas Tech University; and in Madrid, Spain, the research staff at the Biblioteca Nacional, providing direct access to the primary documents in the Miguel de Cervantes Collection—were extremely helpful.

I am indebted to colleagues and friends Daniel B. Hastings Jr., David Perez, Henry C. Dethloff, J. Michael Patrick, Armengol Guerra III, Mike Hall, Miguel Conchas, Baldo García, and Rolly Ortiz. Each assisted me in a variety of ways, as did the great friends of the Jacales Junta who keep me humble and focused on the important things in life: Guillermo "Memo" Treviño, David L. Cardwell, Drew Claes, and the late Guadalupe Martínez. Yvette Medina was most helpful in the preparation of the final draft.

Finally, a great debt of thanks goes to Sherry for her ongoing support and encouragement.

John A. Adams, Jr.

Conflict and Commerce on the Rio Grande

CHAPTER 1

LA VILLA DE SAN AGUSTÍN DE LAREDO

> It is situated on the margin of the Río Grande, or Bravo, on the north bank, in a plain two leagues in extent, reaching to the Hills of Sta. Barbara, which meet it, with two arroyos, of which the upper, to the southwest, is called Arroyo de Lomas Altos, and that on the east side, Arroyo Chacón. . . . This settlement is important, and it is expedient that it increase in size, for the sake of the crossing from the interior provinces of Texas.
>
> AGUSTÍN LÓPEZ DE LA CAMARA ALTA
> VILLA DE LAREDO, JULY 23, 1757

THE LAND AND ITS EARLY PEOPLE

In the time before recorded history, the land of current-day South Texas and northern Mexico was very wild and untamed. In the often-harsh semiarid region, the most distinctive feature was the Rio Grande, known to the people of Mexico as the Río Bravo. Named and renamed by the Indians, seamen, conquistadors, and settlers in various sectors of its course, some of the earliest pre-Columbian designations bestowed by the Indians were *posoge, mets'ichi chena,* and *paslapaane,* all meaning big or great river, a name that would stand the test of time. The Great River, or Rio Grande, flows from its snow-fed headwaters at 12,000 feet above sea level in the present-day southeastern portion of Colorado in the cradle of the Sangre de Cristo Mountains. The river cuts a clear path southward past Taos and Santa Fe, through New Mexico's high desert, and at El Paso del Norte gradually turns southeastward in its flow past the Big Bend area to the Gulf of Mexico. As the explorers and adventurers of the 1500s and 1600s crossed the river in numerous locations, the Rio Grande quickly became the defining physical geographical feature and reference point as the *audiencia* of New Spain gauged the extent of its ability to control the northern reaches of the Spanish colonial borderlands.[1]

Except for isolated settlements at Santa Fe (ca. 1609), San Antonio de Béxar (1718), La Bahía (1721), and Nacogdoches (1721), Spanish efforts failed to define, defend, and occupy regions and rivers north of the Rio Grande. As one historian noted, "within the present day United States, the Spanish regime proved singularly inept and inert." A key example was the unsuccessful early efforts to establish the Nueces River as a key line of demarcation on the northern reaches of New Spain. Occupation of the uncharted and harsh land would define efforts among many to tame the region. As for Laredo, it would in time become one of the few early settlements—*villas del norte*—founded north of the Great River to survive the colonial period; it is the second oldest continuously occupied community in what is today Texas. The roots of the community predate recorded history.[2]

In the era prior to the arrival of Columbus—the late postclassic period, from ca. A.D. 1300 to 1520, the grand Aztec nation centered at Tenochtitlán (the current-day location of Mexico City) had either conquered or entered into trading alliances with the Indian nations and bands spanning an area from present-day Panama to the Gran Chichimeca at the northern lands of the Río Bravo—Rio Grande—down to the river delta on the Gulf of Mexico.[3] The imperial nation was the grand seat of power—all roads led to the Aztec capital. The enormous city, built on and around a series of lakes, was noted for vast hanging gardens, aqueducts, large markets, and decorative temples; it was larger than any European city of that time. The region of the central Mexican plateau boasted a population in 1500 that has been estimated to exceed 25 million.[4] Under the rule of Axayacatl (1469–81) and Ahuizotl (1486–1502), the Aztec empire had conquered its many rivals, expanded trade, and was at the zenith of its power. In 1503, Moctezuma Xocoyotzin, son of Axayacatl, began a reign that would end with the entry of Hernán Cortez and over five hundred Castilian soldiers and sixteen horses (the first ever seen in the New World) into Tenochtitlán on November 19, 1519.[5] In the years prior to the arrival of the Spaniards, trade, not war, was the focus of the empire. The merchants, or *pochteca,* were among the most powerful groups in the Aztec society. In his famed chronicle of ancient Mexico, William H. Prescott exalted the role of the trader-merchant:

> The Aztec merchant was a sort of itinerant trader, who made his journeys to the remotest borders of Anahuac, and to the countries beyond, carrying with him merchandise of rich stuffs, jewelry, slaves, and other valuable commodities. With this rich freight, the merchants visited the different provinces, always bearing some present of value from his own sovereign to their chiefs, and usually receiving others in return, with a permission to trade. Thus their sphere of action was much enlarged beyond that of a humble trader, and they acquired a high consideration in the body politic.[6]

The lingua franca of the Aztec Empire, Nahuatl, emerged from scores of dialects to link the region both as a political and commercial unit. Descendants of these same people were the vanguard of the Tenochtitlán settlers who joined the Spaniards in the 1500s to establish the key northern communities of Monterrey, Saltillo, and Monclova. The Nahuatl legacy remains with us today in native languages. More than 1.5 million farmers in Guerrero and in the southern highlands of Mexico consider this their primary language. Many Nahuatl words are passed down for use in our daily lexicon—tomato, chocolate, coyote, ocelot, and tamale. The goods traded within the vast Aztec empire served not only as much-desired items, but in an age of barter also as a store of value or currency. Among the most traded items in a well-organized market network were bows, flint arrowheads, pottery (of which very little has survived), sea shells, quills of gold dust, cocoa and mescal beans, hides and pelts, salt, and pecans, as well as the highly coveted obsidian, jadeite, and turquoise. In the flow of overland trade, legend maintains that those who traded in the north crossed by way of one of the many corridors on the Great River of the north at "el paso de los Indios"—a low-water ford destined to become the crossroads and gateway for international commercial trade—in time to be known as Laredo.[7]

During this period, long before the arrival of European explorers, the vast arid region bordering the Rio Grande was home to nomadic Indians roaming the region in small autonomous bands. These people were never fully a tribe and never stationary in the land they never tamed. Shaped by the harsh, arid environment, the Indians—the Coahuiltecas, Jumanos, Tonkawas, Kickapoos, Kesale-Terkodams, Carrizos, Tamaulipas (Tamique), Karankawas, and the Apache Lipan—survived on a bleak diet of birds, lizards, deer, rabbits, ants, javelinas, and rattlesnakes. These primary tribes were linked to one another due to the common thread of the Coahuiltecan linguistic family. Thus, the Coahuiltecans, or sometimes called the Tejano tribe, dominated the region southward from the Nueces River into current-day northern Mexico. From this main tribe an enormous number—over 215—of smaller tribes or bands occupied the region. The Coahuiltecans numbered an estimated 15,000 in 1690. In 1886, only a few descendants were identified on the south side of the Rio Grande, yet they could no longer speak the native ancient tongue. And today, none of the Indians of the greater Coahuiltecan tribes are known to survive in Texas.[8]

The ways of the local Indians would have a direct impact on the settlement of the rugged region. One key legacy to those who confronted the indigenous inhabitants has long been the ability to survive off the harsh land. While fish could be found in the rivers, the lack of plentiful wild game forced many to depend on the staples of the land—mesquite beans, sotol bulbs, prickly pear, peyote, and an array of potent drinks, to include *atollé* from maize, chocolate drinks, and *mezcal. El maguey* or *agave Americana* was to prove a useful native species.[9] The *cajeta,* or heart, of the plant yields *aguamiel,* or wort, which when fermented becomes a strong intoxicant known as pulque. One observer traveling in Mexico in the early 1870s noted, the milky white fluid is "put into ox-skins. A little of the old pulque is added for fermentation and the new made worse."[10] The popular drink dating from ancient times was known as *octli* (akin to a strong beer) and played a major role in Aztec rituals. In a separate process, the steeped *cajeta* when distilled produces an "aromatic kind of spirituous liquor" that is clear as pure water—mescal. Additionally, the *quiote,* or stalk, of the plant is cut and baked, and, like sugar cane, is good to chew. And to further mark its multiple uses, the leaves of the maguey yield a fine white fiber called *ixtle,* which has many uses as thread to make mats, ropes, and brushes.[11] The juice of the leaves was considered an excellent "antiscorbutic for old sores and scorbutus diseases," and furthermore maguey was considered to have "great superiority" over lime juice in effecting a cure for scurvy. Confirmation of the healing powers of the maguey was documented by Army surgeon Glover Perin at Fort McIntosh on the outskirts of Laredo in 1851; he conducted what may have been the first limited scientific analysis of the age-old plant.[12]

The maguey was not the only native plant of distinction. Discarded in modern times as an obnoxious tree, the mesquite yielded a crop of beans that were high in protein and of great value to the Coahuiltecans. Considered sweet and nutritious, the beans were dried, crushed by stone into flour, and mixed with berries and pulverized bones to create what the Spaniards called *mezquitamal.* In a region short of wood, the mesquite would prove a primary source of firewood and fence post material. Notwithstanding, most travelers not hardened by the environs avoided this inhospitable and arid semidesert region south of the Balcones Escarpment, known in later years as the *brasada*—Brush Country—or the *monte.*[13] In the classic work, *The Indians of Texas,* W. W. Newcomb Jr. concluded: "Few areas in North America were more difficult for hunters and gatherers to exploit or yield more stubbornly its niggardly harvest than the brush and cactus country of South Texas."[14] An unknown author penned this view of the Rio Grande–Brush Country region:

Paradise in Texas

The devil was given permission one day
To make him a land for his own special sway.
He put thorns on all the bushes and trees
And mixed up the sand with millions of fleas.
He scattered tarantulas along the roads,
Put spines on the cactus and horns on the toads.

He lengthened the horn of the Texas steer
And added a foot to the jack rabbit's ear.
He put three devils in every bronco steed
And poisoned the feet of the centipede.
The rattlesnakes bites you, the scorpion stings,
The mosquito torments you buzzing his wings.
The heat in the summer is a hundred and ten,
Too hot for the devil and too hot for men.
And all who remained in that climate soon bore
Cuts, bites, stings, scratches, and blisters galore.[15]

Las Entradas

The bleakness of daily life along the Rio Grande—Río Bravo or the Río del Norte—is vividly chronicled by the wandering and lost Spanish explorer Alvar Núñez Cabeza de Vaca. For eight years from 1528 to 1536 he—and the few survivors of all ill-fated expedition across the Gulf of Mexico—lived as a captive, surviving on his wits as a trader and would-be shaman and medicine man among a number of South Texas Indian bands.[16] In time, Cabeza de Vaca and his three companions became legends among the many Coahuiltecan and Jumano tribes. This group of four strangers and a few survivors of the Narváez Expedition of the late 1520s became the only contact the Indians of the region had with Spaniards until the mid-seventeenth century.[17]

Cabeza de Vaca survived to wander naked out of the wilderness along the reaches of the Rio Grande, crisscrossing the river near the future site of Laredo, to the *paso del norte* (near current-day El Paso) and back to Mexico City, where he recorded his ordeal.[18] He noted in his account, the *Relación,* tremendous details of his experience, which included numerous sightings of "cattle" and the fine taste of their meat. What he actually saw and recorded was the earliest known description of buffalo (bison) in North America:

> It seems to me they are about the size of the ones in Spain. They have two small horns, like Moorish cattle, and very long hair, like a fine blanket made from wool of the merino sheep. Some are brownish and others black. It seems to me that they have more and better meat than cattle here in Spain. From the small ones the Indians make blankets to cover themselves, and from the large ones they make shoes [moccasins] and shields. These animals come from the North all the way to the coast, where they scatter, crossing the land for more than four hundred leagues. All along the range, through the valleys where they roam, people who live near there descend to live off them, and take inland a great quantity of their hides.[19]

The land and its native people would change little in the years between the wanderings of Cabeza de Vaca and the arrival of the Spanish *entradas* (or overland expeditions), conquistadores, and settlers in the northern reaches of New Spain, or Mexico-Texas. However, the Spaniards had grander desires beyond the mere exploitation of buffalo. Adam Smith in the *Wealth of Nations,* printed in 1776 (and rejoined by David Ricardo in *The Principles of Political Economy and Taxation,* printed in 1817), concluded, "every Spaniard who sailed to America expected to find Eldorado."[20] The Spanish quest for riches was driven by a legend dating from medieval times of glories of wealth to be found in the "Seven Cities of Cíbola."[21] The earliest efforts of the *audiencia* (governing counsel) were directed to the development of the central portions of Mexico and a string of seaports on both the Gulf of Mexico and the Pacific Ocean to facilitate the trans-shipment of galleons of gold and silver to the mother country. The yield of the silver mines of Taxco, Zumpango, Tlalpujahua, Zacatecas, and Guanajuato far exceeded the wildest dreams of the Spanish. Silver forever changed the financial underpinnings of the European markets to become the primary source of funding for the armies and navies of the Spanish Crown. Thus, emerging as the premier producer of silver, the riches of Mexico were the engine that helped shape global trade to include the continental commercial struggles of Europe throughout a period from 1530 to independence in the Americas in 1821 as well as the trans-Pacific "Acapulco ships" galleon trade that "helped establish the Mexican peso as the major underpinning of the Chinese currency."[22] For nearly three centuries, silver accounted for some three-quarters of Mexico's merchandise exports. And to the present day, Mexico remains the primary supplier of the world's silver.[23]

From the seat of centralized power in Mexico City, the land to the far north—the future region of the borderlands, or *la frontera*—had failed to yield the fabled riches so coveted in the myth of the golden cities to the north. Expedition after expedition was organized to promote and pursue the greater glory of Spain with three objectives: gold, God, and glory. Thus the goal was to lay claim to the land in the name of the Spanish Crown, find gold and silver, and spread the word of God by way of converting the Indians as well as establishing a string of missions in all parts of the empire. Ironically, precious feathers, jade, chocolate, and turquoise—not gold and silver—were held in high esteem by the Aztecs and native people of Mexico. Victor D. Hanson, in *Carnage and Culture,* noted: "So bewildered were they by the conquistadores' incessant demands for gold that the Indians of Mexico at first believed the Castilians' ruse that they needed the metal as medicine for 'their hearts'; some more thoughtful Aztecs believed that the Spanish even ate the silly gold dust!" Not until the arrival of the Spaniards did the Indians have a means for the large-scale smelting of ore. Between 1522 and

1650, 180 tons of gold and 16,000 tons of silver bullion were shipped from Mexico and Peru to Spain—representing a quarter of all imperial Spanish revenue. Thus, in an epoch history of the South Texas–Mexico border, Virgil Lott and Mercurio Martínez, in *The Kingdom of Zapata,* noted that the early Spaniards, "were gold-seeking people who cared nothing at all for agricultural lands."[24]

In time, the Spanish realized the only means to a quick, dramatic path to riches in the north was to broaden the occupation and settlement of the region. In the 1600s, the government of Spain was often challenged on the high seas but seldom on the frontier of its New World territories. The lone notable exception was the effort by René-Robert Cavelier, Sieur de La Salle and his small party of Frenchmen in 1685–86. While in the search for the Mississippi River, La Salle walked from Fort St. Louis on the Lavaca River near Matagorda Bay to the Rio Grande and, coincidently, like Cabeza de Vaca, also crossed the river near the future site of Laredo. The wanderings of La Salle energized the French interest in both the Mississippi River valley and in northern New Spain. Reports of the survivors of La Salle's second expedition resulted in cartographer Nicolas de Fer in Paris etching a copper-engraved map of the Southwest in 1705: "*Cette Carta de Californie et du Nouveau Mexique,*" with the Rio Grande prominently noted and labeled "*Río del Norte y del Nuevo Mexico.*" The French government in 1712 claimed that, in addition to Louisiana, it was eager to consolidate its "rights" and the eventual possession of all the lands that comprise current-day Texas to the Rio Grande. Frenchman La Salle's and Louisiana trader Louis Juchereau de St. Denis's visit in the summer of 1714 to the San Juan Bautista Mission (founded January 1, 1700, at the present-day site of Guerrero, Coahuila) was cause for renewed alarm in New Spain. An early account of the competition noted, "The great object [of the French] was to get possession of the rich mines in the interior of Mexico, and to prosecute a trade with the inhabitants." St. Denis returned to the Rio Grande with a horde of questionable merchandise and is credited with being one of the earliest adventurers to make contraband trade a way of life on the borders of Spanish Texas. Thus, given the fact that Spain had no viable settlements dedicated to regional trade north of present-day Monterrey, Mexico, the French endeavored to entice the Spaniards with illicit trade and were eager to cut off and control what they called "Old Mexico."[25]

Notwithstanding French claims north of the Rio Grande, this period of isolation from the rest of the world allowed colonial New Spain to develop a solid hold on central Mexico. The gradual migration of the Spanish to the north of New Spain took on a new urgency with the formation of a group known as the *junta de guerra* and the formal organization of the provinces of "Texas and Coahuila." In the absence of the quick and glorious road to mineral riches, the government in Mexico City reacted by consolidating and controlling trade, increasing tax collection, and protecting its imperial strategic needs on the frontier, first with the positioning of armed garrisons, and second with the establishment of numerous churches or missions. These efforts to fortify and occupy Texas under the direction of Capt. Domingo Ramón were partially realized by 1715.[26]

The provinces of northeast New Spain bordering the Rio Grande were Nuevo Mexico, Nueva Vizcaya (Chihuahua), Nueva Estremadura (Coahuila), and Nuevo Reino de León (Nuevo León). These provinces were viewed in Mexico City as the inhospitable "frontier buffer," and were a no-man's-land viewed as wild with savage tribes and only sparse means to sustain life. These organized and highly structured efforts, or *entradas,* by the viceroy of New Spain and the Spanish Crown to expand and control the territory were placed in the hands of a select few appointed loyalists of the colony. This elite cadre of functionaries of the colonial government was recruited from either the wealthiest families or from the upper ranks of the military. They were trusted for their unquestioned loyalty, their ability to bear arms, their dedication to spread the Catholic faith, and their proven abilities to obtain results. To accept such an obligation was to require the nominee to relocate with family, servants, livestock, and possessions to the uncharted north. The lure for the loyalist was the promise of nearly unlimited land.[27]

Don Tomás Sánchez

From the day of its founding to the present, Laredo has been impacted by global geopolitical forces created far from its present South Texas location on the Rio Grande. The expansion of worldwide trade as nations dueled for control of new lands and markets, and the shift in the wealth of nations due to the surge of silver and gold riches—by the early 1700s flowing into European coffers from Mexico, Peru, and Brazil—fueled the engines of change. Also, religious zeal to identify and convert new peoples to the Catholic Church was a driving force. The mounting competition resulted in tremendous tension among the nations of Europe. The Rio Grande frontier seemed an unlikely place for Spain to draw the line, and thus, as one observer notes, a great deal was at stake on a global scale: "As the eighteenth century advanced, the balance of power in Europe became increasingly dependent upon the power achieved in America, the result in large measure of growing colonial maturity, strength, and prosperity. The trade with each colonial empire in the New World became important not only in relationship to the trade in its European parent, but also in relationship to the combined commerce of the European powers. Mercantilists had always held that trade resembled a pie, the size of the wedge obtained by a particular country determining its power."[28]

The three-way tug-of-war power struggle between England, Spain, and France would intensify after the 1713 Peace of Utrecht. This treaty marked the end of the War of the Spanish Succession. At stake were the control of the high seas, the quest for colonial possessions, and the balance of power in Europe that would entangle the three nations in what amounted to a global war. The English were located on the upper east coast of the Atlantic seaboard, and eager to challenge Spanish territorial claims to the area soon to be known as Georgia and Florida, while the French were positioned in the lower reaches of the Mississippi River valley and eastern Canada. The Spanish Crown's concern was thus intensified over their claim in northern New Spain—stretching from the Texas Gulf Coast westward across the present-day location of the U.S. Southwest extending to the Pacific Ocean. The viceroy and officials in Mexico City, under direct orders from Madrid, moved from purely an exploration phase to adapting an aggressive plan to occupy and populate their northern claims.[29]

The open and vast territory north of the Pánuco River was named the province of Nuevo Santander, as was the custom, after a northern coastal province in Spain. The Viceroy of New Spain, Don Juan Francisco de Güemes y Horcasitas, 1st Count of Revilla Gigedo (r. 1746–55), moved swiftly to appoint José de Escandón y Helguera to organize and lead a formative effort to secure the northern reaches, known as the *Seno Mexicano.* Escandón had been a loyal soldier of the Spanish Crown since the age of fifteen and had risen in the ranks to *corregidor* of Querétaro. During the late 1730s and early 1740s, Escandón had established an impressive string of villas—new towns—and missions in central Mexico aimed at achieving better organization and oversight of the native population. In the process, he had established over a dozen villas in the eastern mountain region of Mexico, for which he was rewarded with the title of El Conde de la Sierra Gorda and appointed lieutenant governor and captain general of the Seno Mexicano.[30] While the level of his knowledge of emerging global rivalries in the Americas is unknown, Escandón's next assignment was to move with haste to reconnoiter, pacify, occupy, and insure a foothold on New Spain's northern frontier up to and beyond the Rio Grande–Río Bravo. In advance of this movement northward, Escandón outlined in detail the objectives desired:

> It is our purpose to explore, pacify, and settle the unknown lands that now form a sort of bay lying between Tampico, Pánuco, Villa de los Valles, Custodia del Río Verde, Nuevo Reynosa de León, and the Bahía del Espíritu Santo—the general reconnaissance of this area can only be practiced by a general entrada. . . . The general point of the lands to be explored lies more or less halfway between Tampico and Bahía del Espíritu Santo, in the vicinity of the mouth of the Rio Grande del Norte.[31]

In January 1749, Escandón launched the most extensive survey to that date of the lands between the Rio Grande and Río Nueces. In the process his scouting parties mapped the region, identified possible sites for towns, and surveyed the indigenous Indian population. His efforts dispelled a persistent notion that the Río Nueces flowed into the Rio Grande. Instead, Escandón confirmed it emptied into a well-protected bay on the Gulf of Mexico—the site for the town of Corpus Christi a century later. By the mid-1700s, mining operations in the area of Monterrey helped spawn a series of small towns and missions that would be staging areas for the movement north. Escandón turned next to the Rio Grande to establish a number of towns along the bank of the river—Camargo (March 5, 1749), Reynosa (March 19, 1749), Mier (March 6, 1753), Nuestra Señora de los Dolores (August 27, 1750), and Revilla (October 10, 1750) (renamed Guerrero in 1827). To colonize the inhospitable frontier, settlers were enticed by *sitios de ganado mayor,* or free land grants, "to be used in common," money to relocate, and the waiver of taxes for ten years. By 1756, Escandón was credited with establishing twenty-four settlements and eighteen missions in the Colony of Nuevo Santander, with only two sites within the present border of Texas—Dolores and Laredo.[32]

The second wave of settlement was planned to be north of the Rio Grande. The Indian influence as the Spanish pushed northward was more pronounced and organized due to the Spanish colonizers' encroachment on ancestral hunting grounds. From experience, Escandón knew the prime means to gain a foothold was to take active possession of the land. Thus, in 1749 the mission of La Bahía was founded at the present-day location of Goliad, Texas, and construction of the Béxar mission was begun at San Fernando de Espada on the San Antonio River in 1751. However, finding no suitable sites along the Nueces, additional efforts north of the Rio Grande stalled. Escandón's efforts now focused on the northern bank of the Rio Grande. For some two decades, Spanish ranchers in the province south of the Rio Grande had routinely grazed their cattle, sheep, and horses on the northern side of the river. In these efforts they had established small ranchos, none with title to the land, at Dolores, San Ygnacio, Carnestolendas (Rio Grande City), and Corralitos. For example, the hacienda of Dolores was the domain of José Vásquez Borrego, occupied by two-dozen families of laborers and herders. In response, Escandón allowed these sites to be recognized de facto, and the claims were reverted to documented land grants with full tax exemption. Little more than a few dirt-floor huts, or *jacales,* existed at each location, yet this was the beginning of organized settlement of the north bank of the Rio Grande. However, Escandón remained eager to move farther north and colonize the Nueces River valley.[33]

The new settlements along the Rio Grande gradually attracted more settlers to the region as well as increased attention from travelers from Monterrey and Mexico City to La Bahía and San Antonio de Béxar—some fifty leagues or 147 miles north of the river. The river crossings increased at Dolores yet proved difficult until shifted to the shallow limestone ford ten miles upstream at a bend in the river known as El Paso de los Indios. In the early 1750s, this low-water crossing was a prime feature that attracted a forty-six-year-old hacendado, or cattle baron, named Tomás Sánchez de la Barrera y Gallardo [Garza] to the region in order to locate additional grazing areas for his herds. The river ford, or *el paso,* well known to the indigenous Indians, was "rediscovered" in about 1746 by Spanish patrol leader Tomás Jacinto de León and soldiers of the presidio of San Juan Bautista del Rio Grande while on a reconnaissance and resupply trip. The Río Bravo crossing was cited as the future "highway" for north-south travel. No permanent rancho or villa had yet been established on either side; however, the new crossing was a significant find, resulting in future expeditions bypassing the Paso de Francia (French Crossing) near San Juan Bautista and the present-day Eagle Pass, Texas, "in favor of a safer" and more direct path at Paso de Jacinto.[34]

In his continuing search for abundant water and grazing lands, Sánchez gained the endorsement of José Vásquez Borrego, a close protégé of Escandón and captain of the small ranching community of Hacienda de Dolores. Sánchez also gained an audience with Escandón to determine the procedure for settlement or use of additional land. In 1753 and again in late 1754, Sánchez, then forty years old, met with El Conde at Revilla to outline his plans and convey his willingness to both fund the development of a new site and assist with the location of families to the north side of the river. Escandón's first response was that he was still very eager to establish settlers in permanent locations and was "desirous of peopling el Río de las Nueces" valley and thus, required that Sánchez first explore a location along the Nueces some seventy miles distant from the Rio Grande. The survey of the Nueces area proved unsatisfactory to Sánchez. On his journey, he found no suitable site and was constantly harassed by Lipan Apaches, keen to protect their hunting grounds.

Generally narrow, the flatland river, without water in times of prolonged drought, would fuel a century-long international boundary dispute until 1848. Notwithstanding, Sánchez returned to the Rio Grande and reported his findings. Upon a second appeal to Escandón, he was granted fifteen *sitios* (sites) *de ganado mayor,* equal to about 66,246 acres, for grazing lands on the Rio Grande. He was also charged to establish a town, or villa, which was originally named for the river ford, Paso de Jacinto de León. However, Don Escandón soon named the new settlement, little more than a few huts and a small ranch, after a town on the Bay of Biscay in his native northern

Table 1.1. First official border census, 1757

Settlement	*Founded*	*Inhabitants*	*Indians*	*Livestock*
Reynosa	March 19, 1749	289	200	16,000
Camargo	May 5, 1749	637	243	81,000
Mier	March 6, 1753	195	150	44,000
Revilla*	October 10,1750	357	0	50,000
Dolores	August 27, 1750	115	2	8,000
Laredo	May 15, 1755	85	0	10,000

Source: José Tienda de Cuervo, 1757
*Later renamed Guerrero

Spanish province—Laredo.[35] Thus, La Villa de San Agustín de Laredo (a name he had first used in 1747 after visiting a small Indian Village near the present-day location of the plaza) was christened on May 15, 1755, on the barren northern banks overlooking the Rio Grande. During the summer the families and settlers moved to this new location, while Sánchez and Escandón agreed to a proposal in early June on the new villa. Escandón confirmed their agreement with the Marques de las Armarillas in Mexico City on August 7, 1755.[36] Tomas Sánchez and his wife Doña Catalina Uribe moved three families from Dolores to Laredo, a total of about thirty persons including his nine children and seven family servants.

Although appointed to the rank of captain by Escandón, Don Tomás Sánchez was first and foremost a rancher. His secondary duties included administration of the fledgling town of Laredo and leading the local (yet unorganized) civilian militia. Unlike most other villas of Nuevo Santander, Laredo during its formative years had neither a mission site for a church nor a formal military presidio or garrison. For special occasions, baptism, and monthly communions, a priest was dispatched from Dolores or Revilla, some twelve leagues distance. Early Laredo was little more than a grouping of crude huts. Short of lumber, building materials literally came from the land. The most prominent structures, prior to the use of stone and brick, were the one-room *jacales,* constructed with a series of slender, unhewn mesquite or bamboo (*carrizo*) posts laced together with reeds or rawhide in vertical rows and covered with a thatched roof to provide shelter. Over time the *jacales* were replaced by adobe structures of mud and straw followed by stone construction. Makeshift adobe ovens were built near the dwellings to serve for baking bread or drying beef into jerky.[37]

In large measure the Laredo ranching community, which quickly grew to

Table 1.2. Inhabitants of the Villa de Laredo, July 1757

Families	*Persons*	*Horse Stock*	*Mules*	*Yokes*	*Sheep and Goats*	*Cattle*
Captain Don Tomás Sánchez, married to Doña Catherina Uribe, seven servants	20	500	125	2	2,000	50
Don Juan Garcia Saldivar, married to Doña Catherina de las Casas, two servants	4				250	
Don Prudencio Garcia, married to Doña Josepha Sanchez	7				740	
Don Joseph Leonardo Treviño, married to Doña Anna Moreno	8	60			700	10
Juan Fran'co Garcia, married to Maria Ritas	9	25			600	
Don Juan Baptista Sanchez, married to Doña Juana Diaz	12				500	4
Don Aug'n Sanchez, married to Doña Fran'ca Rodriguez	4				700	
Leonardo Sanchez, single	2	27			500	
Don Joseph Flores, married	5	30			740	1
Joseph Diaz, single; and mother	2				730	92
Joseph Ramon married to Doña Maria Gertrudis	4	30			200	
Leonardo Garcia, single	1	25			400	
Don Joseph Salinas, married to Ysayvel Treviño	3	15			400	3
Pedro Salinas, single; mother and sister	3				200	
Juan Diego, single	1	12				4
Total	85	712	125	2	9,080	101

Source: José Tienda de Cuervo

ten families, lived and worked to assist Don Tomás with his herd of 2,000 sheep and goats, over 500 range horses, 70 saddle horses, 125 mules, 30 burros, and 50 cattle. Isolated from the center of colonial political power, Herbert Bolton notes, Sánchez "was a veritable medieval lord."[38] To assist the movement of livestock across the river, a second ford, El Paso de Miguel de la Garza, was discovered a few miles south of Villa de Laredo. The two river crossings at Laredo in time became the primary fords, surpassing the Paso de Francia eighty miles upriver near San Juan Bautista. Others in the town owned and worked livestock, yet not until later years did commercial activities in Laredo broaden away from the predominant ranching roots. One critical aspect of Laredo's agrarian beginnings was the lack of water for irrigation. Located high on the bluff, there were few wells and cisterns, and no means to pipe water. Paul Horgan, in *Great River,* noted that for the early Indians, prior to the arrival of the Spanish, "Corn was the staff of life for the river people." However, in the case of the early Laredo settlers, corn planted in the area above the river fared poorly. The mean annual rainfall was 16.6 inches. The only semisustainable agriculture was in the *vega,* or bottomland, along the river, and even then such crops were always susceptible to the whims of the rising river.[39]

The formal written records generated by and for the viceroy and his administrators in Saltillo and Mexico City were a unique aspect of the Spanish frontier. Records of official decrees and "surveys," or inspections of the region, were carefully chronicled, thus leaving a wealth of primary data. Scarcely two years after the Sánchez claim to Laredo, a formal inspection, or "commission," was dispatched to the border by Viceroy Agustín Ahumada y Villalón, Marqués de las Amarillas (r. 1755–60). In late July 1757, eager to gauge the scope and status of this distinct region, Don José Tienda de Cuervo, titled Knight of the Order of Santiago, Captain of Dragoons of the City of Vera Cruz, and Judge Inspector of the Gulf of Mexico, was sent to interview and catalog data on the settlements of the region. Assisting Cuervo in what amounted to the first census of the six Rio Grande villas of Reynosa, Camargo, Mier, Dolores, Revilla, and Laredo was a young engineer, Agustín López de la Camara Alta. Noting that the six border settlements had a combined population of some 2,200 Spaniards and friendly Indians, the carefully described details of the inspector's report proved a gold mine of data and firsthand impressions that were forwarded to the central government in Mexico City and the Crown in Madrid. Many years following, scholars of the Mexican colonial period as well as the Texas-Mexico borderlands also relied on these data.[40]

In addition to his inspection of the small Villa de Laredo, Cuervo conducted three separate interviews, one with Sánchez, and the final two with Juan Eusebio Treviño and Juan Bautista Sánchez. The villa had grown to

Table 1.3. Merchandise and products traded at the border, 1760–80

Domestic Products		*Imported Items*	
salt	tallow	flour	sugar
jerked meat	beef fat	cloth	chocolate
dried meat	hides	tools	tobacco
pulque	wool	paper	wine
candles	leather products	lumber	medicine

Source: Laredo Archives

eleven families by 1757, totaling eighty-five residents. The Spanish frontier historian Herbert Bolton concluded that the three principal family heads had substantially the same observations with few exceptions. If there was any question as to the priorities of the ranchers, Sánchez confirmed to the royal commission, "breeding and the keeping of sheep, goats, and cattle" were the only endeavors of Laredo. In clear words, he stated that Laredo was a trading community limited only by the amount of land Sánchez had been given use of to expand his herds and breeding stock. Within two years of the founding, Sánchez had increased his holdings to over 800 horses, 100 cattle, and over 10,000 sheep and goats. Cuervo noted, "he [Sánchez] is certain they could maintain themselves, because of the great amount of traffic which they have in them, some selling them here, and others taking them to other parts."[41] The early success of the Villa of Laredo, flanked by two strategic river fords, quickly led to the decline and demise of the once bigger ranching community of Dolores about ten leagues downriver. Laredo was destined to be the primary regional ranching and trading center in South Texas and northern Mexico. Hence, the Sánchez settlement launched Laredo as the gateway to regional trade, and the town served from that time forward as a critical crossroads of commerce, connecting over time the heart of New Spain with San Antonio de Béxar, La Bahía, and Nacogdoches in the far northeast of the colonial empire.[42]

Ranching

Don Tomás did not discard farming, but was very clear that while he felt the land was rich in minerals for crops, the intense heat and lack of proper irrigation left few alternatives to ranching. Thus, the primary mainstays of Laredo through the late 1700s were ranching and auxiliary business enterprises. The political, social, and economic impact of ranching was proving

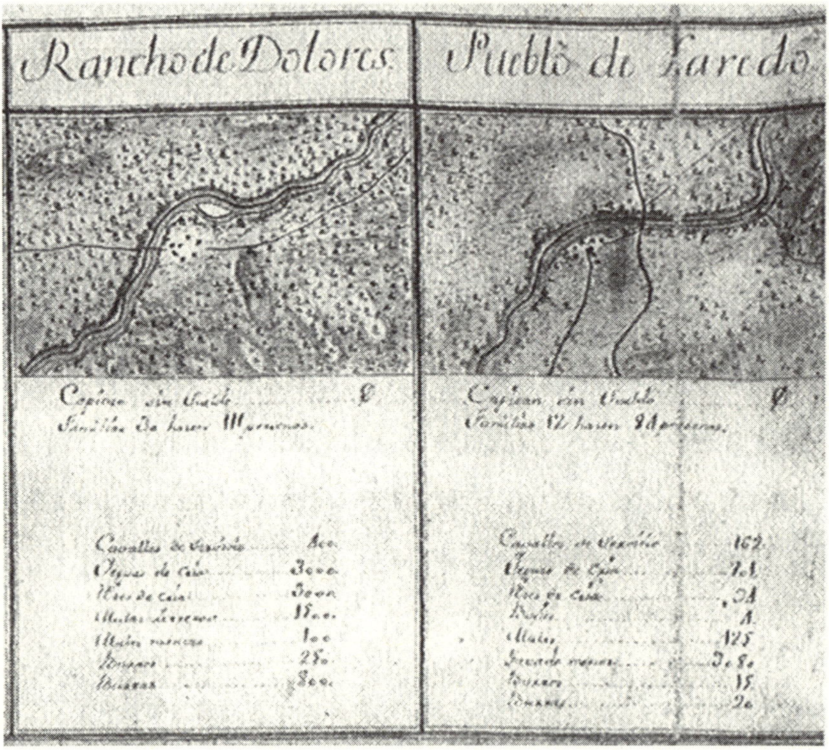

Map 1.1. Rancho de Dolores and Pueblo de Laredo. Courtesy British Library. The Pueblo de Laredo and the downriver Rancho de Dolores were penned by Don Agustín López in 1758 to capture both the topographical features of each location as well as census and general livestock data of the period. Laredo, given its location at a fordable strategic crossing, would in time become the primary trading community in the region.

to be pivotal in gaining a foothold for Spain on the open frontier. Sheep, cattle, hogs, and horses were all imported by the Spanish into central Mexico and gradually moved northward. In this era before barbed wire, the raising of livestock was truly an open range operation, and thus, Sánchez amassed one of the largest haciendas in New Spain. In addition to the goal of occupation of the land and the establishment of villas, the lure for new settlers was directly related to access to large amounts of free grass. A diamond-shaped area formed by the four points of San Antonio, Old Indianola at Matagorda Bay, Brownsville, and Laredo was termed by Walter P. Webb "the cradle of the Western cattle business, an incubator in which throve and multiplied Mexican longhorns."[43]

The harsh land needed not only strong settlers but also hardy livestock that could both survive and thrive in the semiarid region. While sheep, goats, burros, and horses grew in numbers, the mainstay to the ranching growth in South Texas was the famed longhorn cattle. However, by the 1870s, sheep raising was combined with the cattle industry, and in the case of Webb County both sheep and cattle would prove highly profitable well into the early 1900s. The first of this breed of cattle probably entered the Rio Grande region with the Coronado expedition in 1541 and most likely saw its greatest growth beginning in the era following the Alonzo de León *entrada* in 1689. By the time José de Escandón and Tomas Sánchez reconnoitered the region between the Nueces and Rio Grande during 1745–55, wild horses, mules, and cattle were in abundance, but cattle attracted the most attention.[44]

> These animals varied in color from yellows and duns to deep browns, reds, and blacks, they were distinguished by their long, low-swinging heads, formidable horns, narrow sides, and long legs. The Spanish cattle unsuited for dairy or draft purposes, were valued chiefly for their tough hides and stringy beef, and they were perfectly adapted to a frontier existence. They were tough, strong stock, characterized by marked feral instincts and often complete wildness. They were to survive and maintain themselves in country that would have decimated or destroyed a herd of weaker and less self-sufficient animals.[45]

The expansion of cattle ranching and access to markets, as Sánchez noted about the "great amount of traffic," would be key to the solid underpinnings of Laredo's formative years. In addition to regional ranching, Laredo with its strategic crossing became a "market" for traders in cattle and supplies. Relations with the local small bands of Carrizos (Bamboos) and Borrados (Gray) Indians were friendly during the late 1750s and 1760s.[46] Physically isolated from the centers of political and commercial power in New Spain, the Villa of Laredo from its founding was an entrepreneurial venture, and, as previously noted, unlike all other settlements along the Rio Grande, Laredo was developed independently of either a church or a military garrison, or *presidio.* The lack of these two seemingly mandatory cornerstones of Spanish colonial settlement slowed the growth of Laredo and did not go unnoticed by either the viceroy or the church, as was confirmed in a subsequent official inspection visit in mid-1767.[47]

The frontier of New Spain was directly impacted by geopolitical events and a lengthy power struggle in Europe and North America between England and France and their allies during most of the eighteenth century. With the end of the Seven Years' War, the Treaty of Paris (1763) resulted in a victory for Great Britain. In the final agreement, the French threat to Texas ended as it ceded the vast Louisiana territory west of the Mississippi River to

Spain.[48] From this moment forward both the Crown and the viceroyalty in Mexico lowered their guard in all its farthest positions of New Spain, thinking they were no longer bound to fortify their northernmost possessions in America. Notwithstanding, a series of *visitadores*—Bernardo de Gálvez, Teodoro de Croix, Marqués de Rubí, Don Hugo O'Conner, and Don José de Gálvez—were sent north to determine remedies to the problems in the Provincias Interiores.[49] The Spanish Crown soon advised the viceroy of New Spain, Joaquín de Montserrat y Curiana, Marqués de Cruillas (r. 1760–66), to conduct a full examination on the status of the villas and garrisons to insure these areas were gaining a strong foothold and permanence. It is unlikely that Sánchez or his fellow ranchers along the Rio Grande had any knowledge of the European intrigue. Events between 1763 to 1783 among the nations of Europe would in time shape the destiny of not only Laredo and Texas, but also what was to become the western half of the United States.[50] The inspections of the Rio Grande region from 1766 to 1768 would result in a complete realignment of security requirements and priorities by the Spanish Crown.[51]

Viceroy Montserrat was replaced by Carlos Francisco de Croix, Marqués de Croix (r. 1766–71) on August 24, 1766. His counsel in Mexico City surely took note of the 1757 Cuervo commission report, as well as heeding the Crown's orders to secure claims along the Rio Grande and immediately begin an inspection of the northern frontier. As confirmation, he commanded that a "General Visit of the Royal Commission," or *General Visita,* be made to all the communities along the Rio Grande. Don Juan Fernando de Palacios, governor of Nuevo Santander, was selected as *visitor* to lead the royal commission. In addition to a general census survey, the *visita* of early June 1767 had as its primary focus an extensive review and distribution of land grants, following a survey of each town—a formal prerequisite to receiving a formal city charter. Arriving in Laredo on November 18—the inspection officially known as the *Acta de la General Visita al Pueblo de San Agustín de Laredo*—the Crown's agents were instructed to chronicle as much detail as possible. The survey and inspection of Laredo was based on the royal codified standards determined by the *Recopilación de Leyes de los Reynos de las Indias* (Imperial Laws of the Indies) first issued by Philip II in 1573.[52] The lengthy law establishing 148 ordinances of the Crown (based on the Roman and Greek experience regarding the basic grid design and establishment of towns) provided for both the formal Iberian ideal of a city for the founding of colonial towns and the full and detailed recording of lot ownership (*propios*) and adjacent land grants, such as the *porciones* conveyed to Sánchez. One surprise for the *visitadores* of the commission was the interest of some Laredo residents to extend the village limits across to the "south bank" of the Rio Grande—encompassing sixty *jacales* straddling both sides of the river.

This proposal was easily justified due to concerns over grazing rights on the south bank that had not been recorded; these unrecorded rights could result in illegal encroachment by ranchers not affiliated with Laredo. A number of Laredoans had settled across the river on the south side, which resulted in a decree by Governor Palacio that annexed the south bank under the full jurisdiction of the Villa de Laredo. This seemingly benign act to confirm land ownership in the vicinity of present day-Nuevo Laredo nearly proved fatal to the stability of the young community in years to come.[53]

With the south bank question addressed, the surveyors turned their full attention to the survey of the town sites and main plaza. The Spanish were methodical in their efforts to "mark out" the limits of the villa and establish a street grid; however, no street names were assigned. To this day even the most sophisticated survey instruments and a Global Positioning System (GPS) could not improve on the 1767 survey of the near-perfect true north-south orientation of Flores, Convent, and Salinas streets, or the east-west precision of Zaragoza, Houston, Grant, and Lincoln streets.[54] The accuracy of the Spaniards, surveying the land on horseback, "was amazing," noted the renowned Laredo engineer and surveyor John Foster at age ninety in 2004.[55] Many of the original narrow downtown streets laid out in the late 1700s remain today. Not until 1870 were street names selected by Mayor Samuel Jarvis to recognize nationally known personalities, church saints, and heroes of both Mexico and the United States. In large measure, the detailed instructions drafted by Philip II in the Law of the Indies laid the guiding foundation for Laredo, in part stating:

> Having selected the site for the town, it must be in an elevated place, where there are healthy conditions, protection, and fertile lands for farming and pastures, fuel and building materials, good water, natives, convenience of transport, of easy access, and open to the north wind.
>
> The four corners of the plaza face to the four principal winds, because in this way the streets leaving the plaza are not exposed to the principle winds, which would be a great inconvenience. The size of the plaza should be proportionate to the population, taking into consideration . . . the plaza should be designed with such increase in mind. All around the plaza and the four principal streets that start from it there should be colonnades because of the great convenience that they offer to the merchants who gather there.[56]

As was customary, the heart of the 1767 survey of the Villa de Laredo was the establishment of the main plaza. The layout and allocation of lots around the plaza was a standard procedure for the Spanish. The west side of the square was reserved for administrative and municipal government buildings, as well as the alcalde's (Captain in the case of Sánchez) residence. The east side was reserved for the future location of church. Concerned that Laredo had no formal church, the *visita* decreed that a portion of the *canoa* (canoe ferry) toll on the river would be applied toward funding the construction of the church. Once the church was complete, the toll revenue could be used for other civic purposes. Unlike most other communities, missions were funded by the church, and following the expelling of the Jesuits from northern New Spain in 1767, the missions were staffed chiefly by members the Franciscan order. Thus, the first mission at Laredo would be paid by income from a commercial endeavor. The river ferry would be free to the citizens of the villa, and "strangers" or travelers would be charged two *reales* (about twenty-five cents) per passenger and one *real* for each item of cargo. Two decades would pass before the first stone church was completed in 1789.[57]

Homes and adequate space for domestic livestock and barns were located on the north and south sides of the plaza. A total of four lots 20 by 40 *varas* (about 60 x 120 feet) were generally reserved for the leading families of the villa. The harsh dry land above the Rio Grande *vega* was deemed to be ill-suited for domestic crops without the assistance of irrigation. The *Visita General* noted of the lands around Laredo: "son todos de tierra sin riego mas que el que se puede logran de temporal,"—the land was unfit for irrigation, except such as may be caused by the seasonal rains.[58] Residents were expected to build on any assigned lots within two years or forfeit the land. And as an obligation of ownership all residents were to bear arms in defense of the city in case of any invasion. It is interesting to note that the Rio Grande region was seldom referred to in official dispatches as the *frontera,* but instead, the string of communities—Reynosa, Camargo, Mier, Revilla, and Laredo—were referred to as the *villas de la cordillera del margen.* Following a second visit in the fall of 1767 by the Marqués de Rubí (accompanied by military engineer Nicolás de Lafora), it was recommended in 1768 that Laredo be assigned a well-manned garrison as the anchor of the *cordillera.* A semimilitary cordon of outposts was established to hold back Indian incursions, protect communities, and foster economic development. However, in fact, no full garrison was ever assigned to Laredo, only a small element of troops.[59]

As a ranching community, the granting and confirmation of the grazing lands was as important—if not more crucial—than the homesites. Adequate grazing lands on large tracts of free grass (long before fenced pastures) and access to water were critical factors. Throughout New Spain access to water went hand in hand with the determination of the value of and use of the land. To allow maximum individual ownership and access to the river the survey created a number of narrow *porciones,* or sections (tracts). In all, eighty-nine rectangular sections measuring about three quarters of a mile wide at the riverbank and up to fourteen miles in depth were created. The Royal commission assigned sixty-six of eighty-nine *porciones,* drawn by lot, on the north bank of the Rio Grande to thirty-five permanent families in Laredo. Twenty-three *porciones* were held in reserve for new settlement. Don Tomás received two sections as well as a grant of sixty leagues—approximately 265,680 acres—north of the town. Still concerned with the settlement of the territory between the Rio Grande and the Nueces River, settlers were once again encouraged by royal officials to occupy and use as much land as possible.[60]

The final act of the *visita* commission on June 16, 1767, was to confirm a new municipal charter from the Crown, with the mandate to establish a *cabildo* (town council) and hold elections for a *justicia alcalde* and *procurador general* (formal mayor), and two *regidores* (councilmen). Members of the military and clergy, although considered prominent citizens, were expressly forbidden to hold official public office. In the fall of 1767, the second municipal election within Texas resulted in the election of José Martínez de Sotomayor as mayor and Salvador González Hidalgo and Nicolás de Campos Castellanos as *regidores.* In a little more than a decade after the founding, Villa de Laredo was recognized as being "increasingly important as a point of entry to Texas."[61] Furthermore, the detailed survey of the *visita* of 1767, conducted by the Spanish viceroy, was to have a tremendous impact on the future, serving as the basis of legal land titles transferred to and approved by the state of Texas in 1850 following the completion of the Treaty of Guadalupe Hidalgo.[62]

The transition from Captain Sánchez to the newly elected government was at first smooth. The Royal Council of the Viceroy wasted no time in advising the new alcalde that one of his prime duties was the collection of taxes, of which the *alcabala,* an eleventh-century Arabic term for sales, was the primary source of government revenue.[63] The tax on tobacco and pulque produced 40 percent of the total revenue, and collection of these taxes was of great concern given the increased amount of smuggling on the frontier.[64] The collection of duties and tariffs for the central government would, over time, be deemed a key function of the hacienda to generate "domestic" revenue. Documents in archival material in Madrid demonstrate a great deal of oversight by the Crown to have the agents of the hacienda in New Spain regulate and tax commercial activity. Both the demand for tobacco products and the widespread growth of *pulquerías* created an environment that was both inconsistent and difficult to enforce. The tax on pulque was a half a *real* per drink, a rather high sum given the lack of coinage in circulation on the frontier. From these efforts in the late 1700s to enhance tax collection would spring a culture of smuggling that exists to this day.[65] Tax collection was not the only concern.

Table 1.4. Original grantees of Laredo *porciones*

Porcion *No.*	*Name of Grantee*	Porcion *No.*	*Name of Grantee*
1	José Antonio Flores	56	Miguel Garcia
2	Javier Peña	57	Jose Guarjado
3	Jose Jesus Peña	58	Jose P. Garcia
4	Miguel Martinez	59	Domingo Garcia
5	Nicolas de la Garza	60	Jose Cristobal Garcia
6	Tomás de Cuellar	61	Jose de Bustamante
7–12	Unassigned	62	Joaquín Garcia
13	Pedro Garcia	63	Juan Baptista Garcia
14	Salvador Hidalgo	64	Leonardo Garcia
15	Joaquin Cavazos	65	Maria de Jesus Sanchez
16	Blas de J. Sanchez	66	Leonardo Sanchez
17–24	Unassigned	67	Toribio Rodriguez
25	José Tomás de Cuellar	68	Juan Francisco Garcia
26	Jose de Soto Mayor	69	Agustin Sanchez
27	Antonio Lopez	70	Maria Gertrudis Sanchez
28	Nicolas Campos	71	Eugenio Martinez
29	Joaquín Gutierrez	72	Juan B. Villarreal
30	Francisco Xavier Uribe	73	Jose F. Cordova
31	Juan Guerra	74	Jose Treviño
32	Blas Treviño	75	Antonio Treviño
33	Gervacio Badillos	76	Jose Dionisio Treviño
34	Francisca Uribe	77	Jose Antonio Diaz
35	Juan Francisco Uribe	78	Jose Miguel Diaz
36	Juan Diego Treviño	79	Lauriano Salinas
37	Carlos Mendiola	80	Jose Batolo Chapa
38	Juan Mendiola	81	Tadeo Sanchez
39	Juan E. Vasquez	82	Antonio Nasario
40	Martín Morales	83	Manuel Garcia
41	José Antonio Martinez	84	Eugenio Rodriguez
42	Marcos Mendiola	85	Eugenio Sanchez
43	Pedro Mendiola	86	Jose Cayetano de la Garza
44–52	Unassigned	87	Jose Manuel Albino Martinez
53	Tómas Sánchez (Jr.)	88	Tomas Uribe
54	Tómas Sánchez (Jr.)	89	Santo Tomás
55	Santiago Sanchez		

Source: Laredo Archives

With the replacement of Sánchez as the lone, all-powerful authority since 1755 by an elected official, political friction soon surfaced as the new alcalde, Sotomayor, on the pretext of protection from Indian raids on the north bank, directed his staff to move the city records and seat of the municipality to the south side of the river. He further strongly encouraged families in Laredo to leave their homesites and move across the river. Given the recent visit by the governor and the commission of the viceroy, it is hard to determine Sotomayor's motives other than that he was a large user of grazing land on the south bank and thus wanted to further insure his claims to this land. Through the efforts of Sánchez, a large group of citizens loyal to the Spanish Crown rejected the new mayor's attempt to abandon the city. Led by Don Tomás, the citizens filed a protest with the governor of Nuevo Santander, who on July 5, 1770, agreed with their protest. Laredo was not to be moved, and the seat of the municipal government was to be on the north bank, and thus he decreed that Captain Sánchez remove Sotomayor and retake the office as captain and alcalde.[66]

Retaining the title of captain and mayor, Don Tomás would continue to either serve as the lone alcalde of Laredo or exert direct influence on the selection of the mayor for the balance of the eighteenth century. To assist with the administration of the villa, landed male ranchers selected a town council, or *medio cabildo.* While still in day-to-day charge of his vast ranching operations, Don Tomás took a number of actions to address the growth of the city. In 1774, he issued two decrees, or *bandos,* that all residents were to live on the north bank of the river. Unable to enforce the immediate relocation he issued additional decrees. These appealed to the disenchanted on the south bank by family name. Sánchez hired a mounted patrol officer to insure safe streets at night, banned the concealment of small arms, and declared a curfew. Fines for violations ranged from six *reales* to thirty days in jail. To offer further continuity, his son, Santiago de Jesus Sánchez, served as *teniente mayor,* or vice mayor, beginning in the early 1780s. Young Santiago is credited with decreeing the opening of the first formal villa school on March 22, 1783, "for those up to 12 years old." Efforts to improve conditions in Laredo were constantly impacted by the often hostile and untamed countryside.[67]

Residents of Laredo and Mier worked to foster good relations with the Carrizo. However, peace with the Indians was, more often than not, only temporary. While the Carrizos were the first native people to assimilate in numbers, the Comanches and Apaches remained independently hostile.[68] Attempts were made under the Royal regulation decree of 1772 to expand the military presence by adding new troops and continuing with the presidios, yet the Spanish officials were unable to expand operations beyond those villas and presidios already established.[69] Concerned about the ongoing violence and theft, the mayors of Camargo, Mier, Reynosa, Revilla, and

Laredo collectively petitioned the viceroy to stress their plight and to request more protections:

> There are only twenty-five soldiers to defend the frontier together with the inhabitants. . . . to help us defend this territory of more than 100 leagues from Laredo to Reynosa. We haven't been able to irrigate the land so we can't sow crops or raise cattle which is what most of us do . . . these Indian hostilities cause a serious problem for supplies because the merchants don't want to risk traveling the roads. We barely have the basic necessities. These villages will soon be abandoned. We appeal to you to send us troops.[70]

In spite of the ongoing Indian problems, as the number of ranches grew, so too did the population of Laredo, reaching 708 residents and over one hundred friendly Carrizos and Lipans in 1789. By the late 1780s, the villa had over eighty-five homes (a mix of stone, adobe, and jacales), a new very small church of "stone" construction, and a garrison of troops to insure protection against any new disturbances caused by the Apaches. Incidents of smallpox slowed Indian attacks, but did not eliminate pillaging raids by both the Lipans and Comanches on the Rio Grande frontier.[71] To defend the town, a volunteer civilian force of forty-eight men was armed with muskets and rawhide shields to deflect arrows in the event of attack. These efforts at self-defense were crucial to the day-to-day livelihood of the battered town; yet, to truly defend the strategic location would require a greater degree of armed forces. The establishment of a presidio, manned by soldiers of the Crown, was in keeping with the protection of the northern fringe of New Spain, as Adán Benavides noted: "to provide safe routes of travel, to protect frontier settlements, to serve as a line of defense against native Indian and European aggression, and to function as a bastion for Hispanic acculturation."[72]

Armed assistance by a new Spanish garrison at Laredo was established in early 1789. Captain Sánchez, his fellow ranchers, and merchants became increasingly concerned about perennial Indian raids that hampered both ranching and trade; they were unaware of the "Guerra Americana" and the fact that George Washington was inaugurated the first president of the newly independent union of American colonies on April 30, 1789.[73] Laredo's concerns were confirmed by a spectacular Lipan Apache raid that nearly captured the entire villa in April 1790. Upon learning of a raiding party on the outskirts of town, the new commander of the Laredo garrison and unit the *Tercera Compania Volante de Nuevo Santander* (Third Mobile Company), Captain Don Claudio la Comba, responded in hot pursuit to stop the Indians. Once engaged, he realized the band was too strong, so he ordered a retreat back to the plaza. Counterattacking, the Apaches entered the town,

Table 1.5. Villa de Laredo: Census of January 1789

	Mestizos	*Mulattos*	*Spaniards*	*Indians*
girls	22	26	35	11
boys	23	23	38	8
single women	31	30	58	24
single men	33	39	76	33
married women	37	31	65	17
married men	32	39	62	17

Source: Laredo Archives

captured the garrison's powder magazine, and blew it up. As the troops retreated to the homes of the residents for cover, the Indians seized the plaza, where, as one author noted, "throughout the night, they held high carnival, dancing and frightening the people with barbaric noise of drums, shouts, and song."[74] The first battle of Laredo ended at first light when the cautious warriors withdrew, leaving the stunned residents and soldiers in a state of confusion and amazement.

Shortly after the skirmish at the central plaza, José Ramón Díaz de Bustamante was assigned as captain of the Laredo garrison. Reviewing the situation in Laredo, Díaz de Bustamante strongly recommended to the commanding general of the Interior Province that substantial fortification and barracks should be added in the villa. These detailed plans and drawings were forwarded to the viceroy, who chose to delay new construction. In 1794, the Crown, increasingly preoccupied with tax collection and the security of northern New Spain, attempted to station more troops on the frontier and replaced some mayors with appointed military captains, deemed *alcalde primero.*[75] Aware of the increasing unrest, the king ordered additional inspectors to visit and devise a plan to defend the region. In December 1794, the governor of Nuevo Santander, Manuel de Escandón (the founder's son) dispatched Félix María Calleja del Rey to determine the scope of the threat and to explore recommendations to improve the military security and economy.[76] Calleja's report resulted in a reconfirmation of both the strategic location and role of Laredo as a key boundary:

> Peace and war with a single nation needs to be general in all nearby dominions of the King, so that there will no be judicial abuse such as now takes place here. Boundaries should be prescribed over which those who pass may be treated as enemies, thus averting the damages

Fig. 1.1. *Ganadero* of the northern Mexico borderlands. This details the description of a circa 1750s rancher and mount. Source: José Cisneros, *Riders Across the Centuries,* Texas Western Press, 1984.

> the Indians can now cause in the provinces while traveling under the guise of friendship. Laredo could mark such a boundary.[77]

Concerned with the interruption of trade and ranching, the governor of Nuevo Santander ordered the commander of the Laredo garrison to seek a peace treaty and as soon as possible to resume trading with the friendly Indians. The ranching community of Laredo, with a population of some 800 in the late 1790s, welcomed the periods of calm and peace.[78] Occupied with Indian encounters and the day-to-day demands of ranching, these hardy settlers looked forward to any kind of entertainment. Fiestas of the period were highlighted by some of the first rodeos in Texas, allowing the many vaqueros to display their skills. Among the most popular events chronicled in the Laredo Archives was *colear,* or bull-tailing:

> On the appointed day, usually a Sunday or *día de fiesta,* a convivial, lively crowd gathered at the corral. Bulls were released singly at a signal. As the bull charged from the corral, a vaquero pursued him on a horse specially trained for the sport. The bulls were both fast and quick, and if one of them took it into his head to turn and attack horse and rider, the horse had to be nimble and the rider skilled to avoid considerable damage. Once the bull was running on a more or less straight line, however, the vaquero rode up alongside, reached for the bull's tail, passed it under his own right leg, took a turn with it around the pommel of his saddle, and pulled his horse strongly to the left. The bull was violently up-ended and "fell on his face."[79]

As the century drew to a close, Laredo—founded without financial aid or military protection from either the Spanish Crown or Church—was on a firm foundation, notwithstanding an English map of the period that failed

Fig. 1.2. Bull-tailing and rodeo events have been passed down for centuries. Bull-tailing is depicted here at the 2004 Jose Cuervo Traditional Charro Championship as rider Armando Alvarez attempts to bring down the bull by the tail. Source: *San Antonio Express-News.*

Table 1.6. Names for the "Great River": Rio Grande–Río Bravo

Pre-Columbian	
Posoge	big river
Hanapakwa	place of great waters
Tsina	the river
Mests 'ici chene	big river
Paslapaane	big river
to ba-ade	female river
Names given by explores since 1500	
Río de las Palmas	1519
Río de Nuestra Señora	1540
Tiguex River	1540
River of May	1568
Río de la Concepción	1581
Río Guadalquivir	1581
Río Turbio	1581
Río del Norte	1582
Río Bravo	1589
Rio Grande	1598
Rio Grande del Norte	1600
Río Ganapetuan	1691
Río de San Buena Ventura del Norte	1675
Grande River	1806
Río del Norte y de Nuevo Mexico	1700
Río Bravo del Norte	1685
Río Caudaloso	1700
Río del Norte or Río Bravo	1790

Names given by the mapmakers

Great Britain	*France*	*United States*
Rio Grande del Norte, 1862	Río del Norte, 1780, 1832	Río Bravo, 1854, 1862
Río Palmas, 1780	Río del Norte or Bravo, 1845	Rio Grande, 1857
Río Grand, 1850	Río Bravo del Norte, 1851	Great River, 1870
North River or Río Bravo, 1780	Río Palmas, 1682	Río Bravo del Norte, 1842
	Río del Norte y del Nuevo Mexico, 1705	

to identify any features along the Río Bravo, simply inscribing in bold script, "county not particularly known."[80] Laredo's founder Don Tomás Sánchez had endured over four decades of challenges and, at age eighty-seven, died on January 20, 1796. The exact burial site, lost with time, is generally thought to be in the courtyard of San Agustín Church.[81] An unequaled rancher in a wild and turbulent era, he had demonstrated a vigorous, uncommon ability and a rugged individualism that set the course of Laredo. His mark on the second permanent and continuously occupied town in Texas was unmistakable. As noted by historian Jerry Thompson, "The community which was then a gateway to Texas would become a gateway to Mexico." The villa carved by hardy colonists from the wilderness of the Rio Grande frontier would stand the test of time. The era of settlement led by Don Tomás was soon to be followed by the winds of change for Laredo, as well as by the call for independence in both Mexico and Texas.

CHAPTER 2

THE SWELLING STORM

> As the nineteenth century began, Spain's policy on trade across the thinly guarded frontier would, as always, remain out of touch with reality and be its own worst enemy. Concern was expressed . . . it was the demand for trade, more than political or diplomatic considerations, which shaped the Spanish-American frontier during these years and defined the nature of its conflicts.
>
> JACK JACKSON, *LOS MESTEÑOS*

The Rio Grande settlements at the turn of the nineteenth century along the *margen* of the frontier of New Spain suffered from neglect at a time in which they had gained a strong foothold in the still rough and untamed region. A shortage of royal soldiers, too few settlers, hostile Indians, and too much territory to protect diminished efforts to fully develop livestock, to properly manage improvements of the villas and ranches, and to expand trade. By 1800, some dozen scattered settlements north of the Rio Grande had either been abandoned or had been left to die. Laredo remained the only permanent villa on the north bank of the Rio Grande, and only three other small settlements remained inhabited—Béxar, La Bahía, and Nacogdoches. Unlike the early era of Tomas Sánchez, the reason for the precarious straits along the river was the rise of aggressive Indian activity. A grand plan to "*esterminar al enemigos,*" or "exterminate," the Apaches never materialized.[1] Thus, while no single band or tribe of Indians, routinely referred to as "barbarians," of the period were able to mass in large numbers, the small groups that did roam in the area were able to strike with impunity on both sides of the Rio Grande.[2]

The governor of Nuevo Santander, Don Manuel Ygnacio Escandón, eldest son of José de Escandón, gradually attempted to increase the number of troops in the border presidios as well as recruit armed citizens, or *ciudadanos armados.* However, over time, according to Andrés Tijerina in *Tejanos and Texas under the Mexican Flag,* "as years passed other Mexicans [in the central government] developed a condescending attitude toward the isolated *frontera*."[3] Thus, the governor worked to strike a number of peace accords with the Lipans and Mescalero Apaches. Given the preoccupation of the Spanish Crown with affairs in Europe during the late 1790s, Escandón expected no assistance and moved to deal with the problem on his terms. Unable to eliminate the Apaches totally, Escandón urged the alcaldes and commandants at each location to pacify the Indians as much as possible by encouraging them to camp near Laredo for the purpose of trade. Those who rebelled and remained hostile were pursued and killed. These government policy swings by the Spanish, which fluctuated from retaliation to attempts at peace, proved most inconsistent. The Apache threat subsided but did not fully disappear; it was replaced by the Comanches who migrated in large numbers to the Nueces Strip.[4]

Gradually, a small number of friendly Lipan Apaches allied with the troops of the Laredo garrison to fight against their rivals, the aggressive hunting band known by their adversaries as the Comanches—"people who fight us all the time." The fierce level of combat and raid-and-trade tactics on the frontier was not always fully understood by the royal administration, which directed the course of affairs away from the region. While peace was a clearly preferable option, Crown officials were quick to dole out criticism; they did not realize that the Comanches were "bitter enemies" of the Lipan and thus, possible repercussions of incidents among the combatants were not grasped. A case in point is an incident in which "the ears, hair, and part of the skin of three Comanches" killed near Chope were sold to the Apaches. Comandante General Nemesio Salcedo issued a decree of reprimand after, of all things, a complaint by the Comanches. As early as 1787, policies were put in place by the Spanish to induce their soldiers to take the upper hand in dealing with hostile Indians; the policies included an "offer of a bonus for each pair of ears they took during battle or while on patrol—this practice later led to the offering of scalp bounties." Thus, the "tranquility of the provinces" so demanded was not always as simple as a mere decree or proclamation.[5]

The Comanche warriors were some of the most skilled horsemen in the West. They lived and died by their boldness on horseback, their tireless hunts, and a no-quarter approach to combat. Roaming the plains in autonomous bands, they were among the most superior mounted archers in history. One account relates, in the time it took a Texan to reload his rifle, a warrior could ride three hundred yards at full speed and fire twenty arrows.[6] Travelers to the Nueces Strip were warned to be well armed: "tienen que ir buenos armados."[7] The advance of the Comanches into the near "no-man's-land" between the Nueces and Rio Grande was as much a threat to Apaches as it was to the Spaniards. And like relations with the Apaches, peace when attainable with the Comanches was never permanent due to the wide variety of roving bands as well as to the opportunistic whim of warriors who were ever ready to raid and exercise their bravery.[8]

The lightly defended frontier was ideal for the mounted Comanche who could roam hundreds of miles and strike at will. The impact included the near total interruption of overland commerce south of San Antonio to the Rio Grande for extended periods of time. Troop escorts were rare, except in the case of assisting supply shipments or the clergy. Ranchers flocked to the settlements for safety, merchants were reluctant to travel, and the Spanish soldiers (with few exceptions) were ill equipped or not trained to fight on the Comanches' "hit-and-run" terms. The menace of the nomadic Comanches would last long after New Spain gave way to Mexico and the emergence of the state of Texas.[9]

The Indian menace would be a part of South Texas daily life until after the Civil War.[10] A dispatch from Laredo in the records of the Laredo Archives vividly captures firsthand knowledge of the situation facing settlers:

> The Comanches are numerous and daring. They have the greatest advantage in waging war. They have better mounts and arms and are well versed in when to attack and flee as they wish; they know the land thoroughly. They carry on long campaigns with nothing more than horses and weapons because they don't need anything else; they are used to roughing it. The troops are different. They don't have horses or good weapons, nor the necessary experience since most are from the interior [of Mexico]. They don't know the enemy they are fighting, the territory, the way of attacking and pursuing them, their customs and identifying signs . . . we have respectable forces on the frontier but if we want to exterminate the enemy quickly and easily we have to do the same things they do.[11]

Authorities in Mexico City, while repeatedly contacted by mayors and garrison officers along the Rio Grande, remained of little assistance. Instead, the viceroy and agents of the *audiencia* issued decree after decree to be passed along the *cordillera del margen* one by one to each community resting in the last stop of the chain of written communication—in the files of the *cabildo* of Laredo. Instructions ranged from educational procedures to use to teach children to read and write, to a *bando* on mescal (hard to tax), to strict requirements on how citizens were to be armed. By 1800, the *comandante general* became the dominant official figure in the villas under rules known as the Comandante General de Provincias Interna, specifically styled to deal with problems in the northern provinces of the colony. This shift in overall administrative oversight gradually brought Laredo, and other frontier settlements, into the mainstream of the viceroy's control. The collection of the tax, the *alcabala,* was strongly enforced and expanded. Concerned not just with the payment of taxes but also with cattle theft, examination of brands and marks on cattle, as well as who and when cattle were slaughtered came under the daily inspection of the commandant and his staff. This represented a significant shift from the Tomás Sánchez rancher-mayor style to one of bureaucratic accounting and oversight. As trade in Laredo expanded with cities in northern Mexico—Saltillo, Monclova, and Monterrey—one segment of trade that generally eluded the authorities was tobacco. Many tobacco merchants paid tax, however, an ever-present shortage of cigarettes on the frontier made the smuggling trade much more lucrative.[12]

Free Trade and a Noble Bargain

In spite of the agitation on the Rio Grande frontier, New Spain continued to grow; the population doubled from an estimated 3 million in 1750 to nearly 6 million by 1800. The U.S. population in 1800 was approximately 5.3 million people. Thus, colonial Mexico was the most populous and prosperous region in the Americas. Mexico City had some 1,495,140 inhabitants and attracted new migrants from the countryside daily.[13] Growth along the Rio Grande remained stagnant with the Laredo population numbering about 800 in 1800. Indian disturbances and more colonial oversight did not fully slow the shipment of goods (primarily beef and leather products) from Laredo, though, because of its strategic location on the primary road to the markets of Mexico City, Puebla, Veracruz, and Monterrey. To encourage increased trade, on October 12, 1778, Carlos III (r. 1759–88) in Madrid ordered implementation of the Ordenanza o Progmatica del Comercio Libre, or Ordinance and Program for Free Trade. This order expanded on the Free Trade Acts of 1765, slated first for the Caribbean to gradually lower protectionist barriers, abolish the Spanish "fleet system," open more ports to trade, and take away the power of monopoly over any single sector or product engaged in intracolonial shipments.[14] Such monopolies inhibited competition as well as the access to new products in the marketplace; as one observer noted, "Mexico has been crippled by the restrictive commercial system and systematic preference accorded to Spanish born merchants."[15] In this era, over two centuries before the advent of the General Agreement on Tariffs and Trade (GATT), WTO, and NAFTA, of harsh mercantilist control dominated by the Spanish mother country, these steps toward "freer" trade proved to be significant in opening markets—if only for the fact that trade was allowed to expand by extending commercial activities within the colonies. This benign deregulation of colonial trade in 1778 contributed to fostering high levels of merchandise imports, which was offset by increased silver exports to Europe or China. In 1822, the future first U.S.

ambassador to Mexico, Joel Roberts Poinsett, outlined the impact of the new *comercio* decree:

> The exports from Spain [imports to Mexico] were divided into three classes. The articles of growth and manufacture of the mother country, were called free articles, and paid nine and a half percent duty. The second class, consisted of articles of manufacture, but not growth of Spain and paid twelve and a half percent duty. The third class included all foreign goods shipped to the colonies through Spain. They paid fifteen percent entry into Spain, seven percent export, and seven percent entry into America; and with the maritime alcabala [tax], the consulate, and other charges, the duties amounted to thirty-three and a third percent.[16]

The advent of free trade in New Spain was the result of deteriorating economic conditions during the first two decades the nineteenth century. Concern with the expansion of trade and the broadening of overall output was well founded given the fact that gross domestic product (GDP) per capita as a percentage of the U.S. level (factoring in the colonial period) dropped from 89 percent in 1700 to 50 percent in 1800.[17] One reason for this decline was due to some 80 percent of the population in Mexico in 1800 being engaged in small-scale low-productive domestic agriculture. This was in spite of the attention given to the mining sector of the economy. Eric Van Young, in an extensive work on the independence struggle from 1810 to 1821, *The Other Rebellion,* chronicles an extensive review of the period. Unrest prior to 1810 was the result of a 25 percent drop in real wages and rising consumer prices—all impacted by periods of drought that resulted in a shortfall of food supplies, especially maize. Overland commerce was both time-consuming and expensive. Thus, economic conditions had a pivotal role in "setting off" the insurgency of 1810.[18]

Products exported to Spain via Veracruz included indigo, soap, flour, vanilla, cacao, tanned hides, jalap, and peppers. In New Spain, demand for imports ran high as most textiles, finished goods—termed *miserable manufactures*—wines and oil, "cheap trinkets," and farming equipment were imported from Spain—and sold at what Herbert Bancroft termed *enormous-exorbitant prices.*[19] More intracolonial trade resulted in the expansion of wagon roads, presidios, and freight services, as well as gradual improvements of towns. In the larger communities such as Mexico City and Monterrey, education was endorsed with the opening of the Escuela de Minas, consistent with the leading industry of the colony. Thus, over time, the benchmark for the colonial trade system was gauged by the volume of silver exports from some 3,000 mines across Mexico, which by 1810 accounted for three-quarters of the total exports. Since the seventeenth century, the Mexican silver peso had become the world's currency, creating wealth and power between Europe and America; it also created a "peso bound," which linked Europe to Asia by way of Spanish galleons. While the Rio Grande border region was cash starved for lack of ready abundant currency, the Mexican peso, renowned for its purity of silver, served for some three hundred years as the local currency for India, China, and the Philippines. Undermining this seemingly high level of global trade and prosperity were the growing undercurrents of political and social unrest both in Europe and New Spain.[20]

Quite possibly, the precursor to the Texas Revolution and to the colonists' declaration of independence in 1836 occurred in 1800, when Spain secretly signed the Treaty of San Ildefonso. This treaty forced the return of the territory of Louisiana to France with an implied caveat that Spain, at some future date, could reclaim the territory. This was never to be. To secure new territory, President Thomas Jefferson dispatched representatives to France to settle the possession of Louisiana as well as West Florida. In early 1803, strapped for funding for the war against England, Napoléon Bonaparte unceremoniously sold the entire vast possession, 529,912,000 acres of land and inland waterways, to the United States for $11.25 million—a cost of two cents per acre.[21] The American diplomats were astonished by the tremendous Louisiana windfall, since their primary objective had only been to buy the Isle of Orleans, the future site of the city of New Orleans, in order to control access and commerce on the Mississippi River! This action doubled the size and influence of the United States overnight. Control of the Mississippi River would prove a key element in, first, preventing any permanent occupation or advantage for either France or Britain; and second, the first significant action in the western movement of the United States to the Pacific—a pivotal cornerstone in the advent of what was to be termed *Manifest Destiny*.[22] News of the treaty regarding the purchase of Louisiana concluded in Paris on May 2, 1803, and reached Washington on July 3, in time to be boldly announced by Jefferson on the Fourth of July.[23]

Spain's protest of Napoléon's actions went unanswered, and in the course of events the U.S. claimed Spanish "Texas" as part of the Louisiana Territory—of which Jefferson asserted the Río Bravo was the western frontier. Although clearly defined on most contemporary maps of the period as a possession of New Spain, some interpreted the boundaries of Louisiana (the Sabine River, not the Río Bravo), as stated in the treaty, as vague. When asked by the American delegation for clarification of the boundary limits of this extraordinary purchase, French foreign minister Talleyrand quipped, "I can give you no direction. You have made a noble bargain for yourselves, and I suppose you will make the most of it." Thus concluded, no further direction was needed. Regardless of James Monroe's complaint that Jefferson "squandered federal funds when he acquired the *treeless* Louisiana Territory," this was the most important real estate deal—public or private—in history. And, in the heady tug of war between the nations, the first American *emigrados,* or settlers, in small numbers, unfettered by stately treaty definitions and "boundaries," began to enter what is now Texas, and over time these *entradas* proved increasingly more difficult to harness.[24]

DIVIDED LOYALTIES

The Laredo ranching community at the turn of the century was far removed from the intrigue of the European nations. Two-dozen homes surrounded the central plaza, marked prominently by the church and administrative offices of the mayor. The day-to-day life remained focused on ranching and the breeding, shipment, and expansion of the livestock base of the local economy. Traders and eager merchants flocked to the settlement overland both as buyers and wandering travelers looking to find a safe and quick crossing of the Rio Grande. These merchants brought in new goods and supplies; however, most items ranging from salt to cloth to tools were generally overpriced. While poor roads hampered trade, the factor that proved the greatest weakness to economic development along the Rio Grande frontier was the absence of credit and near absence of banks. While the Spanish peso was a rather common means of exchange, a brisk trade in barter also existed.

By 1808, Napoléon had become the most powerful figure on the European continent. With the invasion of Spain, Madrid was occupied by Napoléon, who placed his brother, Joseph, on the Spanish throne—dethroning both Charles IV (r. 1788–1808) and his son Ferdinand VII (r. 1808, 1813–33). A shadow government gathered at Cádiz in southern Spain, and while powerless, proclaimed support of Ferdinand, who eventually returned to the

Table 2.1. Livestock prices at San Agustín de Laredo, 1805 (all prices per each in pesos)

Mares	3.00	Donkeys	18.00
Mules with harness	35.00	Sheep	4.00
Mules not broken	15.00	Cows	7.00
2-year-old bulls	6.00	Heifers	6.00
Calves	9.00	Colts	4.00
Horses—broken	10.00	Stallions	10.00

Source: Laredo Archives

throne in 1814.[25] News of these events did not reach the Texas and the Rio Grande *villas del margen*—San Carlos, San Nicolas, Burgos, Cruillas, San Fernando, Refugio, Camargo, Mier, Revilla, and finally Laredo—until May of 1809.[26]

After years of war, the Spanish Crown soon found itself in a difficult financial position. In spite of the inflow of colonial silver, the national treasury was nearly broke and the Crown's armies were either overextended or defeated. Spain was in a very weak position to dictate to or defend its colonial possessions. Furthermore, these disruptions within the Spanish Crown profoundly impacted New Spain. Scattered business sectors, landed hacendados, and individuals in Mexico had for a number of years became very restless under Spanish rule. However, no one fully gauged the true degree of discontent. Approaching the eve of the three-hundredth anniversary of the arrival of imperial Spain in the New World, a local *criollo* priest, Padre Miguel Hidalgo y Costilla, on September 16, 1810 at Dolores, Mexico near Guanajuato, called for and led what at first seemed a small regional protest, but proved a generally popular uprising that demanded a dramatic redress of the tyrannical rule of the Spanish Crown.[27]

This proclamation—known as the Grito de Dolores—at first was a call for reform and not an outright call for independence. Hidalgo, his call to arms made, would have little control on the final outcome of the revolt that swept across Mexico. During the next decade, Spain's entire Mexican colonial empire would rise in rebellion. Often neglected, the frontier possessions were the last to receive notification of the events as they transpired. This lack of information and lack of good leadership created mixed loyalties. In 1811, a series of rushed decrees from Mexico City to the settlements on the Rio Grande ordered that a curfew of 10:00 P.M. was to be established and no more than six persons could gather together at one time. In a separate dispatch from the governor, the mayors were ordered to "take special care to investigate with the greatest scrupulosity any foreigners."[28] The response was mixed. Residents of Dolores and Revilla expressed sympathy for the revolutionary ideas of Hidalgo, while Laredo under Mayor José Ramón Díaz de Bustamante (1809–10), for the time being remained loyal to the Crown represented by local colonial officials. Concerned with the rising tide of potential "insurrectionists," Texas governor Manuel Salcedo admonished the mayor to recruit and train Laredo citizens as a militia force.[29]

However, in short order the economic impact of the insurgents' uprising in the heart of Mexico led by Hidalgo became a grave concern to those on the frontier, as is noted by Laredo priest José Manuel Pérez:

> Here the storm is swelling us up. We lack everything: no soap, no sugar, no blankets, no fur skins, not even a [trade] fair in Saltillo this

> year. The worst for the people is the lack of tobacco. You can't get a cigarette even for a peso and there are those who pay a real for a cigar. What Usury! But I won't say anything more about that. . . .[30]

Concerned with the shortage of food and supplies, the Laredo alcalde issued a detailed decree on March 29, 1812, to establish a price ceiling on foodstuffs. The details of the mandate may be the first documented evidence of a growing retail and wholesale commercial business sector in Laredo:

> In order to take care of the economy of the village and especially to protect the needy and the poor, I have determined, with the due consent of the councilmen, to fix the prices at which articles of first necessity are to be sold, with reference to weight and measurement in the following way:
>
> I. Anyone who sells meat must give five pounds for one real, including, of course, the weight of the bone.
> II. Persons who sell candles must give four ounces of finished tallow for half a real.
> III. Those selling bread must give twelve ounces of baked bread for half a real.
> IV. No person can kill cattle in the woods and bring the meat to town. Cattle must be killed in the ranch or in this town.
> V. Those who sell grass will give one-half of an arroba for half a real, if the grass is green. If the grass is dry, then ten pounds will sell for half a real.
> VI. Those who sell wood must not charge over a real and a half for each load.
> VII. Those who sell leaf lard must charge two and half reales per pound, and one and a half reales for tallow.
>
> Those who came to sell cannot do so on a wholesale basis without first retailing for three consecutive days at the plaza. Anyone disobeying any of the articles listed above will be fined twenty-five pesos the first time, double that amount for the second offense, and three times the amount for the third offense. In order that no one may claim ignorance of this order, it is posted in the corner of the plaza.
>
> (signed) Manuel Dovalina, Sindico Procurador

Until further notification from the viceroy, General José Joaquín de Arredondo, commander of military operations in Nuevo Santander and Texas, at

Table 2.2. Domestic Mexican products traded at the border, 1816–18

woolen textiles	hats and lace
cotton textiles	tallow
dyes and lime	sheet metal
silversmith's products	ham
chinguirito and mescal	calf hides
leather	belts
carriages	rigging
mats and baskets	bread
fish products	chocolate
cigarettes	bricks
chinaware	wax
firewood and charcoal	timber
iron and steel	shoes
salt	ice
gunpowder	games

Source: AGI, Mexico, leg. 2518, Expedientes del consulado y comercio (1817–18), Memoria de Estatuto

once ordered the fortification of key points on the frontier, to include Laredo. To create a buffer, the town of Palafox, fourteen miles upriver, was reinforced with a garrison captain and thirty soldiers.[31] Furthermore, the general, who visited Laredo in mid-1813, was determined that Laredo, a strategic river ford, would need to be fortified against any rebel action that would come out not only from Mexico in the south but also from the San Antonio-Béxar colony in the north. And through all of this, Laredo remained loyal to the Crown. Plans, never fully realized, were developed by army engineer Lt. José Alexandro that called for construction of an earthen semicircle fortress, anchored on one end by the river. Walls were intended to be three and one half *varas* high (about 10 feet) and four *varas* wide (12 feet), and if time permitted, walls would be raised to five *varas*. The fort was to have nine "turrets," or strong points, to house a total of 314 officers and troops.

Arredondo's prediction was well founded. A force of Anglo-Americans, Mexicans, and Indians engaged the Spanish garrison of San Antonio at the Battle of Salado Creek (Rosalis), eight miles southeast of the Béxar settlements. The Royalist force of over 1,500 regulars and 1,000 militiamen were defeated in less than twenty minutes by 800 revolutionaries—the self-styled Republican Army of the North. In early April 1813, insurgents under the command of Don José Bernardo Gutiérrez de Lara from Revilla captured San Antonio and, in a controversial incident, over a dozen Spanish officers, including Governor-General Manuel Salcedo, were bound and escorted into the countryside east of San Antonio, summarily executed, and their bodies mutilated.[32]

Uneasiness among the rebels following the executions quickly spread among the ranks at Béxar, causing a large number of desertions from Gutiérrez's army. Unfazed by the events, Gutiérrez declared Texas an independent nation on April 6, 1813, and issued Texas' first constitution.[33] This first attempt at independence lasted less than three months. On August 6, Gutiérrez departed and was replaced by a Cuban filibuster named José Álvarez de Toledo. In less than two weeks, news arrived that a massive army under General Arredondo—bent on revenge—was approaching Béxar. Enraged by the slaughter of the Salcedo cadre, Arredondo led a force of 2,000 royals against Toledo's Republican Army in the Battle of the Medina River on August 18, 1813—to date the bloodiest engagement on Texas soil, with over one thousand dead on the field of battle. Ruthlessly pursuing the revolutionaries after the battle, the Spanish counterattacked eastward toward Nacogdoches, capturing and summarily executing over 400 rebels. Accompanying Arredondo was a young officer soon to rise in the ranks to rewrite both Mexican and Texas history—Antonio López de Santa Anna.

Lone Star Revolution

While the power brawl intensified for control of Spanish Texas, so too did the continued attacks from fierce bands of nomadic Indians. During the period from 1815 to 1846, Laredo, and many other fringe frontier communities, became the crossroads in the struggle to determine the future of the region. More attention was given Laredo by increasing the garrison in order to attempt to wrest control from the Indians and to insure that the river crossings at the Rio Grande were kept open and protected. Laredo ranchers constantly struggled to protect their livestock; one rancher noted that many cattle were "scattered far and wide and have reverted to the wild state." In April 1819, thirty-seven of the forty-four major Laredo ranches were abandoned "on account of the desolating war that the barbarous Indians of the north wage against us . . ."[34] Town life was not much better, yet many settlers flocked to the villa for protection. Other than a few sparsely stocked stores, Laredo reported three cobblers, two carpenters, two tailors, and two brick masons.

The Provincias Internas north of Monterrey and Saltillo were seriously impacted by a decade of war and revolution. North-south movement of freight and agricultural commodities to the border, and even *arrierios* (muleteers), were curtailed due to the high demand by the military for transpor-

Table 2.3. Silver coins minted in Mexico, 1809–20

Year	*Number of pesos*
1809	24,708,164
1810	17,950,684
1811	8,956,432
1812	4,027,620
1813	6,133,983
1814	6,902,481
1815	6,454,799
1816	8,325,616
1817	7,994,451
1818	10,852,367
1819	11,491,138
1820	9,897,078

Source: Van Young, *The Other Rebellion,* 81

tation. The colonial revolt was further impacted by a shortage of "coin" in circulation, thus accounting in large measure for the drop in tax collection of the *alcabala.* Paradoxically, the silver-rich colony suffered a severe disruption in the mining and production of coinage and bullion.[35] The shortfall of coins partly accounts for the issuance of the first Mexican paper money in 1823.

This prolonged period of conflict had a direct impact not only on the cross-border trade but also on the future of the northern provinces of New Spain. Notwithstanding that the Adams-Onís Treaty concluded in February 22, 1819 (sometimes referred to as the Transcontinental Treaty or the Florida Treaty), set the boundary between Spanish territorial claims and the United States along the Sabine River on the east and the Red River on the north, Spanish authorities were concerned by the unregulated entrance of squatters. Most of these immigrants were crossing into Mexico-Texas from the Louisiana Territory.[36] Both residents and travelers were required to have documentation and a passport that clearly stated their intent and status. Upon entering a settlement, each newcomer was to report to the magistrate or garrison commanding officer to disclose their intent.[37] The intracolonial mail system along the Camino Real was gradually improved and served as a means of communication as well as a source of much-needed intelligence about new arrivals and suspicious activities. For most, these efforts had little impact since the compromise selection of the Sabine River in the Adams-Onís Treaty by U.S. representative John Quincy Adams was generally not accepted. Many Americans considered the accord a near treasonous "concession" and thus wished to lay claim to the vast unoccupied lands west of the Sabine and north of the Rio Grande del Norte. In fact, the treaty was a stunning victory that gave the westward-expanding nation a cross-continental outlet to the Pacific.[38]

Prior to 1830, few of these American immigrants ventured to the still wild and hostile Nueces Strip and Laredo. A near uninterrupted cycle of unrest and violence hampered growth and expansion of trade. The Villa of Palafox, located fourteen miles upstream from Laredo, was destroyed and permanently abandoned following a massive Indian attack in 1818, sounding an alarm along the Rio Grande.[39] Dolores, San Ygnacio, San Bartolo, and Clareno were either abandoned or all but destroyed. Yet, in spite of the harsh conditions, which caused Laredo Alcalde Ildefonso Ramón to request extra "passports" for those who wanted to leave Laredo, the villa reported a population of 1,418 in 1819. This represented fully one-third of the sparse population of the combined Texas settlements north of the Rio Grande.[40] Furthermore, Ramón proved an able mayor by making great efforts to insure that food and supplies reached the people of Laredo, noting in his official report the means needed to resupply:

> Although they are kept under the protection of the mounted garrison (troop of cavalry), 150 gentle mules to carry packsaddles, these are not grouped in bunches because they belong to many different people, but they are used to bring in grain from the Province of Coahuila, this being done by means of convoys guarded by troops, and we the inhabitants who live here owe our sustenance (bringing in of seeds) although the rigorous and notorious hungers (starvation) that the troops and the people have gone through are well known.[41]

As the revolutionary currents enveloped all of New Spain—with the declaration embodied in the February 1821 Plan of Iguala—the departure of the last viceroy, Juan Ruiz de Apodaca, Conde del Venadito (r. 1816–21), was hastened and he was forced to step down.[42] In the quest for nationhood, the Empire of Mexico was proclaimed under a constitutional monarchy form of government.[43] This burst of enthusiasm for limited democracy with the crowning of the Emperor of Mexico, former royalist leader Agustín de Iturbide, would prove at best a transitional government. John Q. Adams, by 1822 secretary of state, possibly because of the royal overtone of the new Mexican government, declined to offer full diplomatic recognition to Mexico. Mexican historian Enrique Krauze, author of *Mexico: Biography of Power,* fully captured the dynamics of this era of change in Mexico:

> On September 21, 1821, Iturbide's thirty-eighth birthday, the ten thousand men of the "Trigarantine Army," royalist and Insurgents united, entered Mexico City. The army's tricolored flag symbolizing the gist of the Program of Iguala was so popular that it would come to be adopted, with minor alterations, as the national flag. Against a white background, representing the purity of the Catholic religion, flanked by a green that referred to independence and a deep red that conveyed the memory of Spain, the flag bore the emblem of the mythical foundation of Mexico-Tenochtitlán by the Aztecs: an eagle perched on a nopal cactus and devouring a serpent. Thus, Mexico was born of multiple reconciliations, of an embrace between royalist and Insurgents, between gachupines, creoles, Indians, African-Mexicans, mestizos, and Castes, between the pre-Hispanic past and the three centuries of colonialism, between the branch and the trunk.[44]

Laredo, along with the new Republic of Mexico, would be thrust into a seesaw series of struggles for political power. The political battle within Mexico revolved around those who wanted a strong central government dominated in the capital—*centralistas,* and those who championed a decentralized federal republic—the *federalistas.* The leadership in Laredo was concentrated in a small group of landowners and ranchers who were well aware that their priority should be the stability of Laredo, not the mechanics of the transition from colonial rule to a nationalistic structure. The key was thus maintaining flexibility as allegiances would be tested and changed numerous times in the ensuing two decades. However, the Federalist sentiments generally prevailed on the Rio Grande frontier.[45] An example of this Laredo leadership was the rise of Victorino Dovalina to mayor in 1821–22. Dovalina, along with local leaders Fernando García Dávila and José de Jesús Benavides, would form the bases of a transitional political group. In addition to maintaining order in the villa, they were pivotal in selecting Teodocio Treviño as Laredo's representative to the Mexican Constitutional Convention of 1822 that drafted and enacted the Constitution of 1824. Expressing concern over land titles, water rights, and expansion and stability of the commercial trading sector, as well as protection from the Indians, Treviño was but a small voice in a convention dominated by representatives from central Mexico. In the reorganization of the Mexican regions, Laredo became part of the newly created state of Tamaulipas—carved out of the old colonial Nuevo Santander.

The population of Laredo remained unchanged during the early 1820s, yet by 1828 (the same year the new Mexican government officially expelled Spaniards), the villa exceeded 2,000 residents. In 1825, after repeated pressure from the governor, a school was opened in Laredo under headmaster

Juan José Salinas, and via local donations from the sale of wild horses he was paid a salary of twenty pesos per month to teach reading, writing, and "counting."[46] As Laredo endeavored to return to a degree of prosperity, attempts in Mexico City to establish a national government were marked by increased efforts to enhance the flow of commercial trade. The first five years after independence from Spain were chaotic for Mexico as there was a void of political and economic policy. The already failed economy was further constricted by high import duties implemented in the hope of raising revenue for the bankrupt central government; as one observer noted, "the treasury was exhausted."[47] This gradually generated much-needed tax revenues for the upstart government. The importance of the primary seaport on the Gulf of Mexico was confirmed as all ocean bound shipments were ordered to flow through the customs district of Veracruz.[48] Laredo would remain the primary commercial crossing on the Rio Grande—linking old colonial Mexico with the emerging markets north of the river. The concept of *comercio libre* (free trade) was expanded to all ports of the new nation. New regulations on trade were confirmed on December 20, 1821, and as a gesture of goodwill the new commercial policy included a clause that allowed duty-free trade in mules between Mexico and the United States. After 1822, Mexico was freed from the mandatory monopolistic control of trade between either Cádiz and Veracruz or Acapulco to Asia that dated from 1685. The result of this liberalization of trade was the establishment of the port of Refugio in 1823 (renamed Matamoros in 1826), and the long-awaited link to American products direct from merchants and wholesalers in New Orleans. Opening the Rio Grande to commerce and the legalization of trade gradually shifted the economy away from ranching. However, the main source of quick riches for the Mexican government (thus the urgency to reopen the mines) was silver, and the prime specie of barter was tobacco. The tobacco producers were ordered to follow the well-established colonial policies that forbade the planting, growing, selling, or bartering of the very popular leafy product and commodity. Notwithstanding, smuggling flourished. Tobacco, while prohibited, was tremendously profitable. Bought by merchants in New Orleans for $1.50 per hundredweight (cwt), tobacco was baled and smuggled across the border and was sold at between $50.00 and $75.00 per cwt.[49]

Smuggling was not new to the Rio Grande frontier in the early 1820s period as the newly organized government of the Mexican Republic took power. While many hailed the seemingly newfound freedom after over two hundred years of harsh control at the hands of the Spanish Crown, the new regime in fact did little to improve conditions and only modified the old commercial practices and controls—and in some cases tightened the rules of commerce. One observer viewed the continuation of high tariffs as nothing more than "an incentive to the contraband trade, as to reduce lawful trade to a mere camouflage for highly profitable smuggling." As the collection of import duties languished in an atmosphere of contraband, the central government in Mexico City labored under "the erroneous impression that to reduce tariffs would reduce revenue."[50] To solve, yet actually to further complicate, trade and duty collection problems, the government instituted bureaucratic controls such as *guias,* or shipping permits or mercantile passports, a detailed route of delivery to the buyer, and a *tornaguía,* or reply, to confirm merchandise arrived at its declared destination. In spite of the fact that a special purpose decree lowered duties on foodstuffs such as rice, coffee, lard, flour, and bacon, the border permitting process and cumbersome controls in the untamed frontier region only intensified smuggling. Border trade remained cumbersome as most permits were issued either in Matamoros or Monterrey. The U.S. response to border customs, which did not occur until after the Texas annexation, was in its infant stage. On May 17, 1848, the first U.S. customs collection agent, John S. Rhea, was established at Point Isabel. During the period from September 1853 to March 1856, sixteen mounted customs inspectors patrolled the border from the Gulf of Mexico to Laredo. In response, the Mexican government set up a customs inspector, or *contraresguardo,* in Nuevo Laredo, then officially named "Monterrey-Laredo," in January 1856.[51]

The Howling Wilderness

During the early 1800s, poor roads and the perils of transportation inhibited trade and raised the price of products, much as the situation had been for two centuries. Crude maps of the period noted trails in northern Mexico south of the Rio Grande that connected Saltillo, Monterrey, and Monclova via El Camino Real to Laredo and Presidio. From Laredo, the continuation of the Laredo highway crossed the Nueces Strip to San Antonio and La Bahía. Once a village of some one thousand people, Nacogdoches was nearly depopulated yet maintained a poor road to San Antonio and thence to Laredo. One author noted that Laredo, on one of the oldest commercial roads of the North American continent, was then (as well as it is now)—the hub of trade: "for a hundred years the road was used extensively for trade between the French in Louisiana and the Spaniards in Mexico although such trade was in violation of the laws which forbade any trade with the French. The traders bribed the post commanders and were even furnished armed escorts to protect the traders against the Indians."[52] In many respects, during the early nineteenth century Laredo became the crossroads of the first wave of what we have come to know today as commercial globalization. And as Mexico struggled to establish a government, its prime concern was trade and foreign investment from the British and French.[53]

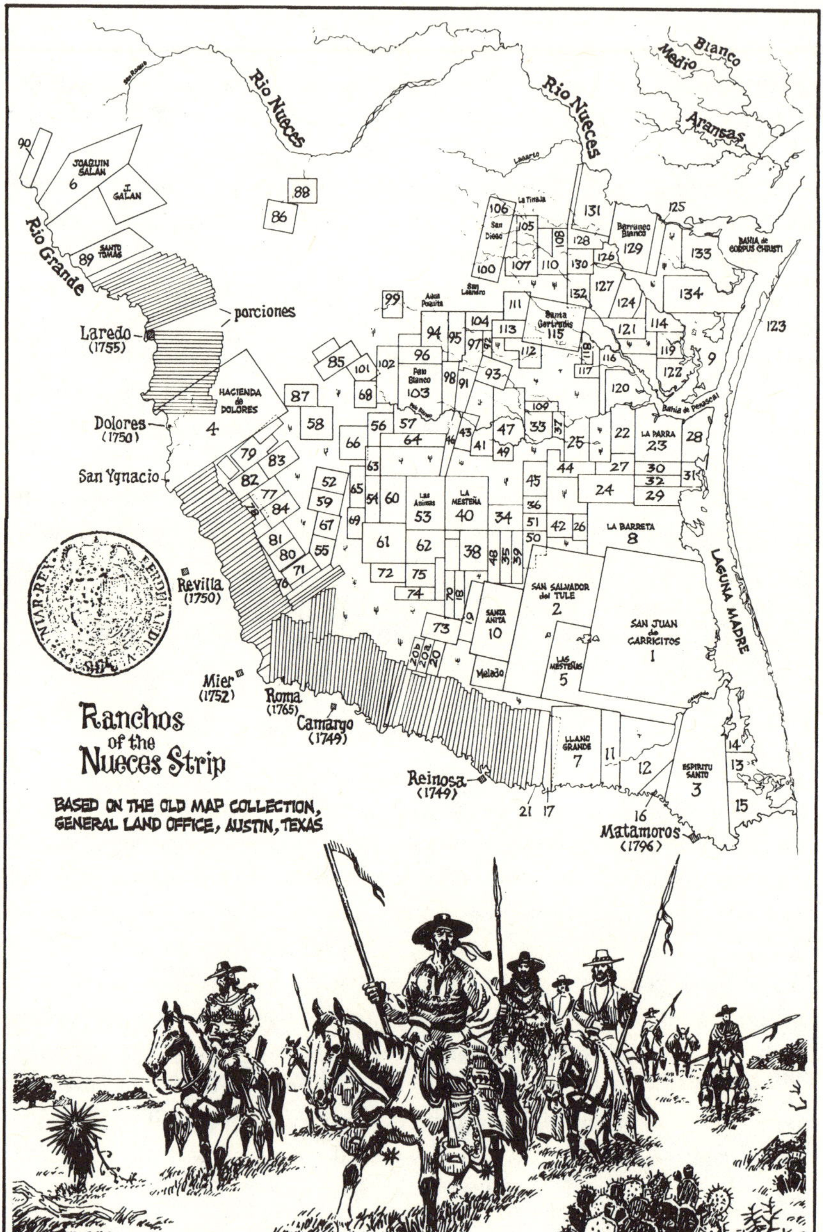

Map 2.1. Ranchos of the Nueces Strip. Courtesy Jack Jackson and Texas A&M University Press. This map shows the *porciones* of South Texas. Laredo, as well as the length of the border region north of the Rio Grande, devised a well-organized means of titling land. Note the slender *porciones* along the river that afforded access to water to as many as possible. Upon the independence of Texas, the General Land Office in Austin accepted these surveys as valid deeds for the transfer and sale of land in the region.

Fig. 2.1. An unidentified Comanche youth with armaments of the frontier. The bow and arrow used by mounted Comanche riders was a lethal match for both their rivals, the Apaches and the settlers. Source: Center for American History, Prints and Photographs Collection (CN 00081).

Ominous reference to the United States would have a profound impact on the future of Mexico's northernmost territories—Tamaulipas, Coahuila, and Texas. In the fall of 1821, few could have predicted that the self-imposed drive of a Virginian transplanted to Missouri, Stephen Fuller Austin, with the founding of fledgling communities at the mouths of both the Brazos and Colorado rivers, would set in motion the first substantial foundation for Anglo-American settlement in Texas. Dealing first with a Spanish colonial grant conveyed to his father Moses Austin by Governor Antonio María Martínez in San Antonio on December 26, 1820, Stephen, upon his father's death in June 1821, assumed the grant claim and became confirmed as an *empresario,* or colonial land agent. Concerned with the change of government in Mexico City, Austin traveled some one thousand miles by horseback via Laredo to confer with the new government of Emperor Agustín I to reconfirm title to his land grant. En route to Laredo, Austin and his small party were captured in a predawn raid by a band of fifty Comanches in the "howling wilderness" north of the Rio Grande, yet all were released when they identified themselves as "Americans." A Spaniard would have been given no quarter! Austin, more accustomed to the abundant water and fertile and rolling hills in the lush green, heavily wooded region between the lower reaches of the Brazos and Colorado River, provided one of the few surviving documented glimpses of the Rio Grande region. In a letter of March 23, 1822, to his younger brother James, he described Laredo in somewhat harsh but vivid terms:

> The Country from the River Medina to this place [Laredo] is the poorest I ever saw in my life, it is generally nothing but Sand, entirely void of Timber, covered with scrubby thorn bushes and Prickly Pear—this place is on the banks of the Rio Grande—and is as poor as sand banks, and drought, and indolence can make it—The river is about the size of the Arkansas, if anything a little larger. . . .[54]

Caught in the euphoria of political change and intrigue in Mexico City, Austin was able to salvage his land claim—an area of over 13,000 square miles—following the passage by the Mexican Congress of the Imperial Colonization Law in January 1823. In much the same way that Tomás Sánchez was conveyed his land grant in Laredo, Austin's grant allowed the establishment of a colony; each family engaged in livestock was to receive one *sitio* of 4,428 acres, and those who farmed received a *labor* (field) of 177 acres. Unlike the traditional Spanish procedures of the 1750s, these new colonial "grants" were not held in common. Instead, very liberal terms of payment (a land fee of twelve cents per acre) by each family land grant proved attractive to new settlers. However, such grants and claim in Texas were greatly influenced by the political stability of the central government in Mexico City. An excellent first-person account of the problems encountered to secure a land grant was penned by an anonymous author in *Visit to Texas: Being the Journal of a Traveller.* Austin's persistence in the Mexican capital bore fruit. In spite of the overthrow of Iturbide in March 1823, which resulted in the cancellation of the colonization act, Austin retained his land title and authority to his vast grant situated astride the Brazos and Colorado rivers—which by 1825 boasted a population of about 1,800.[55]

In time, following the passage of the new Mexican Constitution of 1824, renewed colonization guidelines were once again approved in March 1825.[56] To settle and become a landowner in what was commonly referred to by now as "Texas" (or as the "department" of Texas, which was identified as that region north of the Nueces River), a new American immigrant need only pledge to become a Mexican citizen and join the Catholic Church. The surviving colonial municipalities of San Antonio–Béxar, Nacogdoches, Goliad–La Bahía, and Laredo were joined by new settlements at Victoria (1824) and San Felipe de Austin (1824) on the right bank of the Brazos River—the empresarial headquarters of Austin's Colony. Although Mexico hoped to settle and foster loyal Anglo settlers to strengthen their claims in Texas, the very Mexican Colonization Law of 1825 that encouraged immigration would prove to be the eventual formative roots of the demise of Mexican Texas. In the wake of the American migration to Texas only a few Mexican nationals applied for and received a colonial "empresario contract."[57]

The fate of South Texas and Laredo may well have been sealed in late 1824 had the U.S. Minister to Mexico, Joel R. Poinsett, succeeded in negotiating a draft "friendship and commercial" agreement, the purpose of which was to block British expansionism overtures in the region. Quickly gaining tremendous influence in Mexico, Poinsett, with the approval of Secretary of State Henry Clay and following extensive talks with Mexican officials, offered $1 million for the disputed territory northeast of the Rio Grande—the Nueces Strip—yet the offer was declined, as was a second offer made in 1829.[58] Mexico held fast to its claims to Texas and refused to consider any accord that did not include the boundary provisions of the U.S.-Spanish Treaty of 1819. Poinsett, in spite of his confidence that the disagreements between the two nations about the border and cross-border trade were solvable, was recalled in the fall of 1829.

Poinsett's replacement was Chargé d'Affaires Col. Anthony Butler. President Andrew Jackson instructed newly appointed Secretary of State Martin Van Buren to convey to Butler that he should take a hard line against the Mexican government in order to secure both a conclusive agreement on the border (with the authorization to offer up to $5 million for territory and a treaty) and a comprehensive commercial agreement. British interest in com-

Table 2.4. Diplomatic accords between Mexico and Texas with the United States of America, 1828–1902

Country	*Date*	*Subject*
Mexico	January 12, 1828	Limits and Boundary (Sabine River)
Mexico	April 5, 1831	Amity, Commerce and Navigation
Mexico	April 3, 1835	Modification of Treaty of 1828
Republic of Texas	April 11, 1838	Claims
Republic of Texas	April 25, 1838	Boundary: Rio Grande
Mexico	April 11, 1839 January 30, 1843	Claims
Republic of Texas	March 1, 1845	Annexation
Mexico	February 2, 1848	Treaty of Guadalupe Hidalgo
Mexico	December 30, 1853	Gadsden Treaty
Mexico	December 11, 1861	Extradition and Postal
Mexico	July 4, 10, 1868	Claims and Naturalization
Mexico	November 27, 1872 January 31, 1873 November 20, 1874 April 29, 1876	Claims
Mexico	July 29, 1882 September 21, 1882 June 28, 1883 October 31, 1884	Pursuit of Indians
Mexico	January 20, 1883 February 25, 1885 May 14, 1886	Commerce
Mexico	February 18, 1889 August 24, 1894 October 1, 1895 November 6, 1896	Boundary
Mexico	June 25, 1890 November 25, 1896	Pursuit of Indians
Mexico	March 2, 1897 October 29, 1897 December 2, 1898 February 22, 1899 November 21, 1900 June 25, 1902	Claims and Boundary Extradition

Source: Miller, *Treaties of the U.S.*

mercial access along the Texas coast and the Mexican coast continued with the added threat of a new invasion by Spanish loyalist forces from Havana.[59] While Butler made no progress on the Texas border issues, he did conclude the first extensive U.S.-Mexico binational trade accord, "A Treaty of Amity, Commerce, and Navigation," effective on April 5, 1831.[60] This treaty was to become the cornerstone of all future commercial accords with Mexico, in which was included a most-favored-nation—*de la nació mas favorecida*—clause. The language of the early nineteenth-century trade accord in part agreed:

> The United States of America and the United Mexican States, designing to take for the basis of their agreement the most perfect equality and reciprocity, engage mutually not to grant any particular favor to other nations in respect of commerce and navigation, which shall not immediately become common to the other party, who shall enjoy the same freely, if the concession was freely made, or upon the same conditions, if the concession was conditional.
>
> The citizens of the two countries respectively, shall have liberty, freely and securely, to come with their vessels and cargos to all such places, ports, and rivers of the United States of America and of the United Mexican States, to which other foreigners are permitted to come, to enter to the same, and to remain and reside in any port of the said territories respectively; also, to hire and occupy houses and warehouses for the purposes of their commerce, and to trade therein, in all sorts of produce, manufactures, and merchandise; and generally, the merchants and traders of each nation shall enjoy the most complete protection and security for their commerce.
>
> And they shall not pay higher or other duties, imposts, or fees whatsoever, than those which the most favored nations are or may be obliged to pay; and shall enjoy all the rights, privileges, and exemptions, with respect to navigation and commerce, which the citizens of the most favored nations do or may enjoy; but subject always to the laws, usages, and statutes of the two countries respectively.[61]

This commercial treaty, stressing "reciprocity" and "conformity" with Mexico, failed to address the boundary issues with Mexico, yet represented only the fifteenth nation with which the United States had concluded a bilateral accord. For the balance of the century, U.S.-Mexico bilateral treaties were the subjects of a narrow range of topics: commerce, Indians, and boundaries as well as "claims" to address grievances in each of these three areas. These activities predate the first substantive efforts at "free trade" and NAFTA in the early 1990s. Mexico was one of a number of nations in Latin America with which the United States inked commercial agreements in the 1800s.

Competitiveness, market access, free trade, and tariffs were the subjects of extensive debate between the public and private sector in the United States via an editorial essay series published weekly in the *Banner of the Constitution* during 1831–32. These collective articles and analyses by Condy Raguet appeared in the book *The Principles of Free Trade* in 1835. In the meantime, far removed from the debate on free trade, the fate of Texas seemed on a course that was out of the hands of politicians and policy makers in both Washington and Mexico City.[62]

As east and central Texas grew due to colonization, Laredo in the late 1820s and early 1830s struggled to demonstrate a period of recovery and was coping with the conditions of the day, as noted in the official census report of December 1828 by Alcalde Don José de los Santos Coy:

> The land surrounding this town is chiefly, fitted for all sorts of stock raising. Because of lack of hands, they do not spread out in this, nor in the planting, and principally because of the continuous hostility of the savages. The only seeds cultivated at all are corn, beans, and seasonable wet weather plants because of lack of any irrigation in the district. Building lumber must be hauled from the state of Coahuila sixty leagues away, since in this locality there are only the mesquite and willow of the river bottom.
>
> The constitution of the inhabitants is robust and healthy. Their average height is five feet and of a light color. Their regular diet is corn and meat. Their occupations are the services of arms, cattle raising, mule freighting, and farm work. Their main ailments are wounds in the side from bullets, lance, arrows of the Comanches, and the cause of this affliction is that they do not determine to pursue any campaign against the Comanches until they are exterminated.
>
> The dwellings are earthen houses, and most of them are grass-thatched huts. The town has two plazas, the plaza Principal and the Plaza de arms, and each is a hundred varas square not counting its streets. The wealth or subsistence of these inhabitants consists of a small amount of native commercial exchange, freighting of food for themselves and for Bexar, and some stock raising of all kinds. It is calculated that the town consumes three hundred and sixty five head of cattle, one thousand head of sheep and goats, seven hundred arrobas [25 pounds] of flour and six thousand five hundred fanegas [about equal to one bushel of 110 pounds] of corn.[63]

In spite of the Coy report, Laredo lost about a fourth of its population between 1828 and 1831. In contrast, by 1830, over 25,000 Anglo-American colonists, "principally persons from the Southern and Western states," had settled the new Texas colonies northeast of the Nueces River, joining an estimated 4,000 Mexican-Tejano descendants.[64] Some thirty plus *empresario* contracts in time settled over 9,000 families in Texas. While many of the immigrants moved to Texas from the southern U.S., the rapid growth can also be attributed to media coverage nationwide in feature stories such as those in the Cincinnati *Gazette, New York Statesman,* and the *National Intelligencer,* published in Washington, D.C. In spite of rising tension between Texas and Mexico, Austin was an active promoter of cross-border trade, noting, "everyone who has any knowledge in regard to the commerce of Texas must know that the Mexican markets are the best in the world for the products of Texas."[65] Thus, with the immigration wave started in 1821, Stephen F. Austin did more to populate Texas in a decade than the Spanish Crown had accomplished in the previous century.[66]

Constant threat of Indian attacks, poor roads, and unreliable communications as well as varied weather conditions were compounded by meager means to combat illness and epidemics. Settlement across the Texas territory was greatly impacted by the outbreak of a smallpox epidemic in 1831 followed by a cholera scourge in 1832 and 1834 that spread quickly in the hot and dusty environment and poor sanitary conditions. Many of the upstart Texas cities were near ghost towns as inhabitants fled to the countryside to avoid illness. Survival of complete communities was jeopardized. Laredo officials responded with a prohibition on large gatherings in the market, the cancellation of dances, and efforts to control dust on the city streets. The dead were to be buried immediately in plots, mostly in unmarked graves, "downwind" from the city plaza.[67]

Such outbreaks of illness and epidemics did little to equal the rebellious overtones in the nascent republic.

Victory or Death

Agitation and grievances—both real and imagined—among the growing number of colonists gradually changed both the tone and allegiance of those new to Texas. Concern over taxes and tariff exemptions, greater local political autonomy, and sentiments toward independence fueled a spirit of revolution among the Texas firebrands. One traveler in Texas during 1833 noted, "Texas traders complain of the duties they are often expected to pay; of the necessity of fleeing Mexican officers in order to avoid them; and especially of the inconveniences, expense and imprisonment to which they are not unfrequently [*sic*] subject." From 1833 until 1844, Laredo would be at the crossroads of forces intent on reshaping the destiny of the region.[68]

Gradually the Texas colonists aligned with the Federalist cause in Mexico; they were anchored by their common resolve to restore the Mexican Constitution of 1824. In opposition, the Centralists in Mexico City under Antonio López de Santa Anna had no plans to relinquish their control of the government. In an effort to gain a remedy to their grievances, a convention of the colonists was held in 1833, and Stephen F. Austin was dispatched to Mexico City to address the Texans' concerns. Austin's timing at first seemed ill fated; the central government was in a turmoil that was further aggravated by a cholera epidemic that swept the region. In January 1833, Santa Anna (who would be president of Mexico eleven different times) deposed Gen. Anastasio Bustamante and proclaimed control over the national government. Austin reached Mexico City following rumors that his true goal was to create an independent Texas. He was arrested in February 1834 and jailed for nearly a year in Mexico City prior to his release during a general amnesty decreed by Santa Anna on Christmas Day, 1834. Austin's absence was ill received by the colonists who relied upon his leadership and direction.[69]

In an effort to demonstrate Mexico's control and quell the seeds of open revolt, Santa Anna sent his brother-in-law, Gen. Martín Perfecto de Cos, commander of the Eastern Internal Provinces, and an army of five hundred troops to Texas as a show of force. Austin's response to his infuriated colonists on this "invasion" was equally hostile: "WAR is our only resource—there is no other remedy but to defend our rights, our country and ourselves by force of arms."[70] It is unknown if the Mexican army was aware of his strong sentiments. Moving rather swiftly given the overland conditions, Cos boasted that he would restore order; he arrested numerous agitators and reopened the Mexican customs house at Anahuac. In an equally swift response, the colonists demonstrated their sentiments through the actions of William B. Travis and a small force that recaptured Anahuac. By October 1835, generals Cos and Santa Anna rightly sensed armed revolt. What they did not know was how resoundingly the drums of rebellion were beating.[71]

Laredo, from its vantage point at the crossroads of the Rio Grande and the Laredo highway to San Antonio, would be the primary marshaling point and crossing for troops, supplies, and livestock for the armies moving north from Mexico. Laredo Alcalde Ildefonso Ramón, concerned about the impact on trade as well as about daily efforts to defend against the Indian incursions, petitioned the Governor Francisco Vital Fernández of Tamaulipas for assistance. The magnitude of Ramón's concerns as he faced more demands from the governor, who did little more than urge Laredo to do its best, was further aggravated by ongoing requests from the army for both recruits and supplies. One historian noted: we are "fighting a continuing and often losing battle against [Mexican army] commissary officers to retain enough corn and meat to sustain the villagers, and enough horses and mules to keep the work going on the ranches and maintain the thin stream of commerce that linked the river to its markets."[72]

General Cos moved into Texas, which resulted in a skirmish at González on the Guadalupe River some seventy miles east of San Antonio; he then moved on to Béxar, oddly bypassing San Felipe de Austin on the Brazos, the most likely hotbed and concentration of rebel Texas colonists. Goliad, protected by only a small force of troops, was overrun and captured; supplies and a large amount of ammunition were also captured. Coming with reinforcements, Col. Domingo Ugartechea crossed at Laredo with six hundred men, bound for San Antonio. In the process, the Centralist troops commandeered the best livestock of Laredo, leaving behind—under vocal protest from the alcalde—a weathered *remuda* of worn-out horses.[73]

Ugartechea's efforts proved too little and too late. The Texans at San Antonio, under the command of Col. Edward Burleson, began to apply pressure on the surrounded Mexican army. Following a number of skirmishes and under siege at the Alamo by the Texans, Cos's troops soon became short of supplies. On Wednesday, December 9, 1835, Cos surrendered with the promise that he and his officers would not oppose the colonists' efforts to support and restore the Constitution of 1824 and would agree to retreat to Mexico and never fight again on "Texas" soil.[74] Defeated, Cos retreated south to Laredo where he was joined by the vanguard of Santa Anna's army under the command of Gen. Joaquín Ramírez Sesma. The general was moving northward from Zacatecas with 1,500 troops. The main body of the Mexican army, numbering about 6,000, was resting in Saltillo. By Christmas 1835, the small villa of Laredo was overwhelmed; the main body of Santa Anna's armies was converging from Mexico and the remnant of the Cos force, numbering 1,105 and in total disarray, was headed south.[75]

The loss of Goliad, González, and San Antonio to the Texas rebels left no viable Mexican Texas garrison north of Laredo. Ironically, at a time when the Texans could have consolidated control over the newly gained exercise of authority, the citizen army melted into the countryside as the colonists returned to their farms and ranches. All that remained was a small force of 150 men, under Capt. James C. Neill in San Antonio, headquartered at the old San Antonio de Valero Mission (henceforth, known as "The Alamo"), in addition to two hundred volunteers under Col. James W. Fannin garrisoned at Goliad. Although Sam Houston was designated the commander-in-chief of the provisional army, he, in fact, held only an "advisory" commission and had, at this time, little or no overall command authority over the Texas forces.[76]

Laredo in 1836 was first and foremost a Mexican town caught squarely in the power struggle between Santa Anna and the rebel Texans. Laredo, once again, was in the spotlight as Santa Anna moved north from Saltillo and crossed the Rio Grande on February 16, 1836. Concentrating his forces at

Laredo, including those under General Cos, Santa Anna allowed the men to rest as the leading families of the villa hosted General Santa Anna and his officers to a dinner and *baile,* or dance.[77] Breaking camp, the combined army of some 6,000 men marched directly north to Béxar-San Antonio; the vanguard arrived late on February 23. As Carlos Castañeda concluded, "marching directly to the center of the Texas colonies over a shorter and more convenient route was sacrificed to the desire for revenge."[78] The Alamo, an abandoned mission built in 1718 and surrounded by two-foot-thick, twelve-foot-high walls, was now under the joint command of William B. Travis and James Bowie. Soon, Travis was left in sole command following an illness that confined Bowie to a small corner room of the old mission. On the 24th, Travis penned a dramatic appeal: "To the People of Texas and all Americans in the world" to rise in support of the men of the Alamo—vowing "I shall never surrender or retreat—VICTORY or DEATH."[79] Except for thirty-three men from González who arrived on March 1, the desired reinforcements never materialized. And in the face of battle, on March 2, 1836, Texas declared its independence at Washington-on-the-Brazos as a "sovereign and independent republic."[80]

After a valiant defense by the Texans, the Alamo fell on March 6, followed by the capture and massacre of Fannin and over 350 men at Goliad on March 7, Palm Sunday. Declaring an overwhelming victory, Santa Anna made plans to return to Mexico City. The Mexican government began an aggressive diplomatic effort with the United States throughout March and April in order to secure its territorial position north of the Rio Grande. For example, on April 28, 1836, in a strongly worded communiqué from Secretary of State José María Ortiz Monasterio to U.S. Chargé d'Affaires Anthony Butler, Ortiz Monasterio reminded the U.S. government that the unjust rebellion by Texas colonists was without merit. He bluntly stated, "No one considers it other than a wicked and unheard-of rebellion." To insure a Mexican victory, the border and all Texas seaports were closed, denying access to any foreign carrier "so long as the rebellion may last." And to further insure as much disruption as possible in Texas territory, the Mexican army, following the fall of the Alamo, was ordered to arm the Indians and urge them to "plunder and kill Americans." Reports of this final action by U.S. Army officers gained a great deal of attention in Washington.[81]

To truly end the Texas revolt, Santa Anna reasoned that he must pursue and destroy the remnants of the Texas firebrands and "filibusters" under Sam Houston's command. Moving with haste toward San Felipe (now abandoned) and across the Brazos River at Fort Bend, Santa Anna bivouacked his troops on the west bank of the San Jacinto River. Although outnumbered, Houston moved swiftly to attack the Mexicans on April 21, 1836, routing the larger army in less than twenty minutes.[82] With the defeat and capture of

Santa Anna, Texas independence was virtually assured. Santa Anna expected to be put to death, yet the Mexican president gave the Masonic distress signal and "was shown much deference," according to Sam Houston's son, Andrew Jackson Houston, in his book about the battle of San Jacinto. General Houston, also a Mason, held off those who would lynch the flamboyant general in hopes he would be more valuable alive than dead.[83]

With the secret covenants of the Treaty of Velasco signed by Santa Anna on May 14, Mexico was obligated to grant de facto recognition to the Republic of Texas, with the southwestern border fixed on the Rio Grande. Additionally, both diplomatic recognition and normalization of cross-border commerce was acknowledged in the accord. Furthermore, President Andrew Jackson signed a resolution written by the U.S. Congress on March 3, 1837, his last day in office, that acknowledged the independence of the Lone Star State. Thus, the dramatic victory at San Jacinto would forever change the course of Texas, Mexican, and U.S. history as well as rank among one of the most decisive battles in modern warfare. As Texas historian T. R. Fehrenbach concluded: "the balance of power in Texas had turned. The American West was won."[84] Notwithstanding, the transition would prove difficult.

Following Texas independence, Laredo and the Rio Grande region would continue a decade of unrest. Shortly after the election of Sam Houston as president of the Republic of Texas, the new Congress, at Houston's urging, passed an act on December 19, 1836, that reaffirmed its claim that the southwestern boundary of the new republic was the Rio Grande, with the northern limits stretching to the Arkansas River and the 42nd parallel. This was regardless of the fact that the Texas treasury was heavily in debt and there were few soldiers or settlers to occupy and protect the disputed territory.[85] Clearly this was a bold move on the part of the Texans. However, neither the United States nor Mexico was quick to fully recognize such sweeping claims.[86] In fact, Mexico never officially recognized the Republic of Texas. While Jackson relented with diplomatic recognition and dispatched Alcee La Branche as chargé d'affaires to the Republic of Texas, the Mexican Congress disavowed all claims surrendered by Santa Anna under the Treaty of Velasco. And General Santa Anna in mid-1836 was escorted under armed guard up the Mississippi and Ohio rivers and then overland to visit President Jackson in Washington, D.C. This action probably saved Santa Anna from a summary execution at the hands of Texans displeased with the general. After conferring with the president and officials in Washington, Santa Anna was released and shipped by armed escort back to Veracruz on the U.S. naval corvette *Pioneer.* Officially condemned in Mexico City for his actions at San Jacinto, Santa Anna's public career appeared over.[87]

Commerce on the Rio Grande came to a halt as President David G. Burnet of the Republic of Texas issued a blockade of the river and ports of

Matamoros and Brazos de Santiago.[88] The Rio Grande and the "no man's land" area or "neutral ground" of the Nueces Strip ceded by Santa Anna in the Treaty of Velasco would be hotly contested, both by armed force and diplomatically, for over a decade following 1836 as "South Texas seethed with anarchy."[89] And at the epicenter of this dispute between Texas, Mexico, and United States was Laredo—the lone surviving town on the north bank of the Rio Grande.

Chapter 3

War on the Rio Grande

War, under the most economical conduct, is always expensive and onerous; but most commonly successful in proportion to the insidious liberality of its expenditures—it seldom succeeds under the guidance of those who would value gold above liberty, and life above honor.

Mirabeau B. Lamar, President's Message, November 1839

Laredo is very little more than a heap of ruins. There is scarcely a comfortable home in the place. The desolation was the effect of the most unprecedented rains which fell in 1842, from which it has never revived. The town is divided into two distinct villages by the Rio Grande, both however bearing the common name Laredo. And being governed by the same local Authorities. The original town belongs to the eastern bank; and the joint population amounts to some nineteen hundred souls, about equally divided between the two portions. It is an isolated town, much exposed to the ravages of the Indians and has suffered greatly from that source, seven hundred of its inhabitants have been killed within the last twenty years.

Mirabeau B. Lamar, Laredo, Christmas Eve, 1846

For three decades after the rise of the Republic of Texas, the frontier fortunes of Laredo were impacted by armed rebels, shifting political loyalties, Indian depredations, and periods of famine and drought punctuated by devastating floods. Following the success of the Texas revolution and the declaration of independence, Mexico's efforts to retake Texas spawned attacks, border hostilities, and countermoves that would end in another war with Mexico by 1846—followed by a decade-long borderwide "commercial" war in the 1850s. This sweeping era of war and revolution on the border spelled an end to Civil War Texas and to Laredo as a hub for cotton shipments and smuggling.

Laredo scarcely had time to recover from the chaotic 1836 Texas revolution when fierce Indian attacks resumed in South Texas and as far north—some four hundred miles—as Fort Parker, near current-day Mexia in Limestone County. The only populated settlements in the Texas region in 1837 (other than Laredo) were Béxar, Goliad, González, and Refugio. Each was located north of the Nueces River. In May 1837, the settlement of Dolores, founded in 1753, was abandoned. And the few scattered small communities on both sides of the lower Rio Grande, including Mier, Guerrero, Carolitos, Camargo, and Matamoros south of the river—were struggling to survive. The disputed Nueces Strip north of Laredo and the Rio Grande proved to be an extensive uncharted territory, referred to as *El Desierto Muerto,* in which Indians and bands of "freebooter" smugglers operated. One of the largest bands of smugglers, under the command of Agatón Quiñones, hailed from Laredo. Thus, competing factions of Mexicans, Texans, and Indians waged a tireless guerrilla-like war to gain control over the rugged region.[1]

In spite of the "thoroughly arbitrary" claim by Texas that the Rio Grande was the southern border of the new republic, both the Spanish and Mexicans had defined, mapped, and documented the border as the tiny Nueces River.[2] And, as far as Mexico was concerned, in 1836, this was the fact. The Mexican National Congress flatly rejected any actions taken by Santa Anna after San Jacinto to change the boundaries. In the years after the Texas independence, Mexican troops, though small in number, patrolled the disputed territory of the Nueces Strip. At the same time, Texas Rangers and volunteer agents of the fledgling Texas government—both authorized and unauthorized—endeavored to plant the Lone Star flag on the banks of the Rio Grande *frontera.* In spite of the fact that most Mexican troops had withdrawn south across the Rio Grande, a small garrison of about a hundred poorly equipped soldiers was stationed at Laredo and at the mouth of the river at Matamoros, Bagdad, and Brazos Santiago. However, the greatest fear to Texas officials was the ongoing rumors that Mexico would launch a counterinvasion to attack and occupy Laredo or San Antonio. Such apprehension was with good cause. Mexico had no plans in 1836–37 of giving up either Laredo or its claims to Texas. Thus, the new Texas republic had good reason to be concerned, especially given the large standing Mexican army garrisons stationed across the Rio Grande at Monterrey, Saltillo, Matamoros, and Monclova. In contrast, Texas maintained only a scattered number of organized troop units, relying instead upon a citizen army of volunteers only called to service in times of crisis.[3]

In Texas, the only Texan regulars near the border were the members of a "spy company." This was the identification generally given to troops in the field assigned to gather intelligence and, if needed, conduct covert operations. One such spy company was comprised of some twenty men camped on the Medina River south of San Antonio; they were led by Erastus "Deaf"

Smith. In mid-March 1837, Smith, while reconnoitering Mexican garrison facilities and troop strength along the border, planned to make a dash into the plaza at Laredo in an effort to raise the "flag of independence on the spire of the church." The Laredo garrison of Mexican cavalry were alerted and responded to fight a brisk battle at the Arroyo Chacón, five miles northeast of the central plaza, repelling the Texans.[4] This would be the first of a series of challenges from both sides. In correspondence to an ailing President Houston, recovering from his wounds received at San Jacinto, Thomas J. Rusk, who had taken command of the undermanned and underfunded Texas Army, was concerned that "confusion prevails in the country." He advised the old general:

> The enemy have made three attempts to march from Matamoros but have failed in their plans so far. They are I understand collecting a large force of cavalry up about Saltillo and Monclova. I have our spies and scouts beyond the Nueces and have sent a detachment by Béjar towards Laredo. I have moved all the families back between this [Victoria] and the Nueces and have driven back a portion of cattle.[5]

In addition to these random efforts to counter the threat from Mexico, the small garrison in Laredo was no match for Indians, smugglers, and bandits. Roaming bands of Comanches claimed the area for hunting grounds, while smugglers all but halted merchant trade between the border and Béxar. Texas author Walter Prescott Webb noted, "War was the rule, the commonplace of daily life, and death was the price of defeat, for the savage enemies of Texas knew no mercy."[6] However, the irony was that while a hostile and vast land, the Nueces Strip was reported to be the home to an estimated three million head of stock, ranging from cattle, to horses, to sheep—many under the care of struggling ranchers, yet a large number still in the wild—and free for the taking by those who could capture them. In the unrest of the era, many landed ranchers abandoned their ranches and herds for the safety of Laredo, Béxar, Camargo, or Saltillo. Organized law enforcement was nonexistent. The status of property rights and policing of both branded and unbranded livestock created both opportunities and conflict. And as historian Arnoldo de León concluded, "Anglo arrogance and Texas-Mexican rights became causes for contention."[7]

Frontier Commerce

Even during heightened hostilities, cross-border trade linked Texas and Mexico. Laredo depended upon imports of corn, tobacco, calico, sugar, beans, salt, *piloncillos,* and flour.[8] Furthermore, Laredo was the prime north-south crossing point on the Rio Grande for merchandise bound for Béxar. When possible, Laredo and the border towns shipped beef, hides, tallow, leather products, and wool south across the river to Mexico in exchange for silver specie, flour, cloth, and furniture. One staple of the regional diet was *carne asada,* or *tasajo,* a form of jerky, from the Spanish word *charqui.* The use of dried beef was supplemented by pickled beef in salt brine, known to the Texas settlers as "mess beef," which was packed and sold for $7 to $10 per 200-pound barrel.[9] Cross-border trade was somewhat enhanced by the signing of the first U.S.-Mexico reciprocal trade agreement on tariffs in early 1832 (an agreement that stayed in force for over fifty years), yet barter and smuggling continued to comprise a large portion of the north-south trade. The *Austin City Gazette* had a guarded but optimistic tone toward trade, noting, "Mexican traders have discovered the advantages of open trade . . . a large trading company has arrived [in Austin] with 170 head of cattle and a number of mules and some specie, the whole of which they have left among us, purchasing goods and groceries in exchange."[10] While it is difficult to determine the exact extent of trade following the Texas war for independence, records indicate that as American exports to Texas had a slight increase, in the case of U.S.-Mexico trade, American exports to Mexico experienced a decrease from $9 million in 1835 to some $2 million in 1841.[11]

One driving factor influencing the return of Mexico-Texas trade was Mexico's concern over the deteriorating ability to obtain critically needed government financing from England and the impact of the French blockage of Mexican ports in 1838. Aware of the foreign intrigue, President Sam Houston authorized limited trade with northern Mexico. Texas independence created turmoil in the bond and debenture market in Europe and contributed to growing speculation regarding Mexico's ability to meet external debt payments. In April 1836, Mexico was not able to meet its obligation to the principal debtors in England. To cover the shortage of funds to settle the debt payments, Mexico blamed the United States—attempting to pit the British against the United States. However, angry British bondholders demanded recourse and were assured the "dispute" with Texas would soon be settled. If this did not occur, Mexico offered the concerned English financiers "a tract of country between Río del Norte and Río Nueces fronting one hundred miles of the Mexican Gulf and extending back to the mountains, containing about 30,000,000 acres and being still vacant, could be appropriated to the bondholders."[12] Touted as prime territory for livestock and agriculture, it is quite possible the English bondholders had no idea of the true nature of this land or the ramifications of being offered—the Nueces Strip! However, a few supporters of the Texas independence movement in London, including Texas representative J. Pinkney Henderson, protested to the British Foreign Office that such an action in the area north of the Rio Grande would be strongly opposed by Texas, and no such land transactions to benefit the bondholders would be accepted.[13]

Mexico's problems with England were compounded by the French government's demands for compensation for damages suffered by its citizens. A French naval squadron (following the blockade of the Port of Matamoros) had been deployed to Veracruz in mid-April 1838 to support French demands and grievances for some 600,000 pesos worth of claims against the Mexican government. A blockade of Mexico's primary port followed, which gravely deprived the Mexican government of a prime source of revenue from customs duties on imported products. The resulting skirmish was dubbed the "Pastry War"—Guerra de los Pasteles—because one of the claimants was the owner of a French bakery that had been damaged by Mexican troops at Tacubaya in Mexico City. Unable to negotiate a solution, the French resorted to an intense bombardment of Veracruz. This altercation with France resulted in yet another dramatic return of General López de Santa Anna to defend the honor of Mexico. In command of the army, he organized efforts to defeat the invaders. Due to his actions to retake the Port of Veracruz, General Santa Anna was wounded twice and lost his leg to a cannonball fired from a French ship. After a prolonged standoff and with a guarantee of repayment by Mexico, the French fleet withdrew and Santa Anna regained his status as a popular national hero.[14]

To evade the French Navy blockade of the Mexican coast and ports, a combination of Texas and British blockade-runners delivered goods to Houston and New Orleans for transshipment to Texas and Mexico. Texas, under the leadership of its second president, Mirabeau B. Lamar, and concerned with efforts to gain diplomatic recognition, took great care not to antagonize either the French or the British. Smugglers of merchandise into Texas ports had no concern other than profit. An additional key concern of the debt-strapped Texas republic was the requirement of a reliable currency or specie—mainly the silver *real,* or *onzas de plata*—into the Texas economy. Thus, trade through the Rio Grande border was expected to provide this key secondary benefit. In an effort to stimulate trade, the Texas Congress on July 12, 1837, modified tariffs on imported goods.[15] Congress removed duties from a long list of products, yet maintained a 10 percent ad valorem tax on dry goods and cotton products. Only gold or silver (no paper currency) would be accepted in payment of duties. These actions were well timed as the French signed a Treaty of Amity, Navigation, and Commerce with the Republic of Texas on September 25, 1839 (and opened a French Legation in Austin), thus becoming the first European nation to recognize Texas independence.[16] The treaty with France provided for complete reciprocity as to tonnage, lighthouse charges, and port fees. French and Texan vessels and the products each exported were to enjoy the same privileges, allocations, and duty drawbacks. For example, cotton was to be admitted into France on the same terms from Texas as from the United States, and French silk products were to pay one-half the duty as other countries if carried in either French or Texas flagged vessels. The British, however, were reluctant to extend recognition to the Texas representative in London, Gen. J. Pinckney Henderson, as they watched the reaction from Washington. During the postponement in official recognition, Henderson was assured that all trade with Texas "would be treated as a part of Mexico," and "vessels under the Texas flag . . . would be admitted into English ports under the terms of the commercial treaty between England and Mexico." Soon thereafter, Great Britain, Belgium, and the Netherlands extended diplomatic letters.[17]

However, recognition and commercial treaties with the leading nations of Europe did not automatically result in a willingness to grant loans to the new Republic of Texas. The inflow of specie was critical because Texas was by and large a "cash only" economy. Furthermore, Mexican silver exports to the United States had a direct adverse impact on the U.S. money supply during the 1830s and was credited by some as a primary cause of the broadened national Panic of 1837.[18] In addition to money from the United States in use in Texas, Spanish coinage remained in circulation on the border after the 1821 Mexican revolution. Generated by a historical disgust among Mexicans with the Spanish colonial crown, silver coins were often defaced or "hammered" to remove the royal effigy. This "hammered money" remained in circulation but was discounted by 10 percent as the new silver Mexican pesos were minted and put into circulation. Notwithstanding, the Rio Grande region had no banks and there were few loans. The majority of the wealth of the period was held in asset form—land and property—by either ranchers or merchants. Paper money issued by the Republic of Texas by 1839 was estimated to be over $3.5 million in circulation, yet prone to devaluation. This script was valued at only 16.6 cents to the U.S. dollar. The threat of armed conflict between Mexico and Texas continued to hamper stable economic and monetary conditions in Texas.[19] The irony of tumultuous Mexico is that the first half of the nineteenth century was accentuated by a massive amount of wealth that was being created due to Mexican silver production and the corresponding impact on global commerce, long before "globalization" became fashionable:

> Silver became Mexico's most important export. And by the 1850s it was producing 600 tons or about two-thirds of the world's total output of 900 tons. The silver dollar, which has been aptly described as the traveler's check of the time, was accepted throughout the commercial world, and especially in China where there was a strong demand for both bullion and coins. It was, as *The Times* [of London]

put it, "the coin of commerce." European merchants depended on it for their international trade, and month after month they anxiously awaited the arrival of the ships bringing their supplies from Mexico. In the first decade after independence, before trading companies were well established in Mexico City and Veracruz, there were little or no credit systems in which bills of exchange or other forms of credit could be widely used.[20]

Attack and Counterattack

Many Texans and Mexicans welcomed the opportunity to resume open armed hostilities. This era of endless attacks and counterattacks more commonly represented a state of civil war north and south of the Rio Grande, and Laredo was situated at the crossroads of the vying factions. The new Texas republic's President Mirabeau B. Lamar was powerless to exert authority over Laredo and the disputed Nueces Strip. Designated the area of San Patricio or Wild Horse Prairie by Texas officials on a map of 1839, Secretary of State James Webb (future namesake of Webb County), made the following notation on the contested claim area: "Of this section of country very little is known. From the fact that the Nueces on the south side, and Rio Grande on the north side are without any considerable tributaries, it is inferred that it is mostly dry elevated prairie."[21] Nearly a decade passed before the region reverted to the control of Texas.

While the Centralist authorities in Mexico wanted to hold Laredo and its strategic river crossing, they seldom provided adequate protection and supplies to the Villa de Laredo. Alcalde Don Bacilio Benavides worked with the citizens and ranchers of the villa to secure the central downtown area while he was denied aid requested from regional commanders, Italian-born General Vicente Filísola and his deputy, Adrián Woll. For Benavides's repeated attempts to obtain aid, Filísola, irritated by his vocal persistence, was on the verge of holding Benavides in contempt. The implications were that the independence and self-rule that many border residents desired was not acceptable to the central government. Such hostility toward Laredo and the surrounding region was a primary catalyst for a Federalist uprising along the border and in northern Mexico beginning in late 1838.[22]

In an effort to redress his claims for protection of Laredo, Don Benavides cast his lot with the Federalist movement. These rebels proclaimed the establishment of the independent Republic of the Rio Grande—an action influenced by and modeled after the "Texian" uprising of 1836. Spearheading a meeting of Laredo leaders and citizens, justice of the peace Don José María Ramón and Benavides drafted a resolution on January 5, 1839, proclaiming support for the Federalist cause and the fight to reinstate the Mexican Constitution of 1824. To mark the break with the central government in Mexico, Ramón noted that an eight-hour celebration in the main plaza was followed with, "a constant shouting of '*vivas!*' amid the firing of guns and pealing of bells." Laredo was once again in the center of conflict—encountering its third "revolution" in less than twenty years.[23]

Other communities across northern Mexico, following the lead of Laredo and Guerrero, rose in support of the insurgent cause. With little pomp or ceremony Laredo was selected as the capitol of the Republic of the Rio Grande and Jesús Cárdenas of Reynosa was selected as the first, and only, president to preside over a governing council. In fact, the selection of Laredo may have primarily been a strategic decision to have an announced presence on the *north side* of the Rio Grande, thereby giving credibility to the rebel republic. Having Laredo as the capital of the republic surely assisted in recruiting troops and surely helped in the attempt to form an alliance with the Republic of Texas. Guerrero, south of the Rio Grande, served as the location for major planning and was the home of the official newspaper of the insurgency—*Correo de Río Bravo del Norte.*[24] A newly designed flag consisted of three stars—representing the Mexican states of Tamaulipas, Nuevo León, and Coahuila—set on a field of white, red, and black.

The fledgling revolt gained strength in northern Mexico during a period in which the Centralist government in Mexico City was preoccupied with a French blockade and possible invasion that resulted in closure of the Port of Veracruz. When the French threat was lifted in mid-1839, the Federalists turned their attention to a consolidation and control of Saltillo, Tampico, and Monclova. The Mexican army moved north in late 1839 and recaptured Guerrero, Mier, and Laredo. Federalists under the command of Antonio Canales and Antonio Zapata retreated north across the Río Bravo into the Nueces Strip to resupply and recruit new volunteers. Representatives of the Republic of the Rio Grande contacted President Lamar of the Republic of Texas for support. Canales and President Cárdenas based their request to the Texas president on two factors: (1) if Texas joined the upstart Federalist cause it would be better able to prevent a Mexican invasion of Texas, and (2) cooperation would thwart Centralist efforts on the northern border to incite expanded Indian incursions along the entire Texas frontier. In response, Lamar maintained a guarded policy of neutrality. He was most certainly concerned about the reaction of Britain and France as well as about maintaining good relations with the United States. Most importantly, Lamar anticipated an expanded formal recognition of Texas by the United States to include a much-needed line of credit. Concerned with the growing power of the United States, agents of Great Britain (who feared that the potential success of the Republic of the Rio Grande would lead to a general revolt in an already unstable Mexico) were active in Mexico City and insisted that the best solution was for the Mexican government to "recognize Texas independence in exchange for a commitment that it would not join the United States."[25]

The full extent of the relationship between the two new upstart republics and presidents Lamar and Cárdenas has not been fully explored. The news of the Texas revolution and the rise of the republic was well known in both the United States and Europe, and was the object of wide speculation, as noted in an editorial in the *Austin City Gazette:* "If the Texians understand their interest they will unhesitatingly seize this occasion of insuring forever, at a very slight sacrifice, the existence of their young and frail Republic, which is more precarious than they imagine."[26] The *Gazette,* as both the city paper and the designated "Printer of the [Texas] Congress," carried an extensive debate and details on the merits of dealing with the Republic of the Rio Grande, or, as they styled it, "La República Norte-Mexicana."[27]

The discourse on the means of cooperation between Texas and the Republic of the Rio Grande was the subject of extensive articles; correspondence from Cárdenas and others who aggressively lobbied for a closer relationship between the two republics was also reprinted. As a buffer between Texas and Mexico, the Republic of the Rio Grande gained great attention even as rumors of renewed war fueled the debate in Austin.[28] Yet in his annual Presidential Message to the Texas Congress in mid-November 1839, Lamar expressed strong concern on the course of war as opposed to efforts to expand commercial ties: "Seldom [does war] succeed under the guidance of those who would value gold over liberty."[29]

In spite of the reluctant neglect from Lamar and Texas, Jesús Cárdenas in January 1840 organized a provisional government. Antonio Canales was selected as commander-in-chief of the army and delegates were named to Tamaulipas, Coahuila, and Nuevo León. The army was comprised of Mexicans, Carrizos, and Texans. Taking to the field with Canales were Capt. Samuel Jordan, Col. Jesús González of Laredo, and cavalry commander Antonio Zapata. These officers launched a bold campaign to recapture villas along the Rio Grande and in northern Mexico. After a number of skirmishes, the Republic of the Rio Grande met its high-water mark at the battle of Santa Rita de Morelos in Coahuila. Either unprepared or inept, the Canales forces were defeated and many were captured. In an after-action report, Mirabeau Lamar recorded interviews that indicated Zapata and his troops were "disgusted with his [Canales's] cowardice." While Canales escaped, those captured soldiers who refused to honor the Centralist cause were executed. Most famous among those who remained true to the Federalist revolt of northern Mexico was Colonel Antonio Zapata, who in order to serve as an example was hastily court-martialed for treason, found guilty of rebellion, and executed on March 29, 1840. He was decapitated and his head was placed in a cask of brandy (most likely *vino de mescal*) and returned under armed guard to his hometown of Guerrero to be put on public display for three days as a warning to any who may consider further revolt.[30]

Attempts by the rebels to regain a foothold in the region failed; Canales and Cárdenas surrendered their troops on November 6, 1840. During the period Lamar served as the military commander of Laredo, he interviewed former alcalde Benavides, who "attributed the failure of the revolution mainly to the tardiness of action on the part of the Federals; and especially in their not organizing, promptly, a Federal government to order and direct things."[31] To this day, the government of Mexico has never formally acknowledged the rise and fall of the Republic of the Rio Grande. In Texas, in 1858, the County of Zapata (as well as the county seat in 1898) was named for the dashing cavalry officer—Antonio Zapata. And in Laredo the capitol and headquarters building still stands today on San Agustín Plaza as the Republic of the Rio Grande Museum.[32]

The demise of the Republic of the Rio Grande did not end unrest in Mexico or diminish the real potential of hostilities between Mexico and Texas.[33] The government of Texas was well aware that it needed to secure its boundary claims along the Rio Grande. Thus, as a show of force, Ranger John C. Hayes briefly captured Laredo in January 1841 (and a second time in the spring of 1841), placing the villa on notice to local residents and Mexican officials that the Texas government would soon rule the border region. However, in the meantime, efforts to lay claim to the territory (in the northwest) claimed by Texas resulted in a grand scheme, approved by President Lamar. On June 18, 1841, an expedition of some 320 men, soldiers, servants, adventurers, and merchants was launched to march cross-country to capture Santa Fe in the territory of New Mexico. Over a 1,100-mile distance on the upper reaches of the Rio Grande and within the "boundaries" claimed by the Republic of Texas, the Santa Fe expedition's purpose was for the "the pecuniary advantages of the trade." Once again the control and expansion of trade was used as the reason for action:

> Nothing tends more to reconcile and unite than commerce. *Interest is a tie which all feel.* Again, by directing the profits of the Mexican trade into our own coffers, we are weakening the enemy and adding to our own strength; we are enriching Texas at the expense of Mexico; we are developing our resources, and making friends of our foes. The closer and the oftener the amicable contact of the people of Mexico with the citizens of this country, the better for both parties.[34]

The lofty pronouncements on trade and commerce proved premature. Under the command of Gen. Hugh McLeod, this headstrong attempt by Texas to subvert the influence of Mexico and establish an overland trade route with the New Mexico Territory failed with the capture and imprisonment of many in this adventurous party. The failed Texas expedition had a corresponding impact south of the Rio Grande. In the aftermath, General Santa Anna overthrew Mexican President Anastacio Bustamante's government and assumed dictatorial control of Mexico as Mexicans rejoiced in the failure of the "Texian" Santa Fe Expedition.[35]

In early 1842, with the approval of Santa Anna, Mexico launched a dramatic counterattack across the Rio Grande into Texas near Laredo to briefly recapture San Antonio, yet hastily retreated before the Texans could react in force. In response, President Houston, who was reinaugurated to a second term in December 1841, dispatched Vice President Edward Burleson and Gen. Alexander Somervell to pursue the invaders. Yet as they moved southward toward the border, the retreating Mexican army was able to cross the Rio Grande north of Laredo untouched. Rumors of war swept Texas.[36]

Sam Houston worked to cool demands for revenge among the Texans. But, on September 11, 1842, a second Mexican army under the command of French-born Gen. Adrián Woll again invaded and captured San Antonio, this time taking some one hundred prisoners. In response, General Somervell was recalled and ordered by Houston on October 3, 1842 to organize a punitive expedition to pursue Woll, to move south toward Laredo, and if necessary to "march across the Rio Grande" into Mexico.[37] The ill equipped and poorly disciplined force of approximately 750 men marched from San Antonio on the "Laredo Road" and arrived on the outskirts of Laredo in early December 1842. The small Mexican garrison of eighty men hastily evacuated without opposition. In the lull, Somervell failed to halt the looting of the city by some sixty troops after learning Woll and his army had escaped across the river.[38]

Under strong protest by Laredo's mayor, Don Florencio Villarreal, and many citizens, much of the stolen property was returned, and Somervell at once moved down the northern bank of the Rio Grande twenty miles near the small town of Habitación (later renamed Carrizo), a point across from Guerrero. After a week of delays, on December 19, 1842, Somervell decided not to enter Mexico and ordered a withdrawal back to San Antonio. However, some three hundred of his men bolted ranks to join Col. William S. Fisher in a quest to cross the river and attack the small town of Mier. This renegade band of Texans surrounded and attacked Mier on Christmas Day, 1842, thus launching the dramatic chronicle of the so-called Mier Expedition. This became a controversial episode in history, as Fisher was defeated. His captured troops were marched to Mexico City in chains and incarcerated in the dark dungeons at Castle Perote prison, an old Spanish colonial fort east of the capital. Along with Fisher, survivors of the ill-fated Santa Fe Expedition (of 1841) were combined as prisoners on the trip to confinement.

After suffering harsh imprisonment for nearly two years, Santa Anna, having recently returned to office for his ninth term as president, allowed the few remaining Texan survivors of the two ill-fated efforts to be freed and returned to Texas in September 1844.[39]

This series of cross-border hostilities did little to settle the Mexico-Texas question. From 1842 to late 1845, Texas began the dynamic process toward annexation to the United States. Throughout this period Laredo and reactions to claims to the southern border remained a topic of concern; Texas and the United States asserted the Rio Grande as the rightful boundary. Life in Laredo improved little between the Texas Revolution and 1848. In addition to the Indian menace, Laredo was occupied or claimed by nearly a dozen battling factions in the two-decade period. The city stopped growing and in the early 1840s and actually fell in population, due both to the continued cycle of hostilities and the disruption of ranching and cross-border merchant trade. Laredo was battered in 1842 by a series of uncommon torrential rains and floods, most likely the result of heavy rain from a hurricane that moved inland from the Gulf of Mexico. This first-recorded storm in Laredo inundated the town on both sides of the Rio Grande and destroyed what few crops were planted in the *vega,* and thereby interrupted trade.[40]

Tensions with Mexico were further aggravated by U.S. President John Tyler's initial yet incomplete efforts to annex Texas to the Union. Newspaper reports in the United States of the failed Santa Fe and Mier expeditions, as well as exploits in California, helped fuel a growing number of devotees of Manifest Destiny—as one congressman boasted, "Texas will be annexed. Our republic is to be an ocean bound republic."[41] Thus, the quest of western expansion did not die. With the signing by President James K. Polk of the Texas Treaty of Annexation on December 29, 1845, the Republic of Texas prepared to enter the Union as the state of Texas, and Laredo once again changed hands and was claimed as a part of the United States. Anson Jones and Sam Houston presided over the formal transition and statehood ceremonies on the steps of the Republic of Texas capitol in Austin on February 19, 1846. Shortly thereafter, Houston and Thomas Jefferson Rusk, Texas' first U.S. senators, and Timothy Pillsbury and David Kaufman, the first house members, were seated in the U.S. Congress. Even so, some additional three years would pass before Laredo would break all political ties with Mexico to be a part of Texas and the United States.[42]

While the annexation and political change did little to alter the cultural ties between Laredo and Mexico, the United States moved rapidly to establish a military presence and a federal customs agency to monitor cross-border commercial activities. Shortly after Texas joined the Union, Maj. Gen. Zachary Taylor received orders to move from his camp at Corpus Christi toward the Rio Grande, apparently to occupy the Nueces Strip and the communities along the river.[43] Secretary of War William L. Marcy relayed the president's aims and objectives to General Taylor, noting that any contact with the Mexican army "will be regarded by the Executive [Polk] as an invasion of the United States . . . should depredations be committed on our commerce by her armed vessels, or privateers, acting under her authority, this will constitute a state of war."[44] Following the U.S. annexation of Texas, Mexico resented the action and at once declared a "defensive" war against the United States on April 23, 1846. Inspirited by the western movement, Manifest Destiny "was more reason than excuse for the U.S.-Mexican War."[45] President Polk, following news of fighting along the border, requested and received a congressional declaration of war on May 13, 1846. Laredo remained in disputed territory. A detachment of Texas volunteers commanded by U.S. Army Capt. Richard A. Gillespie, in route to join General Taylor in Mexico, raised the U.S. flag for the first time over the villa of Laredo in July 1846.[46]

The vanguard of the permanent U.S. occupation of Laredo was led by Mirabeau B. Lamar (1798–1859). A former state senator from Georgia, Lamar had immigrated to Texas in 1835 with James W. Fannin. Due to his interest in history, his intent was to visit Texas and study the region. Quickly enthralled by the Texas Revolution, Lamar enlisted as a private and rose in rank through a number of military and political assignments. His experience included a battlefield commission as a cavalry commander at the Battle of San Jacinto in April 1836.[47] He was elected by acclamation the second "president" (December 1838–December 1841) of the Republic of Texas—when both of the opposing candidates committed suicide! As president, Lamar opposed annexation and lobbied to have the Republic of Texas expand its boundaries and territory to the Pacific Ocean. Both the British and French labored urgently to prevent such action in order to curb and contain the prospect of the rising North American giant.[48] The ill-fated Santa Fe Expedition of 1841 was intended to be a key part of Lamar's expansion strategy. Lamar selected the Colorado River site of Austin on the edge of Indian territory as the Republic's capital in late 1839 in order to push settlement westward. However, by 1844 he supported entry into the Union and thus, the annexation of Texas. After leaving office in December of 1841, Lamar continued in an active political role while developing his plantation near Richmond, Texas; he was then called back to military duty by Gen. Zachary Taylor. His reenlistment at the rank of captain was largely based on the strong recommendation of Texas governor James P. Henderson. While eager to serve with Taylor in Mexico, Lamar was dispatched in November 1846 to the strategic river ford at Laredo in the role of military commander of the newly mustered Laredo Guards, numbering seventy-three men.[49] Events in late 1846, such as the dramatic arrival of the seemingly enormous 150-foot-long side-wheeler *Major Brown* and its curious crew and cargo of troops, astounded the local residents. Within days Lamar arrived on the border with the detachment of Laredo Guards.[50]

Lamar, an avid reader and writer, provided some of the most detailed accounts of conditions in Laredo as it approached the century mark of its founding in 1855. He chronicled his observations in hundreds of letters, part of which he hoped to use in a future writing of a history of Texas. Unfortunately for all, no draft was completed before his death by heart attack in 1859. His candid and vivid reports to General Taylor are displayed in a first letter, dated Christmas Eve, 1846, observing that Laredo was "little more than a heap of ruins" due to massive rains and flooding in 1842, as well as to general neglect. Over a two-decade period, the ravages of Indian attacks, revolution, and a harsh climate reduced a once-vibrant villa and ranching community to a collection of abandoned properties. The Indian "depredations" were staggering, with an estimated seven hundred killed at the hands of the various marauding bands. Trade with Mexico was on the decline.[51]

Lamar quickly worked to develop a good relationship with alcalde Don Andrés Martínez and the citizens of Laredo—who surely were somewhat surprised to have as their commanding officer a former president of the Republic of Texas! Early cooperative measures included orders that all visitors to the town must register at the commandant's office. Learning of the full extent of Indian attacks, he worked to secure the town and in the process conducted an extensive census that indicated a population of 1,891. The slight drop in population was largely attributed to Indian attacks, but also included, as Lamar noted, that "an epidemic [most likely smallpox] has prevailed to an alarming extent." Reacting to this emergency, he ordered the quartermaster to provide medicine and assistance to the local residents.[52] Lamar's second concern was obtaining adequate food for both the troops and citizens:

> Corn is rather scarce, and is worth $3.00 pr. Fanega. It is a matter of some doubt if there is a suffici[e]ncy to last until the coming crop. Mexican flour can be had from the towns above this, enough to supply the garrison at $600 pr hundred pounds in the bran—Beef is abundant of excellent quality and worth from 1 1/4 to 3 cts pr pound, when bought on foot, the mode of purchasing which we have thus far adopted.[53]

Mexico Has Lost Laredo Forever

General Lamar, his customary title in spite of his captain's commission, while at times bored with his often-dull assignment in Laredo, proved highly capable in stabilizing the immediate region around the settlement. Sporadic

Indian attacks and harassment by bandits continued. However, after a decade of unrest, most citizens welcomed peace. In one last effort to keep Laredo a part of Mexico, several influential Laredo citizens attempted to turn back the clock. Former alcalde Bacilio Benavides (r. 1843–44), future mayor José María González (1851), and José María Ramón, all previously very active in the Republic of the Rio Grande, launched a written protest.[54] Addressing General-in-Chief John Ellis Wool, regional U.S. military commander in Monterrey, the three petitioned redress, claiming as justification that Lamar had failed to protect Laredo from the Indians and poorly administered the town. Thus, they sought to allow Laredo to take its own course and remain with Mexico.[55] Not mentioned in the letter to Wool was the lingering concern by landed gentry with the future of Laredo property and inheritance rights. Learning of the protest to Wool, Lamar strongly objected in a clear and concise letter to the trio:

> I cannot accept your Excellencies' proposal . . . Texas extends from the Sabine to the Rio Grande, and no portion within these limits has belonged to Mexico since the year 1836, when Texas won her independence.
>
> The government of Mexico has not employed you to sustain its right; it pays you nothing for your assistance; and the vindication of its cause cannot benefit the town of Laredo. For more than twelve months the inhabitants here have been contented and happy. Their property rights have been protected and their families been defended from the Indians, and you Excellencies cannot deny that they have enjoyed the greatest liberty, prosperity and peace under the laws and institutions of the United States.
>
> I am sorry that it is my duty to state that you can never realize desires for re-establishment of the authority of Mexico on this side of the Rio Grande. I have often told you this truth. Such a thing is impossible. Whatever you may believe to the contrary, Mexico has lost Laredo forever.[56]

General Lamar gave three options to those who would incite any civil disruption in Laredo. They could, first, uphold the laws of Texas and the United States; second, leave the country; or third, "take up arms—[thus,] I speak frankly to you as a friend, not as an enemy, because I sincerely desire the prosperity and happiness of the town of Laredo."[57] No response or action was taken by General Woll. Establishment of the new municipality in Nuevo Laredo continued without interruption. To foster tranquility, Lamar maintained an open dialogue with the citizens of Laredo and also administered a state of martial law into the summer of 1848. Any seeds of local rebellion were quickly dashed when news reached Laredo that the Treaty of Guadalupe Hidalgo was inked. Lamar was quick to point local citizens to the Spanish legacy to the successor property rights provisions embodies in Article 8 of the Treaty: "In the said territories, property of every kind, now belonging to Mexicans not established there, *shall be inviolably respected.*"[58] Hamilton P. Bee in Laredo was very active in contacting the General Land Office in Texas to perfect land titles as well as rights of access to the river.[59] Concern by local landowners in Laredo were further calmed when an act of the Texas legislature on September 4, 1850, authorized Governor P. H. Bell to appoint what became known as the Bourland-Miller Commission to gather abstracts of titles in order to make recommendations to recognize all valid grants and land titles north of the Rio Grande made before March 2, 1836. Donald Chipman notes that such grants and land titles, "as a consequence [totaled] approximately one-seventh of all private lands in Texas." Thus, the long disputed border war between Texas and Mexico, fueled by commercial interest and expansionist fervor, was considered resolved. Independent Texas, once it became a part of the Union, sealed the final border along the Rio Grande. And in the process, Mexico ceded approximately one-half of its territory in the far north to the United States. The Rio Grande was at last the permanent boundary—and Laredo a part of Texas.[60]

Assisted by Lt. Hamilton P. Bee, a native of Charleston, South Carolina, and future general in the Confederate army, Lamar endeavored to incorporate democratic procedures into Laredo's political structure.[61] With the help of Basilio Benavides, Agustín Dovalina, and Andrés Martínez, Lamar declared elections of city and county officials beginning in mid-1847. Thus, in mid-July forty residents of "Laredo, Texas," part of Nueces County, elected by ballot a new mayor, Florencio Villarreal, and two justices of the peace, Lee T. Tucker and Agustín Soto. Tomás Flores, running unopposed, was elected the first county commissioner.[62] With the Rio Grande as the boundary dividing Mexico and the United States, Laredo was split into two communities. Concerned about the inhabitants on the south bank of the river, Lamar invoked his authority, and, symbolically on the eve of the 26th anniversary of Mexican independence, September 16, 1847, appointed Don Andrés Martínez (the last alcalde of Laredo under Mexican rule) as the first mayor of the independent municipality of "Nuevo Laredo." The newly formed cross-border town was named Monterrey de Laredo, or Monterrey-Laredo, for a brief period, most likely to distinguish it from "Laredo, Texas." However, by mid-1850, the accepted name was Nuevo Laredo. A seemingly bold and unusual move by Lamar, the appointment of Martínez was fully justified given the fact the U.S. military occupied all northern Mexico under martial law with authority to maintain civil-political tranquility.[63]

The war with Mexico during 1846–48 had little direct impact on Laredo. The presence of Lamar's troops and the quartermaster's purchases added to the gradual recovery of the local economy. Lamar was further instrumental in creating stability before Texas legislative action created Webb County on January 28, 1848, from portions of Béxar and Nueces counties. The county of Webb, named for Virginian and former Texas secretary of states James Webb and close personal friend of Lamar's, originally covered 4,507 square miles and was one of eleven counties, to include Starr and Cameron, organized during February and March 1848. The city of Laredo, incorporated by approval of the state legislature on January 29, 1848, was officially designated the Webb County seat on March 16, 1848. On August 6, 1849, James A. Wilkinson was elected the first Webb County judge. In 1858, with Texas legislative approval, Zapata County was created out of eastern Webb County. Encinal County was carved out of the northern portion of Webb, yet was voided and reannexed to Webb County in 1898.[64]

Lamar's irregular Laredo Guards became one of the last Mexican War units to be discharged from duty—many members of the unit elected to remain and live in Laredo. On March 3, 1849, the first in a long history of federal presence that extends to the present, a company of thirty-three blue-clad troops of the 1st U.S. Infantry were dispatched from Ringgold Barracks at Rio Grande City to establish a garrison at Laredo. Bivouacking west of Laredo, commander Lt. Egbert L. Viele noted the strategic significance of the site and on March 3, 1849, established Camp Crawford and an earthen fort on the riverbank across from the age-old ford at Paso de los Indios. By 1850, this site became the permanent U.S. Army post, renamed Fort McIntosh, and the garrison under command of Capt. J. H. LaMotte expanded to two companies of troops. Fort McIntosh was one of a string of military posts ranging from the mouth of the Rio Grande at Brownsville to El Paso. Total army troops in Texas by the mid-1850s numbered over two thousand, with most dispatched along the border.[65]

Laredo, Texas—1850

General Lamar departed Laredo in 1849; he left local citizens in control of the destiny of the town and region. Upon the end of hostilities, Lamar returned to Georgia briefly and then traveled back to Texas in April 1851 to marry Henrietta Moffitt of Galveston. Until January 1855, he led a quiet private life, whereupon he became president of the organization of planters and exporters, the Southern Commercial Convention, which held a meeting annually in New Orleans. In early 1857, he was recommended for a diplomatic post in the Buchanan administration. And on July 23, 1857, Secretary of State Lewis Cass appointed him as minister plenipotentiary to Nicaragua.

Arriving in the capital of Managua, in the wake of the expulsion of the William Walker filibustering expedition to take over the country, Lamar's primary efforts were to assist the American Atlantic and Pacific Ship Company (a.k.a. Accessory Transit Company) secure a contract with the Nicaraguan government for an exclusive overland transisthmus route. The California gold rush fueled demand for a faster means to travel from the east coast of the U.S. to the west coast, which in turn created a rush of transisthmus schemes in Panama, Costa Rica, Nicaragua, and across the Isthmus of Tehuantepec in southern Mexico. Thus, a half-century before completion of the Panama Canal, the strategic and commercial importance of an isthmus crossing was well known. Intrigue by British and French agents unraveled the formal ratification of a final U.S.-Nicaraguan treaty, whereupon Lamar requested recall to Washington in July 1959. He died suddenly on December 19, 1859, at this home in Richmond, Texas.[66]

The population based only on the Laredo side of the border numbered 1,173 and consisted of 264 families. The 1850s were an era of adjustment to the requirements of both state and federal authorities. The period was also

Table 3.1. Immigrants to Laredo, 1850s

James A. Wilkinson	(1807–)	North Carolina	military interpreter
Hamilton P. Bee	(1822–1897)	South Carolina LG	county clerk
T. J. Miller		LG*	sheriff
R. M. Williams		LG*	district clerk
Tandy K. Anderson		Tennessee	justice of peace
I. W. Lillig		Maryland	county clerk/merchant
William Davis		LG*	sheriff
William F. Alexander	(1819–1882)	Kentucky	merchants
Raymond Martin	(1828–1900)	France	merchant/rancher
Edmund J. Davis	(1828–1883)	Florida	attorney
José Dolores Garcia		Monterrey	mayor 1853
David M. Level	(1824–1890)	Virginia	U.S. Customs/wagon maker
George W. Woodman	(1832–1890)		hardware
John L. Haynes	(1821–1888)	Virginia	state representative
John Z. Leyendecker	(1827–1902)	Germany	merchant, customs agent, ranching
Garner W. Pierce			
José Maria Rodriguez	(1829–1913)	San Antonio	Webb County Judge 1879

*LG: former members of Lamar's Laredo Guards: 1846–49

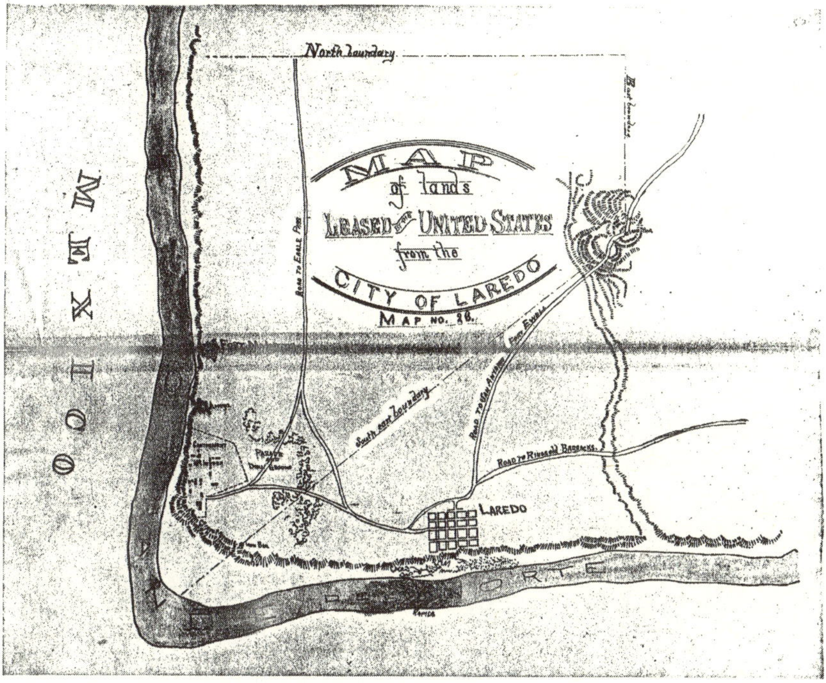

Map 3.1. Land leased by the U.S. from the City of Laredo, 1855. A map of the land surrounding Laredo and the road system. This is one of the earliest maps that depicts Fort MacIntosh and highlights the connections to the military outposts at Eagle Pass, Fort Ewell, and Ringgold Barracks.

first time in over five decades that the border had in-bound migration; as one author noted, "the mid-nineteenth century was the critical moment when Mexicans [north of the Rio Grande] became Mexican Americans, at least nominally."[67] In preparation for petitioning and securing historical land rights, one of the first actions of the Laredo city council was to translate the Royal Visita of 1767—the cornerstone document on land deeds in Webb County. In time, a state commission confirmed the validity of the original Laredo grants. However, the not-so-smooth struggle would be between the key Mexican families that survived the post-Texas revolution period and the Anglo-European investors and adventurers drawn to opportunity on the Rio Grande frontier. Some two-dozen members of the former Lamar Laredo Guards became a large part of the new political and commercial sector in Laredo.[68]

The dual challenge of politics and business would set the tone for the balance of the century. The entry of increasingly larger numbers of Anglo-American and European immigrants to Texas in general and to south Texas in particular resulted in a gradual shift in legal processes, land and water use, and to the general social order.[69] For the most part this shift was peaceful.[70] Gilberto Miguel Hinojosa noted of Laredo:

> Sharp divisions among the townspeople along ethnic lines seem to have been avoided. Interaction between Mexican Americans and Anglo-Americans was to a great extent characterized by cooperation. Gestures toward getting along included the publication of ordinances in both English and Spanish, celebration of American and Mexican national holidays [a practice continued to this date], and division of political offices more or less equal. Anglo-Americans and Europeans in Laredo, according to local tradition, learned Spanish, mixed socially with the Mexican American upper class, and intermarried with them. They often appeared more Mexicanized than Mexicanos appeared Americanized.[71]

News of the final approval of the Treaty of Guadalupe Hidalgo by the Mexican Congress on May 30, 1848, officially marked the transfer of Laredo to Texas. There was an extensive national debate on the final treaty and settlement with Mexico. Expansionists felt the moment was ripe to extend the U.S. boundary southward to the Isthmus of Tehuantepec; however, the debate over slavery in 1848 prevented further annexation.[72] The transition of sovereignty required the election of numerous officials to join mayors Florencio Villarreal (1848) and Basilio Benavides (1849–50). The first election in newly incorporated "Laredo, Texas" was held on June 28, 1850. Lamar's former troops fielded a number of candidates in the early years of elected government in Laredo. Most notable was Capt. Hamilton Prioleau Bee, who was married to Andrea Martínez, daughter of the revered alcalde. Bee held a number of elected positions in Webb County, including district representative from 1849 to 1859 and a stint as speaker of the Texas House of Representatives from 1855 to 1857. Other soldiers that stood for office were T. J. Miller, elected sheriff; North Carolinian R. M. McWilliams, district clerk; Gardner W. Pierce, notary public; Michel Lidwell, city alderman; and Lamar's interpreter James Wilkinson was elected the first Webb County judge. General Lamar was elected to a single term in the second Texas Legislature, he represented Nueces and San Patricio counties. Thus, a new political elite gained ground in South Texas.[73]

A notable example was Florida attorney Edmund Jackson Davis, who did not achieve overwhelming riches but would leave a mark on Laredo and the state. The political career of Davis closely paralleled his alliance with the Benavides family, in war and peace. Davis was elected a Laredo alderman in 1851, selected by the U.S. Treasury as inspector and deputy collector of U.S. Customs at the port of Laredo from 1849 to 1853, and in August 1853 was elected the district attorney in the 12th Judicial District at Brownsville. Strongly opposed to the Confederacy, he fled Texas to New Orleans in May 1862.[74]

Anglos, primarily from the southern United States, and foreign arrivals from Europe in the 1850s provided for a diverse mix on the streets of Laredo. John Z. Leyendecker was the vanguard of a German family that has had commercial interests in Laredo since 1847. New merchants in downtown included Joshua W. Littig, William F. Alexander, Alfred P. George, and José María Rodríguez. Rodríguez, a descendant of the Canary Islanders clan that settled in San Antonio, became the Webb County judge in 1879. Other new arrivals to Laredo included David M. Level, Santiago Sánchez, and George Woodman. French entrepreneur Raymond Martin, at age twenty-nine, arrived in 1857 from France to seek fame and fortune in Laredo. These men and their families mixed commercial and ranching success with political patronage to become influential and wealthy in South Texas.[75]

Mayor William F. Alexander worked with the aldermen of the city council to bring order to the city. Their primary concern was generating revenue by selling town lots and collecting income from fines, such as the twelve-and-a-half-cent fine placed on "owners of hogs found running at large." Laredo was a small community, with a total population in 1850 of about two thousand, and these men and their ambitions were known to their fellow merchants and political rivals. Such relationships would shift as allegiances, influence, and competition launched an era of freewheeling free enterprise, matched with the growth and expansion of cross-border trade with Mexico. Then, as now, commerce with Mexico was a key factor in the future of Laredo.[76]

In the years after 1848, many Mexicans moved south of the Rio Grande in order to avoid newly installed U.S. policies and laws, while others crossed into the U.S. to establish new Texas towns: Brownsville, across from Matamoros, as well as Eagle Pass, Edinburg, Rio Grande City, and Roma. Furthermore, trade between Laredo and Corpus Christi grew rapidly after the opening of an improved road in 1848, as Mexican ox-drawn carts staged merchandise in Laredo for export to Mexico. And for the governments of both the United States and Mexico, the border presented a tremendous struggle because the Rio Grande region remained infested with banditry, Indian depredations, runaway slaves, unrest by factual political groups (primarily in Mexico) looking to secede from the Mexican central government, and a growing, unchecked smuggling industry.[77]

In addition, the existence of wild horses, mules, and cattle dominated reports by travelers. One observer noted a large herd of horses led "by stallions with long wavy manes, and flowing tails which almost touched the ground."[78] The armies and government agents on both sides of the border

MEXICAN MULETEER.

Fig. 3.1. Mexican muleteer. In the era of wooden carts and oxen, the muleteer was a forerunner of the modern-day cross-border truckers. Averaging only a dozen miles per day over rugged terrain, the carts carried loads of up to 4,000 pounds. Source: Haven, *Our Next-Door Neighbor,* 1875.

were ill equipped to deal with the Comanches and Lipan Apaches, or with the large-scale illicit trade in contraband. Unrest persisted on both sides of the Rio Grande. As an example, in a bold move, Indians on the night of February 1, 1850, attacked the center of Nuevo Laredo, stealing cattle and disrupting trade. And trade across the Nueces Strip from Corpus Christi overland to Laredo was never totally safe for merchants or travelers; as the *New York Times* noted: "today a report came in that the [weekly] mail-rider was killed near Laredo." In a skirmish with Indians on the outskirts of town, 2nd Lt. Walter W. Hudson was mortally wounded on April 7, 1850. Alarmed at the increased number of attacks, the citizens of Laredo, following a town meeting, directed their concern for assistance with the unrest on the border to Governor Peter Hansborough Bell in Austin. Over forty-five community leaders and merchants signed a detailed letter on May 18, 1850. The protest requested swift dispatch of additional law enforcement and/or enhanced military protection. There was no action from the capital, so more protests and petitions from Laredo followed. In August 1852, Governor Bell, no stranger to border trouble since he had served in the Texas Rangers with Capt. John C. "Jack" Hays in the early 1840s, eventually wrote President Millard Fillmore for assistance. The correspondence stressed that the region is "depopulating and on the verge of ruin."[79] Notwithstanding, through it all emerged a merchant class who "were true believers in free trade."[80]

Alcabala

In many ways the Mexican approach to trade was much more complex than new U.S. Customs rules, and was more closely controlled by the central government in Mexico City. Merchants and government officials in the Federal District and in Veracruz had monopolized foreign trade and its regulation for most of Mexico since 1530. The northern frontier was thus more prone to trade outside established legal channels. Neglect of the northern region was partially addressed with the official opening of the Port of Matamoros in 1826. However, daily operations were limited; Monterrey agents were the official "middlemen" for all goods shipped into the interior of Mexico. In the case of trade with the United States, two vast differences accented what merchants and traders encountered. First, the United States maintained low tariffs, imposed no export tax, and no taxes on interstate or internal trade. In contrast, Mexico demanded high tariffs on both imports and internal trade. This was a manifestation of the colonial *alcabala.* The result, the cost of doing business in Mexico legally was often as much as four to six times more than in the United States and Texas. The burden on the Mexican merchants, the high tariff regime, and the stagnation of the Mexican economy is vividly captured in a gloomy commentary authored by "Varios Mexicanos" titled *Consideraciones sobre la situación política y social de la República Mexicana, en el año 1847.*[81]

Such centralized state control, noted the anonymous authors, inherited from the early days of New Spain, foretold continued government response and expectations from Mexicans on the influential and generally unproductive role of government in the nation's fragile economy. This characteristic also partially explains decades of underdevelopment. Yet by the 1850s, the concern was with adjustments to cross-border competition in trade and new rules of the border. One such heated rivalry was the Cart War in the late 1857 that pitted Mexican Texan and Anglo-Texan freight haulers of millions of dollars of merchandise and supplies from Corpus Christi and San Antonio via Laredo to Monterrey and Saltillo in Mexico. Protecting trade routes and clients often turned violent. The centralized government in Mexico City and their U.S. counterparts were ill staffed to police traders and shippers on the 1,952-mile-long border. As demand for merchandise grew, cross-border smuggling thrived.[82]

Spurs and Saddles: Army on the Border

Lamar's former cadre of troops who chose to remain in Laredo after their discharge from the Army, along with new Anglo and European immigrants, had a distinct impact on the Laredo downtown commercial sector and the ranching community. The primary injection of investment and hard currency into the cash-poor Laredo economy came from the post–Mexican War U.S. military operations at Fort McIntosh. Established in 1849, by 1855, following the construction of a small field fortification with two corner bastions, the fort numbered ten companies of infantry troops, one artillery battery, and three rifle companies. In total, the garrison comprised over three hundred federal bluecoats. While the number of troops fluctuated during the 1850s, the monthly payroll, the supplying via locally sourced provisions, and services to the military (as well as federal lease and purchase of land) provided a tremendous boost to the local economy.[83]

With the growth of Fort McIntosh, the Laredo economy in the 1850s became increasingly more dependent on local spending by the military. The improved supply and the support of the U.S. Army was unlike the support of the soldiers during either the Spanish colonial era or during the time of the ill-equipped Mexican garrison, between 1836 and 1845. Then, troops lived in tents with no furniture except a web cot and a trunk. Lumber was very scarce and the few boards available from the old wooden "bacon boxes were reserved to make coffins."[84]

The Army Quartermaster's Department in the postwar years established a small depot at Corpus Christi in November 1850 to supply Fort McIntosh. North of Laredo, at the bend in the Nueces River, Fort Ewell, founded in 1852, was established to provide protection for overland supply, mail, and travel on the Laredo–San Antonio Road. The bulk of supplies was shipped from New Orleans to Corpus Christi, and some moved up the Rio Grande on flat boats to Davis Landing at Ringgold Barracks across from Camargo,

Table 3.2. Laredo beef and forage contractors of U.S. Army supplies at Fort McIntosh, 1849–58

	Contractor	*Hay–price per ton*
1849	H. P. Bee and I. W. Lillig	
1850	H. P. Bee	
1851	B. Benavides and G. W. Pierce	
1852	B. Garcia	
1853	W. F. Alexander	
1854	E. J. Davis	E. J. Davis, 300 tons @ $20.00
1855	E. J. Davis	E. J. Davis, 500 tons @ $20.00
		H. P. Bee, 400 tons @ $13.40
		M. Lidwell, 400 tons @ $14.25
1856	H. P. Bee	
1857	———	R. Martin, 140 tons @ $12.00
1858	M. Lidwell	

Source: Smith, *U.S. Army and the Texas Frontier Economy,* 203–13

and from there by wagon to Fort McIntosh. Two-wheeled *carretas,* pack trains, and army issue "prairie schooners" drawn by six mules, dominated the frontier in the era prior to the arrival of the railroad. Building materials were in short supply given the absence of timber. Lumber shipped up the Rio Grande cost $65 per 1,000 feet and shingles $10 per thousand, delivered. The cost of the initial post buildings in 1852 at Fort McIntosh, with the use of local masons and carpenters, was $2,508.[85]

The supply of forage—corn, hay, and oats—as well as beef for the troops had a tremendous economic impact on all communities near the army post. Numerous Laredo citizens and merchants were involved in providing foodstuffs to the Army. Hamilton P. Bee and E. J. Davis, from 1849 to 1856, filled numerous requests for hay and beef. Hay for Fort McIntosh commanded a premium price; it sold for as high as $20 per ton when the average price in Texas was $12 to $13 per ton.[86] The *Texas Almanac* of 1857 supports the growing capacities of Webb County to supply livestock with the report of 274 horses and 3,539 head of cattle with a total valuation of $24,075. All manner of supplies and foodstuffs were in high demand: corn, flour, beans, coffee, pickled pork, large quantities of beef, as well as sugar and, occasionally when available, vegetables. The variety of available food was limited. In fact, the bland diet of the troops resulted in a higher incidence of scurvy for the soldiers, which inflicted more suffering than from wounds from skirmishes with the Indians or bandits. To cure as well as prevent cases of scurvy, the surgeon at Fort McIntosh issued each soldier a mandatory daily ration of *pulque*.[87] One young U.S. Army border officer posted at Laredo, Philip H. Sheridan, recalled:

> I was often detailed to march the company out about forty miles, cut the plant [maguey], load up two or three wagons with the stalks, and carry them to camp. Here the juice was extracted by rude press, and put in bottles until it fermented and became worse in odor than sulphurated hydrogen. At reveille roll-call every morning this fermented liquor was dealt out to the company, and as it was my duty, in my capacity of subaltern, to attend these roll-calls and see that the men took their ration of pulque, I always began the duty by drinking a cup of the repulsive stuff myself. Though hard to swallow, its well-known specific qualities in the prevention and cure of scurvy were familiar to all, so every man in the command gulped down his share notwithstanding its vile taste and odor.[88]

Many new local jobs were created in Laredo to move equipment and supplies: blacksmith, wheelwright, guide, interpreter, and teamster. The overland trip from Laredo to San Antonio was an eleven- to twelve-day journey by wagon.[89] However, these jobs, even when combined with the relatively large military purchases, did not fully revive the town's state of disrepair. Years of neglect and unrest took time to remedy. Newly elected members of the Laredo city council, much as their colonial Spanish forefathers, issued a broad number of ordinances (formerly called *bandos*), printed in both English and Spanish, to foster order. To curb any unrest in the city, saloons and billiard parlors were regulated, and visitors to Laredo, termed "strangers," were required to register with the sheriff's office. Firearms were prohibited, and speed limits were set on horse- and mule-drawn buggies. *Fandangos* were closely monitored, and bathing in the Rio Grande in sight of the city was closely patrolled. In spite of the poor economic conditions, the injection of money from the U.S. Army, coupled with high aspirations for expanded trade with Mexico, proved critical for the long-range development of the city.[90]

In a "special correspondence" to the *New York Times* signed only "Texas," readers on the East Coast received numerous vivid reports such as the following, headed "The Rio Grande Frontier."

> *Laredo (Texas) Wednesday, June 7, 1854*
>
> Incidents thicken here to make a New Yorker stare. In the first place, this town is the farthest from "white" land, in fact in distance,

> the nearer the famous identical jumping-off place to the pit than any other in Texas, though several be thereto than any man East can imagine. It is such a place here you would wonder to get a letter from it. Game cannot subsist anywhere within 15 miles of the river, and yet the town has nearly a thousand people, all Mexicans. They subsist almost solely of corn (of which, wetted and broken, they make their tortillas), smuggled from 60 miles in Mexico.
>
> But a worse enemy is within our borders, viz.: the Indians, lawless Comanches and others. Smaller outrages are "too numerous to mention." Single individuals move not through the country but with escorts, nor through the town but with revolvers. *Viva el Colt.* The scouting parties frequently see Indians but that is all. Everything is in a state of siege. The fact is, bad people sell bad brandy which drives bad men mad, and they devour each other. The practice of carrying weapons, imposed by a few upon all, makes them suspicious and hasty. The climate is choleric. When a man has to undergo three hours a day of temperatures of 115 degrees even in the shade . . . with an atmosphere filled with clouds of the fine dust, he is apt to grow "hot."[91]

Zona Libre

In spite of a near "lawless" region, the expansion of commercial activities in Laredo, while augmented by local military expenditures, expanded into the larger market of cross-border trade. Laredo, still the only town of any size on the Texas side of the Rio Grande, began to slowly grow during the 1850s. This occurred as poor economic conditions attracted many Mexicans to Laredo for higher wages and much lower prices for basic everyday goods such as clothes and food. During the immediate months and years after the Treaty of Guadalupe Hidalgo of 1848, traders on both sides of the border attempted to adjust to the new government regulations, poor transportation, and cross-border "federal" customs monitoring. The treaty had provisions that stipulated that American goods in ports or inland in Mexico during the U.S. occupation would not be subject to import tariffs, local sales tax, or confiscation once the U.S. Army withdrew. If any tariffs were to be levied, they would be determined by the U.S. government. Not surprisingly, the Mexican authorities categorically ignored any such agreements or implied policies; the result was a decade of unchecked smuggling and undeclared commercial warfare.[92]

Hoping to capitalize on the final weeks of the postwar U.S. occupation, a number of border tobacco merchants flooded the Mexican market with thousands of pounds of tobacco. This was to avoid duties and make a windfall due to the demand and popularity of tobacco products. Those who sold their products prior to the end of the U.S. occupation garnered a high return on their investment, and the rest were subsequently subject to confiscation and hefty fines. What resulted was a "merchant's war" throughout northern Mexico between U.S. dealers, Mexican importers, and Mexican state officials. One objective of U.S. dealers behind the increased American exports to Mexico during the war and occupation was to disrupt the British tobacco monopoly. In a classic case of trade following the "flag," U.S. merchant Samuel A. Belden shipped 565 bales of tobacco to Mexico, which was seized without recourse. In a petition to the president of the United States and the Senate Committee on Foreign Affairs he strongly requested that the U.S. government intercede to recover his loss. Belden represented that, "he and others were induced to engage in a very extensive business in Mexico, [encouraged by] our government in 1847, establishing war tariffs and inviting merchants into" the Mexican market to sell their products, and Americans were "promised protection."[93] Furthermore, Belden's claim cited that his loss, valued at U.S. $500,000 was a part of the merchandise and property protection provisions in Articles 17, 18, and 19 of the Treaty of Guadalupe Hidalgo—which included the renewal of articles in the 1831 Treaty of Amity, Commerce, and Navigation for an eight-year term.[94]

Fined $26,000 by the magistrate in Saltillo, Belden narrowly avoided arrest by returning to Texas. In addition to Belden, there were some dozen similar claims. Untangling the claims and counterclaims involved diplomatic negotiations over a twenty-year period. Belden was eventually awarded $128,000 in 1885.[95] In addition to numerous merchants' claims for tobacco and other exported products, constant political unrest and problems in northern Mexico continued for a decade following the end of the Mexican War and resulted in increased smuggling and cross-border attacks against both merchants and ranchers. In spite of the constant dangers, merchants in Laredo and other cities along the Rio Grande worked to establish new customers in Monterrey, Saltillo, Monclova, and Ciudad Victoria. The continued bandit activity, high duties, and Mexican domestic taxes (*alcabala*) resulted in shippers, merchants, and vendors locating in Texas towns along the Rio Grande. This avoided having merchandise stored and taxed in Mexican border towns until shipments were requested. Notwithstanding the official establishment of a U.S. Customs port of entry at Laredo in 1851, growth of Texas border towns outpaced their cross-river Mexican counterparts as merchants, as well as smugglers, legally took advantage of what was viewed as a safer heaven on the U.S. side of the river.[96]

During the 1850s, as border towns south of the river lost population, Mexico felt threatened by what they determined was unfair competition and viewed the merchant activity as an attack on the growth and prosperity of the Mexican towns. Texas merchants increasingly preferred storage of goods on the left bank of the Rio Grande. In response to the loss of business and of tax revenue, Ramón Guerra, governor of Tamaulipas, on March 18, 1858, signed a state legislative decree, apparently without the approval of the central government in Mexico City, to establish a *Zona Libre,* or *libre comercio,* free trade area. The twelve- to fourteen-mile-wide zone, or belt, along the river from Laredo to the Gulf of Mexico (later expanded to El Paso) authorized the importation of U.S. goods duty free (except for a 2.5 percent municipal tax) into the cities of Matamoros, Río Bravo (Rio Grande City), Reynosa, Camargo, Mier, Guerrero, and Monterrey, Laredo, and Nuevo Laredo.[97] Furthermore, merchants on the Texas side could move their entire inventories across the river into Mexico with little or no payment. Guerra's decree was termed a defiant "revolutionary act" and in violation of the Mexican constitution, thereby abrogating revenues to the central government. Laredo and the other Texas border cities were certain they would be heavily impacted by this action. Over five decades of debate would follow on the creation and impact of the Zona Libre. The U.S. Congressional Committee on Foreign Affairs (also concerned with the loss of revenue for the Treasury), in 1878, twenty years after the duty-free zone had been in effect, noted: "The object expressed in the decree was to prevent the decay of the towns of the northern frontier of Mexico. The towns on the opposite side of the river, in Texas, were then flourishing and rapidly increasing in trade and population, and it was feared that all the local trade would move from Mexico over to Texas."[98]

The Zona Libre and the border would be much-contested issues within Mexico, and would be at center stage in the commercial relations between Mexico and the United States. At the time of the Zona Libre implementation, relations continued to be badly strained between the two nations, not so much over trade but over concerns about border disputes, continued cross-border raids on ranchers, and a lack of law enforcement. Cross-border trade issues in the late 1850s prior to the outbreak of the Civil War were a regional, not a national issue in the U.S. What was of more concern was the continued Indian and bandit raids across the border to steal cattle and property. The U.S. Army commander of the Department of Texas, Brevet Col. Robert E. Lee, advocated an in-person inspection of the Texas-Mexican border from Fort Duncan at Eagle Pass to Fort McIntosh at Laredo and continuing downriver to Brownsville. Fort McIntosh, located on the bluff above the famed Paso de los Indios crossing, was initially a "star-shaped" earthwork designed by army engineers and built by the troops.[99]

Colonel Lee noted in an official report to Washington: "The commerce and intercourse between Mexico and Texas continued, though the feelings of the Mexican and American population seemed much embittered against each other."[100] Such unrest resulted in a prolonged borderwide power struggle with a new "opportunist" entering the scene. Juan Nepomuceno Cortina was a legendary rogue Mexican bandit; he was categorized by the popular serial magazine *Frank Leslie's Illustrated* as a "freebooter and marauder . . . reared in the saddle." In northeast Mexico, Cortina (a native of Camargo), along with lesser-known hit-and-run thieves, waged an ongoing series of raids that neither the U.S. Army nor the Texas Rangers could fully control. Unlike the Indian depredations, Cortina, a Robin Hood figure to the people of northern Mexico, harbored contempt for the U.S. invasion of Mexico and the impact on the region.[101] While rumors abounded in 1859–60 that Cortina might threaten Laredo, his raids and disruption of border commerce were generally confined to the vicinity of Brownsville, Matamoros, and Rio Grande City.[102]

Outraged by the continued hostilities, especially in the lower Rio Grande region and the entire border, U.S. president James Buchanan addressed this issue in his annual message to Congress in 1859. He boldly repeated a previous recommendation advocating that the president be given authority to "establish one or more temporary military posts across in Mexico . . . to protect the lives of American and Mexican citizens," and curb the "state of lawlessness and violence that prevails on the distant frontier."[103] No action was taken and hostilities continued unchecked. An appeal to the U.S. government in April 1860 for attention to the harsh conditions was echoed by newly elected Texas governor Sam Houston. Tension along the border escalated with both the regular U.S. Army and Texas Rangers crossing the Rio Grande into Mexico. Houston, as the former U.S. Senator from Texas in 1858, had supported Buchanan and strongly advocated in the halls of Congress that a U.S. military protectorate be "imposed" on Mexico:

> Texas willingly yields to the federal government the settlement of the Rio Grande difficulties. Its entire means of defense now in the field is inadequate to the protection of the country from Indians. Believing that when the facts are presented to Congress the dictates of humanity will rise above all party or personal considerations, I yet look for aid from that quarter. The American heart must feel for a people of like race and kindred; and though sectional considerations may prevail at times, they will, I believe, be forgotten when the catalogue of barbarities, by which our frontier has been devastated, is remembered.[104]

Laredo's population by 1860 was still unsettled. While numbering 1,306 in the official census, a new influx into the region brought change and new aspiring settlers—only 186 Laredoans listed in the 1850 Census as residents appeared in the 1860 Census. The number of households increased in town from 265 to 280, while only twenty-seven active ranches were listed in 1860, half the number of 1850. Unrest in the *monte,* or open range surrounding Laredo, not only reduced the number of ranches but also contributed to the increase in various occupations, beyond those required to support the military at Fort McIntosh. Included in the list of over a dozen active merchants was Raymond Martin, who over time became one of the leading Laredo merchants and office holders. In spite of a report by a military inspector, who noted, "It is difficult to say what sustains this town," the census of 1860 included a gunsmith, a bookkeeper, numerous tailors, a lawyer, several carpenters, and what may be the first doctor and fifty-eight cart men. The primary property owners were Martin, Charles Callaghan, Alphonse Martin, John Rigos, and Santos Benavides. The steady diversification of the Laredo economy soon was placed in conflict at the crossroads of the approaching American civil war.[105]

Cotton Times

Sam Houston's cautionary words that "sectional considerations may prevail at times" became reality with the secession of Texas in support of the states' rights platform of the Confederate States of America. Although Texas seceded on March 16, 1861, Houston, a stubborn Unionist, refused to honor the Texas secession and resigned as governor. However, once the southern states opened hostilities in April 1861, Houston acquiesced, "the time has come when man's section is his country."[106] In Laredo, there was no hesitation. Behind the leadership of mayor Santos Benavides, Laredo and Webb County voted overwhelmingly with the southern Confederacy, yet much pro-Union sentiment continued along the border as U.S. "agents" and spies recruited many on both sides. These individuals were known as *enganchados* and conducted guerilla attacks to disrupt Confederate supply lines and trade with Mexico.[107]

Laredo sentiments remained with the Southern cause and were marked by the service of a number of citizens in the Civil War. Santos Benavides and his brothers, Cristóbal and Refugio, were among the key Confederate leaders from Laredo. From the war's inception in 1861 to 1863, Benavides raised and trained a company of cavalry. This South Texas unit patrolled both sides of the border for union guerrillas, holding attacks against Laredo at bay until late 1863.[108] In November 1863, war was thrust upon Laredo following the Union capture of Brownsville by General Nathaniel P. Banks and seven thousand troops. Closing access to the mouth of the Rio Grande for Confederate trade resulted in the Confederate States of America (CSA) quickly looking for alternative land routes to Laredo, Roma, and Eagle Pass. This was necessary to transship cotton destined to the foreign textile mills in Europe across the border via Mexico. Once across in Mexico, the cotton was moved overland downriver to Bagdad, Mexico—deemed a "wretched place" by one observer in the late 1850s—at the mouth of the Rio Grande.[109] Since the southern Confederate states produced less than 10 percent of manufactured goods, compared to the northern region of the United States in 1860, it became imperative that cotton exports were made available to the foreign buyers in exchange for war material. Southern cotton, in the case of England, was in competition for British imports from Brazil, Egypt, Turkey, Italy, West Indies, East Indies, and China.[110] Hard currency and supplies for the Confederacy depended heavily on cotton exports. Thus, those of the period referred to this era as "Cotton Times." And Texas contributed extensively to cotton exports, raising production from 58,161 bales in 1850 to 431,463 bales by 1861.[111]

General Banks wasted little time and moved rapidly to seal off of the U.S.-Mexico border. He ordered former South Texas attorney Col. Edmund J. Davis and the First Texas U.S. Cavalry to Rio Grande City to stop and destroy all cotton shipments. From November 1863 to mid-1864, southern shippers were able to save and cross into Mexico thousands of bales of cotton. Former Lamar aide, now CSA Brig. Gen. Hamilton P. Bee ordered Col. Santos Benavides to protect the "all important trains [i.e., wagons] of cotton now approaching the Rio Grande" and keep the trade routes from San Antonio and González to Laredo as well as downriver to Rio Grande City open and to consolidate the movement of cotton bales to Laredo and across the river to foreign buyers.[112] The concerns and call to arms by Colonel Benavides became statewide news during December in the Austin *State Gazette* and the Houston *Tri-Weekly Telegraph:*

> *H'dqr's Line of the Rio Grande*
>
> LAREDO, TEXAS, DECEMBER 3, 1863
>
> To the people of the Frontier:
>
> This frontier is now invaded, the enemy have advanced and taken the line of the Rio Grande, as far as Roma. They have armed all the Mexican thieves on both sides of the Rio Grande. A few brave and determined men will drive them back to Brownsville and keep them within the lines of their fortifications. I have 150 fighting men. With 350 more I can drive back the enemy, I appeal to every man on the frontier, old and young, to come to the protection of his country. Mount and bring guns. I will furnish you with ammunition and rations, and any property taken from the enemy is yours.[113]

Table 3.3. Rio Grande merchandise trade, 1860–65

alabaster and spar ornaments	anchovies	sardines
billiard and bagatelle tables	furniture	brandy
sweetmeats preserved in sugar	molasses	cut glass
kirchenwasser	absynthe	arrack
cigars, snuff, paper cigar	curacoa	ratafia
Madeira, port, sherry	ebony	mahogany
almonds, raisins, currants, dates	German silver	satinwood
embroidered cosmetics	bay rum	beads of amber
tinctures used for the toilette	shell boxes	playing cards
brooms and brushes of all kinds	card cases	carriages
canes and sticks for walking	cider	clocks and parts
artificial feathers and flowers	cotton lace	plated and gilt ware
manufacturers of papier-mache	jewelry	stained glass
beer, ale, and porter in the case	muffs and tippets	marble
carper, hearth rugs, bed kinds	bricks	silk and fur
dolls and toys of all kinds	pavlog and roofing	stationery
angora, Tibet goat hair	velvet in the piece	engravings
fire crackers, sky rockets	roman candles	bananas, cocoa, nuts

Source: New Orleans *Times-Picayune,* March 21, 1865; Houston *Daily Telegraph,* January 9, 1865 and November 16, 1864

During this period, this area along the river gained a widely reported reputation as a rowdy, chaotic, and near-lawless region. Union and French naval ships boarded numerous ships in an effort to patrol the gulf waters, which raised protests from shippers about such harassment and seizures. However, trade flourished as Union warships were unable to patrol the shallow Rio Grande. The river, an international boundary under Article 7 of the Treaty of Guadalupe Hidalgo, was considered "free and common" to all vessels. In spite of the fact that 80 percent of the shipments to the border eventually entered Texas to supply and arm the Confederacy, the Union soon realized that an "effective naval blockage is impracticable." By 1863–64, the mouth of the Rio Grande at both Bagdad and Matamoros became one of the busiest shipping locations in the world and also the scene of constantly patrolling Union warships, confederate privateers, and blockade runners, as well as American, British, German, Dutch, French, Danish, Russian, and Spanish merchant carriers. Up to four hundred ships rode at anchor offshore, awaiting the signal from their onshore agents to unload merchandise for lighter transfer beyond the treacherous bar at the mouth of the river and then reload outbound Confederate cotton.[114]

The key to maintaining southern cotton exports by late 1863 was the protection and defense of Laredo and the ford across the Rio Grande to northern Mexico. General Bee, confident in his troops, stated candidly that without a good defense "at most, we have two or three months within which we have the advantage of the cotton trade."[115] And a good defense depended on not allowing the Federals to capture Laredo. In response, Banks dispatched Maj. Alfred E. Holt up the left bank of the Rio Grande with two hundred men to halt and destroy cotton shipments. He arrived at the outskirts of Laredo in mid-March 1864. On the 19th he divided his force in an attempt to lay siege to the strategic border villa and burn some five thousand bales of cotton stacked in San Agustín Plaza. Defending his hometown, Col. Santos Benavides reported to Col. John S. Ford, Commanding, Expeditionary Forces, that with "about 60 men all told, we have done all we could," and repelled three Union attacks along Zacate Creek.[116] Expecting the Federals to reinforce and counterattack, Benavides and Bee were both surprised when the Union troops withdrew toward Brownsville, remaining along the gulf coast in an uneasy standoff for the balance of the war. Benavides was prepared to torch the military supplies and cotton stored in Laredo. Direct orders to burn his home on the main plaza if the city fell to the federals were unnecessary. The defense of Laredo proved pivotal. It was estimated that 200,000 of the over 350,000 bales, from as far away as Louisiana and Arkansas, shipped to foreign buyers were sold and shipped via Laredo to the Port of Bagdad.[117]

In addition to the expansion of both seaborne and land-based activities along the Rio Grande to halt Confederate shipments, merchant-middlemen, such as the firm of P. Milmo and Company, owned by Patricio Milmo, conducted a competitive, brisk cross-border business in cotton and merchandise. Milmo, son-in-law of Nuevo León governor Santiago Vidaurri, had arrived in central Mexico in 1848, before settling in Monterrey. Milmo, the first border merchant to establish brokerage and forwarding agencies in multiple Rio Grande communities, moved swiftly to relocate operations up the Rio Grande from Matamoros to Roma, Laredo, Piedras Negras, and Eagle Pass. Each time he took great care to protect his overland shipping routes as well as his supply of merchandise. In the process, Milmo and Vidaurri amassed tremendous wealth and power. Cotton exports to Europe far exceeded the value of the goods imported into Texas and the Confederacy, thus shippers and speculators deposited the difference in merchandise and bank credits in the north (New York and Boston) or in England. Laredo, only 170 miles from Monterrey, by the Civil War's end became Milmo and Company's primary Texas border operation. As Milmo made money brokering cotton and contraband, Vidaurri, a near dictatorial *caudillo* of northern Mexico, maintained power in an era of Mexican unrest due to the French invasion and the inability of Benito Juárez to consolidate control of the weak central government. Customs revenue collected at customs houses in Nuevo Laredo and Piedras Negras by Vidaurri's special agents were as much as $175,000 monthly. Profits made by Milmo and other border merchants "became the economic foundation" of the postwar border region.[118]

Largely because of the Civil War, trade in Laredo boomed as a lucrative cross-border business grew. For the border merchants and traders, the "cotton times" and the lucrative cotton-induced trade fueled commerce much as tobacco exports had done following the Mexican War in 1848. The Port of Bagdad south of the mouth of the Rio Grande had grown to a population of some 15,000 and was a hot bed of both legal and illegal commerce. Smuggling became a way of life. The Union blockade of the Port of Matamoros delayed but did not stop trade in the region. As trade was diverted upriver in 1863 and 1864, Laredo gained notoriety among merchants and shippers in New Orleans, Boston, Mobile, and New York, as well as Cuba and the British Caribbean islands.[119] Goods and merchandise "from all quarters of the world"—with the exception of cotton and wool—entered border trade "duty free." The New Orleans *Times Picayune* hailed Matamoros and Laredo as the leading "Free Ports" during the final months of the war.[120]

Laredo in the mid-nineteenth century had prospered during wartime with the expansion of the number of merchants, traders, and new service activities to support the commercial sector and the military. The inflow of immigrants began a second wave, following the first influx on the 1850s. The cotton business, along with the merchant exports, created the beginnings of the Laredo forwarding agents and brokers, thus solidifying fast ties not just with San Antonio and Monterrey but also with shippers from New Orleans and the eastern seaboard of the United States.[121] Such excitement in boomtown Laredo was dampened by the greatest recorded flood of the Rio Grande to date on Saturday, June 10, 1865. Surging to a level of 62.5 feet above normal, the floodwaters of 1865 exceeded the rise of June 29–30, 1954, which measured 61.35 feet.[122] There are only a few accounts of the flood of 1865, as captured in this verse:

El sábado fue un día atroz,	Saturday was a terrible day,
que amaneció lloviendo,	Which dawned raining,
El Río también creciendo,	The river also flooding,
Con un aumento veloz.	With a increased speed.
Todos rogamos a Dios,	We all asked God,
No permitiera del agua el brinco,	Not to let the water leap,
Para el pueblo corría	Toward the town it ran
El año de sesenta y cinco.	In the year sixty-five.

Table 3.4. Rio Grande flooding at Laredo, 1842–2004

Date	*Gauge ft.*	*Date*	*Gauge ft.*
1800	Unknown	June 20, 1922	50.90
Spring 1842	***	September 8, 1923	23.50
June 10, 1865	62.50	May 31, 1925	39.90
September 9, 1883	Unknown	September 3, 1932	52.20
May 14, 1887	Unknown	September 9, 1932	23.40
September 27, 1894	32.20	October 2, 1932	22.47
September 21, 1896	34.30	October 8, 1932	22.37
June 15, 1899	37.40	June 16, 1935	35.10
April 7, 1900	35.70	September 7, 1935	32.28
May 15, 1900	22.00	June 30, 1936	20.96
September 25, 1900	22.00	September 14, 1936	18.44
June 15, 1903	21.30	July 26, 1938	27.40
September 17, 1904	32.30	September 20, 1941	20.31
July 1, 1905	36.60	August 29, 1944	22.44
August 14, 1906	27.70	October 10, 1945	22.80
June 19, 1912	27.70	June 26, 1948	47.83
October 6, 1914	32.80	July 6, 1948	26.97
September 29, 1917	27.20	February 27, 1949	20.41
October 23, 1918	20.90	June 29, 1954	61.35
September 18, 1919	40.30	August 27, 1998	32.20
September 24, 1919	36.10	October 13, 2003	23.10
September 11, 1920	19.90	April 6, 2004	28.30

***Exact date and flood level are unknown, yet reported by M. B. Lamar in a December 24, 1846, letter to General Zachary Taylor.

Source: IWBC, Laredo Archives, *New York Times,* O.R.

No state or federal assistance came to the aid of Laredo in June 1865. Notwithstanding, the two-decade era between the Mexican War and the end of the Civil War transformed the role of Laredo as a leading commercial center. Once again firmly in the Union, the "gateway" to trade in Laredo was faced with local and federal mandates of the coming postwar Reconstruction era.

CHAPTER 4

GATEWAY TO INTERNATIONAL COMMERCE

> We must enhance the utmost friendliness and good will that now exists between the two Republics and which cannot fail to be strengthened and go hand in hand with the grand commercial relations that are now being inaugurated.
>
> JAMES S. PENN, EDITOR, *LAREDO TIMES,* JULY 6, 1881

The post–Civil War era proved a harsh adjustment for both the state of Texas and the overall South. The return to normal commercial activities was now more so than ever under the close watch of the U.S. federal government. The carpetbaggers and "radical scalawag" Republicans that arrived in Texas during this period remained suspect through the Reconstruction period and the administration of Governor Edmund Jackson Davis, a former Laredo attorney, former general officer in the Union army in command of the First Texas Cavalry, and reputed South Texas native.[1] Davis was vocal in opposing economic development and opposed particularly Jay Gould's early interest in railroad projects across the state of Texas. Not until the defeat of Davis by Richard Coke in the contested election in the fall of 1873 did Texas truly begin economic recovery and growth. In the case of Laredo, from the postwar period through the 1870s, the economic and physical environment remained one that fully reflected all aspects of the Wild West. In spite of the fact that ranching and commerce were hampered by a bold increase of Indian and bandit hostilities along the Rio Grande, U.S. demand for livestock gradually increased. Cross-border raids on cattle and horses, as well as attacks on citizens of the region, required the added attention of both the U.S. Army stationed along the border and the reluctant Mexican government—neither of which ever fully established the upper hand.[2]

The region along the Rio Grande was in constant turmoil. Local governments and law enforcement were placed in a secondary role—both in authority and inability to maintain order—in light of a federal mandate from the U.S. Congress. The Reconstruction Act of March 1867 divided the South into a number of geographic military districts to be administered by the U.S. Army. Texas, along with Louisiana, comprised the Fifth Military District under the initial command of Gen. Philip H. Sheridan. The general (who had once served at Fort McIntosh as a young lieutenant) had little desire to deal with the critical issues facing the economic recovery of the Southern states and particularly Texas—whereupon notification by Washington of his assignment, legend has it, he quipped, "If I owned hell and Texas, I would rent out Texas and live in hell." Soon Sheridan was transferred to Missouri and a string of commanders followed in his place over the next decade.[3]

The Rio Grande border and Laredo in particular were not a high priority for the U.S. Army.[4] Units sent to the various forts along the border were undermanned, ill equipped, and generally unable to deal with the harsh realities of the cross-border region. Few if any officers were bilingual. In August 1867, the 9th Cavalry was assigned to Fort McIntosh west of downtown Laredo. In addition to garrison duty, the commander of the unit had the additional responsibility of monitoring the Laredo political structure and the qualifications and actions of local "elected" city and county officials. In the case of Laredo, as well as other South Texas towns, the majority of the local leadership was replete with former soldiers, officers of the Confederacy, and those who had supported the "lost cause." Divided loyalties would lead to numerous breaches of cooperation between the U.S. Army and the citizens of Laredo.[5]

In mid-1869, Brevet Lieutenant Colonel Prime, commanding officer at Fort McIntosh, determined that most, if not all, of the elected Webb County officials were not eligible to hold public office under federal Reconstruction guidelines because they were former Confederates. Efforts to find replacements failed and Prime became the de facto military commander of the county and the city. The one exception was the appointment by Prime, and confirmation by Governor Andrew J. Hamilton, of Samuel Mattias Jarvis (1822–1893) as mayor. The only Republican mayor in the history of the city and a dedicated "Unionist," Jarvis brought to his permanent home in Laredo a varied past. A native of New York City, as a captain in the U.S. Army he fought in the Mexican War of 1846–47 at the Battle of Chapultepec, then worked as a civilian clerk to Army quartermaster Maj. William Chapman at Fort Brown in the early 1850s, and subsequently signed on for a brief period with Col. William Walker's filibustering expedition to Nicaragua in 1856. His close dealings with wealthy lower Rio Grande merchant and land baron Charles Stillman led Jarvis to invest in Mexican mines. Fluent in Spanish, he managed a silver mining operation in Vallecillos, Nuevo León, during the early 1860s, where he married Inocencia Flores. In 1865, at age forty-three, Jarvis moved to Laredo and for the next three decades had a tremendous impact on the political structure, planning, and commercial development of the city.[6]

Colonel Prime, wielding absolute authority, issued numerous directives. He banned the custom of citizens carrying weapons, open or concealed, on the streets of the city. Visitors and traveling salesmen, however, maintained the right to carry arms, yet only in the course of their travels. Rules were issued to prohibit gambling, which included the favorite pastime of cock fighting. *Bailes* or *fandangos* required an armed military sentinel posted at the door to aid the city marshal in the event of disturbances. Mayor Jarvis mandated that the streets be clean and that sanitary facilities be built. The slaughter of cattle in the city was outlawed unless all offal was hauled out of town a distance of a least one mile. The mayor was offered the use of a quartermaster wagon to assist in the removal of waste.[7]

In the midst of efforts to organize and clean up the city, the region along the Rio Grande throughout Reconstruction was subjected to numerous Indian and bandit raids. Staging in safe sanctuaries across the border near Santa Rosa and Monclova, Mexico, renegade bands of Comanche, Lipan, Kiowa, and Mescalero Apache, as well as Kickapoo, were able to roam the border with ease.[8] Most of these Indians had been displaced from their ancestral homelands and hunting grounds. Their historic primary prey of buffalo was all but gone, and, thus, they began to raid for cattle, horses, and sheep as substitutes. The ease of crossing the Rio Grande facilitated their raids. The vast area between the Rio Grande and the Nueces, the Nueces Strip, afforded the Indians a place to hide and introduced the element of surprise in their attacks. The raids turned increasingly more violent with the taking of hostages and the killing of dozens of ranchers and shepherds. Often, the gradually more aggressive Indians were led by Mexican bandits who encouraged the contraband trade in cattle and horses.[9] Stolen cattle and horses were part of a smuggling ring headed by Mexican bandit Juan Cortina. Cortina, who had a contract with the Cuban government to supply beef, sent the stolen cattle to the Mexican port of Bagdad at the mouth of the Rio Grande for shipment to Cuba. Shipments from Bagdad came to an abrupt halt when the city and port were totally destroyed (and never rebuilt) by a massive hurricane on October 29, 1867—killing more than one hundred residents. Cortina then simply switched to a new port: Tampico, Mexico, a few miles south on the Gulf of Mexico.[10]

By 1870, the assessment of the military commanders at Fort McIntosh and Fort Duncan at Eagle Pass, in reports to their respective headquarters, was that allowing hot pursuit by the Army across the Rio Grande would be beneficial. However, in spite of scattered incidents of hot pursuit by troops, the U.S. Army would never fully officially sanction this. The state of Texas provided little or no assistance prior to the mid-1870s, and the Army proved ineffective against the cross-border raiders. Hence, the enlistment of the Laredo citizens to help repel attacks began, due in large part to the vastness of the region. The Army recruited local men, which resulted in the formation of four companies of irregular volunteers under the leadership of captains Santos Benavides, Bernardo Mendiola, Bartolo García, and Juan García Soto. Poorly armed and underfunded, these units and their commanders saw little or no service.[11]

The repeated official reports from the border commanders to the U.S. War Department resulted in a directive from President U. S. Grant in 1872 to appoint a commission to investigate the unrest along the Rio Grande. Shortly thereafter, Mexico also appointed a committee to survey conditions on the border. After numerous investigative visits, a detailed report was completed and forwarded to Washington. The findings noted that the U.S. commission was able to identify the main Indian tribes involved in the incidents, but due to the understaffed military units, poor communications, and meager supplies, there was little the Army could or would do. One solution that did prove workable was to relocate the Indian tribes from Mexico to U.S. reservations. Following a U.S. congressional appropriation of $25,000, agents of the Department of the Interior were dispatched to persuade the Indians to relocate. The Mexican national government concurred with the removal. Yet, local Mexican authorities in the northern areas were "loath to lose the profitable trade caused by their presence." Notwithstanding, over a three-year period, some groups of the Kickapoo and Seminole tribes agreed to the terms of the relocation.[12]

While the Indian raids waned, Mexican and Anglo bandits on both sides of the border were an ongoing threat to citizens, shippers, stagecoaches, ranchers, and merchants. Dubbed the "G.T.T.s"—Gone to Texas—adventurers, get-rich-quick novices and desperadoes from the North and South arrived in the Nueces Strip, many on the run from the law and eager to make a quick buck rounding up "stray" cattle.[13] J. Frank Dobie, in the classic book *The Longhorns,* noted, "Cattle were so common and money was so scarce that a 'cow and calf' represented the medium of exchange." Both were a form of payment and collateral.[14] Border leaders strongly requested that the state step in and eliminate the bandits. This strategy was paramount; strong commercial interests ranging from Monterrey, Mexico, to San Antonio and Corpus Christi (raided in March 1875) demanded that action be taken to reduce the menace. A change of government in Austin was a first step. Following the election of Governor Richard Coke on a pledge to restore law and order, one of the new governor's first actions in early 1874 was to reorganize and staff the Texas Rangers. In the spring of 1875, Capt. Leander H. McNelly was ordered to organize a new company of Rangers to patrol South Texas. These lawmen were to be fully empowered as peace officers to pursue and arrest all that violated the laws of Texas, as well as in cases of "hot pursuit" they could cross any county, state, or national boundaries. And once organized, they were instructed to move at once to the border. While the Rangers' efforts provided some element of law enforcement south of the Nueces River, there was little they could do to fully halt cross-border raids. In one seventeen-day period, Captain McNelly reported that "upward of 2,000 cattle had been crossed into Mexico by raiders . . . the stealing of cattle is extraordinary, and almost past belief."[15]

The population of Laredo in 1870 numbered 2,046. Trade in Texas struggled to recover in the wake of the Radical Reconstruction in Texas and an era of political unrest in Mexico. The three leading Texas cities at the time were Galveston with 13,818 residents; San Antonio, 12,256; and Houston, 9,382. As trade via the Port of Laredo slowly recovered, so did the increase in staffing for the U.S. Customs agency. Key to merchant travel and commercial dispute settlement was the assignment of U.S. commercial agent Thomas Gilgan to Nuevo Laredo on October 12, 1871. The office of commercial agent was dispatched under the jurisdiction of the U.S. Consulate in Matamoros. Nuevo Laredo was not designated a consulate-level station until February 6, 1880. In the meantime, Gilgan and the agents who followed during the decade became active players in representing the commercial interests of local border merchants in both Laredo and Nuevo Laredo. Inconsistent Mexican commercial and customs policies, zealous local officials, and political intrigue on both sides of the border confirmed the need for location of the formal U.S. commercial agent to monitor cross-border trade.

In a dispatch from Nuevo Laredo to Washington in April 1872, Gilgan candidly captured in detail the dynamics of commercial affairs at the U.S.-Mexico border:

> The Customs House and other offices controlled by the Treasury Department of the Republic are in possession of the revolutionist. The import duties are now being collected under the Tariff of January 31st 1856, instant and additional duties established by that tariff, and about 42% discount from the duties lately collected here under the Tariff now in force in ports under control by the revolutionist.
>
> Flour, coffee, sugar, rice, lard, and all classes of grain for seed, are permitted to be imported at a duty of 5% on the value of these articles at the port of introduction.
>
> The trade of this place has considerably increased for the past three months, owing principally to the low rate of duties collected. A good many foreign goods have been imported, these are generally for the interior market. The principal goods imported for consumption here are manufactures and produce of the United States, and are exchanged at from 10% to 15% advance on cash and charges for produce of this country such as wool, hides, goat and deer skins, which with lead from the mines of Villicillo, about 100 miles from

> this place, owned by citizens of the United States, are the principal articles of export.
>
> The business here is principally carried on by native merchants, who control very little capital of their own, they act as commission merchants. The capital occupied is owned chiefly by the United States. There is very little money in circulation here. The country about this place is but sparsely inhabited, and the people devote themselves entirely to the raising of sheep and goats.[16]

As the turbulence of the 1870s subsided, Laredo turned to the more productive endeavors of building a city and expanding cross-border commerce in spite of the continued tendency of Mexican agents in the Free Zone to disrupt trade. It soon became clear that the heroes and icons of Laredo's role in the "late unpleasantness"—as the Civil War was referred to in the South—became the stalwarts of development and progressive improvements in South Texas during the years prior to the turn of the twentieth century. Leadership in and for Laredo meant active participation in both the commercial and political dynamics of the city, region, and state. Among those who rose to the challenge were the Benavides brothers, Santos and Refugio. Santos Benavides (1823–1891) returned from a distinguished military career to serve as Webb County judge in 1856–57, and as a state representative to the Texas legislature from 1879 to 1885. Refugio Benavides (1821–1899), the older brother, returned from the Civil War to serve during a critical period as mayor of Laredo, from 1873 to 1875. Half-brother Cristóbal (1838–1904), also a Civil War veteran, established a mercantile store, S. Benavides and Brother, and remained an active civic leader. The commercial sector of Laredo grew with much common ownership of city businesses and ranching interest in Webb, Encinal, and Zapata counties.[17]

On the rangeland around Laredo, cattle, horses, and sheep flourished. The hardy longhorn rapidly multiplied; in 1870 there were estimated to be nine hundred head of cattle for each citizen of Texas. It was further estimated that the Nueces Strip held an estimated one million head of cattle and horses. This vast amount of cattle proved critical to meeting the post–Civil War demand for beef in the eastern and midwestern markets. In 1870, before the arrival of the railroad, some 300,000 head of Texas cattle were driven up the Chisholm Trail to the railhead in Topeka, Kansas, followed by 700,000 head in 1871. The average price per head of cattle "delivered" was $20. Laredo functioned as a central market for hides, tallow, salt, and leather products. Webb County established a charge of three cents to inspect cattle hides and another three cents' fee for recording. However, many hides sold by the independent "skinners" and traders went uninspected due to prevalent smuggling. In 1870 and 1871, Webb County ranchers reported 12,000 cattle and 67,000 sheep, followed by 20,000 cattle and 124,000 sheep, respectively.

Webb was considered the third largest county in sheep production in Texas, behind adjacent Nueces and Starr counties. However, by the early 1880s, due largely to the extensive 100,000-sheep operation on the Callaghan Ranch in northern Webb County, Laredo handled in excess of five million pounds of wool annually destined for eastern milling markets around Boston. Sheep tended to be popular because they were more difficult to steal, and wool was in high demand due to a growing and lucrative eastern market.[18]

The Laredo of the 1870s was a hot and dusty city in which growth had all but stalled in the wake of the Radical Reconstruction (1865–76) period.[19] Indian depredations, cattle rustling, and bandit hostilities throughout South Texas and northern Mexico slowed the community's growth. As the commerce of Texas gradually recovered so too did the economy of Laredo.[20] And in spite of reports and rumors of unrest south of the Nueces, extensive efforts by promoters attracted new immigrants as growth became a high priority statewide. Individual investors, land speculators, traders, and the railroads created books and pamphlets that touted Texas in order to attract settlers and investment to the Lone Star State. Three classic accounts of the Texas frontier were widely circulated: the anonymously authored *A Visit to Texas: Being the Journal of a Traveler,* 1834; German author Viktor Bracht, *Texas Im Jahre 1848* (1849); and Josiah Gregg's *Commerce of the Prairies,* which was first published in New York and London in 1844 and then was reprinted in 1850, 1855, and 1857 to include an edition in German. Other accounts were also published: Frederick Law Olmsted, *A Journey through Texas* (1857); *What I Saw in Texas* (1872); and *Texas: Its Climate, Productions, Trade, Commerce, and Inducements for Emigration* (1870).[21] The lure south of the border rivaled Texas with the widely published classical historical account of Mexico by W. H. Prescott, *The Conquest of Mexico,* and numerous travelers' chronicles of the era penned in the first person: Gilbert Haven, *Our Next-Door Neighbor: A Winter in Mexico* (1875) and A. B. Clarke, *Travels in Mexico and California* (1852). And immigrants flocked to south Texas. The last two decades of the nineteenth century were marked by dynamic efforts in Laredo to, first, enhance city services (water and electricity) and the infrastructure (streets) of the community; second, link Laredo and thereby the Texas economy and markets to Mexico by cross-border railroad; and third, expand the economic vitality of downtown with the addition of new merchants, housing, and financial institutions.[22]

The Power of the Penn

The expansion of Laredo city services and economic development was first and foremost driven by the downtown business merchants and owners. The array of improvements touched every segment of the Laredo economy and included financing for and installment of a streetcar service, a telephone system, and improved streets. The U.S. census of 1880 reported a Laredo population of 3,500, which was considered locally as a significant undercount, and in fact should have exceeded 5,000.[23] Laredo's growing commercial sector and cross-border trade helped attract new immigrants and investment as well as fuel a public demand for improvement. The growth of the Laredo business sector came from the outside as buyers and customers depended on the services of the town to support operations not only in South Texas but also throughout northern Mexico. The inflow of these buyers, commonly termed "strangers" by the locals, was critical in setting the foundation for the broader trading community that was to follow. Growth and the attraction of new investors was a priority, as the *Laredo Times* noted. Editor J. S. Penn, on the same day that President Garfield was reported shot, wrote that the "Laredo boom is very much in ascendency."[24]

The improvements were not expected to be left to only the city and county government. The private commercial sector and merchants increasingly took a larger role in the planned improvements. Improving access for travelers, salesmen, ranchers, and merchants was good business, and was a priority. Still without a bridge, access across the Rio Grande in the early 1880s was very difficult. Complaints persisted that the river ferries, small flat-bottom boats known as *chalanas,* did not provide enough service, and thus strong demands were made to extend the hours of operation beyond 8:00 P.M. The larger concern was the pressing need for a bridge spanning the river to connect with Nuevo Laredo. To address the construction of a wooden suspension bridge for wagons, the Union Laredense Bridge Company was formed to raise financing for the structure. Driven by the collection of tolls, final ownership had yet to be determined. And at the same time, planning was underway for construction of a railroad bridge.[25]

One of the most vocal advocates of civic improvements for Laredo was James Saunders Penn (1846–1901), owner and publisher of the *Laredo Times.* The *Times,* which inaugurated publication on June 14, 1881, was one of a group of papers of this era, in English and Spanish, that chronicled events in both Laredo and Nuevo Laredo. The *Two Eagles* was published for a few years in the early 1870s, followed by the biweekly *El Horizonte.* In the early 1880s, the *Laredo Times* vied for readership and advertising with the *Laredo Enterprise,* the daily report *Gate City,* Ridge Paschal's *The Two Laredos,* J. C. Hart's *Laredo,* as well as *La Voz de la Pueblo, La Colonia Mexicana,* and Juan Zardeneta's *El Mutualista.* Yet, the entrepreneur Penn would rise to dominate the Laredo media.[26]

Penn was born in Mississippi and moved with this family to Fayette County, Texas, as a child. He rose to the rank of major after enlisting in the Confederate Army and joining Tom Green's Texas Regiment. He, as well as numerous other postwar Southern veterans, was so disenchanted with the

South's defeat that he departed the United States to seek his fortune abroad. Penn chose Rio de Janeiro, Brazil, yet, after five years, he returned to Texas in late 1870, and worked at various jobs in Houston, Galveston, and San Antonio before moving to Laredo. Within six weeks of arriving in Laredo, on May 1, 1881, he opened a stationary-printing business and shortly thereafter began publishing of the *Laredo Weekly Times.* The *Weekly Times,* which added a daily edition in September 1883, would prove a catalyst of opinion on reform measures and political intrigue. It was also a promotional tabloid and a venue for comments from concerned citizens. The four pages of this weekly, published each Wednesday, were filled with national and state news, often delayed up to three or four days after the occurrence of the events. The paper also focused on commercial-merchant advertisements and notices, as well as on editorials and news of local interest. Penn edited and controlled the content, thereby promoting many of his personal ideas about the improvements needed in Laredo. During July and August of 1881, Penn repeatedly addressed the poor, dusty conditions and disrepair of the main streets of the town as lead items in his editorial column:

> Dust! Dust! Dust!
> Hot! Hot! Hot!
> Oh! For some water
> Sprinkled on the street
> Oh! To see the streets graveled!

Shortly after his pointed columns, Penn proudly reported that the "dirt streets were graded and graveled."[27] The dust did not fully subside, but if and when it rained—the mud would be reduced to a minimum! Notwithstanding his endless campaign to fix the dusty streets, Penn was an avid promoter of the strategic location of Laredo as both a commercial center and "gateway" (a term he coined) to the growing markets of Mexico.

Gateway of Commerce

Economic and political interest had been long intertwined in the South Texas ranching industry. The stakes were raised as manufacturing, railroad transportation, and banking expanded nationwide. In the case of Laredo and other border towns, the expanded linkage to international markets became a driving force. In addition to Governor Coke taking a personal interest in the border, Mexico's new government under Porfirio Díaz began, in 1876, a four-decade reign over the fortunes and future of Mexico. Díaz, in the years before he ascended to what his followers termed the "imperial presidency," was well versed in border affairs; he had planned his overthrow of the Mexican government from Brownsville. He resided for over two years in Piedras Negras—a small town across the Rio Grande from Eagle Pass. Once in office, Díaz's actions were swift. To curb the bandits, he ordered generals Severano Canales and Geronimo Treviño to dispatch and expand the *rurales,* local constables, to immediately curb the cross-border raids.[28] Díaz, while heavy-handed, had a larger vision for the development of the Mexican economy and infrastructure. His tenure in office would parallel the American industrial revolution in the 1870s and 1890s, the greatest period of industrial expansion and capital investment of any nation in the annuals of recorded history. Laredo was at the crossroads of these events. Investment during this period in Mexico, and the scramble for new markets, was dominated by both European capitalists and American industrialists.[29]

The catalyst that would link manufacturers, markets, and customers in the late nineteenth century was access to improved transportation and communications. Into the late 1870s, people and merchandise in quantity were moved by three methods—first, on foot; second, by horse, ox, and mule-drawn wagons and carts; and lastly by boats and ferries, where waterways permitted passage. The steam engine and canals defined early industrial expansion and transportation in the northeast portion of the United States. Texas and Mexico for the most part had no satisfactory river navigation and hence gained no advantage from these eastern developments.[30] The Rio Grande above Roma was generally too shallow for large watercraft. An exception was a spectacular upriver visit on October 24, 1846, by the side-wheeler steamboat the *Major Brown*—a 125-ton, 150-foot-long vessel with a draft of three feet loaded. Captained by Mark Sterling and accompanied by Army Lt. Bryant P. Tilden Jr. and twenty soldiers, the steamboat navigated the unknown course and anchored at Laredo on the north bank of the river; the ship's crew were welcomed by a crowd of "astonished" citizens.[31] Following an inspection of Laredo, Tilden noted in his report: "This town lies on both sides of the river [and] contains about 1,500 inhabitants. This town is important in a commercial point of view, being on the direct route from San Antonio de Bexar, in Texas, to Monterrey," but "has few points for the agriculture or the manufacturer."[32] Tilden's reference to too-few manufacturing sites is based on his perception of New England–style mills that were located on steady-flowing streams and rivers. This fact would be better understood and appreciated when low water prevented a downriver return by the *Major Brown* for nearly two years.[33] No other vessel of this size would ever again venture up the Rio Grande to Laredo. In future years, small freight boat operations such as the company of Blas Uribe, established in 1860, navigated between Brownsville and Laredo, yet such shipments ran generally only during a near-full flood of the river.[34] Laredo historian Jerry Thompson noted, "The anchorage of the *Major Brown* at Laredo is now the site of an international bridge which serves as the link between two cities, two nations, and two civilizations."[35] Notwithstanding, for the balance of the nineteenth century, waterborne trade destined for Texas and Mexico used the fledgling seaports along the Gulf of Mexico at Galveston, Indianola, Corpus Christi, Brownsville, Bagdad, Tampico, and Veracruz.[36]

Other than by foot or horseback, overland journey in South Texas was by stage and the movement of goods by six yokes of ox-drawn *carretas*. These handmade two-wheel carts driven by *arrieros* were the mainstay of shipping for some four hundred years. With an axle of hardened live oak or pecan, the solid wooden wheels, as high as seven feet in height and seven feet apart, could carry over five thousand pounds. The grinding of the wooden axle against the heavily ladened wheels created a high pitched screech, which was lubricated by prickly pear leaves.[37] All manner of goods, grain, and manufactured equipment including building materials, farm implements, printing presses, and sewing machines were routinely hauled. The Gil brothers of Laredo were among the leading freight companies of the region in the 1860s, moving goods into northern Mexico and to San Antonio and Corpus Christi. Competition was fierce as carts were improved and mules introduced to replace the oxen.[38]

> Mexican mules [were used] to pull both the stages and the freight wagons. They were small but wiry, quick, and apparently tireless. They pulled a stage at a lope, and the only way the driver could stop them was to circle as he pulled them up. If he had a passenger who wanted to get off between stations, he drove the stage in a circle, and his maneuver slowed it just enough for the passenger to jump. Indians or robbers had to shoot the mules to stop the stage. In the freight business, 10 mules were needed to pull one prairie schooner loaded with about 7,000 pounds of cargo.[39]

In this era before modern just-in-time logistics the volume shipped and the time of delivery was as important as it is today. However, lead times varied. For example, a round trip by ox-drawn cart from Laredo to Zapata on the old cow trail, or "trace," along the river some fifty miles took an estimated eight days. From Laredo to San Antonio the journey was of some fourteen days by cart or wagon. While carts continued to be key to South Texas transportation well into the twentieth century, by the late 1870s change was on the horizon.[40]

Ribbons of Steel

From the East Coast and Midwest a new breed of industrial tycoon burst on the scene to expand and compete for three emerging enterprises: railroads, large-scale manufacturing, and commercial banking. The "rise" in large-scale, capital-intensive industries, "signaled the coming of a new economic order in the land."[41] In Texas and the Southwest, the great leap in commercial activity came with the arrival of the railroad. For Laredo it was the most significant event in the history of the town since its founding in 1755. Inadequate transportation had hampered growth throughout the western United States. The railroads "transformed American life on the plains,"[42] with railroad construction nationwide totaling 40,962 miles in the 1870s and a "staggering" 71,212 miles in the 1880s.[43] And in Mexico there was less than five hundred miles of track in 1873 and only about five thousand miles by 1883. However, Laredo was not just a passenger or freight stop along internal domestic markets. Instead, the city stood as "the great international gateway of the two republics" to enhance border trade with emerging markets in Mexico and points south. The strategic geographic location of Laredo would not be lost as the rail moguls fought over right-of-way concessions, bridgeheads, and terminals critical to link the markets of the two nations.[44]

Confirming the distinct strategic location of Laredo, local city leaders and merchants were notified that the International Railroad Company had obtained a charter in August 1870 to build a line from St. Louis, via Texarkana, Austin, and San Antonio, to its proposed terminus at Laredo! In February 1872, as planning was underway, the International Railroad merged with the Houston & Great Northern to form the International & Great Northern Railway (I&GN).[45] These actions did not go unnoticed in Laredo. Samuel Jarvis, as well as the architect of urban planning for the city of Laredo, in 1872 correctly envisioned the potential dynamic impact rail linkage to Laredo would have on the local economy. The key determinant for a border city to secure rail investment was a civic agreement to provide adequate acreage for rights-of-way as well as land for a terminal and repair shops within the community. In advance of the arrival of representatives from I&GN, the Laredo Board of Alderman (city council) composed of Mayor Jarvis and Aldermen José María Rodríguez, Clemente Salinas, and Evaristo López were solicited in April 1872 by an agent of the Rockport, Fulton, Laredo & Mexican Pacific Railroad (RFL&MP) to determine the interest of the city to donate land for track right-of-way, a rail yard, and depot. This extensive request for donated land was unprecedented in South Texas, yet in short order the aldermen agreed to deed the railroad "100 lots of land" (or about 100 acres) within the city limits if and only if the railroad completed its work on or before December 1, 1879. If not, all grants, deeds, and rights-of-way were null and void. The RFL&MP Railroad, for unknown reasons (possibly they hoped to tie up key rights-of-way concessions in Laredo in order to leverage a merger with the I&GN), failed to accomplish their objective, yet the probusiness public-private precedent established by the Laredo city fathers in 1872 would prove timely for the attraction of rail investment soon to follow in the early 1880s.[46]

In the wake of the demise of the RFL&MP, the I&GN in a separate transaction acquired charter rights to the Victoria Columbus Railroad Company that included a branch to Laredo, thus moving gradually closer to their goal of connecting with the border. Notwithstanding, the I&GN was preoccupied during the balance of the 1870s with rail improvements away from the border. In the interim, competition from Corpus Christi would soon change the race to determine who would be the first to connect the border by rail at Laredo. In contrast, and to the credit to the Laredo aldermen and merchants, they identified and acted on the opportunity that new rail investment would bring to Laredo, in spite of the fact that during the early 1870s the region remained a hotbed of Indian spoliations and bandit activity. Reports of the unrest were reported in the print media in Texas, as well as nationwide, as the "Texas Frontier Troubles"—with one observer noting, "commerce languished and profitable industry is unknown" along the border.[47] Furthermore, President U. S. Grant and the U.S. Congress gave an ample focus on the border in a series of hearings and official commissions to evaluate the magnitude of the border disturbances. The rejuvenation of the Mexican-imposed *Zona Libre* trade area paralleling the right bank of the Rio Grande resulted in commercial as well as diplomatic irritations in Mexico City and Washington, D.C. These events drew attention from the highest political level in Washington, D.C. and also drew critical commercial concerns from investors in New York City. In the case of irregularities and smuggling along the border, President Grant specifically referred to the impact of the *Zona Libre* in his annual State of the Union reports in 1870, 1871, and 1872. Thus, it is well to surmise that the officials and merchants in Laredo (as well as the competition in other border towns) viewed the securing of a railroad hub as a possible vital reprieve from the troubles of the times.[48]

The first substantive efforts to link Laredo by rail began in mid-1874, when entrepreneur Uriah Lott began plans to build a narrow gauge railway from Corpus Christi to Laredo. A dozen shareholders, including Laredoans Meyer M. Levy, C. M. McDonnell, and Henry Goldsmidt, formed the Corpus Christi, San Diego, and Rio Grande Narrow Gauge Railroad Company (CC, SD & RG) on September 18, 1875. Construction of the railway stalled near the tiny town of El Mesquite, ninety-five miles northeast of Laredo. Lott, strapped for cash, threatened to run the line to an alternate Rio Grande site, possibly Mier, Rio Grande City, or Roma, if Laredo did not pay an immediate cash "bonus." Unmoved by the demand, Laredo felt their strategic location was enough of an "inducement" for Lott to push forward to Laredo. Well aware of the rail competition by the I&GN coming south from San Antonio, as well as reports of the Ferrocarriles Nacionales de Mexico (Mexican National Railway) building a line south from Nuevo Laredo toward Monterrey, Lott raised new funding to reorganize the CC, SD & RG Railroad as the Texas Mexican Railway Company on June 30, 1881.[49] Stockholders, including ranching caudillos Capt. Richard King and Mifflin Kenedy, in this newly capitalized company—with $1,380,000 in 6 percent bonds issued on July 1, 1881 and due in 1921—strongly recommended construction toward Laredo. A second rail line, the Texas Mexican Northern Railway, was charted on February 17, 1882, with the intent of constructing a line from Laredo up the river to Eagle Pass, about one hundred miles. Due to the lack of capital, only about 1.5 miles were constructed, which soon became a side track for stock pen access for the Texas Mexican Railroad. Lott and the famed 163-mile-long (from Laredo to Corpus Christi) narrow-gauge "Tex-Mex," one of the most profitable short line railroads in the nation, was soon to become a key part of the regional and international trade hub to Mexico via Laredo.[50]

Merchandise trade between the United States and Mexico in 1860 totaled only $7 million and gradually doubled to $15 million in 1880.[51] This stimulation and growth in international trade along with the impact of the railroad (there are no navigable rivers in Mexico) was the rallying cry for economic development and commercial expansion of both agricultural and mining in Laredo in the late 1870s and 1880s. The potential benefit of rail was apparent in Mexico as early as 1857 when the governor of Nuevo León and Coahuila, Santiago Vidaurri, endorsed the newly founded Monterrey and Rio Grande Railroad Company, noting, "a railroad from the Río Bravo to Monterrey . . . is a solid base for the development of commerce and industry." A constant reminder and proponent of the impact of rail service, *Laredo Times* editor James Penn, noted the strategic location of Laredo, given the excellent supply of high-grade bituminous coal fifteen miles upriver along the Rio Grande. The magnitude of the economic impact on Laredo as a rail and commercial hub surely exceeded even his wildest expectations; the railroad barons planned not one, but four, separate lines to service Laredo.[52]

As the railroad moguls prepared to push both railroads and massive capital investment via Laredo into Mexico, they were fully encouraged by a protrade policy from Washington. To address a broader trading partnership, Mexico agreed to denounce the dated commercial treaty of 1831 and the January 1858 tariff amendments in order to broaden market access and lower tariffs in exchange for more direct foreign investment from the United States. The key component of the new trade treaty negotiated between Secretary Frederick T. Frelinghuysen and Mexican minister Matías Romero was a "reciprocal" approach to cross-border commerce and investment. For the first time, each country submitted a list of "duty free" products they desired to export. Protectionists in both countries protested the reciprocal accord (with some in Mexico fearing the agreement would isolate European investment), yet the agreement was ratified. Mexico's duty free product list included exports of coffee, vanilla, wood, and henequen, and the U.S. exports to Mexico included railroad equipment, coal, oil, agricultural machinery, and mining supplies—all of which would have a tremendous impact on the Laredo economy. However, the linchpin to the future of trade between the United States and Mexico was connecting the two countries by railroad.[53]

Texas became a major battleground in the domination of the east-west southern route that pitted industrialist Jay Gould against Collis P. Huntington, Charles Crocker, Gen. William J. Palmer, and Charles L. Perkins.[54] All were speculators in the development of railroads and real estate, but few could match Gould's tenacious and legendary no-holds-barred drive. It was Gould, along with his not-so-silent partner former President U. S. Grant, who realized the importance of gaining control of the Texas market and, thus, being first to own and open the north-south railroad connections to markets in Mexico. By the late 1870s, President Díaz had extended a near carte blanche policy to convey liberal concessions with an open invitation to foreign companies seeking to invest in railroads, mining, harbors, and manufacturing. Railroads were equally important to the economic development of both the Mexican and Texas economy, which, according to the San Antonio *Herald*, "would constitute the biggest bonanza that could possibly be conferred."[55]

Huntington struck first in the race to connect with Mexico by arranging for the expansion of the Southern Pacific Railroad from Phoenix to El Paso. Palmer followed by running a line from Denver to Pueblo, Colorado. Both these actions were a potential blow to Gould's Texas and Pacific line. The combination of distrust and rivalry pitted Gould against Huntington in a fight over Texas concessions. Actions taken by both tycoons in Texas, who together controlled over half of the railroad mileage in the state, had a profound impact on the financial empire of each. Huntington, in the fray, was quick to invoke a maxim given to him by his father: Do not be afraid to do business with a rascal, only watch him; but avoid a fool.[56] And Gould was no fool.

Gould's and Huntington's bullish plans were nearly derailed by a potential diplomatic impasse between the United States and Mexico. The powerful northern Mexico caudillos who controlled the army, and the governors in the states of Nuevo León, Tamaulipas, and Chihuahua were reluctant to agree to the complete and total "open door" policy of Don Porfirio. In addition to efforts by the state of Texas to curb random violence and banditry, the U.S. State Department added diplomatic pressure that was welcomed neither in Mexico City nor by the border caudillos. The uneasiness of border affairs was further aggravated by reports of the U.S. Army crossing the Rio Grande numerous times in force into Mexico in "hot pursuit" of bandits and Indian cattle rustlers. Reciprocal concurrence of pursuit across the border into Mexico to reduce what was termed *depredations* would not be formally signed between the United States and Mexico until the Frelinghuysen-Romero Agreement of July 29, 1882.[57] In the meantime, the national media in the United States noted the concern with the border hostilities, some calling for action, to include the establishment of a "protectorate" along the Rio Grande—to include much of northern Mexico.[58] Still pending U.S. recognition of the Díaz government, John W. Foster, U.S. ambassador to Mexico, strongly admonished Díaz:

> The condition of affairs on the Río Grande frontier is the most serious and present case of danger of the interruption of peace between the United States and Mexico. . . . When the honor of the American flag is involved, or the lives, liberty, and property of American citizens are concerned, it is difficult to weigh in scales and precisely designate the relative importance of one question of outrage over another.[59]

The strong words of Ambassador Foster, the continued cross-border incursions on both sides of the river, and the lingering apprehension by Díaz officials that construction of international railroad bridges and rail lines might only assist the United States in "another" invasion of Mexico nearly brought both nations to the brink of war.[60] The Mexican Congress stepped forward to express opposition to any U.S. firm that would be involved with bridge and rail construction; this construction would be viewed as a veiled "annexationist plot." The Mexican concerns were not without cause; as early as the late 1850s Washington officials, including President James Buchanan in his December 19, 1859 message to Congress. stated emphatically:

> I repeat the recommendation contained in my last annual message that authority be given . . . to establish one or more temporary military posts across the Mexican line . . . to protect the lives and property of American and Mexican citizens. A state of lawlessness and violence prevails on that distant frontier.[61]

President Díaz did not want U.S. invaders or a war. Instead, he wanted foreign direct investment in Mexico that would enhance economic development, improve the agrarian system, and create jobs which resulted in the widespread granting of concessions to railroad and mining interests.[62] To help calm the situation, Díaz sent Gen. Geronimo Treviño to Laredo to negotiate a cooling-off period. Meeting with U.S. Gen. Edward O. C. Ord, U.S. Army Commander of the Department of Texas, the two men came to a peaceful solution that resulted in reduced friction on the border. In short order the northern Mexico caudillos grudgingly supported Díaz; the U.S. government granted de jure recognition of the Díaz government in April 1878 and rail negotiations resumed.[63] The I&GN, which had been chartered by the state of Texas under Governor Davis's administration, was given a permit that provided grants of twenty sections of land (12,800 acres) for each mile of new track as well as exception from state tax for twenty-five years. Shortly thereafter, U.S. Senator Richard Coke, also a former governor of Texas, introduced a bill in the U.S. Senate backing "the promotion of the rapid and immediate construction of the International and Great Northern Railway of Texas from San Antonio to the Rio Grande, at or near Laredo." The commercial dynamics and intent of the rail development were very evident. The language read: "it is intended not only to build up trade with Mexico" but also to build a connection with the Mexican railway.[64]

Possibly with the two American tycoons in mind, Díaz, and his calculating finance minister José Yves Limantour, arranged for two prime railroad concessions from Mexico to link with two U.S. border sites on the Rio Grande—the Mexican Central Railroad running to Juárez-El Paso and the Mexican National Railroad from Mexico City to Laredo. Don Porfirio envisioned a network of railways across Mexico as the "path to progress," often saying the development of "the railways has played a great part in bringing peace to Mexico."[65] The price of progress and peace would prove very expensive. Gould hoped to avoid a bidding war, but in the rush to have access to the mineral resources and markets of Mexico this was nearly unavoidable. Discoveries in Mexico of rich deposits of copper, silver, coal, oil, and iron ore energized foreign investors wanting access to these critical raw materials for the expanding industrial sectors in America. The haste to source and develop these raw materials was further fueled by the reversal of a Mexican law dating from the colonial era, which revoked government ownership of subsoil minerals.[66]

Thus, Gould in late 1880 and early 1881 gambled to obtain the cross-Texas access to both El Paso and Laredo simultaneously, but decided to abandon the El Paso route in favor of building the Laredo route under his lead corporate entity—the International & Great Northern Railway, or I&GN Railway. The arrangement allowed Gould the standard gauge line (4 feet 8 1/2 inches) from points in the Midwest via Longview and San Antonio (with a branch to Galveston, location of the primary seaport of Texas) to a terminus on the Rio Grande at Laredo as well as pending trackage rights via Laredo to Mexico City.[67] The monopolization of the north-south I&GN lines from central Texas connecting with the Missouri Pacific Line to St. Louis allowed

Gould to dominate the region's rail traffic.[68] News of the I&GN Railroad moving south from San Antonio raised intense investor interest in South Texas as well as in financial circles in New York. Eager to induce the railroad to extend to Laredo via La Salle County, rancher Joseph Cotulla in 1881 deeded a townsite of 120 acres to create "Cotulla Station," later known only as the city of "Cotulla," with an adjacent rail depot.[69] The Mexico City segment of the rail line was "to agree to a fusion of their several interest" and was brokered over dinner at Delmonico's Restaurant in New York City by Gould, Collis Huntington, former president U. S. Grant (who had since lost his bid for a second term in the White House), and former Mexican minister to Washington, Matías Romero.[70]

To further secure his rail empire, Gould in June 1881 purchased a second line concession between Laredo via Ciudad Victoria and Mexico City, with spurs to Tampico and Veracruz, christened the Mexican Oriental Interoceanic & International Railroad Company. The City of Laredo worked both with the Tex-Mex Railroad and the I&GN providing rights-of-way and sites for depots. Both the city council and the local merchants understood the tremendous economic impact of the railroad on the future of Laredo. A few weeks after the completion of the 153-mile short line, the Texas Mexican Railway from Corpus Christi to Laredo, the Tex-Mex Locomotive No. 4 upstaged the mighty I&GN by being the first railway to cross the temporary wooden pontoon bridge over the Rio Grande into Mexico on November 21, 1881. The final trackage of the I&GN track from Cotulla to downtown Laredo was finished on December 15, 1881. Mindful of the significance of the merger of the three primary rail lines, Laredo and Nuevo Laredo celebrated their newfound distinction as the primary cross-border route between the two nations with a week-long fiesta that lasted from Christmas Eve 1881 until New Year's Day, January 1882. The drive and entrepreneurship of Lott and Gould would forever change Laredo by securing the first strategic cross-border trade link with Mexico.[71]

The key pieces of the railroad puzzle were in place with the final completion of the 842-mile narrow-gauge road by the Mexican National Railroad from Laredo to Mexico City in 1882. The first "through shipment" of freight by rail from Mexico crossed at Laredo on March 3, 1882. A few days later Gen. William T. Sherman, representing the I&GN, headed a festive delegation on the first passenger car to cross the Rio Grande via the temporary "low-water" wooden bridge, which was sturdy enough to cross voluminous construction supplies for the Mexican National Railroad. A sudden series of river floods in 1882, on May 18–19, August 21 and 28, and again September 4–6, were deemed sufficient to suspend rail crossings in favor of using a ferry, yet proved an omen of nature and accelerated completion of the more massive steel girder International Railroad Bridge high above the

Table 4.1. Railroad facilities investment in Laredo, 1881–84

Railroad	*Track & Switching*	*Depot*	*Machine Shops*	*Warehouse*
I&GN	$80,000	$60,000	$100,000	$50,000
Tex-Mex	$70,000	$60,000	$300,000	$40,000
RG&EP	$60,000	$20,000	$10,000	$10,000
Mexican National	$60,000	$0	$400,000	$20,000

Source: *Laredo Times*

river.[72] With the completion of the cross-border international rail system, the journey by train between New York and Mexico City via Laredo was cut from two weeks to five days. The *Galveston Daily News,* the largest newspaper in circulation in Texas at the time, hailed the success with the notation, "progress is the watchword for Northern Mexico."[73]

From this time forward the fate of the Mexican economy was directly tied to that of the United States. In the waning years of the nineteenth century, U.S. entrepreneurs' investments in railroads throughout Mexico enabled the completion of a system of tracks and stations totaling some 14,500 kilometers. Laredo and El Paso were the key border terminals, followed by the addition of a crossing at Nogales. And communications by means of the telegraph followed the railroad lines, linking some of Mexico's most remote areas. Both in direct capital investment and in transfer of technology the railroads helped to bring Mexico into the first stages of the mainstream of industrial development and commerce. Expanding trade in the region included a resolution passed in the Texas Legislature, introduced by Laredo attorney and state senator E. A. Atlee, to establish at the earliest possible date a deepwater port on the Texas coast.[74]

As long as jobs were created and the Mexican elite was included in the transactions, there was little protest over the growing foreign ownership. In the 1880s, the Díaz administration was touted as progressive and probusiness. Trade data confirm these results. U.S.-Mexico commerce jumped from $36 million in 1890 to over $64 million in 1900. Train shipments by the I&GN and Tex-Mex Railway exceeded a combined total of over 925,000 tons of freight in 1891 and grew annually. American investment in Mexico was substantial; the railroad comprised over 70 percent of the value of total foreign direct investment. American railway ownership in Mexico mushroomed from $300 million in 1902 to over $650 million in 1911. During this same period, 81 percent of the external capital invested in the Mexican mining industry came from the United States. In addition to French and

German investment, the British represented about 12 percent of railroad and 14.5 percent of mining investment in Mexico.[75]

The U.S. investment in railroads and the supplying of the mines and agricultural equipment in northern Mexico placed Laredo in a very strategic location, and as one historian of the period noted, "permanently altered economic relations between the [two] nations."[76] In the rush to attract and secure rights-of-way and depot sites for rail operations, over 688,203 acres were either "granted" by the city and Webb County or acquired in the name of some twenty railroads companies looking to gain a foothold in Laredo. In spite of numerous corporate reorganizations of railroad companies during the 1880s and 1890s, Texas provided lucrative incentives to subsidize railroad construction with grants of twenty sections (12,000 acres) of land and in some cases exemption of taxes for up to twenty-five years. For example, the Tex-Mex Railroad between Laredo and Corpus Christi was destined to be one of the most profitable "short lines" in the nation. In the early 1880s, the Tex-Mex operated seventeen locomotives, ten passenger cars, 195 flat cars, seventy-five boxcars, and twenty-five construction cars. With more efficient and cost-saving access into both the U.S. and Mexican markets, large volumes of freight were shifted from the Matamoros-Brownsville border crossing to Laredo. The development of the deepwater port of Corpus Christi, linking by rail industrial business with Monterrey and Mexico City, further enhanced the strategic cross-border role of Laredo in international trade.[77]

The Laredo of the 1880s resembled a Wild West boomtown. The population nearly tripled from 3,811 in 1880 to 11,319 in 1890. The numbers of visitors and merchants passing through the city increased rapidly. Civil War veteran and representative to the Texas Legislature Sam T. Foster presided over the organization of the Laredo Masonic Lodge No. 547, which held its first meetings at Charles Keller's Saddle Shop at 1410 Iturbide Street. From the pages of the *Laredo Times,* Penn noted the shortage of housing and hotels and the urgent need for a hospital. In a building frenzy in the spring of 1882, over one hundred buildings, at a total valuation of $220,000, were under construction. The demand for building materials was so high that, at one point, two hundred carloads of lumber delivered by the I&GN was used in a single week. City and county services were expanded to include better land use requirements, and the first Webb County courthouse was completed in June 1882 at a cost of $41,000—a brick, two-story Victorian structure topped with an ornate cupola and located at the current corner of Matamoros and Flores streets.[78]

Direct capital investment in railroad facilities, land acquisition, and labor in Laredo from 1881 to 1884 exceeded $1.3 million. This infusion of capital into the city had a tremendous impact on housing demands from the migra-

Fig. 4.1. Webb County Court House. Built in 1882 in the center of the city, in its day it was the most majestic structure in all of South Texas. The massive building was topped with a distinctive cupola that was visible for miles. A tragic fire of unknown origins razed the structure in 1906. Source: John Keck Collection.

tion of new workers and the steady increase in cross-border travelers. Laredo in the late 1880s experienced its first real estate boom as homes were added west of the city along Santa María Street. Formal banking operations in Laredo began with the Rio Grande National Bank, located on the first floor of the Hamilton Hotel; the Milmo National Bank was chartered on July 1, 1880. Both banks were very involved with community development. The Milmo National Bank was organized by Patricio Milmo [formerly Patrick Mullens], an Irish immigrant who first settled in Monterrey prior to investing in an extensive number of enterprises on the border, which included extensive investments in railroads, ranching, banking, and mining.[79] Milmo's banking background began with the opening of Casa Milmo in Monterrey, one of the first financial institutions in Mexico to establish international banking with New York, London, Paris, and Shanghai. After one year of operation, the Milmo National Bank boasted $300,000 in total assets and reported a "paid in capital" stock of $120,000, $80,000 in loans, and $59,305 in deposits.[80]

The Milmo brothers, Pat and Daniel, announced the construction of an extensive two-story banking headquarters at the corner of Lincoln Street and Salinas Avenue in January 1883. Designed by British architect Alfred Giles, the $29,000 facility included a warehouse, residence for bank president Daniel, and additional public offices. Penn at the *Times* seized upon this major downtown investment in his weekly editorial: "The building is an ornament to our city, and shows the enterprising character of the Milmo's—a character that some others of our capitalists might well emulate."[81] Penn's idea and promotion of the Laredo commercial "gateway" was becoming a reality.

Table 4.2. Railroad operations and land grants in Webb County, 1888–1900

Railroad	*Estimated Land/Acres*
Buffalo Bayou, Brazos & Colorado Railway Company	1,280
Corpus Christi, San Diego & Rio Grande Narrow Gauge Railroad	183,359
CT & MC Railway	2,560
Central & Montgomery Railway Company	40,120
East Line & Red River Railroad Company	10,240
GB & CG Narrow Gauge Railroad	8,320
Gulf Colorado & Santa Fe Railway Company	128,431
Georgetown Railroad Company	5,120
Gulf Western Texas & Pacific Railway Company	7,680
H & OB Railroad	16,640
Houston East & West Texas Railroad	34,361
Houston & Great Northern Railroad Company	65,013
International & Great Northern Railroad	97,883
Rusk Transportation Company	9,600
San Antonio & Mexican Gulf Railroad Company	2,240
Texas & New Orleans Railroad Company	24,960
Tyler Tap Railroad Company	15,360
Texas Western Narrow Gauge Railroad Company	2,560
Texas Trunk Railway Company	3,840
Texas Central Railroad Company	17,280
Texas-Mexican Railway Company	11,406
Total:	688,253

Source: Webb County, City of Laredo, Texas Land Office; Texas State Archives; Laredo Realty Co. Indexed Block Map of Webb County, circa 1910; Reed, *A History of Texas Railroads,* 1941.

U.S.-Mexico trade from 1870 to 1900 expanded, first, as Mexico opened its markets to foreign investment and, second, due directly to the tremendous expansion of cross-border railways at four locations: Laredo, El Paso, Eagle Pass, and Benson. As north-south commerce increased with Mexico, an annual average of 45 percent of all merchandise trade crossed the southern border, and of that amount a majority crossed at Laredo, followed by lesser amounts via El Paso, Brownsville, Roma, and Nogales. Total U.S.-Mexico merchandise trade grew from $9 million in 1870 to $64 million by the turn of the twentieth century.

Table 4.3. Value of U.S.-Mexico merchandise trade, 1870–1900 (in millions of U.S. $)

				Mexico border only		
	Exports	*Imports*	*Total*	*Exports*	*Imports*	*Total*
1870	$6	$3	$9	$2	$1	$3
1880	$8	$7	$15	$4	$2	$6
1890	$13	$23	$36	$6	$9	$15
1900	$35	$29	$64	$22	$5	$27
1910	$58	$59	$117	$29	$23	$52

Source: U.S. Bureau of Census

Immigrants and Entrepreneurs

As detailed previously, beginning in the late 1870s, Laredo attracted a broad cross-section of immigrants. Most were part of an influx of immigration from Europe; many landed at the ports of Galveston and Indianola. James Penn was also instrumental in promoting Laredo through the *Laredo Times.* The leading nationwide periodical of the era, *Frank Leslie's Popular Monthly,* ran numerous specials on Texas and the Southwest, including a feature on "our Southern Frontier," in which Laredo was prominently noted. In addition to the growing trade with Mexico, the catalyst for the balance of the decade was the railroad. Immigrants and investors from a score of countries were attracted to Laredo, with one promotional document boldly noting that the city's "population represent[s] almost every nation beneath the sun."[82] The first period of significant growth came in the early 1880s. In 1881, Raymond Martin opened the first large hotel, the Commercial Hotel, managed by Frenchmen Joseph Christen and his son Louis. The new hotel joined the smaller Exchange Hotel that had been opened by a Welsh immigrant, Tomkins Jefferson Guernsey. The primary mercantile stores were Joaquín Villegas and Brothers Dry Goods (1874), the Bruni Store (1877), the Joe Sielski grocery (1878), George C. Woodman and Brother (Albert V.) Hardware, George Pfeuffer Lumber Yard (1882), and Deutz Brothers Hardware (1880) specializing in railroad and mining equipment. El Precio Fijo opened in 1881 and was subsequently purchased by August C. Richter in the early 1890s. A number of *boticas,* or apothecaries, were opened—Laredo Drug Store and City Drug Store, known also as *Botica del León,* owned by Dr. L. M. Berg. The Laredo Ice Plant was expanded and the Laredo Steam Laundry established. In April 1884, the first telephone exchange service began and the central city market was opened at Market Hall, at a cost of \$60,000 in 1885.[83]

The growing city needed services, the first of which was potable water. Wells and some cisterns existed but did not meet the needs of the expanding population. Thus, the Rio Grande became the primary source of Laredo's water. It was delivered by cart and mule, by salesmen/water deliverymen known as *aguadoras* or *barrileros.* These independent entrepreneurs hauled water from the river and delivered it in forty-gallon barrels, at a retail cost of three cents per barrel. Crude pumps were added to fill reservoirs, and eventually Laredo Waterworks built an elevated water tank in late 1883, and by early 1884 Laredo Waterworks boasted ten miles of distribution lines. The pump station was located at Flores Street on the riverbank, with a daily capacity of 2 million gallons of water. Service rates ranged from \$24 per annum for residential locations to \$36 for irrigation purposes. Three "ice works"—one each in Laredo, Nuevo Laredo, and at Fort McIntosh—manufactured over 10,000 pounds of ice per day. Yet, even then the *barrileros* flourished due to

No

Laredo Texas June 30 1883

Mr Charles Wickland

Bought of A. M. BRUNI & BRO.,

WHOLESALE AND RETAIL

Dry Goods, Groceries, Liquors & Tobaccos,

Laredo, Texas, and Nuevo Laredo, Mexico.

1883

March 14 To Cash \$231.00 U.S. cy

The State of Texas
County of Webb } Before me W. N. Mowry Clerk of the County Court in and for Webb County Texas, on this day personally appeared A. M. Bruni of the firm of A M Bruni & Bro who being by me duly sworn deposes and says that the above account against Charles Wickland is, within the knowledge of affiant just and true; that it is due and unpaid and that all just and lawful offsets, payments and credits have been allowed.

A M Bruni

Sworn to and subscribed before me this 30th day of June AD 1883
W N Mowry
Clerk Co Court W. C.

Fig. 4.2. With the growth of the railroads, merchant trade in Laredo boomed. One of the leading businesses to gain an early foothold was A. M. Bruni. This 1883 document reflects the flamboyant letterhead used by merchants to draw credibility to their commercial endeavors. Source: John Keck Collection.

Table 4.4. Origins of Laredo immigrants, 1870–1900

August C. Richter (1863–1940)	Cork, Ireland	merchant
Antonio M. Bruni (1856–1931)	Bedonia, Italy	hotel/merchant
Raymond Martin (1828–1900)	Auzas Huate, France	merchant
Abraham Kazen Sr. (1868–1967)	K'nat, Lebanon	merchant
George Reuthinger (1858–1926)	Keunkirch, Switzerland	saddlery shop
Andrew Hans Thaison (1849–1898)	Haderslew, Denmark	brick manufacturer and mayor
Joseph Deutz Sr. (1827–1912)	Coblenz, Germany	hardware
Hamilton P. Bee (1822–1897)	South Carolina	BG CSA & Speaker of the House
Joaquin Villegas (1844–1910)	Santander, Spain	hardware
Patrico Milmo (1826–1899)	Ireland via Monterrey	banking, ranching
John L. Haynes (1821–1888)	Virginia	Texas State Legislature
Samuel M. Jarvis (1822–1893)	New York, New York	surveyor, mayor
Edmund J. Davis (1827–1883)	Florida	customs agent & Governor
Salis N. Johnson (1857–1932)	New York	beverage distributor
James S. Penn (1846–1901)	Mississippi	editor/publisher *Laredo Times*
Herman Poggenpohl (1848–1886)	Czechoslovakia	tanner and rancher
Jose Armengol Rangel (1840–1898)	Nalech, Spain	grocery
Joe Sielski (?–?)	Poland	grocery
Alphonse Siros (1848–1923)	Greece	merchant
John O. Buenz (?–?)	Germany	lumber yard
Paul Sauvignet (?–?)	France	ice plant
Alexander C. Hunt (1825–1894)	New York	Former governor of Colorado
Sam T. Foster (1828–1919)	South Carolina	Texas Legislature/JP
William H. Mims (1840–1953)	Mississippi	merchant
Eduardo Cruz (1860–)	Cadereyta, Nuevo Leon	retail merchant

the high demand. The Anheuser-Busch distributor, Silas N. Johnson, who arrived in Laredo in 1880, provided a selection of beverages; his became one of the oldest distributors in the company's worldwide network.[84]

A. C. Hunt, in late 1887, obtained a permit to set up "machinery" and poles along the narrow dirt streets to supply Laredo's first electricity. The primary objective was to provide residential service. On April 18, 1888, the first electrical "lamp" was turned on at the Hunt home at 1313 Lincoln Street. In short order the city contracted Hunt to provide one hundred streetlights

Fig. 4.3. Turn-of-the-century horse-drawn jitneys still navigated the dirt streets of Laredo well into the 1930s. Pictured here in front of the Federal Building in downtown against a backdrop of newly minted Ford Model Ts. Source: John Keck Collection.

at $2.25 each per month. Residences in Laredo were able to obtain lighting at $1.50 per light. Efforts to expand potable water followed when the city offered private contracts to pipe water in to replace the *barrileros,* who remained active into the early 1920s supplying the surrounding areas. On February 8, 1890, Laredo Waterworks obtained a franchise to provide water from a plant located at the foot of Convent Street on the bluff above the river *vega.* Due to an absence of meters, residences were charged a flat rate of $2.00. Arrangements were made to have customers pay their utility bills at the Milmo National Bank.[85]

Two Laredo merchant "societies" led the promotion of growth and investment opportunities during the late 1880s. The first was the Laredo Immigration Society. Leaders of this group billed themselves as an "impartial" source of information; they were led by A. L. McLane, president, and S. T. Foster, secretary. On the eve of the 1890 census, Laredo was boldly promoted as a town with a population of "15,000 souls"—which in fact was officially numerated by the U.S. Census at only 11,319. The shortfall, which many believed was an undercount, did not dampen enthusiastic efforts to promote both Laredo and Nuevo Laredo. The "gateway" theme highlighted the "capital, muscle, and pluck" of Laredo as a "dry, salubrious, and mild climate" and the key to commerce between the United States and Mexico. To chronicle the advantages of Laredo, the society contracted correspondent E. R. Tarver of the *Galveston Daily News* (the leading daily paper in the state in the 1880s and 1890s) to write an extensive narrative that was sponsored by the I&GN

Railroad, the Laredo Bank (not yet a national bank), and Pierce and Pierce Real Estate Agency and printed by Penn at the Daily Times Print Shop—grandiosely titled *Laredo the Gateway between the United States and Mexico: An Illustrated Description of the Future City of the Great Southwest.*[86]

In August 1888, the Laredo Improvement Company (LIC), the second and more commercial society, was formed by a group of merchants and investors to expand promotion, attraction of immigrants, new industry, expansion of local business, and to encourage land development—complete with project financing. As an inducement for new investment, manufacturing establishments were exempt from taxation for ten years. The LIC was a joint stock company chaired by president J. M. Hamilton along with a broad group of stockholders from Laredo and San Antonio, and business investors with interests in South Texas and Mexico. Of the extensive investment in Laredo growth, the nationally circulated and widely read tabloid *Frank Leslie's Illustrated Newspaper* noted (in what was the first featured nationwide article on Laredo): "these eminent men are interested in Laredo and they have reason for the confidence they express in the future of the city, old in history, but new in the progress of Texas."[87] In addition to becoming in essence the first large site developer and economic development organization in Laredo, the Laredo Improvement Company invested in the narrow gauge electric streetcar system, with electrical power provided by overhead lines. Hunt, distracted by interest in mining, sold his interest in the financially strapped electrical company to the Studebaker Wagon Company and Drake Lumber Company of Austin—who jointly served as "receivers"—"merely to take it over to save the loss of money due them from the electric company." In 1889, G. Bedell Moore purchased the firm, assumed all debts, and merged the electric company with the street trolley firm into the Laredo Electric Railway Company. The streetcar line—touted as the first electrically operated system west of the Mississippi River—reflected a vision of development that included service running from downtown at the I&GN Depot eastward over a steel bridge across Zacate Creek and down Market Street to Meadow Avenue.[88]

In time, the line—well in advance of the trolley wave that swept the nation in the early 1900s—was extended across the river into Nuevo Laredo to the Mexican Customs House. The Laredo line was the only known twin border city interurban trolley on the U.S.-Mexico border. Furthermore, the streetcar line running down Market Street became the east-west axis of growth in Laredo and changed the social landscape well after the turn of the century. Mayor E. A. Atlee, a local attorney, in his inaugural address of April 18, 1889, highlighted the robust Laredo economy:

> The importance of Laredo is being recognized, as is evidenced by the influx of population and the large investments of capital. Our

> borders are being enlarged, and cottages of newcomers are rapidly dotting the slopes. An era of prosperity has dawned upon the city. A liberal [business friendly] policy in the past has done very much to bring the city to its present condition. It shall be my purpose from time to time to recommend such measures as in my opinion shall tend to make our city more attractive and more prosperous.[89]

In spite of a tornado that hit the city in May 1890, causing heavy damage to both the electrical system and buildings, the emphasis on growth continued and brought in further investment. J. M. Hamilton completed the Hamilton Hotel in early 1890 at an estimated cost of $100,000. An ornate opera house was constructed, and the Masonic Temple was moved to the second floor of the Werner Building above Guajardo's Drug Store. Warehousing was expanded in the area along Market Street, and the Yguana Smelting and Refining Company and Foundry also expanded. New facilities were added near the I&GN Railroad train depot on Santa María, and the Tex-Mex Railroad moved its corporate headquarters to Laredo from Corpus Christi. The trolley was a pivotal element in expanding growth of the city east across Zacate Creek to a new residential area known as the "Heights." Situated on gently rolling high ground east of downtown, these new home lots were promoted by the Laredo Improvement Company and quickly grew into Laredo's first commercial housing development.[90] However, such growth was not without a price, while political unrest during the era threatened to hamper progressive urbanization of Laredo, many who visited the border city hailed its growth and progress:

> In Laredo, Texas, the Americans are laying out broad streets, putting up imposing business houses of brick and stone, erecting residences that would be handsome and creditable in any American city, and making things hum generally.
>
> The electric motor road that is now operated a distance of four miles (and still building) runs from Fort McIntosh, where Uncle Sam has an extensive military force, with spacious quarters, through the main part of the city out to what is called "The Heights.". . . It belongs to the famous Laredo improvement company, and there is where the solid, handsome and costly building of the future will be—it is already anchored there and no power can stop it. Money has been liberally lavished on "The Heights" to a degree scarcely to be believed without an inspection. The people who own it have a theory that for every dollar spent in originally purchasing land it will pay them to spend two in developing and beautifying the purchase. It was this spirit that induced the Laredo Improvement company

to build the electric motor system, the elegant Hotel Hamilton, to put in an extensive system of arc and incandescent lighting, water-works, etc. They take stock in every hopeful enterprise that comes to Laredo, from a bank down to a broom factory; erect costly business houses and residences, and explain by saying that they expect to get back every dollar with good interest. The secretary of the company, an affable and intelligent young Englishman, made the remark: "It does not matter to us in what part of Laredo a man settles, what line of business or enterprise he represents, what his politics or religion may be—if he comes and stays the value of our investment is just that much enhanced. If we don't sell land or houses to one man we will to another, and as for all our investments in stocks, plants, factories, buildings, etc., we earn money on those, too, for we are not here simply to sell real estate." These words are the keynote to Laredo's boom, and it may be remarked that but for just such a spirit the great growth which has been witnessed could not have taken place. An intelligent observer can see, however, that the impetus is too great now to be stopped. The amount of capital already planted is immense, and it keeps rolling in.

What will impress an observant outsider is the start Laredo has made, and in so short a time, as a railroad, manufacturing, mercantile and banking center. Four railroads run into the city, the chief being the International & Great Northern and Mexican National. The next important is the road running to Corpus Christi, and what is called "the coal road," running now to the rich coal mines twenty-five miles up the Rio Grande and to go on to Eagle Pass. The next to come will be the San Antonio & Aransas Pass, which has been subsidized and will undoubtedly be built within a few months. There is much to talk of other projected roads, but the writer cannot say how substantial those projects are. The railroads are a bonanza to the town, for they have all located extensive shops there that pay out large sums of money every week. The smelting works, foundries, planing mills and dozens of minor industries now under way employ big forces of skilled men, and these added to mechanics and citizens of all kinds give this city just what a town needs—a large wage-earning and money-spending population.[91]

Botas and Huaraches

Laredo's dynamic growth following the arrival and expansion of the railroad was also the cause of a political crisis that threatened to harm commercial expansion. The progressive image of the city actively promoted by the Laredo

Immigration Society and the *Laredo Times* was also at risk to local political rivalry. The population of Laredo grew from 3,521 in 1880 to 8,000 in 1886 and over 12,000 by 1890—leading the state with an increase of 225 percent. The increasingly more cosmopolitan diversification of the city became the stage for a protracted power struggle for the political control of City Hall and the county government.[92] Since most voters in South Texas were Democrats, two political factions within the party emerged in Laredo—with dramatically different leadership and political agendas. Those asserting nonpartisan views aligned themselves as the Citizens Party, comprised of what they claimed were the "common people." In their efforts to attract a broad following among the citizens they took as their slogan or name Huaraches. The symbolic name it represented—sandals, footwear worn by the lower class in Mexico—served as a rallying cry. Leading this upstart party was Dario González, the former county sheriff, and Stephen Boyard, Laredo city marshal.[93]

In opposition, a vocal group calling themselves the true Democrats was comprised of the merchants and more aristocratic citizens of Laredo. In response to the Huarache slogan, the Democrats adopted the Bota, or boot, as their icon. Immigrants Raymond Martin from France and Irishman C. M. McDonnell, both longtime residents of Laredo, acted as the principal leaders for the Botas. The membership of both factions of the parties was comprised of Anglos, Mexicans, and immigrants as well as a mixture of poor and affluent, city dwellers and ranchers. At issue was the outcome of the city-county elections of April 6, 1886. One observer noted, "The principal difference was between those who were out wanting in and those who were in wanting to stay." Prior to the election, the two factions split the existing elected positions—the mayor, E. A. Atlee, the sheriff, and county officials were backers of the Botas; and the city marshal and two of the city councilmen were backed by the Huaraches. The two vocal political factions by early 1886, in advance of the citywide election, developed large memberships.[94]

Weekly meetings of each group were peppered with dramatic speeches, cheers, and occasional gunfire to accentuate the excitement. The Botas met in their private hall to develop strategy. The Huaraches, with a reclaimed pre–Civil War cannon provided by postmaster John Z. Leyendecker, staged vocal outdoor evening rallies, with speeches and the ceremonial firing of the cannon. The numerous saloons of the day became the hotbeds of debate and electioneering following each rally. On the eve of the April election, city councilman Henry Douglas, a Bota member, was shot and killed at the Commercial Saloon located at the corner of Flores Avenue and Grant Street. Bota Sheriff Sánchez deputized a number of men in order to avert any mob violence, an action the Huarache party strongly protested. In spite of their concerns, the election on April 6 was conducted without incident. The Botas won nearly all the offices with the exception of two city council positions.[95]

To celebrate their victory, the Botas followers issued a handbill notice in Spanish that stated that it was their intent to gather on the evening of Wednesday, April 7, in the meeting hall above Los Dos Republics department store owned by Eduardo Cruz, to celebrate and stage a mock funeral to bury the "effigy" of the defeated Huarache party. Printed "invitations" were made and distributed, with a small, miniature leather sandal attached. To insure a large gathering, notices were also widely distributed in Nuevo Laredo. Leaders from both groups requested that demonstrations be peaceful and limited, yet both parties indicated they would parade at will.

During the evening, tension increased with the gathering of each party. Parading through the dimly lit Laredo streets with bands playing, each of the armed factions grew in numbers as they proceeded. Gunfire erupted as the marching partisans converged at twilight and entered San Agustín Plaza. Open street fighting ensued, followed by a heated gun battle that was halted only with the hasty arrival of a detachment of U.S. troops from Fort McIntosh. Over two thousand rounds were fired in and around the plaza in "one of the biggest gun battles in the entire history of the American West." Bullets peppered the buildings and church. When the smoke cleared, over two dozen were "reported" killed in the altercation, and many more were reported wounded.[96]

Citizens and merchants, alarmed at the violence, sent a special petition to Governor John Ireland requesting that he at once dispatch the Texas Rangers to guard the city.[97] The attention to the Laredo violence greatly concerned the merchants because newspapers across the nation and Texas carried sordid headlines—"Battle on the Border," "The Great Laredo Riot," "Bloody Streets," "The Woeful War on the Rolling Río Bravo," and "Blood Lust."[98] Although the Laredo weather remained hot, tempers cooled and both factions of the Democrats gradually merged into a single party known as the Independent Club. However, the events of April 1886 left a marked impact on Laredo. Reacting to the outcry of the Election Riots of 1886, veteran Laredo leader Col. Santos Benavides, called the event a "great disorder," noting, "The devil takes advantage of a weak spot."[99] The refrain of an old cavalry trooper echoed loudly in the stillness of Benavides's concern for his home on the Río Bravo:

> The Devil was granted permission one day
> To select him a land for his own special sway;
> He looked around for a month or more,
> And ripped and snorted and terribly swore;
> But at last was delighted a country to view,
> Where the prickly pear and mesquite tree grew;
> After a survey brief he took up his stand
> On the eastern shore of the Rio Grande.

CHAPTER 5

ORE, ONIONS, AND OIL

> Laredo is by far the leading port on the Rio Grande frontier, importing and exporting as much as all the other ports combined. Laredo is a wonderful city, with a wonderful but at the same time substantial growth.
>
> *NEW YORK TIMES,* MAY 1890

> The cannel coal of Santo Tomás, Webb County is of unique interest, both economically and geologically . . . it is probably the largest body of coal of bituminous rank in the United States, if not in the world.
>
> GEORGE H. ASHLEY, U.S. GEOLOGICAL SURVEY, 1918

The growth of trade in Laredo was directly related to the arrival of and dynamic economic impact of the railroads during the 1880s and also to the construction of bridges across the Rio Grande that connected Laredo and Nuevo Laredo. Long a strategic crossing between the United States and Mexico, Laredo was crowned by the *New York Times* in 1890 as "by far the leading port on the Rio Grande frontier."[1] The city fathers and merchants of Laredo gained a much-needed stimulus of the local economy from the railroad. Surely these events predicted a prosperous future for an era of newfound "riches." Overland travel from either Monterrey or San Antonio to Laredo was reduced from four days by horse and wagon to some four hours by steam locomotive. With cross-border trade providing a sold base for growth, turn-of-the-twentieth-century economic development and investment in Laredo would be identified by coal mining, farming, and ranching as well as by the exploration for oil and gas. Efforts to develop light manufacturing helped to diversify the Laredo economy. However, the main efforts of the 1880s focused on the expansion of trade via the bridges and border crossings.[2]

Following the Mexican National Railway's completion of the seven-span 1,700-foot iron railroad truss bridge in November 1881, Laredo petitioned

Washington, D.C. and Mexico City to approve construction of a multipurpose pedestrian bridge. Since the 1750s, *chalanas,* or flat-bottomed ferries and canoes, were the only method used for the crossing of passengers and freight. The Spanish Crown mandated that the municipality collect funds beginning in 1767 to build the central church; crossing tolls were collected—at two *reales* for passengers and one *real* for freight at that time. Once the church was completed, revenue reverted to city projects. Never substantial in the era prior to the arrival of the railroad, revenue from bridge crossing fees would become a key cornerstone of the municipal budget. Over time, the *chalanas* were replaced by a ferry service.

Operation of the cross-river ferry from 1810 to 1850 required the city of Laredo to issue a concession to a private vender to operate this vital link daily between the two cities. In the early 1850s, following formal recognition of both the city and county, the Laredo city council leased the rights with full power to only one approved river ferry, causing others to contemplate a competing ferry. The leading contender to challenge the exclusivity of the city was the newly formed Laredo Ferry Company, owned by Raymond Martin, C. M. MacDonnell, and E. F. Hall. The group Martin led began ferry service in 1874, only to be abruptly sued by the city to halt operations. After a lengthy court battle the final appeal was taken to the Supreme Court of Texas and the city of Laredo prevailed. The resolution of legal challenges to ferry operations soon proved inadequate for the times as increased trade in the 1880s demanded construction of a bridge and rail expansion to link the markets of Mexico with Texas.[3]

After two centuries of canoes and small flat boats connecting the two border cities, the first action taken to bridge the river was by Dr. Plutarco Ornelas, Mexican Consul in Laredo, who petitioned Mexico City to grant a bridge concession. As the Díaz government reviewed the application, legislation was submitted and passed in the U.S. House of Representatives on March 29, 1884, to approve the creation of the International Bridge and Tramway Company (IBTC) to "build and lay on and across said bridge ways for passage of animals, foot-passengers, and vehicles of all kinds." The bill further stipulated that the owner might "charge a reasonable toll." The congressional provision, ever mindful of the strategic value of border bridge crossings, reserved the right of the U.S. Secretary of War to reasonable review of all projects across the Rio Grande.[4]

Financing for the IBTC bridge was arranged with the Holland Trust Company of New York. In spite of the fact that the financing was in place in 1885, construction did not began until June 1887, when President Díaz simultaneously approved two bridges across the "Río Bravo del Norte el uno a Piedras Negras con Eagle Pass, y el otro a Laredo de Tamaulipas con Laredo, Texas." With the Díaz decree, construction moved swiftly and the bridge was opened on April 6, 1889.[5] The steel-truss twenty-foot-wide bridge and steel cylinder pier were covered with wooden planks, walkways, and a set of parallel steel tracks that allowed the Laredo Electric and Street Railway Company electric streetcars (successor in 1892 to the Laredo Improvement Company) to cross to its Nuevo Laredo terminus at the Mexican Customs House. This bold move was reputed to be the first and only electrical trolley across the U.S.-Mexico border. Tolls were set based on the dollar-peso exchange rate, which, in the early 1890s, was five cents on the U.S. side and ten centavos in Nuevo Laredo. The only interruptions to service on the bridge prior to the Mexican Revolution were, first, in 1895 when a tremendous flood twisted the piers of the bridge and, second, when two spans of the bridge were violently blown into the river in 1905 by a tornado—which also tore off the ornate cupola on City Hall. The spans were replaced with heavier gauge steel trusses and the cylinder piers were encased in reinforced concrete.[6]

The increased commercial trade driven by the railroad, inauguration of the new bridge, the arrival of both the Tex-Mex Railroad and the I&GN Railroad as well as the opening of the Mexican market was for Laredo somewhat stifled by an extended drought across South Texas and northern Mexico from 1891 to 1894. In spite of the arrival of the railroad, mail and news arrived by overland stage or the rail. Communication from Laredo with "the outside world" was established on November 15, 1893, by Sam P. Wreford of Laredo. He completed a $17,000 contract awarded by the Army to build a telegraph line to Brownsville. Intended for sending military dispatches and weather reports, Thomas T. Smith notes, "By 1900, the majority of 17,990 messages sent along the Brownsville-Laredo military telegraph were private or business communications of local citizens."[7]

In spite of numerous efforts to capitalize on and expand large-scale commercial agricultural production by such new companies as the North Laredo Land, Irrigation, and Water Company, the arid South Texas climate confirmed that conditions were not suitable to gain a foothold along the Rio Grande. In lieu of cultivation, new investment during the 1890s increasingly was directed to mining, both in the support of operations in Mexico as well as mining and smelting in the outskirts of Laredo. Additionally, light manufacturing expanded in Laredo with the opening of a large tannery, a boot and shoe factory, a gristmill, an ice factory (five cents per pound), a paper mill, a foundry and machine shop, a wooden mill and a cotton factory, and four brickyards. The southbound movement of high-value capital equipment to the major mineral fields in Mexico and the northbound shipment of ore were important for trade volume. The total U.S. merchandise exports in December 1893 to Mexico totaled $1.4 million, and of the thirty-four port-of-entry Mexican customs houses, Nuevo Laredo ranked as number one on the border and as the number two port of entry, trailing

Table 5.1. Mexican imports by Customs House revenues, December 1893

Veracruz	713,001	Juárez	53,366
Nuevo Laredo	108,406	Porfirio Díaz	40,364
Mazatlán	101,357	Nogales	34,545
Tampico	96,227	Matamoros	6,106

Note: Total for thirty-four Mexican Customs Houses: $1,403,479. A majority of imports to Veracruz were European products, many of which were transshipped to the United States via Laredo.
Source: *Laredo Morning Times*

the centuries-old Mexican gulf coast seaport of Veracruz. Goods shipped via Laredo into Mexico totaled $108,406 for the final month of 1893. While this appears to be a seemingly low figure by today's levels of trade, the amount exceeded the combined U.S. merchandise exports shipped through El Paso, Eagle Pass, Porfirio Díaz (Acuna), and Matamoros. Laredo–Nuevo Laredo from this date forward would be the dominant U.S. cross-border port of entry on the 1,952-mile U.S.-Mexican border. Laredo was promoted and hailed nationally: "It [Laredo] is at the gateway to Mexico, the gateway, too, of the nearest, shortest, direct line from the commercial centers of the North to the commercial centers of the Mexican Republic. . . . Laredo is a great centre [*sic*] of business."[8]

The rising cross-border trade spurred the Laredo commercial sector to continue to diversify and attract new merchants by catering to the buyers and travelers drawn to the border and Mexico. Laredo had a dozen each of bakers, blacksmiths, and attorneys; twenty-four barbers; eleven butchers; and two dairies. The Sisters of Mercy Hospital opened in October 1894 and was supported by six local doctors. A continued influx of international immigrant merchants to Laredo brought a variety of products and services. The Celestin Jaque Shop offered a mix of exotic European wines, cognac, fancy groceries—and ammunition and arms! Chinese and Japanese "fresh goods" could be found at 1216 Iturbide Avenue in the store of Wing Hing Lung—importers and exporters.[9] The Commercial Hotel, the Wilson House, and the Hamilton Hotel routinely listed their varied roster of "special" guests in the *Laredo Daily Times*—in all Laredo had seven hotels in 1900. Seven churches and a dozen local civic organizations flourished, such as the Laredo City Ladies Social Club, which annually hosted a stage play at the Market Hall in the center of the city each fall. Also, a dozen private and fraternal clubs—such as the Aztec Club located on the second floor above the

Fig. 5.1. The Hamilton Hotel, shortly after it was built in 1890. Note the horse-drawn stagecoach and the electric trolley cars operated by the Laredo Development Company. One of Laredo's first financial institutions, the Rio Grande National Bank occupied the corner office. Source: John Keck Collection.

Milmo National Bank—catered to the local merchants and their visitors. Evening events were sponsored by such ad hoc groups as the Laredo Casino Association, which held occasional gatherings such as the fall "Hop and Lawn Party."[10]

Across the river in Nuevo Laredo, bullfights were a popular diversion. The much-advertised so-called therapeutic waters at Topo Chico Hot Springs and Resort in the mountains west of Monterrey were also popular. Only a two-hour train ride south of Laredo, proprietor Jules Randle routinely promoted the oasis-like springs as a "cure for rheumatism, catarrh, blood poison, and skin diseases."[11] A much-touted sign of Laredo's growth and prosperity was the approval by the U.S. Postal Service in January 1894 to initiate citywide door-to-door mail service. Laredo was divided into four mail districts and twenty-six mail collection boxes were placed around the city, thus ending the window-only pick-up of general delivery mail at the old main post office. Across the street from the post office, the Sisters of Mercy purchased the Steffian home on Jarvis Plaza in 1894 to establish the first full service hospital, Mercy Hospital, which when completed consisted of four wards and fifty-one private patient rooms.[12]

Interest in Laredo was further stimulated by sensational rumors in February 1894 of large amounts of gold in the riverbed of the Rio Grande near the city. Coal mining had begun some fifteen years earlier upstream, yet no gold had been found. And it is unlikely that the traces of gold dust found in small quantities along the river, as reported in late 1846 by Army Lt. Bryant Tilden following the grounding of the steamer *Major Brown,* was known at the time. Thus, always eager to promote the city, the *Laredo Weekly Times* began a series of articles about the grand and glorious gold rush days of California of the 1850s, whereupon unnamed mining experts envisioned a large potential in the Rio Grande for placer gold as a result of the "run off" from the Rocky Mountains over 1,500 miles upstream! Also included in an article were unfounded predictions that gold could "most likely" be found forty feet "under" the main riverbed—yet the article failed to mention that there was no economical means available to mine such deposits. J. S. Penn, the *Laredo Times* editor, filled the paper with numerous hypotheses yet with few supportable facts or results. As would-be prospectors went in search of the so-called gold of Laredo, one intriguing theory was put forth that the gold might be as common as oyster shells! Large deposits of petrified oyster shells, dating back forty-two million years, had been uncovered northeast of town. The vast deposit of well-preserved cameo-white shells resulted in a group of entrepreneurs "mining" them with the intent of grinding them into what was then termed—"lime." Both the oyster-shell project and the rumors of gold were short-lived.[13]

Mining, Smelting, and Bricks

Large-scale development of coal mining in Laredo dates from 1881, when Alexander Cameron Hunt, governor of the Colorado Territory from 1867 to 1869, arrived in Laredo in the early rail development and boom days to explore options to own or invest in a local rail line. Following a stint as the general manager of the Mexican National Railroad being built southward to Monterrey and Mexico City, Hunt established the Rio Grande and Pecos Railway and Telegraph Company. This rail and communications system was planned to traverse from Brownsville to El Paso via Laredo. Co-owners of the bold project were J. W. Throckmorton and Albert W. Wilcox. Hunt expanded this $500,000 railroad investment when, according to the *Laredo Weekly Times:* "He heard a story that Mexican *vaqueros* used a black rock they took out of a ravine near the Rio Grande twenty five miles above Laredo, to burn in their camp fires. . . . Hunt visited the ravine, confirmed it was coal and opened one of the finest coal mines in all Texas." Hunt was the first to develop Webb County's coal reserve but was not the first to realize the potential commercial and strategic value of the coal.[14]

In fact, knowledge of coal in the Laredo area dates from the colonial era. Settlers in the ill-fated town of San José de Palafox surely had contact with the shallow veins of rich, black coal that were exposed along the Rio Grande and small streams in the area. Although Palafox was abandoned in 1818 due

Fig. 5.2. Alexander Cameron Hunt (1825–1894) was pivotal in the development of the first electrical and water system for Laredo and was a major investor in the expansion of coal mining and railroads throughout the region. In his earlier career, prior to coming to Laredo, Hunt was governor of the Colorado Territory (1867–69) and was responsible for the relocation of the future state's capital from Golden to Denver in late 1867. Source: Colorado State Archives.

to Indian raids and was then reoccupied in 1829 and 1846, no clear records on coal exploration have survived. One who did provide what may be the first detailed written record of the Rio Grande region was French naturalist and explorer Jean Louis Berlandier, who surveyed and drew a map of what was to be the present-day Mines Road area, noting the presence of coal and evidence of past mining along a small creek known as El Astillero.[15] Later, British promoter William Egerton, in the early 1830s era of early Texas colonization fostered by Stephen F. Austin, formed the Rio Grande and Texas Company to advance his grand scheme to establish a colony of 3 million acres between the Rio Grande and Nueces River. In order to lure prospective immigrants from Britain he published a pamphlet claiming that, "coal, of pitchy quality and equal to Liverpool coal, [had] been discovered upon the grants." It is unclear how and when broad knowledge of coal deposits became known, but beginning with the Mexican War numerous official accounts were filed by members of the U.S. Army. Lieutenant Tilden, scouting the Rio Grande north of Laredo, gave a detailed report about coal "of superior quality" that he and scout Alpheus Rackliff found in November 1846. Shortly thereafter, a notation by surveyors lieutenants Nathaniel Michler and Martin L. Smith followed; they had been dispatched by Col. William H. Emory during the 1848 U.S.-Mexican boundary survey, when they found (fifteen miles above Laredo) a "strata of coal three or four feet thick . . . of great prospective value." This report was followed by a second confirmation by Michler and Smith in August 1850. In 1852, Army surgeon Glover Perin, stationed at Fort McIntosh, noted in an official report to the War Department in Washington, D.C.: "Coal of a very bituminous character is found in small quantities in the bank of the river a few miles above the post." These reports of coal in South Texas and in Coahuila were followed by limited commercial efforts during the Civil War to barge coal downriver to steamboats at Brownsville. In the early 1870s, a joint venture by rancher Charles Callaghan and Refugio Benavides was launched to mine and ship mule-drawn cartloads of coal overland to Corpus Christi for use by steamers along the Texas gulf coast.[16]

However, Governor Hunt's action that gained greatest notoriety was when the *New York Times,* on September 24, 1881, ran a small article titled, "Coal Discovery in Texas," followed by articles in two leading Texas newspapers of the period, the San Antonio *Express* and the *Galveston Daily News,* which carried feature stories in March 1882 announcing that there was a "discovery of coal oil near Laredo [that] arose from the appearance in a well dug in the coal bed north of Laredo . . . an oil which is pronounced to be petroleum."[17] This is the earliest known report of oil in South Texas and the Laredo area. Knowledge of this did not at once begin an oil boom, an event that would not occur for another three decades. Instead, Hunt began to buy land in

U. S. GEOLOGICAL SURVEY BULLETIN 691 PLATE XXIX

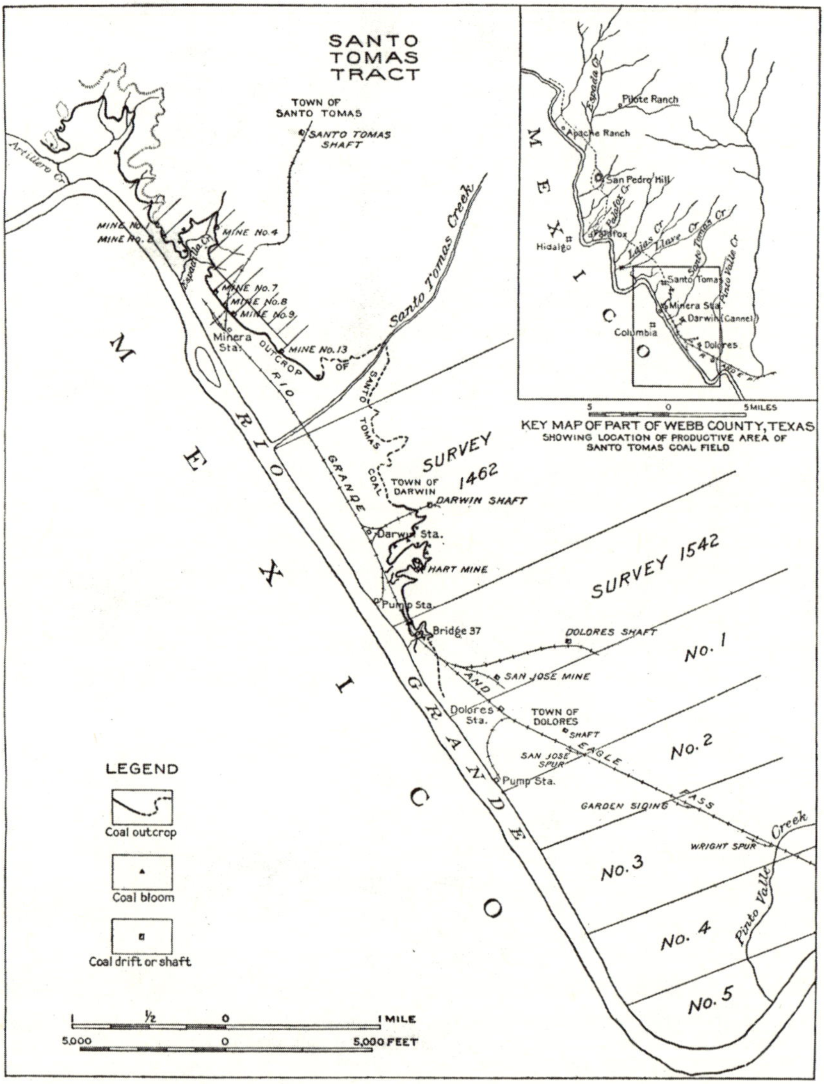

SKETCH MAP OF PRODUCTIVE PORTION OF SANTO TOMAS COAL FIELD, WEBB COUNTY, TEX.

Map 5.1. Santo Tomás Coal Field. This 1918 sketch map of the Santo Tomás Coal Field shows that it extended upriver from Laredo some ten miles. At its peak production between 1914 and 1918, over a dozen mines produced high quality bituminous coal. Note the existence of the towns of Santo Tomás, Dolores, Minerva, and Darwin—all little more than ghost towns today. Source: U.S. Geological Survey.

Laredo and Webb County in March 1881, and by December had amassed over 15,000 acres upriver from town, and soon thereafter concentrated on mining and shipping the coal reserves.[18] In time, and unlike the false Laredo oyster shell and gold rush, multiple coal mining companies were established to extract some of the largest volumes of high quality bituminous coal in the nation—rated at a burn "under guaranty of 12,500 British thermal units in 'dry coal'" (i.e. coal with low moisture content).[19]

The development of coal reserves in Webb County in the late nineteenth century was the direct result of three factors: first, the convergence of the Tex-Mex Railroad, the International and Great Northern, and the Mexican National Railroad at Laredo; second, the expansion of mining and smelting in northern Mexico; and third, an urban and industrial demand in both Texas and northern Mexico for a more efficient source of fuel. As a source of fuel for the railroads, coal was highly preferred over wood. Up until the mid-1880s, the railroads that traversed South Texas and northern Mexico depended on mesquite as fuel for their boilers. Sensing a major potential customer in the railroads, A. C. Hunt would pioneer the opening of the coal industry north of Laredo with the formation of the Mexican National Construction Company (MNCC), headquartered in the lower floor of the former governor's Laredo home. Employing hundreds of "hands," the first objective of the MNCC was the construction of a short line railroad due north of town to the Santo Tomás coalfield. MNCC then signed a contract to build the main line of the Mexican National from Nuevo Laredo to Monterrey and on to Mexico City.[20]

Hunt and MNCC's development was considered "one of the first sustained industrial coal mining operations in Texas."[21] This judgment was confirmed by the U.S. Geological Survey's (USGS) report *Mineral Resources of the United States, 1882,* which termed the coal reserves in Webb County to be "extensive." This was evidenced by the fact that the Santo Tomás Mine near Minera, Texas, at the height of operations produced about 130 tons of coal per day, yet normally averaged 80 to 100 tons per day. Laredo and Webb County mining and railroad activities became statewide news when Texas governor John Ireland, accompanied by Laredo's state representative Santos Benavides, visited the Hunt mines. Other mines along the narrow gauge Rio Grande and Eagle Pass Railway included the San José Coal Mine at Dolores and extensive operations at the Hunt Mine at Darwin.[22]

Speculation, mergers, and financial difficulties marked a steady stream of new investors and owners of the mining concerns and the local short line railway. The MNCC, for example, was merged into the newly incorporated Rio Grande & Pecos Railway Company (RG&PR). Investors flocked to invest in both the railroads and the adjacent mining discoveries. Stock of the RG&PR traded freely and generated a large capital reserve. Hunt's role as

Fig. 5.3. The Santo Tomás Coal Mine, which opened in the mid-1880s, proved highly profitable as the railroad and industries shifted to using coal as a fuel. The processing facility loaded hundreds of rail cars per day. In the background can be seen the leftover slag that grew into a hill that is still visible today. Source: U.S. Geological Survey.

land developer and rail owner changed in May 1882 when, after less than a year of ownership, he sold a portion of his share in the RG&PR for $2 million, as well as a portion of his coal mining interest (*porciones,* or tracts, 1, 2, 3 and a tract known as Webb County School Lands) for $4 million to railroad magnate Jay Gould.[23] Hunt's total investment in property, equipment, and rights-of-way had been less than $20,000. This series of transactions attracted great attention, bringing in new interest and immigrants to Laredo.[24]

Hunt remained as the president of the RG&PR as well as the principal mine operator, but hired experienced railroad-man Col. W. W. Hungerfor, who formerly supervised construction on the Texas-Mexican line, to take over construction. Hunt, meanwhile, traveled north to purchase rails, bridge materials, and supplies to keep the project on track. Rails were obtained from mills in Kansas City and I-beams for the bridge across Santa Isabella Creek were purchased at the Bethlehem Steel Works in Bethlehem, Pennsylvania. On May 24, 1882, Hunt led a procession of local city officials and prominent merchants to a spot west of town to ceremoniously lay the first cross tie with the sinking of a silver spike. With much of the roadbed already in place, by late June 1882, Webb County mines were producing and shipping hundreds of tons of coal per day.

The influx of new investors resulted in increased competition. By mid-1884, a fluctuation in coal prices and the rising cost of equipment created a cash flow problem for many of the new coal speculators. Furthermore, the

RG&PR came under pressure of foreclosure in December 1884 and was sold to Philadelphia investors Charles Barstow Wright and his son Charles Jr. in June 1885.[25] Wright recapitalized the twenty-seven-mile track with ten stockholders, the Laredo investors James J. Haynes, E. A. Atlee, Joseph Deutz, D. H. Randolph, W. M. Sharpe, and John Z. Leyendecker as the Rio Grande & Eagle Pass Railway Company (RG&EP). The 1892 annual report filed with the Texas Railroad Commission by RG&EP Railway noted a unique feature that allowed maximum operations: "our track is laid with *three* rails and we pull standard and narrow gauge cars on the same train."[26] Wright's $100,000 investment included control of 20,000 acres of land along the rail line, properties he actively promoted to potential speculative investors and small ranchers.[27] Furthermore, Wright offered company-paid excursions to promote land development along the river. In addition to construction of a depot and terminal, three stations (or stops)—Sánchez, New Boston, and San Pedro—were established. Near San Pedro, on the banks of the Rio Grande, Wright in 1886 created the first recreational park, which became one of the few local excursion destinations in Webb County (see map 5.1).[28]

The Santo Tomás mines gave rise in the mid-1880s to the small mining town of Minera, Texas, sometimes called Carbon, which grew to over two thousand residents. The inflow of workers, primarily immigrant Mexicans, was critical to the labor-intense mining industry. In 1886, the Kansas Ore Company established a sampling works to process ores, and in 1887, the Guadalupe Mining Company of Philadelphia occupied twenty acres of land donated by the city to building a smelting and concentrating plant—with a 300-ton daily capacity.[29] The railroads in Mexico and Texas were the primary customers for the coal, followed by Mexican smelters in Torreón, Monterrey, San Luis Potosí, Monclova, and Sabinas. The prime by-products of the Mexican smelter operations were, of course, gold and silver, followed by a rising demand for the industrial metals copper, zinc, graphite, antimony, and lead. Much of this ore was exported to Britain. The early years of mining proved lucrative; coal sold for $6 per ton, yet by the late 1880s, in spite of the fact that demand increased, competition with the opening of new mines resulted in the price dropping to $1.85 delivered to Laredo.[30]

The demands of the railroads and mining industry resulted in extensive industrial investment in northern Mexico. By 1900, Webb County became the second major producer of "clean" bituminous (cannel) coal in the state, behind Erath County. Laredo coal was used by over eight railroads in the United States and Mexico and was shipped to industrial plants in San Antonio, Austin, and Corpus Christi.[31] To supply railroad coaling stations, the I&GN Railroad shipped Webb County coal from the Santo Tomás mines to depots at Pearsall, Taylor, and New Braunfels. And Laredo's high-quality bituminous coal was the first fuel to burn in Mexico's first steel and iron plant, Compañía Fundidora de Fierro y Acero de Monterrey, which opened operations in 1902. The Fundidora, as it was commonly called, became a symbol of Mexico's "modernization" and the national economic development drive during the Díaz era; it was the first to obtain the latest manufacturing technology.

Cross-border trade was halted due to massive damage caused by tornadoes that struck the city on the evening of April 28, 1905, killing two dozen citizens.[32] The roundhouse and depot of the Mexican Railway and the Laredo Cotton Gin and Ice House were destroyed; few homes and businesses escaped damage. Some $6,000 damage was done to the barracks, commissary, and officers' residences of Fort McIntosh. Of greatest concern was the collapse of two spans of the International Bridge, yet repair to the vital link with Mexico commenced almost immediately. Thus, with the link between the commercial and industrial growth of northern Mexico soon restored (particularly to Monterrey), Laredo would become critical to the region's economic development, of which the broader implications were captured by Juan Mora-Torres in *The Making of the Mexican Border:*

> Northern Mexico became a permanent zone in which the economies and cultures of two nations that were in many ways worlds apart engaged in each other, creating a unique region different from the interiors of both Mexico and the United States. Substantial foreign (mainly U.S.) investments in railroads and mining sparked the development of capitalism in the north, which spread more rapidly and thoroughly in this region than in the rest of Mexico. Two of the major outcomes of this process were that the northern economy became an extension of the U.S. economy and that the north [Monterrey] turned into the center of Mexican capitalism. Mexico modernized by following an outward (export-led) strategy of economic development: one-third of all exports passed through northern [border] ports of entry by 1911, compared to less the 2 percent in 1878.[33]

The first boom phase of mining north of Laredo was abruptly interrupted by the flood of 1912 that destroyed the mines and processing facilities at Minera. Much of the small mining town resided in the river *vega* (flood plain), and thus was flooded with the mines. This resulted in destruction of the equipment and collapse of the shallow earthen shafts. A new town was founded on higher ground above the river, Santo Tomás, which replaced Minera.[34] Retooling after the flood resulted in a shift from shallow surface mining to the emergence of three active mines. These all-shaft mines were the Santo Tomás mine about 165 feet below the surface; the Darwin mine,

50 feet; and the Dolores mine, 200 feet. These mines and their rail stations and communities of over five thousand Mexican workers depended heavily on Laredo merchants for food, imported timber for shafts, clothing, and equipment.[35] The down hole operations, using "electric chain machines," were at the time some of the most sophisticated commercial mining operations in the hemisphere:

> The Dolores mine is worked by the room and pillar method. The rooms, which follow the face "slips," or cleavage planes, are 35 feet wide, and the pillars 15 to 18 feet. Rooms from adjoining entries are driven together, and the pillars are taken in retreating, so that practically no coal is left. Height is obtained in the entries by taking up the floor and taking down the roof. Because of the thinness of the beds much of the floor is taken up. Part of this is "gobbed" in the middle of the room, and the rest is sent to the surface. The air intake follows down one rib of the room across the face and back on the outgoing track. The coal is undercut, then drilled and shot down, yielding from 75 to 80 percent of lump over 1 1/4 inch bar screens.[36]

Numerous new investors entered Webb County to mine coal, and recovery from the flooding was swift. R. C. Bateman, secretary of the Laredo Chamber of Commerce, displayed a two-ton "lump" of coal from the Minerva Mine in the lobby of the downtown chamber offices in Laredo. Prospective investors were given an opportunity to buy shares in the 9,000 acres of the Llave Coal Mines (formerly the Manuel García Grant) north of and bordering the Llave Creek and six miles from Minerva. The excitement over the mines caused Mexican investors to consider the renewal of an old plan to extend rail service to the small ranching community of Columbia, seventeen miles upriver from Laredo. The Rio Grande coal near Laredo was highly touted by the industry tabloid *Coal Age,* which noted that the coal "readily sells for three times as the best grade of bituminous coal in the coal fields of west Pennsylvania and West Virginia . . . the demand for it exceeds the supply." Reaching its peak in 1918, coal production continued as a strong regional industry.[37]

By the 1920s, a combination of a post–World War I downturn in the national economy and the need for new capital investment in equipment slowed mining operations. The era of multimining operations came to an end in 1933, with the abandonment of the rail line by the Rio Grande and Eagle Pass Railway in 1942. Notwithstanding, the railroads and mining activities greatly impacted the growth and improvement in Laredo, which included significant improvements in commercial and residential construction. Thus, Laredo had commercially mined coal continuously since 1881 and had slowed large-scale operations by World War II. Today the Farco Mining Company, mining coal just beyond the original Santo Tomás site near the old town of Palafox, remains one of the leading exporters of bituminous coal to Ireland.[38]

To build a community in the 1880s required not only lumber that arrived in quantity from East Texas via the railroad, but also bricks. Laredo by 1900 became the largest center for commercial brick production on the Rio Grande. Brick makers in Laredo outnumbered the combined total in the other border counties of Starr, Hidalgo, and Cameron. The initiation of large-scale brick manufacturing and construction was led by Danish immigrant and future Laredo mayor Andrew Hans Thaison, who arrived in Laredo in late 1881. The Thaison brickyard and ovens were located a few miles downriver (on what became the Slaughter Farm) and used the natural powder loess deposits in the river *vega* for manufacturing bricks. The first significant masonry structure was the multipurpose two-story Milmo National Bank located at the corner of Salinas and Flores streets, completed in April 1883. Others entered the brick industry along with the leading local companies of the era: the Laredo Brick Company owned by Thaison, the Page Company, and A. Ligarde, Valdez and Ortiz Companies, as well as the Johnson Brick Company. The Johnson Brick Company was pioneered by S. N. Johnson, the future Anheuser Busch beer distributor and owner of the Laredo Coca-Cola Bottling Company (est. 1910).[39]

Bricks and lumber by 1890 had a tremendous impact on the architecture and building standards in the city. Commercial downtown buildings took on a permanence with the construction of numerous two-story structures. A common feature in downtown Laredo was a store on the first floor and a warehouse or residence on the second. The Hamilton Hotel, the Deutz Brothers Hardware store, and the Masonic Hall built in the late 1880s changed the skyline of Laredo. Homes were being built entirely with brick facades; those constructed of lumber were in the Victorian style. The former residence of B. J. Salinas on the corner of Salinas and Matamoros, which was restored by the Union National Bank in the late 1980s as the Heritage House, is a prime example. Most houses had brick foundations and many had brick-lined cellars. The manufacture of bricks and improved lumber distribution—with the opening of the Laredo City Lumber Company by Peter P. Leyendecker Jr. on August 15, 1895 and the Texas Export Lumber Company (specializing in mining timbers and railway materials)—furthered the construction boom that continued into the early twentieth century. This boom created hundreds of jobs. One key example of the construction boom was the new Webb County Court House that was designed and built by architect Alfred Giles in 1909 following the fire that destroyed the first seat of county government. Bricks from Laredo were sold throughout the region, in northern Mexico, and to Texas markets. The Laredo brick industry would thrive until the early 1960s when competition from Mexico lowered prices and shifted production.[40]

The Bermuda Onion

Earning a profit from the land in South Texas up until the turn of the twentieth century had been limited to mining and the age-old livestock-ranching industry. Cattle and sheep, and to a lesser degree horses and mules, were the main focus of the livestock-ranching industry. Texas ranchers' investment in the cattle industry between 1890 and 1910, as well as the expansion of Mexican ranching, created a profitable export-driven business due to demand in the United States. Much of the cattle that crossed by rail at Laredo was bound for Texas ranches and feedlots and on to markets in the Midwest. From 1900 to 1910, Mexico exported an average of 75,000 head of cattle per year. The outbreak of the revolution in Mexico in 1910 disrupted shipments for nearly a decade.[41]

However, in 1898, efforts to expand agriculture in the Laredo area gained major backing with the commercial construction and improvements in electrical power pumps and "modern" irrigation techniques. Rich alluvial soil deposited for ages along the river was adequate for crops; however, without irrigation crops of corn, some vegetables, cotton, and hay had not proved sustainable in the dry climate. Dry farming techniques used in other parts of the state did not have commercial acceptance in Webb County. Leading a major agricultural development was Thomas Carter Nye, who introduced both large-scale irrigation and the Bermuda onion to Webb County in 1899. Water from the Rio Grande was pumped via wooden pipes north of downtown to elevated tanks that provided for gravity irrigation for an initial 2,000 acres. The onion needed a minimum amount of water and, once rooted was resilient to heat. More importantly, it met the taste and culinary demands of a growing market both in Texas and nationally. To assure timely loading of the annual onion crop, a rail siding on the I&GN was built north of downtown; the station was named Nye. While the downtown commercial sector, ranching, and mining all remained healthy, during this period the onion crops added an entirely new dynamic to the Laredo economy.[42]

Water from the river was pumped to tanks as far as ten miles away. The expansion of drip irrigation and the fertile soil along the river and northeast of Laredo helped produce a yearly increase in the output of onions in what became known as the South Texas winter garden, or truck farming, district.[43] Once the onion fields were established, it was estimated that an irrigated acre would yield 20,000 pounds, or $1,200 per acre, in 1908. In spite of calls to diversify to other crops such as cantaloupes and tomatoes, onions became the mainstay. To gain broader access to produce markets outside of Texas, Laredo growers bolted the Texas Truck Growers Association and formed the Bermuda Onion Association of Laredo. Its first officers were J. J. Haynes, president; G. L. Woodman, vice president; and E. H. Sauvigent, secretary. By 1908, Laredo growers shipped some eight thousand railcar loads of onions, representing 45 million pounds of production.[44] The John Armengol San Rafael Farm, on the Rio Grande ten miles south of downtown Laredo was hailed as the largest Bermuda onion farm in the world, pumping over 300,000 gallons of water per hour from the Rio Grande during the growing season and producing an annual yield of 450,000 pounds.[45] In addition to Armengol, active Laredo growers included A. C. Richter, S. N. Johnson, Geronimo Treviño, John H. Davis, and G. C. Jones. In response to a claim by a group of California growers that the San Jose region grew the most onions, in 1908 Rufus Jones, executive secretary of the Laredo Board of Trade (LBT) drafted a spirited response: "The onion center of the *universe* at present happens to be Laredo, Texas, where the finest onions known to ancient or modern history are produced."[46] Laredo, by 1915, produced some 75 percent of the onions grown in the United States. And in spite of increased competition by onion imports from Spain, Egypt, and England, Laredo would remain the undisputed center of U.S. onion production until the early 1950s.[47]

Fig. 5.4. During the period from 1900 to 1925, the production of Bermuda onions in Webb County led the nation. The significance of this cash crop is the honored attention it received each year in the annual downtown Washington's Birthday Celebration parade. Pictured here, the Bermuda onion float, ca. 1920, with a soldier sitting on an onion crate. Source: John Keck Collection.

Table 5.2. U.S. production and import profile of 1926 onion markets

U.S. Production	*Bushels*
Texas	2,552,000 (75% grown in Webb County)
California	894,000
Louisiana	294,000
Onion imports by origin	
Spain	1,341,000
Egypt	600,000
England	294,000

Source: USDA, Year of Agriculture: 1926

At the turn of the century, prior to the formal establishment of the Laredo Chamber of Commerce in 1915, the Laredo Board of Trade was pivotal in promoting the commercial interests of Laredo and Webb County. Rufus Jones was active in promoting industrial visits to South Texas, negotiating rail rates for passengers and freight, as well as promoting the mining and agricultural sectors. One long-range project of the LBT was to develop a downriver rail connection with Rio Grande City and Brownsville. This rail line that was to parallel the river was never fully completed, yet the planning and community awareness was important for the border towns, which were eventually connected by a series of farm-to-market roads built in the late 1930s.[48]

Fostering commercial relations with San Antonio and Corpus Christi was an additional objective of the Laredo Board of Trade. Promoting the interest of Laredo and Nuevo Laredo as the "gateway communities" long before the advent of the Pan American Highway, Interstate Highway 35, or the maquiladora twin-plant industry, the city hosted numerous business groups, for example, members of the Jobbers and Manufacturers League of San Antonio, to an industrial tour of the twin cities. Arriving on six Pullman passenger railcars, the 150 businessmen were greeted by a band and then were given a reception at the Hamilton Hotel, at which the *Laredo Weekly Times* noted, "all did justice to the refreshments" of tamales, sandwiches, pickles, onions *a la souvenir*—followed by beer and cigars.[49] And to spur tourism, one key enticement was the offer of special passenger rail rates such as a round trip excursion fare via the Tex-Mex Railroad from Corpus Christi to Laredo for $3.20.[50]

The dynamic expansion of the Laredo economy, backed by railroads, ranching, mining, and onions, during the first decade of the century transpired concurrently with economic and political unrest that emerged in Mexico. In spite of the tragic loss of the Webb County Court House located at Flores and Matamoros streets to a highly questionable late-night fire on October 16, 1906, trade flourished with Mexico. Most tax and district court records stored in the basement of the old courthouse were saved, including the Laredo archival information (later known as the "Laredo Archives") dating back to the founding of Laredo in 1755.[51] However, the industrialization of northern Mexico and the backlash to foreign investment in the three decades of the Díaz era resulted in a complicated pattern of social and economic unrest on the doorsteps of Laredo, as noted by John Mason Hart in *Revolutionary Mexico:*

> The destabilizing results of foreign penetration of the Mexican political economy were manifold, but the salient impacts were economic vulnerability through dependence on sometimes unavailable alien finance capital; an increasing rate of inflation characterized by wildly fluctuating food prices; peasant displacement as a result of agricultural commercialization; the proliferation of small industrial enclaves that failed to provide the employment opportunities needed for the economy successfully to complete enclosure; the defeat and exclusion of regional elites and *pequeña burguesia* in competition with foreigners for access to opportunities; the political exclusion of regional and local elites by the metropolitan regime; incipient famine in much of the country brought about by reduced acreage committed to domestic food production; and prolonged dictatorship made possible by an alliance with foreigners, which upset the previous interregional balance of power.[52]

Saddles and Wings and Revolution

Fort McIntosh, established in 1849 on the northwestern edge of the city along the Rio Grande, remained a sleepy cavalry post, outlasting many Texas Army posts that were closed in the early 1890s. The winds of revolution in Mexico caused grave concerns about the security of the border. As in the days of the Indian raids, the border served as a safe haven for bandits and rebels looking to dash across the Rio Grande to avoid their pursuers. Of concern, given the extensive concentration of rebel forces in the northern Mexican states, were any attempts to embroil cities and inhabitants on the Texas side of the border. Mexican exiles ousted by Díaz and coming to the United States organized a number of efforts to overthrow the aging dictator. The leading anti-Díaz movement was the Partido Liberal Mexicano (PLM), organized in July 1906. In response, the United States invoked neutrality laws that prohibited the organization of any paramilitary expeditions launched from U.S. territory. Notwithstanding, isolated incidents would take a new course in 1910 with the rise of political activist Francisco I. Madero. It would prove a defining era for Mexico. As one author noted, "It started out as a simple if drastic shift in political power; it ramified into one of the complex revolutions of modern times."[53] Unrest in Mexico and along the border would result in the decade-long Mexican Revolution, once again placing Laredo in the path of history-making events.[54]

Following a failed effort to unseat Díaz, who was overwhelmingly elected to his eighth term as president in 1910, Madero fled to Texas disguised as a railroad mechanic and walked across the steel rail bridge at Laredo on October 7, 1910. Declaring the 1910 Mexican election a fraud, Madero released the Plan of San Luis Potosí. In an attempt to avoid a violation of the neutrality accords, the document, drafted in San Antonio, was backdated to make it appear that it was issued in Mexico. Madero nominated himself as provisional president of the government of Mexico in exile. Fully aware of the U.S. neutrality laws, Madero, joined by his brothers and a small group of supporters, secretly operated from the Hutchins Hotel in San Antonio. U.S. Secret Service agents were assigned to monitor their activities, yet failed to notice his departure by train to Cotulla. Transferring to a carriage, the Madero party attempted to disguise themselves as miners and proceeded to Carrizo Springs where their intent to return to the U.S.-Mexico border to foment revolution was uncovered.[55] The alarm signaled by the newspaper headlines caused concern in Austin and Washington. As a response to increased armed Mexican bands along the border, as well as rumors of large quantities of guns and ammunition being shipped to the rebels (presumed to be slated for Madero), the governor dispatched additional Texas Rangers to Laredo, and the U.S. Army was ordered to mobilize to move to the border to assist federal marshals and customs agents. In the process of the army mobilization in Texas, aviation history was soon to be made in Laredo.[56]

The 1910–11 period was the infancy of military aviation. The role of aircraft in the army had not been fully determined. Before the creation of the Army Air Corps (1926) or the U.S. Air Force (1947), early military pilots of fixed-wing aircraft were assigned to the Army Aeronautical Division, U.S. Signal Corps. Among the early pioneer aviators was Lt. Benjamin D. Foulois, who was assigned to Fort Sam Houston in San Antonio. He was instructed to test, first, the remodeled Wright Flyer and, second, to evaluate the "new" Wright Type B airplane, the Scout. Once initial testing was completed, Foulois made plans and gained permission to conduct a series of reconnaissance missions along the Mexican border in conjunction with troops at Fort McIntosh. The army ground crew in San Antonio disassembled and crated the thirty-nine-foot wingspan Wright Scout and shipped it by train to Laredo on February 27, 1911. News of the arrival of the Scout spread fast through Laredo, and hundreds of onlookers gathered at the fort to watch as the army ground crew unpacked and assembled the cloth-covered biwing aircraft. Once prepared, the strange-looking "flying machine" was positioned on the drill field for takeoff as thousands of spectators lined housetops on both sides of the river to watch the spectacular first airplane flight around the city.[57]

After reviewing army field intelligence reports, Foulois and his copilot Philip O. "Phil" Parmalee, planned a nonstop flight upriver to Eagle Pass. The terrain they covered was the same route taken by the overland recon of Lieutenant Tilden in November 1846. It was also some of the roughest terrain along the river, thus causing the pilots to fly low and close to the river. History was made in Laredo on March 3, 1911, when the Scout and its pilots set a world's record for distance—flying 106 miles nonstop between Laredo and Eagle Pass in two hours and ten minutes. There were no sightings of rebels or bandit activity by the pilots, and if there had been, the frail unarmed aircraft would have been an easy target. The return flight to Laredo on March 6 proved nearly a disaster when the airplane encountered a flock of wild ducks in flight, which resulted in the pilots inadvertently shutting down the engine, followed by a crash landing in the river. The plane was recovered, loaded on wagons for transit back to Laredo, repacked, and shipped to Kelly Field in San Antonio by train. There it was repaired for future flights. Notwithstanding the minor accident (also the first military "water crash" and recovery), the report on the Laredo–Eagle Pass recon mission greatly impressed the Army because of the potential expanded use of the airplane.[58]

The specialized Foulois recon mission at Laredo was the first of a large deployment of troops and aircraft to the border that soon followed. The buildup along the border began with an initial deployment of 20,000 soldiers to augment the 5,000 already on duty in early 1911. The Taft administration proved vocal in its concerns to protect the 40,000 plus Americans residing in Mexico and the multimillion-dollar U.S. investment in Mexican mining, railroads, and ranching. With a quarter of the entire U.S. Army deployed to the southern border, Laredo became a staging area for the U.S. Army as well as for smugglers attempting to cross arms and supplies to the Madero army. Additionally, U.S. Customs in Washington, D.C. ordered J. J. Haynes, collector of U.S. Customs for Laredo, to have all agents concentrate on detection and interception of arms and munitions. In the process, a politically and diplomatically sensitive debate surfaced among the Taft administration, the U.S. State Department, and Mexican officials over the full extent and degree of enforcement of the U.S. neutrality laws. At issue was the official "diplomatic" status of the Madero faction in Mexico. The Taft administration was fully aware of the importance of Mexico for U.S. investment during three decades of Porfirio Díaz's rule. Yet, approaching eighty years of age, Díaz' days as president were numbered.[59]

Fighting in northern Mexico in March and April of 1911 resulted in Madero's rebel army capturing the border towns of Ojinaga, Agua Prieta, and Ciudad Juárez across from El Paso. The tension in the north soon created political instability in the capital of Mexico City. What followed was a negotiated departure of Díaz from Mexico on May 25. Under the terms of the Treaty of Ciudad Juárez, Díaz was allowed to "escape" to Europe, and Francisco León de la Barra, formerly the Mexican ambassador in Washington, was named interim president. In spite of the seemingly peaceful departure of Díaz, both the border and the U.S. government braced for a period of unrest.[60]

The United States took a measured response to the early stages of the Mexican Revolution yet was constantly petitioned by border residents and governors of border states to increase the number of American troops on patrol. By 1915, total U.S. federal presence on the border would exceed 160,000 militia, National Guard, and Border Patrol. The 14th Cavalry and battery of the 3rd Field Artillery at Fort McIntosh were augmented with 250 troops of the 3rd Cavalry from Fort Sam Houston. The Army also tested balloons for use in reconnaissance.[61] Within a few years a borderwide air patrol operated with the deployment in Laredo of the 8th Aero Squadron flying single engine DH-4 De Havillands.[62] In addition to increased troop strength at Fort McIntosh, Laredo merchants such as Deutz Hardware conducted a brisk arms and munitions business. Clearly, the militarization of the border was a direct response to the internal revolution in Mexico.[63]

Revolution on the Border

Following the near dictatorial rule of the Díaz regime, the winds of change in 1910 enveloped Mexico in a decade-long revolution. The release of the best-selling book *Los grandes problemas nacionales* by Andrés Molina Enríquez in 1909 coincided with the first-ever meeting between the presidents of the United States and Mexico. Díaz was seventy-nine years old and President William Taft feared the destabilization and crisis that would follow in the event of the demise of the Díaz regime.[64] The fear was well founded given the fact that U.S. investors controlled over 40 percent of the total foreign investment in Mexico. Americans owned 75 percent of Mexico's silver mines and two-thirds of the 16,000 miles of railway south of the Rio Grande. Total direct U.S. investment by 1909 was valued at over $1.2 million. The power struggle caused by political instability in Mexico placed the border once again at the crossroads of war. Crossing the border provided a safe haven for many of the revolutionaries. The incursion by Mexican revolutionary leader Francisco "Pancho" Villa across the border into Douglas, Arizona, resulted in the United States taking action to once again intervene in Mexican problems. Cross-border arms shipments flourished throughout the Mexican Revolution. Movement of contraband across the river exceeded previous smuggling activities; border merchants on both sides worked to protect their business while freebooters endeavored to supply the warring factions. In one incident five coffins arrived at the I&GN depot in downtown Laredo for "general delivery" to an unknown buyer. Although listed as containing mining equipment, under close examination the coffins were discovered to contain Winchester rifles. There is no record of anyone claiming this cargo.[65]

In 1911, tension between the Texan-Mexican landholders and the large number of newly arriving Anglo settlers from the North and Midwest escalated along the border. Many of these new settlers were seeking subdivided ranch land. The rapid purchases of age-old family homesteads and property kindled a volatile atmosphere. This was further aggravated by a large number of land fraud cases. In an effort to quell the unrest, Governor Oscar Colquitt sent the Texas Rangers to South Texas in force. Land fights resulted in the deaths of sixteen Texan Mexicans, many of which were blamed on the heavy-handed tactics of the Rangers. In response, a broad group of concerned citizens convened a week-long meeting of four hundred Texan Mexican leaders. Mexican consuls in Texas and the invited media in Laredo met on the Dies y Seis de Septiembre—September 16, 1911—Mexican independence day holiday. Known as the Congreso Mexicanista, the gathering denounced the wave of violence, looked for means to protect land claims, and strongly encouraged larger voter participation. With a rising concern "with the situation on the border," Texas governor O. B. Colquitt in March 1913 instructed state attorney general B. F. Looney to draft a bill to address the protection of persons and property in the border counties. The strongly worded bill that would have imposed martial law along the border was never introduced for consideration, yet did set the tone of the Colquitt administration on border issues. In the meantime, the rebellion intensified across the border.[66]

Concerned with the smuggling of arms as well as the pockets of resistance, the Carranzista Constitutionalist rebel army under Gen. Pablo González began a sweep of the border. Skirmishes were fought between the Constitutionalists and the Federalists at Minera on May 31, 1913, and at Piedras Negras on June 28. In the path of the fighting, millions of dollars worth of mines, smelters, railroad facilities, and ranches were destroyed. The next objectives for González, Nuevo Laredo, and Monterrey, were spurred on by news that Villa had captured Ciudad Juárez. Thus, early on New Year's Day, 1914, the Constitutionalists entered a startled Nuevo Laredo and attacked the Federal garrison commanded by Col. Gustavo Guardiola, resulting in a pitched door-to-door battle. As the battle in Nuevo Laredo raged, casualties mounted and were estimated to be over two hundred killed and wounded. As border historian Jerry Thompson notes, "Laredo was in a state of panic." U.S. troops of the 3rd Cavalry from Fort McIntosh closed and guarded the Rio Grande bridges, under protest from the U.S. Consul in Nuevo Laredo. A company of reserve troops known as the Milmo Rifles from the local National Guard unit were mobilized. All commerce came to halt as citizens of Laredo flocked to the banks of the river and to rooftops to witness the Battle of Nuevo Laredo. Fully armed, U.S. troops, under Col. A. P. Blocksom, were very cautious and did not engage in the fighting. As hostilities subsided, the bridges were reopened on January 5. Stray bullets raised havoc but did not seem to dampen spectator interest, even as a prominent Laredoan, Manuel Lugo, was struck and killed while crossing the plaza in front of San Agustín Church. Once the battle of Nuevo Laredo waned, many of the wounded Mexican troops were moved across the bridge to the hospital at Fort McIntosh for treatment. After two days of intense battle the fighting halted long enough for long lines of wagons piled high with the dead to pick up and burn the deceased combatants in order to avoid growing fears of an epidemic. The engagement proved to be a standoff as the Federals held the city and González and the rebels regrouped and moved south along the river in preparation to attack Tampico. At the same time, Pancho Villa lay siege to Torreón.[67]

As the revolution intensified in northern Mexico along the border, many families chose to immigrate to the safety of the United States. Many professionals, primarily physicians, attorneys, and engineers, viewed the unrest as a threat to both their families and business interests. An example was the exodus in 1914 of Dr. Aureliano Urrutia to San Antonio and the arrival in Laredo of his associate Dr. Francisco R. Canseco, a practicing surgeon in Monterrey and former mayor pro tem of the city, and his wife Margarita Zambrano. After establishing a residency in Laredo, Dr. Canseco secured his medical licensing in Baltimore, Maryland, and returned to Texas to complete the requirements for certification there. Thus began his active role as a surgeon and a pillar of the development of Laredo's lone hospital, owned and operated by the Sisters of Mercy. His civic activities were many and included his investment in the Merchants State Bank & Trust Company in 1924. He was elected its president, and his brother-in-law Adolfo Zambrano Jr. joined the organization as chairman of the board. Following his sudden death in May 1928, Dr. Canseco's position as president of the bank was assumed by Zambrano until 1934.

The momentum changed in April 1914 when the Constitutionalists gained the upper hand and drove the Federalists from Nuevo Laredo. Commercial concerns were felt as far away as New York because bond holders

Fig. 5.5. Dr. Francisco R. Canseco (1875–1928) with his wife Margarita, son Francisco Manuel, and daughter Margarita, pictured shortly before leaving Monterrey, Mexico, to immigrate to Laredo. The family was one of many who left Mexico in the wake of the revolution that swept the northern border region. Source: Canseco Family Collection.

of the Laredo Bridge Company (LBC) were concerned with the safety of the bridge. B. M. Alexander, manager and auditor of the LBC, sent a steady stream of reports on the bridge security, concerns with the abnormal circulation of counterfeit currency, and the cooperation with Nuevo Laredo officials:

> When the Federal garrison evacuated they burned all the business houses and important buildings. The Constitutionalists are now in charge of Nuevo Laredo and they have opened up [bridge] traffic again. The rebels are now working on the railroad to Monterrey and they expect to have it reopened within the next 10 days which will help our business materially.
>
> During the last two weeks that the Federals occupied Nuevo Laredo all kinds of money that was current here became vary scarce, and we were compelled to take the worst sort [counterfeit] of Mexican bills. We worked off a large part of it, but had about

> $1,000.00 Pesos left on hand when the final exodus came. We disposed of the Mexican money at the end of the month at a discount. We also have on hand $175.00 of money issued by the Mexican Government "Pagares de Nación" which money is forced circulation where the Federals have their soldiers . . . but the last days of excitement when everyone rushed to this side we had to take what we could get or nothing.
>
> We had a great deal of excitement here when the Federals evacuated, and they tried to dynamite the railroad bridge and exchange shots with our soldiers. I got busy and had search lights placed on the bridge, besides kept in touch with Ft. McIntosh and received protection. We had sharp shooters stationed along the river and bridge on our side who had instructions to shoot if anyone attempted to destroy the bridge.[68]

The Vergara Incident

In large measure the outcome of the Mexican Revolution would be determined by the power struggle among the northern Mexico caudillos. Victoriano Huerta, who deposed and executed Madero, was faced with the growing threat for control from Venustiano Carranza, Álvaro Obregón, Emiliano Zapata, and Pancho Villa. The political and military situation in Mexico was being reported to the Wilson administration by special U.S. agents (both official and unofficial), such as George Carothers and John Lind, who was the de facto U.S. ambassador in role only, but not in title. Lind was acutely aware of the revolution's extensive impact on American investments in railroads, ranching, and mining throughout northern Mexico and strongly contended in dispatches to Washington "that northern Mexico's proximity to the United States was the single most important determinant" to the guide U.S. policy. The unofficial Washington response was one of measured concern and a wait-and-see attitude. And throughout this tense period troop strength continued to increase on the U.S. side.[69]

Flamboyant Gen. Francisco "Pancho" Villa, born Doroteo Arango, soon changed the entire dynamics of the Mexican Revolution. Unlike most of the warring chieftains, the reputed cattle thief and bandit favored cooperation with the United States. As Washington searched for a government to extend recognition, Villa seemed to be a possible option over the autocratic and criminal *golpe de estado*–created administration of Victoriano Huerta. President Wilson, who became very involved while monitoring the hostile events in Mexico, totally dismissed Huerta as a "bloody tyrant."[70] Villa's seeming amity toward Americans did not extend to other foreigners in Mexico. In the northern region of Mexico, Villa ordered all Europeans, and especially

Spaniards, to leave Mexico within ten days or be shot. American disgust with Huerta's and Villa's actions was front-page news in the *New York Times* and the subject of much diplomatic correspondence both with Washington and with European capitals.[71]

Anticipating a gradual resolution of the unrest in Mexico, the Wilson policy since late November 1913 had been termed *watchful waiting*.[72] A key overriding factor was to weigh intervention, neutrality, and the lifting of the arms embargo against the commercial disruption and expanded rebel activity south of the border. In so doing, Wilson by December had pressured the European powers to remain out of Mexico, in return for the president's pledge that the United States accepted full responsibility "for protecting the interest of all foreigners in Mexico." Secretary of State William Jennings Bryan notified U.S. ambassador W. H. Page in London: "No one [European nation] outside Mexico can now accommodate her affairs." This was a diplomatic phrase often repeated into 1914 and the official policy of the U.S. Furthermore, U.S. citizens were also warned by U.S. border consulates that under the current circumstances the Huerta government could not protect them, and they were strongly urged to seek safety. Secretly, the Wilson cabinet issued orders to the U.S. armed forces to draft plans for an armed invasion in force of Mexico if needed to protect American investment in strategic areas such as oil, copper, and rubber. And Wilson's announced policy commitment to prevent European intervention in exchange for providing a pledge to protect the safety of foreign nationals in Mexico was soon tested.[73]

The sacking of homes and businesses owned by Chinese and some Europeans (primarily Spaniards) had occurred in northern Mexican towns occupied by Villa's troops. This activity was curtailed in a number of areas upon the protest of U.S. consuls in the region. These actions received some but not extensive media coverage. What did receive global coverage was the detention near Ciudad Juárez in mid-February 1914 of American Gustavo Bauch and rancher William S. Benton, a Scotsman. The final fate of Bauch is still unknown and from the available records did not receive a lot of attention at the time, but not Benton's. The Scottish rancher and investor, a British citizen, after approaching Villa at his headquarters with vocal complaints of damage and theft on his ranch, was detained and summarily executed. Benton's wife, via the U.S. Consul and the British Embassy in Mexico City, protested; she urged the U.S. State Department to investigate. Claims by Villa that Benton had been arrested and tried for a crime were totally discredited. In response, the British government raised a cry to Washington that was quickly exploited in the press; they questioned the course of affairs in Mexico and the safety of British citizens. In spite of the U.S. pledge, the Benton affair remained unresolved for months due to the Mexico's growing civil war in the north.[74]

The hostilities in Nuevo Laredo in early 1914 were briefly overshadowed by the New York and European coverage of General Villa across the border from El Paso in the northern area of Chihuahua. In late 1913 and into 1914, the Wilson administration struggled to assess their policy in relation to the mounting number of revolutionary factions. With the United States continuing to refuse to recognize Huerta, the U.S. arms embargo to Mexico dated March 12, 1912 was lifted by a presidential proclamation in Washington on January 31, 1914. This action, opening the border and ports to arms and munitions, gave tacit support to the Constitutionalist faction and Gen. Venustiano Carranza's revolutionaries, further raising confusion. The British as well as Wilson's U.S. political opponents and a number of newspapers vehemently protested the administration's arms policy. Call for an armed intervention in Mexico to insure the safety of foreigners also resurfaced. Furthermore, border citizens and merchants (many making profits from smuggling arm and munitions) raised vocal concerns that the so-called protection by the central government in Mexico City did not provide adequate safety. In an effort to calm border tensions, Washington ordered U.S. troops, assigned to patrol the river to enforce the embargo, recalled. Merchants and mayors on the border protested the troop withdrawal. In response, Texas governor O. B. Colquitt contacted the secretary of war, Lindley M. Garrison, requesting him to rescind the order, reimpose an embargo, and protect the border from rebels, bandits, and mercenaries. And if needed, Colquitt noted he would send Texas troops at once to the border.[75]

There was cause for concern. Both militarily and diplomatically the situation was chaotic. At precisely the same time as the Benton incident, a Laredo rancher and U.S. citizen, Clemente Vergara, was taken prisoner along the banks of the river by Federalist Mexican soldiers reportedly during an effort to resolve a dispute over the recovery of stolen horses on an island in the middle of the Rio Grande near his ranch about fifteen miles upriver from Laredo.[76] The disputed ownership of the river island dated from 1849 when the Texas General Land Office Commissioner, in reviewing "all Empresarios and commissions" claiming title on the border, noted, "I have thus far refused to patent lands on any part of the Rio Grande." To this day, it is unclear if Mexican officials knew this; regardless, Mexican Federal authorities jailed Vergara without charges on February 15, 1915 in Hidalgo, Mexico, a few miles south of the border. The U.S. Consul in Nuevo Laredo reported the incident to Washington. Unsure if the harassment and detention of U.S. and foreign citizens was a new pattern by the military forces along the frontier, Secretary of State William Jennings Bryan cabled a protest to Mexican officials. He strongly urged that Vergara be immediately released, only to learn instead that on February 28 the Webb County rancher had been beaten and shot three times without formal charges or a trial, his body left hanging from a tree. Much like the Benton incident, which gained broad nationwide media coverage, the Vergara murder became front-page news across Texas and in the nation. The *New York Times* headline read: "Federals Hanged American." In a number of news accounts it was implied the Texas Rangers had failed to prevent the incident, but in fact they had no initial part. Webb County sheriff Amador Sánchez had arranged the river crossing for Vergara to recover what were deemed stolen horses in Mexico. Reaction from Texas was swift as continued pressure was directed to Washington to uphold justice on the border. Governor Colquitt responded by dispatching additional Texas Rangers to Laredo to take local charge of the case and "intimated that the [Texas] National Guard might be dispatched to the border."[77]

The governor's unilateral action to deploy the Rangers and mobilize state troops was of grave concern to the Wilson administration. Within days, the Vergara incident would reach the highest diplomatic attention in both Washington and Mexico City when ranger-in-charge Capt. J. J. Sanders, in recovering Vergara's body, created what some termed an international incident. Without formal authorization, Sanders and his Rangers "allegedly" crossed the border and "reportedly" traveled through Mexico to Hidalgo. Unable to apprehend those responsible, the Rangers recovered Vergara's body and returned across the Rio Grande. While this action was intended to reassure the Laredo community that all efforts would be used to limit further rebel incursions, in Washington and Mexico City tensions were high.[78]

Recovery of Vergara's body did not quell the calls for immediate action to protect the border. As the Texas Rangers lingered in Laredo in the aftermath of the incident, there were calls from the floor of the U.S. Senate for the immediate movement of additional U.S. troops to the border. The president and Secretary of State Bryan received repeated pressure from Governor Colquitt to take bold and aggressive action. A period of calm prevailed whereby Venustiano Carranza, known as the Primero Jefe, or First Chief, assured U.S. diplomats on the scene in Mexico that he would take full charge of and responsibility for the Benton and Vergara incidents. Careful in his handling of both the British and Americans, Carranza cooled any ideas of an invasion by forcefully challenging the U.S. insistence on invoking the Roosevelt Corollary of the Monroe Doctrine. Developed in 1905 by then President Teddy Roosevelt, the corollary stated that the United States and only the United States would enforce any and all issues of international law and/or negotiations of grievances in Latin America. Escalation of tensions on the border and military build-up were avoided as Villa was soon overshadowed by the First Chief's actions and Governor Colquitt was quieted.[79]

To improve relations and reduce border tensions, newly elected Texas governor Jim Ferguson traveled to Laredo and met with de facto Mexican president Venustiano Carranza in Nuevo Laredo in late November 1915. The

Table 5.3. Laredo banking, 1914

	President	*Assets*
Milmo National Bank	R. Y. Benavides	$1,392,068
Laredo National Bank	J. K. Beretta	$1,193,125
First State Bank and Trust	M. T. Cogley	$55,858

Source: *Laredo Weekly Times,* January 18, 1914

popular Ferguson arrived early in Laredo to meet with the local business leaders. He was escorted by Mayor Robert M. McComb and Gen. R. H. Evans, commandant at Fort McIntosh, to the center of the bridge to be greeted by the governor of Tamaulipas, Luis Caballero, who made the introduction to Carranza at the Nuevo Laredo Municipal Palace. Ferguson's "international" meeting with the First Chief in Nuevo Laredo caused a tremendous stir in Washington, yet the governor's only action was to assure the Mexican president of the importance of trade between Mexico and Texas as well as to express his concern for the safety of all citizens along the border.[80] Ferguson's next major meeting (following a whirlwind tour of the Midwest) was with President Woodrow Wilson at the White House on December 3, 1915 to review the Carranza meeting and stress the importance of trade and security to the border region.[81]

The revolution had created a tremendous amount of disruption in cross-border trade. All were eager to return to a state of calm and "business as usual." The *Laredo Weekly Times* noted the recovery with the increase of imports-exports with Mexico (primarily foodstuffs—corn, lard, soap, sugar, and flour), the rebuilding of the smelting industry and railroads (hampered by a shortage of locomotives), continued expansion of the onion and produce sector, and the prophetic prospects for Laredo to become a merchandise wholesale-distribution center. Optimism for Laredo was further demonstrated with the announcement by the Laredo National Bank to build a new three-story bank in downtown.[82] Shortly after the Carranza-Ferguson meeting the *Laredo Weekly Times* noted:

> Our communal relations with Mexico have been of the closest nature. For many years the Mexican money [silver] circulated in all the stores and business houses of Laredo. Not only is Laredo the gateway into Mexico, but it was always the greatest port of entry from that country with the results that hardly anything shipped to our friends of the North went by any other route. Merchants from all

> over northern Mexico found their trading center here, and there was hardly a day in the year that hotels were not filled with merchants. The re-establishment of peace across the border means a great wave of prosperity for Laredo.[83]

Revolution in Mexico and border disturbances did not dampen plans for the annual Washington Birthday Celebration (WBC), chaired by Joseph C. Netzer. The festive week of activities, centered on the only extensive and continuous recognition of President George Washington, was founded in Laredo in 1897. The WBC organization committee focused the activities for the local citizens as well as visitors arriving mostly by rail from San Antonio, Corpus Christi, and Monterrey. Laredo merchants and hoteliers viewed the annual event as an economic boost and showcase of the local economy. Events at the turn of the century included the staging of a "sham battle" (pitting Indians against cowboys), street parades, a shooting tournament, military maneuvers by the troops from Fort McIntosh, "hose" racing by the newly organized Laredo Volunteer Fire Department, and a "Grand Bull Fight" hosted in Nuevo Laredo.[84] The Washington's Birthday Celebration is still celebrated yearly.[85]

The Mexican Revolution only temporarily dampened the commercial activities in Laredo. Merchants were able to maintain ties with customers in Mexico, overtly and covertly. Silver and gold coins disappeared from circulation in Mexico; this resulted in the printing of paper currency. Yet U.S. silver dollars became the preferred currency. With no firm backing of the near-worthless paper currency, hyperinflation followed in Mexico, and in large measure a functioning market, the banking system, and the national economy came to a halt.[86] However, for goods purchased on the border, payments were almost exclusively in Mexican silver or U.S. dollars and gold. Capital flight from Mexico resulted in increased deposits in border banks, with total banking assets in Laredo exceeding $3 million in early 1914. In spite of revolutionary rumblings, to address the changing cross-border trade dynamics in Laredo, the Laredo Chamber of Commerce was incorporated on March 26, 1915, replacing the Laredo Board of Trade as the prime business organization "to promote the interest of trade and increase of facilities of commercial transaction." The first board of directors included John H. Davis, Samuel W. Brown, Royle K. Mims, J. E. Trout, John A. Applewhite, Frank Lattig, and Charles F. Kenney.[87]

One additional ramification of the Mexican Revolution was the change in cross-border immigration patterns. For the first time, large numbers of Mexicans (and some Chinese) crossed the border into Laredo and moved north to avoid the hostilities. Many never returned to Mexico. Up until 1910, day workers with "border permits" crossed the border in small numbers for daily jobs and agricultural work, yet most returned home. While the Laredo merchants welcomed the new customers, public services did not exist to fully handle the inflow. In the absence of a clear immigration policy, enforcement of undocumented aliens was lax and no major legal actions were taken. The only exceptions were scattered reports of rebel actions near Nuevo Laredo and frequent health quarantines, such as that caused by the Nuevo Laredo–Laredo Christmas Eve typhus epidemic of December 1915.[88]

The outbreak of war in Europe reordered priorities in the U.S. government. Germany looked to entice an accord with Mexico, to oppose the United States, with the promise to return land lost in the Southwest in 1848. A reputed coded note, known as the Zimmermann telegram, was intercepted in mid-January 1917 and deciphered by the British secret service; it was then passed on to the Wilson administration. Expecting Mexico to remain neutral, Wilson recalled Gen. John J. "Blackjack" Pershing and the Punitive Expedition back north of the Rio Grande. The U.S. invasion of northern Mexico and months of bandit pursuits ended without the capture of Pancho Villa, who continued to foment unrest along the border until June 1918. The period of the U.S. Army expedition and bandits' unrest only added to the northern migration of Mexicans.[89]

It is estimated that a million and a half people migrated into the Southwest from Mexico between 1910 and 1920. By the early 1920s, over one-third of all immigrants entering the U.S. on the border were processed via the Port of Laredo. And much like today, there was a major concern with funding to provide adequate processing facilities and federal inspectors. While immigration fees prior to World War I were a major generator of revenue for the U.S. Treasury, the shortage in staffing and assistance along the U.S. southern border was attributed to the failure of Congress to provide funding.[90] Notwithstanding, the new immigrants provided a boast to the local economies along the border.

Concern over the safety of bridges diminished with the ending of the revolution, but concern was heightened following the September 18, 1919, flood of the Rio Grande. Floodwaters reached 34.2 feet and nearly covered the bridge. Further concern was caused due to a massive fire that destroyed three spans of the oil-soaked wooden planks on the American side of the International Bridge. While some asserted that Mexican revolutionaries set the fire, its trigger was never conclusively determined. A temporary low-water wooden pontoon bridge was added, as plans were completed to build a durable concrete structure to replace the old wood and steel structure. The new bridge had scarcely been opened when the river crested to a 43.9-foot flood stage on June 20, 1922. This fourth-highest recorded flood at Laredo, covered the top of the bridge with water and debris, yet no apparent permanent damage occurred.[91]

Fig. 5.6. On April 25, 1920, a fire engulfed the International Bridge. While the superstructure was of iron and steel, the intensity of the heat from the oiled wooden planks of the roadbed resulted in the total destruction of three spans on the American side. Cross-border trade came to a halt until a temporary wooden bridge was constructed. Some suspected sabotage; yet conclusive evidence was never forthcoming. Source: John Keck Collection.

The 1920s were formative years for Laredo. As the downtown commercial district gradually expanded so too did cross-border trade. The 1920 Census indicated that Laredo had grown by an astonishing 53 percent over the past decade. The gain of over 7,800 new citizens was hotly debated in South Texas as concern swirled that in fact there was a gross population undercount.[92] In a survey of the industrial and commercial opportunities in Laredo, an independent study for Central Power and Light, the local electric utility, concluded, "Laredo ranks as the most important exporting center on the Texas Mexican border."[93] The rise of the customs brokerage and freight forwarding industries placed Laredo as the hub of transborder shipments. A broad cross-section of shipments consisting of mostly finished goods and industrial supplies was transferred, such as lumber, automobiles, brick, soda ash, pipes, gasoline, paper, silica sand, mining machinery, and light trucks. Agricultural products shipped south to Mexico in quantity included eggs, wheat, corn, malt vegetable oil, and lard. Northbound products from Mexico (in spite of the disruption of the Mexican rail system) included copper, lead, arsenic, beans, cotton, bone meal, istle, tomatoes, hides, iron, and bananas. Laredo's strategic location, augmented by the enhanced rail linkage, construction of a new half-million-dollar Rio Grande "concrete" bridge, and warehouse facilities along Santa Maria Street, proved critical to the city's sustained growth. The Port of Laredo handled 59.5 percent of all southbound merchandise shipments across the U.S.-Mexico border, followed by Eagle Pass at 20.3 percent, El Paso at 18.1 percent, and Brownsville at 2.1 percent.[94]

With the addition of the Merchants State Bank and Trust Company, founded in April 1917, Laredo boasted four financial institutions with combined assets of over $8 million. A large number of stores and supply shops led retail and wholesale distribution in Laredo during the era. Richter's; I. Alexander and Bro. Clothier; A. Deutz and Bro. Hardware; Joseph Netzer Hardware; P. M. Sauvignet Laredo Ice Factory; Moser's Store; G. A. Stover Furniture Company; Eduardo Cruz "Los 2 Republics" Department Store; City Drug Company; Casso, Guerra, and Company; Laredo Novelty Company; L. Villegas and Co. Wholesale Grocers; John O. Buenz Lumber Company; the Hotel Hamilton, proprietor D. J. MacDonald; and the Webb County Lumber Company comprised much of the commercial district. The *Laredo Times* named Houston Street "Automotive Row" due to the location and variety of car and carriage dealerships as well as automotive supply shops that covered over six city blocks. Major car dealers included Laredo Auto Sales Company (Ford, Cadillac, and Dodge), National Motor

Fig. 5.7. U.S. Customs House, Laredo. As cross-border trade grew, so too did the role of the U.S. Customs House at Laredo. Pictured here in 1892, Laredo–Nuevo Laredo was the number one port of entry for merchandise moving north and south. At desk: A. R. Kahn, Fred Thomas, and Mary Devine; inside the counter: Ed Cotulla; outside the counter: Will May, Messrs. Carpenter and Lewis. Source: Western History Collection, University of Oklahoma Library.

Company, Wormser Brothers Vehicles (Hercules buggies, Milburn Wagons, and Hudson Super-Six), Rio Grande Buick Company (Republic Trucks), Auto Supply Company of Laredo, Guarantee Auto Company (Oakland and Chandler cars), and Citizens Garage and Auto Company. With the distinction of being the first and oldest Ford dealership in Texas, Laredo Auto Sales was jointly owned by W. S. Sames and J. R. Moore. Their opening inventory in 1910 was three automobiles. Agricultural packing and produce shipping was led by United Trading Corporation, John Armengol, S. N. Johnson, Valls, and the Nye Farms. The growth of the commercial sector fostered civic activities. Programs and plays at the Royal Opera House and Strand Theater became key social events for the citizens. Also during this time, the St. Anthony Hotel, located at the corner of Salinas and Victoria Streets, was opened.[95]

The growth and diversification of local industry included increased sales and exports of brick statewide and into Mexico. Local promotional materials touted the town, "as the central point between St. Louis and Mexico City, Laredo has the best location for the development of an immense business with Mexico and as a distributing point [that] has a distinct advantage over other Texas cities—Laredo is the logical center for distribution of American products sold into Mexico."[96] The aggregate capital, excluding the over $6 million in railroads and mining, invested in industrial plants in Laredo in 1928 alone was estimated to be $790,500. This produced an average annual value of manufactured goods at $1 million. Construction was also begun on the six-story addition and renovation of the Hamilton Hotel at an investment of $150,000. Fort McIntosh in the early 1920s was the quarters to some 1,600 soldiers and a support detachment; each payday boosted the Laredo economy. The three largest manufacturing operations were meatpacking, small-scale oil refining, and hat making. Other smaller operations included a bottling plant, cotton gin, foundry and machine shop, ice cream and ice plant, and a mattress factory. In all, some six hundred workers were directly employed in manufacturing. Dramatic growth, leading the region in cotton, onion, citrus, and vegetable production, new streets and sewage system, and the rumored windfall in oil and gas was reflected on July 20 in the *Laredo Weekly Times* with well-founded headline enthusiasm: "Great Prosperity Ahead for This City and County."[97]

Black Gold: Oil and Gas

Cross-border trade via the railroads in consumer and capital goods, together with coal mining and a growing ranching and agricultural industry in onions, cotton, and fruits provided for a balanced and diversified economy. But the key to the 1920s was the extensive focus on exploration for oil and gas. The presence of oil in the Laredo area was common knowledge among coal miners, water well drillers, and ranchers since the 1880s. Many in Webb County dug water wells only to find the fresh water they sought laced with oil. Most of the early water wells were very shallow, and as the *Laredo Times* in early 1920 noted, "in some instances it was necessary to abandon the well because the flow of oil was so heavy the water could not be used for [live] stock."[98] In contrast, those within the city benefited from the newfound energy source. The development of natural gas from Reiser Field, located twenty miles east of Laredo, shortly after World War I proved profitable and allowed Laredo to be the first and only of the year to extensively use natural gas as an urban fuel source. However, the big race was not for natural gas (often considered a nuisance in the 1920s) but instead to find large deposits of crude oil—petroleum.

Laredo and all of South Texas would benefit from the quest for "black gold." Oil exploration had floundered during the last quarter of the nineteenth century in Texas, following development of the first commercial oil well at Nacogdoches in 1866. Texas provided less than 1 percent of all the oil produced in the continental United States in 1899.[99] The average price per barrel of crude in 1900 ranged from sixty-two cents to $1.20. Demand was sluggish due to limited refining and distribution. In Mexico, American and British investors in oil exploration also had only marginal success. However, reports of oil, due to observations of seepage along the shoreline of the Gulf of Mexico, were deemed a sign of potential substantial petroleum fields.[100]

The formative years of the oil and gas industry in Mexico and Texas abruptly ended, first, on January 10, 1901, when the Spindletop site three miles south of Beaumont, Texas was struck and, second, on May 14, 1901 when a major discovery was made at El Ebano, southwest of Tampico, Mexico. The twin unrelated gushers would forever change the economies of Texas and Mexico. Only some 250 miles apart, both wells flowed unchecked for over a week until brought under control. At Spindletop it was reported that the well flowed during its first nine days at an estimated 100,000 barrels per day. Over a million barrels poured onto the surrounding prairie as thousands of sightseers flocked to get a glimpse of the "gusher" and wooden derrick. Overnight, "oil fever" and the scramble to be part of the "black gold" rush, swept the region, escalating land prices and igniting fierce competition among wildcatters, con men, speculators, and land men. All sought to lay claim to the future fuel of the twentieth century.[101]

In the years that followed Spindletop, 1,600 new oil companies were started nationwide; most incorporated in Texas and California. However, during the early years after 1900, Mexico made more progress than South Texas in the development of oil, because most of the attention prior to 1920 in the state was focused on exploration north of Beaumont in East Texas.

This occurred in spite of Mexican president Venustiano Carranza's hard-line stance against foreign investment in the Mexican oil fields.[102] By 1920, Mexico's petroleum production represented 23 percent of the world's total, but the "actual output of the Mexican wells [was] never equal to their potential capacity, either because of lack of markets and shipping facilities or because of a desire to conserve the oil supply."[103] In the mid-1920s, the "nationalization of petroleum exercising clauses" were written into the Mexican Constitution of 1917, which resulted in much foreign investment leaving Mexico, and hence a sharp drop in the country's total production.

A combination of factors would impact increased energy usage as the United States and the world began to make the change from coal to fuel oil. The demand for oil was driven by a broad cross-section of inventions and technological innovations, including the invention of the internal combustion engine. Demands for oil during World War I, conversion of locomotive and steamships from coal to oil, and a series of crippling coal-miner strikes between 1918 and 1922 also contributed to the oil boom. These factors coupled with improved refining technology and enhanced means to transport both oil and natural gas via tanks, tank cars, and pipelines redefined consumer and industrial demand for petroleum products—kerosene, diesel, gasoline, lubricants, and liquefied natural gas (LNG). Gradual increases in oil prices did not reduce demand, yet did spur investment in expanding exploration and refining. Thus, the post–World War I commercial market drove the wave of exploration in South Texas and Webb County. This demand more than doubled the average U.S. price per barrel of crude oil at the wellhead from $1.56 in 1917 to $3.51 in early 1920. Furthermore, oil quickly became a "global" commodity. Predictions of U.S. domestic oil shortages and a perceived shortfall of new proven reserves caused some concern that the United States would be "frozen out" of overseas markets. As the United States emerged as a postwar world power, the dynamics of global access to petroleum was key to the nation's industrial and military power.[104]

The rise of the oil production in 1919–20 coincided with the apex of coal production and consumption in the United States. The gradual demise of the coal industry and the growing acceptance and demand for oil was demonstrated in the dramatic doubling of crude production from 220 million bbls in 1911 to 443 million bbls by 1921. In terms of the production of gasoline, U.S. refineries produced 7,425,825 gallons in 1911 and by 1921 gasoline production reached 5,647,207,818 gallons.[105] Coal mining did not slip at once nationally, but in Webb County most mining operations along the "Mines Road" corridor northwest of Laredo were dramatically reduced by 1930 with a few operations surviving into the late 1930s. The dramatic shift to oil from coal is demonstrated by the fact the Rio Grande and Eagle Pass Line in 1920 hauled 1,844 carloads of Webb County coal compared to

Table 5.4. Comparative U.S. production of coal and oil, 1911–21

Year	*Bituminous Coal millions/tons*	*Petroleum millions/bbls*	*Gasoline Production millions/gallons*
1911	405	220	7
1912	450	223	8
1913	478	248	42
1914	422	268	43
1915	442	281	130
1916	503	301	2,162
1917	552	335	3,068
1918	579	356	3,852
1919	466	361	4,309
1920	568	432	5,247
1921	407	433	5,647

Source: Payne, *Mining Journal Congress,* 1922

only thirty-one carloads by 1930. The heyday in coal dwindled to nominal levels as South Texas was eager, as was the rest of the nation, to take part in the growing oil industry boom.[106]

The reaction to the tremendous jump in crude oil prices resulted in an overnight rush by wildcatters and novices alike to explore for new fields and riches in South Texas. During the month of February 1920, speculators, drillers, and land men arrived in Laredo to begin the first major exploration efforts in Webb County. The Rio Grande Oil and Gas Company of Tulsa, Oklahoma, was the first to drill a deep well west of Laredo in the Santo Tomás Tract near the mining sector; they boasted that they had "spud in an 18 inch hole" and were going deeper. The Rio Grande Company was soon joined by the Imperial Oil and Development Company of San Antonio, drilling on the T. A. Coleman Ranch; Bor-Tex Oil Company drilling in the Ortiz pasture; and the Cactus Oil Company of San Antonio. These efforts became a part of the first dozen oil wells in what was known then as the Laredo District, a sector within a twenty-five-mile radius of the city. Most of these early companies set up their headquarters in the Hamilton Hotel.[107] By spring of 1920, the *Laredo Weekly Times* ran a banner headline "Laredo Almost Encircled by Drilling Operations" as the North Texas Oil and Refining Company, the Mirando Oil Company, the Webb-Zapata Oil Company, and the Hughes Petroleum Company joined the rush to "work double shifts for the honor of bringing in the first gusher."[108]

Oliver W. Killam pioneered South Texas oil development from 1920 until his death. Mirando City became the first boom town in the area, having been built by Mr. Killam. Picture shows Mr. Killam, after age 80, on location at one of his rigs. One of his goals was to make as much money after he reached the age of 80 as he had before. He did.

Fig. 5.8. The era of South Texas oil and gas exploration and production in the 1920s was pioneered by Oliver W. Killam, pictured here at age eighty on location at one of his rigs. Source: Killam Oil Co., Ltd.

Given the fact that by late 1920, well after well in Webb and Zapata counties came into production, it is difficult to determine who was the first. Headlines in the *Laredo Times* proclaimed the discoveries. Wells came in at Benavides and the Reiser Oil Field east of Laredo, and on the Joe Jennings Ranch a huge "gasser" was reportedly struck. However, the most extensive early find to be developed was the Mirando Field beginning on April 17, 1921, led by Zapata Oil, Mirando City Oil, and the Killam Oil Company headed by forty-seven-year-old wildcatter and Missouri-born attorney Oliver Winfield Killam.[109] The Killam strike, 1,461 feet deep at the Hinnant No. 3 well created a tremendous level of excitement in Laredo. Overnight, thousands from Laredo traveled to Mirando City to get a glimpse of the well and be a part of the festivities. Within a week, visitors, investors, and con men from as far away as New York and California arrived in Laredo. A carnival-like atmosphere prevailed as a building boom raged in both Mirando City and Laredo. Concerned with the access over poor roads to the new oil fields, the Laredo Chamber of Commerce organized a committee to address new road construction. The immediate action was to use crushed coal and slag from Santo Tomás Mines as an improved base for the new roads.[110]

The development of the Mirando Field was one of the first extensive commercial ventures in South Texas, it resulted in the construction by Killam of the Texpata Pipe Line Company to carry oil to tank yards and the rail depots on the Tex-Mex rail line as well as the establishment in 1923 of the Misko Refineries in Mirando City. Overnight a group of small "oil" towns east of Laredo near the Webb-Zapata county line flourished—Bruni, Oilton, Aguilares, Ojuelos, and Pescadito. The success of these efforts and those of dozens of drillers resulted in over three hundred producing wells in 1924 and some 650 oil wells by 1927—a 317 percent increase in production

Fig. 5.9. One key to the success of the Santo Tomás Mine and the others that sprang up northwest of Laredo was the integrated system of mining and rail access developed by Alexander C. Hunt to rapidly move the coal to markets in Monterrey, Mexico, and Corpus Christi. The tracks seen in the foreground of the short line Rio Grande & Eagle Pass Railway connected in Laredo with the Tex-Mex Railroad, the I&GN Railroad, and the Mexican National. Source: U.S. Geological Survey.

from 765,790 barrels in 1923 to 2,416,774 barrels in 1927. Additional refineries were established to supply local demand for fuel oil and lubricants. And 160 natural gas wells produced 4.5 billion cubic feet of gas per day.[111]

The *Laredo Weekly Times,* as always, was quick to tout the new economic success in verse:

> Drilling east, drilling west,
> In old Webb they will rush-er
> Some are making a deep test,
> To try to get a real gusher.[112]

By 1929, the dramatic increase in petroleum production in South Texas allowed the state of Texas to lead all states in oil production—representing some 20 percent of total world supply. By 2005, Webb and Zapata counties ranked as the two leading natural gas producing counties in the nation.

In the excitement to find the "next gusher" near Laredo, it became evident that the community was on the verge of entering a new period of a transition from what had finally become a productive and profitable agricultural region to one that was transfixed with the quick wealth from oil and gas. More critically, Laredo moved toward international trade. In the early 1920s, Laredo struggled with a shortage of onion packing crates and availability of refrigerator railcars yet managed to ship over two thousand cars of the "odorous bulbs" to hungry eastern markets. Ever mindful of foreign competition, primarily from Spain and Egypt, South Texas congressman and future vice president John Nance Garner expressed concern that the foreign suppliers were working hard to undercut U.S. domestic prices. Laredo growers heeded this and other warnings with new efforts to expand and diversify production. As soon as the onion crop was ready to harvest in late March, Webb County boasted of a crop transition and planted over 12,000 acres of cotton in April, of which 3,000 were irrigated, producing an annual yield of over 5,000 bales by early September. This all occurred in the face of rising land prices due to the local oil boom. By 1920, Mexico, after a decade of revolutionary strife, was left in economic shambles. For example, Mexico's cattle herds in 1911 dropped from over 10 million head to 1.3 million head in 1921. The only Mexican exports of any volume during this period were carloads of bones, hides, henequen, and ixtle.[113]

Laredo soon entered a nationwide trend toward organized business–civic clubs. The charter meeting of the Laredo Rotary Club at the Metropolitan Club was held on March 26, 1920. Selected as the chairman of this first of its kind organization on the border was F. A. Matthes, who, along with the organizing committee of J. S. Penn, J. R. Moore, and J. E. Trout, noted: "the benefits of the organization are for the commercial interest of Laredo."[114]

Table 5.5. Laredo Rotary Club charter members, 1920

J. Alexander	haberdasher
R. L. Babbitt	lawyer
Dr. M. P. Cullinan	Border Gas Company
J. J. Christian	superintendent of schools
J. B. Da Camara	automobiles
C. Deutz	hardware
C. M. Fish	railway traffic
W. L. Guyler	lumber
Dr. H. C. Hall	surgeon
Dr. G. C. Hiatt	dentist
Frank A. Lattig	oil
S. E. Leonard	customs broker
F. W. Mally	Chamber of Commerce
F. A. Matthes	Laredo Water Company
R. K. Mims	wholesale grocery
R. R. Moore	city alderman
J. B. Morton	electric light street railway
James S. Penn	*Laredo Times*
L. M. Purwin	hides
Carlos Richter	dry goods
J. E. Trout	U.S. Immigration Service
J. S. Westbrook	commission merchant
L. H. Wharton	clergyman
J. H. Winch	druggist and rancher

Source: *Laredo Times*

The charter membership reflected a diverse cross-section of the business and professional interests in the community.

Many of the Rotary's organizing members were also active in the Laredo Chamber of Commerce. The Chamber was an extensive promoter of Laredo and South Texas both statewide and in Mexico. The chamber was active in positioning Laredo as the "gateway" between both nations during the 1920s. Few issues were off limits. In the period immediately following the Mexican Revolution, the chamber drafted a strongly worded resolution signed by president W. L. Guyler and executive secretary Fred W. Mally for presentation in Washington, D.C. to the president. The resolution urged swift recognition of the new Mexican government of Adolfo de la Huerta (who assumed the presidency following the assassination of Carranza) in order to encourage "peace and commerce."[115]

Quick recognition by federal officials in Washington of South Texas much-needed highway improvements was seen as key to expansion of cross-border trade, specifically exports of agricultural products. In 1920, there were eight primary highway crossings on the United States–Mexico border: Laredo opposite Nuevo Laredo; Brownsville opposite Matamoros; Mexicali, Baja California, across from Calexico; Ciudad Porfirio Díaz (Piedras Negras) opposite Eagle Pass; El Paso opposite Ciudad Juárez; Douglas, Arizona, across from Agua Prieta; Nogales, Arizona, across from Nogales, Sonora; and Naco, Arizona, across from Naco, Sonora. Laredo leaders worked to expand local highways.[116] One key local infrastructure project was an improved "border military highway" to replace the narrow old *camino* along the river between Laredo and Brownsville.[117]

Concerned with the wider market to attract national business, the Laredo chamber hosted one of the first U.S.-Mexico conferences on international cross-border infrastructure in June 1920. U.S. representatives were eager to develop what was then known as the "Bankhead Highway," sponsored by House Speaker William Bankhead, which ran from Laredo, Texas across the nation to the East Coast markets (very similar to the proposed route of I 69). Following a spike in U.S.-Mexico cross-border trade from 1923 to 1926, efforts were spearheaded in Mexico to expand the highway system to Laredo. President Calvin Coolidge in 1927 worked for better roads nationwide, with also an international connection to Monterrey and Mexico City as well as to the Isthmus of Panama.[118] This highway planning was the forerunner of the Pan-American Highway, running southbound from Laredo to Panama and on to South America, which was completed in mid-1936. The railroads still remained vital to local commerce and the chamber worked with the I&GN to schedule a "special" (nonstop) Pullman train to the annual Texas State Fair in Dallas each October.[119]

Hailed by *Business Week* in 1936 as the "New Trade Route to Mexico," the broader impact of the Pan-American Highway, south from Laredo to Mexico City some 765 miles, was first promoted as a boost to *turismo*—always welcomed by Laredo merchants.[120] However, the long-term impact, predating the rise of the maquiladora (twin plant) manufacturing facilities in the late 1960s, was the possibility it opened for greater trade with Mexico. In spite of mounting antiforeign (particularly American and British) overtones in Mexico, by the mid-1930s U.S. multinationals such as General Electric (light bulb factory in Monterrey), Ford and General Motors (automotive plants near Mexico City) and Standard Oil (fuel distribution), pioneered the way for the hundreds of manufacturing facilities and joint ventures that followed over the next four decades.[121]

As Mexico opened to more manufacturing, Laredo by 1935 remained an active trade community regardless of the nationwide economic downturn. Boasting thirty miles of "paved" streets, the community had 3,350 water connections and 4,396 electrical customers. The convergence of four railroads was good for hotel (830 rooms citywide), retail, and wholesale businesses. Bank deposits exceeded $6 million, and the freight forwarding–brokerage sector was in the hands of eight firms. And it was estimated that 3,400 "manufacturing" workers were employed in the hat industry, mining and smelting, oil refining, and cotton seed mills.[122]

In spite of the much-touted Good Neighbor Policy of Franklin Delano Roosevelt's administration, commercial and diplomatic relations between the two nations hit a low point; in 1938 the Mexican government expropriated all foreign-owned oil interests and property. A new wave of nationalism swept Mexico and electrified a feeling of newfound independence. These actions in Mexico dramatically diminished foreign investment and also curbed cross-border trade. War clouds on the distant horizon would soon change the U.S.-Mexico relationship.

CHAPTER 6

WAR, FLOODS, AND TRADE

> The geographic and economic position of Laredo makes it the logical port of entry from Mexico, and because of its location, it will continue to lead other border cities for generations to come.
>
> K. DA CAMARA, 1949

> If you think big, give big, and act big, you will receive big.
>
> O. W. KILLAM, 1954

In spite of a marked downturn in the Texas economy during the 1930s, Laredo and the surrounding area weathered the Great Depression with little damaging economic impact. Oil and natural gas operations in the region along with cattle ranching and crop production sustained the local economy. While Roosevelt's New Deal agencies of the federal government, such as the Works Progress Administration (WPA), Public Works Administration (PWA) and Civilian Conservation Corps (CCC), provided funding for a number of employment programs and projects across Texas and in Webb County during the late 1930s, Laredo was not much different than it had been during the past decade. Webb County judge Justo Penn (from 1928 to 1939) was the driver behind securing WPA projects and New Deal job placement in Laredo. The private sector was brisk, and with some 60 percent of all international commercial freight crossing the U.S.-Mexico border at the Port of Laredo, cross-border trade with Mexico insured a healthy mix of investments by shippers, brokers, and freight forwarders in transportation equipment and warehousing. A majority of Laredo cross-border trade in the mid-1930s was processed by customs brokers at the following firms: American Customs Dispatch Company, Corrigan Dispatch Company, H. H. Earnst, A. F. Ochoa, H. L. Spindle, Wells Fargo, Peña and Flores, and Roberto Zuñiga and Company. The Laredo banking sector deposits grew annually during the 1930s, and in 1940 Laredo boasted two main financial institutions, Laredo National Bank and Union National Bank, with combined assets exceeding $9.2 million. The population of Laredo on the eve of

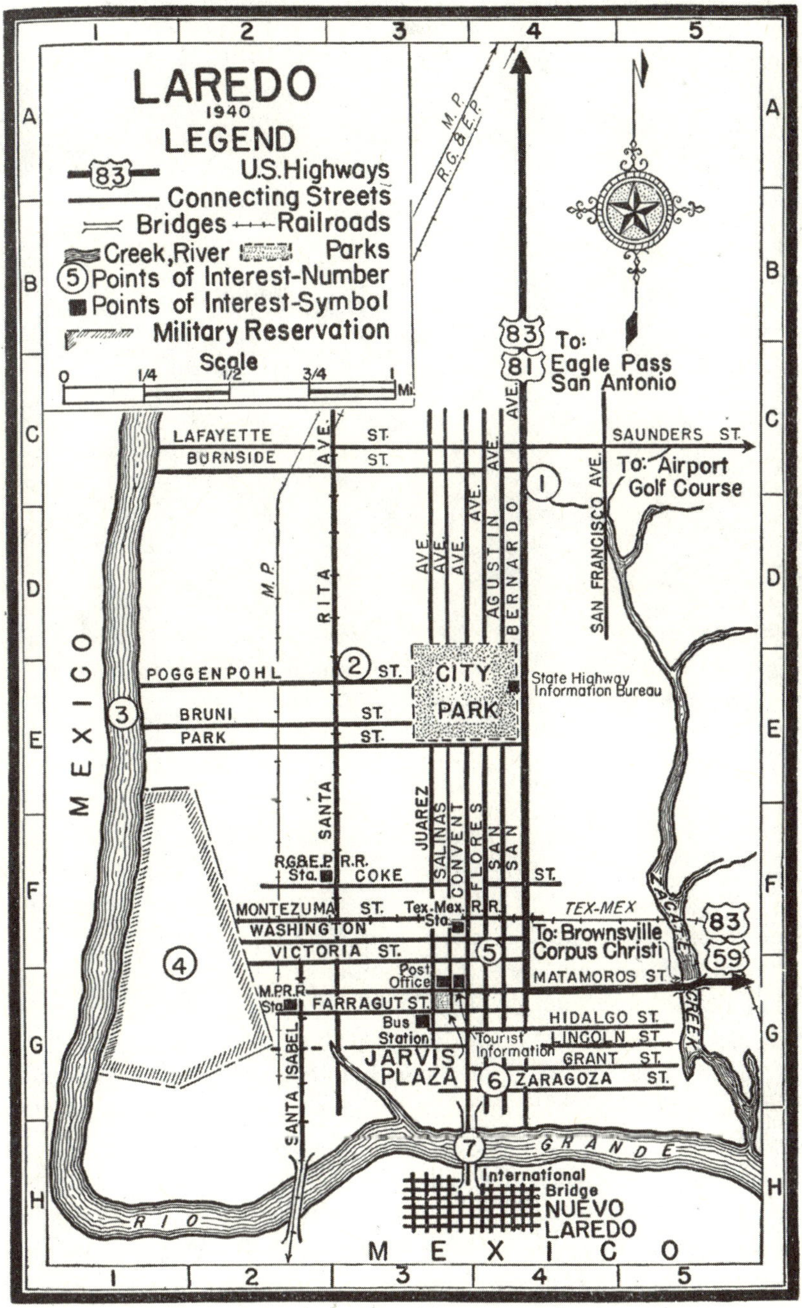

Map 6.1. Laredo, 1940. By 1940, Laredo had reached a population of nearly 40,000. With the improvements to Highway 83, growth continued to the north and east toward the Heights. The legend of this WPA map prepared for the Texas Highway and Tourism Department include: (1) Shiner Cactus Nursery, (2) U.S. Border Patrol Quarters, (3) Indian Crossing, (4) Fort McIntosh, (5) Texas Harvest Hat Company Plant, (6) Martin Plaza, and (7) International Bridge. Note that in downtown there were three railroad stations. Source: Texas State Highway Commission.

Fig. 6.1. By the 1930s, the Laredo Chamber of Commerce worked closely with the Laredo Port Commission to promote the city as a hub of north-south trade. The diversified economy included not only international trade but also a growing produce market, an expanding oil and gas industry, and coal. Pictured here in the lobby of the Laredo Chamber of Commerce is a "lump" of coal weighing over two tons, with R. C. Bateman, secretary of the chamber. Source: Center for Texas History, Austin.

World War II was 40,000, a modest increase from the 1930 census of 32,618. Nuevo Laredo was estimated to have a population of 25,000.[1]

As the city expanded, the new center of growth in Laredo was City Park, on San Bernardo Avenue, also designated as U.S. Highway 83, the location of Laredo High School. The first modern high school in the city was built in 1936 with $353,000 of PWA labor and funds; it was renamed the Raymond and Tirza R. Martin High School in late 1937.[2] The last eight miles of this improved state highway to Laredo were finished in mid-1939, and the highway was viewed by civic leaders as key to maintaining a competitive inflow of commerce and tourists. Both the State Highway Information Bureau and the headquarters of the U.S. Border Patrol were located near City Park. To promote the new highway linkage for the Laredo merchants to the surrounding region, Laredo Chamber of Commerce president Matías de Llano forged ties with the Winter Garden Chamber of Commerce in Cotulla, chaired by Stockmens National Bank president Ray M. Keck. In the decades prior to the completion of Interstate 35, the northernmost development of the city was to Lafayette and Saunders streets. Beyond lay irrigated fields for numerous vegetables, citrus fruit, and melons as well as the prime cash crop of Webb County, onions. On average, 2,180 railcar loads of onions per year were shipped from Laredo between 1938 and 1942. The onion crop was so important that during harvest and shipping season each May the *Laredo Times* carried a daily front page "box score" on the number of railcars loaded and sent to northern U.S. markets. In addition to the produce sector, the livestock industry remained strong; Webb County boasted the seventh-largest contiguous ranch in Texas with the 218,500-acre Callaghan Ranch north of Laredo. This diversified crop and livestock base helped to maintain a strong, yet often seasonal, job market. The regional agricultural sector continued a close commercial tie with the merchants, brokers, railroads, and banks in Laredo. City buses replaced the electric trolley cars in December 1935 and connected the city, at a fare of five cents with a two-cent charge for transfer. Taxi fares were twenty-five cents for up to three persons, and the charge for crossing the International Foot Bridge at Convent Avenue was five cents for pedestrians and fifteen cents per passenger car.[3]

Fig. 6.2. In October 1928, Laredo was connected to mail markets with the introduction of international airmail service. Flights were soon expanded to key markets in both Mexico and the United States. Source: Mary Cook Collection, Nuevo Santander Museum.

The hub of Laredo trade, warehousing, and shipping was on the recently completed Pan-American Highway, which ran from Nuevo Laredo to Panama via Monterrey and Mexico City and through Central America a distance of 3,349 miles, as well as in the three downtown central railroad terminals. The Rio Grande & Eagle Pass Railway, chartered in May 1885 after acquiring the Rio Grande and Pecos Railway Company, continued to run a twenty-seven-mile narrow gauge short line upriver from Laredo to the Santo Tomás Mines, yet filed to abandon the line when the mines were temporarily closed in early 1939. The direct northbound rail connection was provided by the Missouri Pacific Line, which acquired the International & Great Northern Railroad in 1925. The Texas Mexican Railway served the eastbound connection to the Port of Corpus Christi. The railroads operated stations, docks, and warehouses in the five-block area of Santa Isabel and Moctezuma streets adjacent to Fort McIntosh. New warehouse and forwarding agencies were added along Santa Maria and new hotels and offices were constructed on Farragut. On December 22, 1939, Laredo was designated the headquarters of the 23rd Customs Collection District by the U.S. Department of Treasury. To assist with the promotion of trade and commerce, the board of the Laredo Chamber of Commerce created the Laredo Port Commission (LPC). As one author noted, it was "made up of men particularly interested in this phase of Laredo's industrial life." This group actively promoted enlarged and efficient port facilities as well as lobbied for adequate federal funding for U.S. Customs and Immigration personnel and facilities. The first LPC commissioners were E. H. Corrigan, chairman; W.W. Stein; A. E. Villarreal; Hugh S. Cluck; and A. M. Gault.[4]

In April 1940, a probusiness and protrade attitude prevailed as Hugh Cluck, the handpicked candidate of the Laredo Democrats' Independent Club political machine, began a fifteen-year tenure as mayor of Laredo. Downtown Laredo remained unchanged as new housing gradually expanded east of Zacate Creek to the Heights area, where the first HEB food store in South Texas opened in a new shopping center on Guadalupe Street. City improvements in the downtown included paving with brick and creosoted blocks as well as efforts to plant trees in parks and along the roadways. By the early 1940s, the ten-story two-hundred-room Plaza Hotel on San Bernardo Street replaced the Hamilton Hotel as the choice for businessmen and tourist visitors, further boasting Laredo's first "year round air conditioned" facility. To highlight the availability of utilities, United Gas Company's large advertisement in the *Laredo Times* promoted its service during the weeklong annual February Washington's Birthday Celebration; it proclaimed, "[George] Washington's Cook Burned Wood—Laredo Cooks Use Natural Gas." In all, Laredo had ten hotels and five motion picture theaters by 1940.[5]

Mexico in 1940 had two primary commercial ports of entry, Veracruz and Laredo. Ocean cargo entered via Veracruz, with most inbound merchandise moving 187 miles by rail to Mexico City. Laredo serviced overland connections via the Pan-American Highway and railroad service to Monterrey and central Mexico. The "continued aggressive policy" of the Laredo business and trade community that the Chamber of Commerce touted led the *Laredo Times* to boldly promote Laredo as the "City of Destiny" and the north-south crossing as the "Greatest Inland Port in the Nation." The widely acknowledged strategic border location was enhanced by a growing working relationship via the Tex-Mex Railway and the opening of the deep-sea channel at the Port of Corpus Christi. Laredo was promoted as "connected via Corpus Christi and the Tex Mex to the greatest amount of traffic shipped by rail to every commercial and manufacturing center in the U.S. and Mexico."[6]

Prior to World War II, the United States supplied 62 percent of all Mexican imports, followed by Germany at 16 percent, and Great Britain and France each with less than 5 percent. The primary prewar U.S. exports through the Port of Laredo included agricultural implements; construction and mining equipment; automobiles; electrical appliances; and consumer goods such as shoes, clothing, and housewares. In contrast, the United States absorbed some 72 percent of Mexico's exports, including silver, lead, zinc, and copper as well as henequen, cotton, grains, vegetables, and cattle. One interesting import was some 25,000 live quail per year for restocking game preserves on Texas ranches. The increased cross-border trade with Mexico proved helpful in attracting new investment to Laredo.[7]

The British-owned Texas Mining and Smelting Company, which relocated to Laredo in 1930 from San Luis Potosí, Mexico, continued its growth throughout the late 1930s. The operation north of Laredo on fifteen acres employed over one hundred workers to process ore from Mexico, Peru, and Bolivia for the manufacturing of antimony oxide and antimony metal.[8] Laredo's rail hub on the Missouri Pacific line was critical for obtaining raw production ore and for shipping the finished product. Antimony, a lustrous hard-brittle scalelike crystal, was a critical raw material for the production of lead, batteries, ammunition (tracer bullets), and specialty chemicals. When the Japanese blockaded China, heretofore the primary producer of antimony, in the late 1930s and early 1940s following the outbreak of the Sino-Japanese War, U.S. imports of the key product were halted. The Laredo smelter then gained a near monopoly of the American antimony market.[9] As the price of antimony rose by over 50 percent in 1941, the U.S. War Department was concerned with production levels if war should expand in Europe. Known by some as Lead Industries, Texas Mining & Smelting, the production facility was considered the largest antimony smelter in the world in 1945. Renamed National Lead Company in 1976, the ownership reverted to the Cookson Group of England under the name of Anzon.[10]

Adjacent to the smelter operation, Central Power and Light (CPL) built the first large-scale electrical power plant in South Texas. CPL began construction in 1946, completed the plant in 1951, and doubled in size in 1955 to supply the surrounding area with 66,000 kilowatts of electricity. Oil refining and shipping, along with brick and tile manufacturing, were major local employers. The Texas Harvest Hat Company, located downtown on Victoria Street (current site of the Webb County Jail) was established in 1921, employed over one hundred citizens, and specialized in remanufacturing (or molding) straw hats imported from the Dutch East Indies, Mexico, and China. The remanufacturing included (a first for its time) "enameling" the finished product with paint spray guns. By the early 1940s, under the slogan Texas Hats Shade the Nation, the company, owned and managed by Matías de Llano, processed and sold five million hats annually in two hundred styles.[11]

U.S. demand for raw materials from Mexico dramatically increased during the war. Initially, Mexico was not enthusiastic about assisting the United States in fighting against the Axis nations, due in large part to the growing amount of German investment in Mexico during the 1930s. Furthermore, ardent postrevolution Mexican nationalist sentiments remained strong and were carried over from two decades of land and oil rights disputes with U.S. and British firms. Attitudes were also accented by the Mexican nationalization of the railroads in June 1937 and expropriation of foreign oil and mining interest after March 18, 1938.[12] During 1941 and early 1942, Mexico was officially neutral, having broken "diplomatic relations"—but not necessarily commercial interaction—with Germany and Italy on December 11, 1941. Beginning in late May 1942, public opinion quickly shifted when German U-boats sank the Mexican oil tankers *Potrero del Llano* and *Faja de Oro.* Laredo once again would find itself at center stage in world affairs.[13]

The *Potrero del Llano* (Plains Keeper) was sunk on May 14 in the Gulf of Mexico off the coast of Miami with a shipment of crude oil destined for the United States. In the unprovoked surprise attack, fourteen crewmembers and their captain were killed. There were twenty-one survivors, and only one body was recovered. For the return trip to Mexico, the survivors and the lone casket were sent by railroad via Laredo. Mayor Hugh S. Cluck ordered flags flown at half mast. He requested that the Laredo Chamber of Commerce and U.S. Army officials at Fort McIntosh prepare a welcome for the returning seaman, perform a flyover, and provide an escort and honor guard to and across the border. The goodwill gesture received extensive media coverage in Mexico. Arriving in Laredo, the crew received a hero's welcome. And on the morning of the crew's departure to Mexico bold headlines carried a second news item, "Another Mexican Tanker Sunk!" with the loss of the *Faja de Oro* (Golden Belt) and its entire crew on May 21. The neutral public opinion in Mexico soon changed.[14]

Mexican president Miguel Avila Camacho protested to Germany, demanding "complete satisfaction and damage reparations." There was no official response, which resulted in a congressional declaration on May 22, that a "state of war" existed between Mexico and Germany, Italy, and Japan. By early June 1942, Mexico and the United States were formal allies, endorsing the Mexican-American Joint Defense Commission. Fearing a possible German or Japanese landing on Mexican soil, Avila Camacho allowed the extensive operation of U.S. secret forces in Mexico, primarily to neutralize German espionage agents. These spies sought to disrupt U.S.-Mexican relations by sabotaging Mexico's oil fields or attacking U.S. aircraft production in San Diego. A possible dramatic attack on the Panama Canal, which would close the vital transisthmus connection, was anticipated.[15] Furthermore, Mexico also struggled to regain foreign oil market export revenue that was lost following expropriation in 1938. This was due largely to the expropriated oil firms' promotion of a boycott of Mexican oil that made it difficult for Petróleos Mexicanos (PEMEX) to acquire tankers for export shipments of crude. Now, Mexico lifted the quota and began unlimited oil exports to the United States at a reduced cost and rate of duty.[16] It appears that while the Mexican public and some politicians were initially reluctant to take action, the inner circle of Avila Camacho's cabinet, headed by the Secretario de Gobernación (Secretary of State), felt otherwise. The Secretario de Gobernación position was occupied by Lic. Miguel Alemán, a future president of Mexico. On April 24, 1942, Alemán, forty-one years old, made a special visit to Laredo, well before the incidents on the high seas. He sought to determine how Mexican industry, with the support of the government, could enhance cross-border trade in raw materials and labor. Exhaustive meetings, hosted by federal district judge and former Texas governor James V. Allred, were held at the new Plaza Hotel with Mayor Cluck, Webb County judge M. J. Raymond, various government officials, and representatives from the private sector attending.[17]

The results of this gathering soon became apparent. Airmail service and cargo were expanded between the two nations. The U.S. also signed an exclusive agreement with Mexico to buy all of its rubber production through the end of 1946. New rules were established to enhance rail traffic, and a temporary guest worker plan was launched on August 4, 1942—later known as the Bracero Program. The Port of Laredo received an increase in shipments, which included copper, lead, silver, gold, zinc, and graphite. In addition to oil and minerals, imports of guayule rubber, henequen, istle, bananas, chickpeas, salt, coffee, cattle, and chicle grew. The final confirmation of the new and improved U.S.-Mexican relations resulted in a meeting of the two heads of state, one year later on April 20, 1943, when President Franklin D. Roosevelt traveled by private train via Laredo to confer "on continental defense" with President Avila Camacho in Monterrey, Nuevo León. This was the first trip to Mexican soil for an incumbent U.S. president. To seal the relationship, presidents Roosevelt and Camacho created the Mexican-American Commission for Economic Cooperation, whereby there would be a joint effort to increase the production of strategic materials needed for the war by reducing import duties and quotas. In exchange for better relations, Mexico would also provide an air force squadron for duty in the Pacific Theater and receive in return much-needed technology, capital, and infrastructure enhancements. These benefits came primarily in the domestic development and commercialization of the chemical, metallurgical, glass, cement, and electrical industries—the pivotal foundation industries that would drive and expand the Mexican economy in the 1980s and 1990s.[18]

Given the wartime concern about the U.S. president's whereabouts and travel schedule, the U.S. Secret Service arranged for President Roosevelt's unmarked train to cross the rail bridge at Laredo under high security nonstop at 11:00 A.M. on Tuesday, April 20, southbound for Monterrey. Following a lavish state dinner in Monterrey that same evening, the president returned directly to the train. Due to a bomb threat at the Laredo Bridge in early April, the Secret Service again altered the travel schedule on the return trip; the president crossed the border at 4:00 A.M. on Wednesday, April 21, and remained in the Laredo rail yard only about fifteen minutes. The U.S. Secret Service log of the trip noted: "In Laredo, iced, watered, and delivered [train from the Missouri Pacific Railroad] to the Tex-Mex" for the continued trip to Corpus Christi.[19] By mid-1943, 90 percent of Mexico's foreign trade was solely with the United States, and Laredo was repeatedly proclaimed "the most important rail gateway to Mexico."[20]

Mexican scholars Josephina Zoraida Vázquez and Lorenzo Meyer conclude that the relationship between the United States and Mexico in the early 1940s was not forged in terms of military support but instead on economic interaction in strategic raw materials and much-needed labor.[21] This strongly contributed to the U.S. war production industry and agricultural sector. At the same time, the expanded commercial ties generated a 20 percent increase in direct foreign investment by 1945 from U.S. firms and financiers in Mexico manufacturing operations. It was noted:

> Between 1942 and 1945, a substantial change in Mexico-U.S. relations took place: confrontation was replaced by cooperation. Mexican exports increased in value from $177.8 million in 1940 to $262.3 million in 1945. The temporary disappearance of a number of con-

> sumer goods from the international market set the scene for Mexico's substitution of locally made products for former imports. This in turn promoted the development of capitalism, strengthened the national bourgeoisie, and stranded the social projects of Cardenism.[22]

In the early 1940s, the *Laredo Times* continued the vigorous promotion of Laredo that it started in the 1880s with the publication of two weekly special reports: "Laredo Business Review: Builders of a Greater Laredo," and a weekend oil and gas column, "Weekly Review of Oil Activities around Laredo."[23] Annual retail sales in 477 stores in the downtown grew from $9.6 million in 1941 to $18 million in 1946. With a continual demand from customers in Mexico, annual wholesale trade experienced the most dramatic increases; wholesale trade grew almost sixfold, from $5.6 million in 1941 to $35 million in 1946. For the fiscal years ending June 30, 1946, U.S. Customs collected $3,415,567.66 in duties at the Port of Laredo. In the cross-border trade, freight to Mexico via Laredo represented $150 million in merchandise exports in 1946, with annual two-way trade accounting for 29,000 carloads. Trade was further enhanced with a wave of U.S. multinational companies that began production in Mexico. Maytag, Bendix, Kraft Paper, Studebaker, Gillette, and John Deere all built plants in Mexico after the war. In 1946, 575,355 passenger vehicles crossed the bridge. Confirming the vital location of Laredo as the "terminus for motor traffic," Texas Highway Department engineers in July 1946 released a detailed map of the Texas highway system labeled, "All Roads Lead to Laredo."[24] According to the Laredo Port Commission and facilitated by over thirty-six Laredo customhouse brokers, "Sixty percent of the freight and ninety percent of the passengers pass to and from Mexico at the Port of Laredo." And in the same year the manufacturing sector of the Laredo economy, to include the Texas Harvest Hat Company, Laredo Manufacturing Company, the Mexican Palm Hat Company, four milk dairies, twenty-seven produce packers, Amedee Frock, Inc., and Salo Manufacturing Company generated $7.8 million in manufactured and processed items.[25]

Promotion of Laredo and international trade via the port continued during the war. Nationwide publicity was garnered through the expanded Washington's Birthday Celebration each February. Reports of the 1943 festivities appeared in a reported 1,400 newspapers and gained added attention with a special appearance by entertainer and western actor Gene Autry, "the greatest movie drawing card" in the nation. Guests from Texas and Mexico were hosted by city officials, merchants, and the International Good Neighbor Council at dinners, military demonstrations, bullfights, and parades over a three-day period.[26] One unheralded reason to celebrate was the expanded investment in Laredo due to the opening of the Laredo Army Airfield.

ZACHRY FIELD

Aviation in Laredo dates from February 1911, when officers of the Army Signal Corps conducted historic testing of one of their first bi-wing "aeroplanes," the Wright Scout, from an unimproved dirt strip at Fort McIntosh. Reconnaissance aircraft and a small ground crew were assigned to the Fort during World War I as an auxiliary field unit when Kelly Field in San Antonio reached peak operations. During the 1920s, the Laredo field beside the Rio Grande was the site of the first delivery of domestic correspondence and small packages by the U.S. Airmail Service and the first international airmail service from Laredo to Mexico City on October 1, 1928. It was also the headquarters and hanger of the 8th Aero Squadron, which provided border surveillance. The Army Air Service unit at Fort McIntosh under the pioneering instruction of Lt. Harrison G. Crocker was one of the first military installations in the nation equipped with a parachute jump school. However, as the federal funding appropriation for military aviation waned nationwide during the interwar period, so too did Air Corps activity in Laredo.[27]

In the late 1930s, following the loss of the lease with Fort McIntosh, the city drafted plans to construct a municipal airport. Laredo contractor Henry Bartell "Pat" Zachry was selected to develop a 320-acre site to contain a single runway and a new facility. This WPA-funded project was named in the honor of the late Colonel John H. Zachry, H. B. Zachry's father. The senior Zachry, a banker and South Texas businessman, died in a single car automobile accident on January 20, 1937 near the Callaghan Ranch. City officials in late 1940 encouraged Army Air Corps officers from San Antonio to consider Zachry Field as a possible aviation training site. Mayor Cluck, Judge John A. Valls, and prominent leaders contacted Texas U.S. Senator Morris Sheppard, chairman of the powerful Military Affairs Committee, to encourage the War Department to be favorable to the South Texas site.[28] The experience H. B. Zachry gained in Laredo would have a far-reaching impact.

The H. B. Zachry Company had roots in South Texas dating from the establishment of the construction-engineering firm in Laredo on August 23, 1924. Zachry began work as a surveyor for E. J. Foster and later was the Webb County Engineer following his graduation from Texas A&M in 1922. Zachry's private firm began with road and bridge construction projects for the Texas Highway Department between Laredo and Corpus Christi.[29] By the late 1920s, the projects, using rented teams of mules and harnesses, included street paving in Laredo, remodeling projects, and commercial buildings. The Laredo remodeling projects include Sulak Men's Store, Borcher's Bakery, and the Laredo Seminary or Holding Institute. The 1930s were lean depression years that allowed the company to contract a number of diverse construction projects. These included highway projects, the Laredo municipal airport, dormitories, and buildings for the Texas State Hospital System in Austin. By the late 1930s, Zachry had completed over twenty building projects, including the Colonia Guadalupe Public Housing Project, Zachry's first contract to exceed one-half million dollars. The *Laredo Times* hailed the upstart construction firm as, "H. B. Zachry Company One of the States' Greatest." This was a compliment to its young energetic founder, who confidently purchased a full-page company advertisement in the *Times* with the heading: "The Master Power of Progress."[30]

The construction of Zachry Field and the confidence generated by a variety of other projects were precursors of the future, as the primary expansion of the firm came during the war years. The Zachry Company completed over $50 million in U.S. defense projects, including air bases and extensive military installments at Laredo, El Paso, Hondo, Brownsville, and Harlingen during World War II. Postwar activity included pipeline projects, grade work for the Texas-Mexican Railroad, construction of the Addicks Dam near Houston, and the engineering and construction of Texas' first expressway system in San Antonio. An organizing charter member, along with A. W. Pettit, Philip Kazen, and Ed Russell, of the Laredo Boys Club built in 1940, Zachry funded the new club when the community project ran short of construction money, and for a time Pat Zachry was owner of the Rio Grande and Eagle Pass Railroad Company until it sold to the Missouri Pacific. He also served briefly as president of the Merchants State Bank and Trust Company following his father's death in early 1937, which subsequently was acquired by Union State Bank and Trust, which then changed its name to Union National Bank. As the global scope of the firm's engineering and construction projects grew, Zachry moved the corporate offices from Laredo to San Antonio in June 1952.[31]

Following the December 7, 1941, Japanese surprise attack on the U.S. Pacific Fleet at Pearl Harbor, the nation was engaged in wartime efforts. In Texas alone, sixty new Army Airfields were added. In mid-May 1942, Mayor Cluck was notified of the War Department's intentions to not only come to Laredo but also to vastly expand Zachry Field. Cluck told the *Laredo Times,* "we are not authorized to make public the details an air training center." Within months, Zachry Field was expanded to the 2,085-acre Laredo Army Airfield (AAF) northeast of the city with a hard-surface 4,000-foot runway. In addition to new base housing, hangers, additional runways, and training facilities, the AAF contracted 725,000 acres north of Laredo for use as a flexible aerial gunnery target range and established the Chupadero Auxiliary Army Airfield four miles northeast of the main base. The *New York Times* reported that the Laredo Army Airfield and Laredo Flexible Gunnery School opened three months ahead of schedule. Of the program for the new aerial gunnery training, the *New York Times* noted, "Skeet and trap shooting are the students' introduction to the art of knocking enemy planes out of the sky. It helps him learn to 'lead' his flying target and estimate range." Skeet shooting was only the precursor of hours of in-flight target practice for thousands of graduates of the aerial gunnery school. Thus, the South Texas Brush Country became a vital part of the national war effort; spent brass .38 and .50 caliber machine-gun shell casings cover the open *monte* to this day.[32]

By the fall of 1942, over 14,000 military personnel and 250 aircraft (to include B-17, B-25, B-26, B-29, B-32, P-40, and P-63) were assigned to Laredo. Hundreds of civilian workers were hired locally. The military leased Casa Blanca Country Club for one dollar per year for use as an officers' club. In late 1943, the federal government purchased the airfield from the city and county for $185,000, an amount equal to what was paid by the city for the property in 1940. The extensive economic development generated by the airbase and its monthly federal payroll came to an abrupt halt with victory over Germany and Japan in late 1945. Training ceased and the Laredo Army Airfield was soon closed. Returning the airfield to the city of Laredo, the War Department retained the right to reactivate the field on a thirty-day notice.[33]

Laredo adjusted slowly to the postwar era after the closing of both Fort McIntosh and the Laredo Army Airfield. The federal government paid little or no attention to the economic ramifications of closing the Laredo installations and the scores of other military facilities across Texas and the nation. Returning GI veterans were expected to have a big impact, particularly as many returned to college. On September 28, 1946, Laredo Junior College, funded by the Laredo Municipal Junior College District, was opened and held classes in the vacated buildings at Fort McIntosh. These facilities were obtained through a federal grant from the War Assets Administration. Further changes included the sales of the Laredo water system owned by CPL to the city of Laredo for $1.3 million following a ruling by the Securities and Exchange Commission to divest "integrated systems" in August 1945. Webb County postwar oil and gas production was a key part of a Texas-wide economic boom that wiped out the $42 million Depression era state debt. However, the postwar release on the oil price freeze from $.92 per barrel in August 1945 to $2.32 in December 1947, along with the rise in demand for natural gas, helped stimulate the state's economy. By 1950, in spite of the fact that South Texas continued a vibrant ranching industry, the state shifted from a rural to an urban-based population, and the Laredo census totaled 51,910.[34]

On April 1, 1952, following the outbreak of the Korean War, the U.S. Air Force reopened the field as Laredo Air Force Base (LAFB) with an initial investment of over $10 million. Its purpose was to provide basic flight training for jet pilots in T-41, T-33, T-38, and T-37 aircraft. Hirsch Auxiliary Airfield No. 2, known to scores of student pilots as "Bar Fly," was set up near

Aguilares east of Laredo for Visual Flight Rules (VFR) patterns. The reactivation of the LAFB impacted the Laredo economy positively. For civilian air travel and cargo, a new Laredo Municipal Airport with a 7,700-foot runway, ramps, and hangers was located three miles north of the city on the north side of Mines Road. While commercial air cargo of high-value items—electronics, perfumes, and medical equipment—brought revenue to Laredo, the engine that ran the Laredo economy in the 1950s and 1960s was the federal investment in the base. The city benefited from base's the monthly payroll, local purchases of supplies and services, and from federal stipends for the local school system. The LAFB housed and trained thousands of pilots; from these, over forty Air Force officers who had earned their wings at Laredo attained the rank of general. The base was closed during the final years of the Vietnam War in 1973 when the demand for pilots dropped. Once again the facilities were returned to the city to be used as a municipal airport, the Laredo International Airport. By 2000, the airport had become one of the primary U.S. air cargo hubs to Mexico and Latin America.[35]

The Great Drought and Flood of 1953–54

The reopening of Laredo Air Force Base in 1952 gave a much-welcomed injection to the Laredo economy. New jobs, housing, and retail businesses flourished. The growth raised concerns with city officials on the availability of ample water to meet the needs of the town and base. This concern was well founded given the drought that began to sweep Texas and the Southwest beginning in mid-1950. Concern about available water became a statewide crisis by late 1952. The normal runoff of snowmelt in the Colorado Rockies and the spring rains in the vast West Texas and Mexican watersheds paralleling the Rio Grande had dropped to near unrecordable amounts. Further tension grew as New Mexico and Texas quarreled over the impounding of low supplies of the Rio Grande water at Elephant Butte Dam in New Mexico. Texas' governor Alan Shivers appointed a "water master" to enforce water use priorities, effectively pitting the demand of urban areas against farm irrigation. To compound the problems, on June 5, 1953, the Texas Water Conservation Association announced that for the first time in recorded history the flow of the Rio Grande at Laredo "had stopped!" and the city of over 52,000 had only a one-day supply of water.[36]

Although Lake Casa Blanca (originally named the Country Club Dam) at Chacon Creek had been completed in late 1951, there was not adequate off-river storage in the 1,500-acre reservoir, or producing water wells, to address the daily needs of the city. Water for basic needs returned after a few weeks once there was a ban on irrigation upriver. At the same time as the city was addressing its immediate water concerns, the International Boundary and Water Commission was in the process of completing the Falcon Dam and reservoir that the U.S.-Mexico Water Treaty of 1944 stipulated. This project was of little help to Laredo since it was located seventy-five miles downstream. Touted as a three-prong multipurpose project for flood control, generation of hydroelectricity, and irrigation, the $50 million project split between the United States and Mexico was constructed primarily to benefit the Lower Rio Grande Valley. As the Texas drought continued, the presidents of the United States and Mexico, Dwight Eisenhower and Adolfo Ruiz Cortines, toasted the dedication of the new Rio Grande Dam and reservoir on October 19, 1953. Following the ceremonies, Eisenhower crossed the dam to visit Nuevo Guerrero, Mexico. This was the president's first visit to foreign soil since taking office. He toured the new city built for those displaced by the dam and lake. The president's motorcade then proceeded upriver from Zapata to Laredo Air Force Base, where he conferred with local Laredo officials and then boarded Air Force One for Washington, D.C.[37]

The drought persisted during the early 1950s and into 1954. Except for brief showers in April and early June little relief was experienced. Further bad news threatened the Laredo economy when Mexico devalued the peso for

Fig. 6.3. The great Rio Grande flood of June 30, 1954, created extensive damage throughout the city. By early July the U.S. Army Corps of Engineers had constructed a temporary pontoon bridge as seen in the upper left of this picture, downstream from the total destruction of the International Bridge. Source: Patricia Martin Galo.

the third time in six years on April 19, 1954, from 8.65 peso/dollar to 12.50. Devaluation of the peso, which generally has an adverse impact on Mexican consumers in U.S. border towns, and drought have long been twin concerns on the border. However, shipments of produce from the fields of Laredo continued (by May, 644 rail cars of onions and 346 cars of cantaloupes). The increased U.S. exports of assembly parts through the Port of Laredo for the Mexican industry remained vibrant—led by sand for glass factories, oil and oil products, butane, and machinery. Investment in downtown remained dependent on trade, ranching, banking, and oil and gas. While the number of irrigated acres in Webb County dropped from 9,122 in 1949 to 7,654 in 1954, the value of all farm and ranch products sold in 1954 from the county was $5,784,812. Banking flourished at the Union National Bank ($9.9 million in assets) under the direction of Ed S. Russell and key investors J. O. Walker and N. D. Hacher, as well as at the Laredo National Bank ($17.1 million in assets) backed by Ramiro Sánchez, Payne Briscoe, George W. Spence, and L. G. Alexander. Merchant retail and wholesale business remained steady. One new addition to downtown was the construction of the Killam Office Building on the corner of Salinas and Washington to house the O. W. Killam Company, Killam and Hurd, Ltd., the Texpata Pipe Line Company, and the Killam Land and Cattle Company, headquarters of the vast oil, gas, and land empire the *Laredo Times* claimed totaled a net worth of $500 million. Reflecting on his success in the oil and gas business, O. W. Killam noted, "If you think big, give big, and act big you will receive big." A devaluation of the Mexican peso to 12.50/dollar, unlike other currency disruptions in decades to come, had little impact, however, this time the cycle of drought and floods took center stage.[38]

Historically, floods along the Rio Grande have defined periods of change. Texas revolutionary leader Mirabeau B. Lamar, in his first written correspondence from Laredo following his dispatch to the border in December 1846, noted the dramatic flood destruction that had preceded his arrival in Laredo. He wrote that the town is a "heap of ruins" and has yet to recover. Massive floods at Laredo followed in June 1865, September 1919, June 1922, May 1925, September 1932, and June 1935.[39] These events had a far-reaching impact along the entire watershed of the Rio Grande. Most of the communities along the river, built very close to it, faced sudden disaster due to rapidly rising water with little or no warning. Of primary concern were the bridges that spanned the Rio Grande. Each bridge in each cross-border community was the direct link with its counterpart. On nearly a dozen occasions prior to 1954, the bridges at Laredo had been threatened, damaged, or destroyed. Following the 1920 bridge fire, Laredo engineers worked to take into account the potential threat to the bridge and designed what they deemed was a sturdy structure. Based on the floods during the previous five decades they were correct. Few imagined the new "concrete" bridge at Laredo, completed in early 1922, would be threatened. The test came on June 29, 1954.[40]

The hot and dusty calm of the extensive Texas drought of the early 1950s that had brought the Rio Grande to a virtual standstill was dramatically broken on the evening of Tuesday June 29, 1954, following the aftermath of Hurricane Alice, which moved inland from the Gulf of Mexico. Flash floods following over thirty inches of rain across the broad Texas plains northwest of Laredo produced a surface runoff led by the Pecos and Devil's rivers that could not be handled in the dry watershed and riverbed of the Rio Grande. News of the catastrophic damage and death in the town of Ozona on June 28 was graphically reported in Eagle Pass and Laredo. As the water rose during the night of the 29th, the maximum river flow crested at over sixty feet above the Laredo flood gauge on June 30 and included a number of water surges that did extensive damage in both Laredo and Nuevo Laredo. The combined population of the two cities was about 87,000. As water backed up at Manadas, Chacon, and Zacate creeks and into the streets of downtown Laredo, inland over six blocks, roads were closed into the city. Air Force personnel from Laredo Air Force Base, unaffected by the rising water, assisted with search and rescue operations. Reports of damage in Eagle Pass, where the river crested at fifty feet, posed even greater concern when two sections of the International Bridge were swept away. As the raft of the floodwaters piled debris against the Laredo Bridge, the sections of the fallen Eagle Pass bridge floated downriver and also smashed into the submerged bridge. When the water that was over thirty feet deep above the bridge receded, the extent of the damage was realized, having taken out the middle three 150-foot spans of the structure. Built of reinforced concrete in 1922, the bridge was well anchored in the riverbed but could not withstand the powerful surge of the flood and debris. Extensive damage was also done to the Laredo railroad bridge.[41]

The business and residential districts on both sides of the river were inundated, in some areas as deep as six feet; several buildings collapsed under the pressure of the floodwaters. The flood left lasting memories. Odie Arámbula, a 1954 graduate of Martin High School, recalls the water creeping rapidly through the streets until leaving his home on Santa Ursula waste deep in muddy water: "We picked up what we could and headed for high ground in the Heights."[42] Daniel B. Hastings Jr., vividly recalled the water flooding the family customhouse brokerage office adjacent to the bridge, owned and operated by his aunt, Jovita Pérez (the first woman on the Texas border to hold a customs brokers license), and father, Daniel B. Hastings Sr. Hundreds were left homeless as officials of the International Boundary and Water Commission ordered the newly constructed flood gates at Falcon Dam opened to relieve pressure on the new structure and to prepare for the

Table 6.1. Largest Rio Grande floods at Laredo, 1865–1955

Date	*Flood Crest/Feet*	*Discharge C.F.S.*	*Bridge Status*
June 10, 1865	62.50	950,000 Est.	No bridge
September 18, 1919	40.30	192,000	Heavy damage
June 2, 1922	50.90	312,000	Partial damage
May 31, 1925	39.90	189,000	Partial damage
September 3, 1932	52.20	335,000	Partial damage
June 16, 1935	35.10	176,000	Partial damage
June 26, 1948	47.83	299,500	Partial damage
June 29, 1954	61.35	716,900	Destroyed

Source: U.S. Geological Survey

surge of some 2.3 million acre-feet of floodwater. President Eisenhower, who had just months before dedicated the dam in October 1953, declared the region a disaster area—the first ever designated for the region. This action allowed the border cities to be eligible for federal aid. The damage to the five wrecked bridges in Laredo, Eagle Pass, and Del Rio required millions of dollars in repairs.[43]

With the bridge still covered in floodwater, the trustees of the Laredo Bridge Company (LBC)—Payne Briscoe, L. P. Botello, Louis Kowalski, Frank Y. Hill, A. M. Gault, Woodie Y. Bunn Jr., and former Mayor Hugh Cluck—convened early on June 30 with newly elected Mayor Joe C. "Pepe" Martin Jr. to assess the damage and determine options for recovery. The bridge was severely damaged and the city was cut off from outside assistance. All commercial activity across the river came to a halt and brought a loss of toll revenue and the prospects of months of rebuilding. While the U.S. portion of the bridge was insured for $250,000, concern rose about the ability and commitment in Nuevo Laredo to rebuild the Mexican end. To insure swift cooperation, the LBC retained Nuevo Laredo banker Octavino "Chito" Longoria to negotiate a rapid response from Mexican officials. Reconstruction began almost at once when the water receded; both cities contributed.[44]

Amid concerns of a typhoid fever outbreak, the American Red Cross, personnel and rescue helicopters from the Laredo Air Force Base, and the U.S. Army assisted by bringing immediate medical care, drinking water, and a field kitchen for those left homeless.[45] After a closer survey, the Red Cross estimated that 605 homes were destroyed in Laredo and over 2,500 families were affected by the disaster. The unsightly Laredo sanitary landfill, located in an old gravel pit in the river below Santa Cleotilde Avenue and Juárez Avenue below Water Street between the International Bridge and the railroad bridge, became a major health concern. To insure future safety the landfill was closed and converted to a recreational area along the Rio Grande.

To address the overall regional flood recovery, Governor Allan Shivers and Mayor "Pepe" Martin held a meeting with public and private sector officials in Laredo. Reopening the link to the Pan-American Highway and cross-border trade was a priority. The mayor via the American Red Cross contacted Gen. Hayden L. Boatner, commander of the 4th U.S. Army, who approved the dispatch of combat engineers from Fort Hood, Texas. These seasoned military engineers established operations on both sides of the Rio Grande; near the foot of the damaged bridge they connected Los Dos Laredos with a temporary low-water pontoon bridge. For weeks, cross-border traffic was by a single vehicle at a time. Repairs to the railroad bridge were completed ahead of the commercial bridge.[46]

In spite of the damage from the June 1954 flood, the Laredo economy continued to expand through local growth and increased international trade. While the Webb County oil and gas sector flourished, the value of farm products produced in the county exceeded $6 million in 1955, with 70 percent of the sales derived from livestock. The total value of retail sales in Laredo exceeded $50 million; annually, over $4 million in new construction was added. Over 180 railroad cars crossed freight daily, and the trucking in-

Table 6.2. Laredo utilities and bank assets, 1940–55

	Electrical Connections	*Water Meters*	*Gas Meters*	*Telephone Connections*	*Bank Deposits ($mil)*
1940	4,360	4,871	5,351	3,493	9.2
1941	5,042	5,017	5,581	3,578	9.7
1942	5,466	5,211	5,951	4,184	12
1943	5,767	5,445	6,245	4,198	14.5
1944	6,684	6,033	6,656	4,290	19.1
1945	7,505	6,677	7,150	4,405	22.4
1946	8,289	7,041	7,635	4,460	22.7
1947	8,461	8,069	7,721	5,342	22.9
1948	8,579	9,125	7,802	6,118	23.1
1950	10,356	8,489	9,031	7,838	23.4
1955	11,876	9,825	10,576	10,752	30.2

Source: Da Camara, 1949; Industrial Committee, Laredo Chamber of Commerce, 1955

Fig. 6.4. Full-scale cross-border trade was restored with the completion and dedication of the new international bridge in 1956. Pictured is Agustín Arriaga Rivera, Director of Major Federal Projects, Mexico, and J. C. "Pepe" Martin, mayor of Laredo. Source: Patricia Martin Galo.

dustry was rapidly growing. Southbound exports to Mexico in the mid-1950s were concentrated in the following areas: bulk sand for glass fabrication, oil, butane gas, and machinery.[47]

A prime catalyst to commercial development was Carlton Whitworth, district manager for Central Power and Light (CP&L) in Laredo. Whitworth, an Army Air Corps pilot during World War II, was sent to Laredo to expand the customer base for CP&L. Arriving on the day of the 1954 flood, he quickly became a part of the Laredo business community. As chairman of the Industrial Development Committee, he filed for and received a formal charter for The Laredo–Webb County Industrial Foundation, Inc. from the Texas secretary of state dated September 9, 1960; this was a forerunner of the Laredo Development Foundation. The workforce expanded from 17,460 in 1950 to 20,205 in 1955. As Laredo's population in 1955 reached 55,385, there were extensive efforts to expand city services and utilities. In addition to the need for citywide paving, an all-purpose auditorium, and expanded wastewater treatment facilities, customer accounts for water, gas, telephone, and electrical utilities exceeded 10,000 customer connections for the first time—each of these four key services was more than double the local service provided from 1940 to 1955.[48]

Trade with Mexico remained brisk; Laredo maintained its role as the primary cross-border port between the two nations. With the devaluation of the peso in 1954, imports from Mexico dropped slightly, while southbound exports expanded over 25 percent and Laredo banks gained new deposits. Retail sales were not impacted as the annual total value of goods sold at retail stores in Laredo rose from $46.441 million in 1950 to $52.814 million in 1957. Community investment, with the value of permitted "authorized construction" within the city during the same time period, more than tripled from $1.1 million to $3.9 million. Traffic on the International Bridge increased at an average annual rate of nearly 10 percent. With the addition of the "new fashionable" Sands Motel on Highway 81, Laredo boasted four hotels and twenty-three motels with a combined 1,100 rooms.[49]

CONCLUSION

On the two hundredth anniversary of the City of Laredo in 1955, the community had solidified its place as the primary north-south point across the border between Mexico and the United States. Annual growth of the community and the commercial sector benefited from the ongoing diversification of the economy as well as the underpinnings of a region rich in natural resources. What the arrival of the railroad solidified in the 1880s, the market forces and expanded highways on both sides of the border reaffirmed in the years that passed. Governed under seven flags since 1755, the constant factor for the *villa* founded by Tomás Sánchez on the right side of the Rio Grande is that Laredo is the strategic north-south crossing and international trade center. Weathering the uniqueness of the natural environs and decades of political intrigue and conflict, first as New Spain and Mexico, and then as Texas and the United States, Laredo has charted a successful course as the primary *gateway* to Mexico.

EPILOGUE

Events during the first two centuries of Laredo's history would have far-reaching implications for the city and state as well as a direct impact on the growth of international trade between the United States and Mexico. The founding of Laredo in 1755 was driven largely by the dual desires to populate a hostile region and to secure a strategic commercial foothold in northern New Spain across the Rio Grande into what would become Texas. Trade across the low-water river ford on the Rio Grande at the *Paso de Indios* just north of the original townsite was initially sporadic. Yet the north-south railroad link that followed and the bridges and the Pan-American Highway, effectively joined two national markets. Laredo has historically been the center of commerce and conflict brought on by territorial and political dynamics. Few observers over the first two centuries of Laredo's colorful history could have envisioned the role the tiny frontier town would play in the future of world commerce. Yet many did envision that the future was ripe with opportunity, notwithstanding the rugged environs and challenges to realize its full potential. The story of Laredo's pivotal role in international trade and commerce on the southern U.S. border did not end in 1955, but arguably began a new chapter in the late 1950s.

In the years that followed the two hundredth anniversary of Laredo in 1955, the community and the trade links between Texas and Mexico continued to expand. Of the some two dozen twin city points for border crossings between the United States and Mexico, Laredo and its cross-river neighbor Nuevo Laredo have emerged as one of the primary inland ports for trade and commerce in the hemisphere. The groundwork established in the formative years gained new direction and momentum in recent decades with the expansion of infrastructure, national and international manufacturing coming to the region, and the advent of free-market agreements that enhance commerce throughout the world. Thus, the broader contemporary story of Laredo during the second half of the twentieth century—the dynamic growth in commerce, investment, and international trade with Mexico—has yet to be fully told.

In recent decades the agricultural sector has greatly diminished in the Laredo–Webb County region. Cattle ranching has continued while the raising of sheep on a large scale has all but vanished. The one constant since the 1920s, outside of ranching and international trade, is the dominant role of the oil and gas industry in Webb and adjacent counties in South Texas. As the energy industry has become more technically sophisticated and efficient, oil and gas has played a sustained role in the economy of the region. Webb and Zapata counties have ranked in the top two energy-producing areas in the state and nation over the past three decades. New diagonal drilling and capture methods have shifted much of the mineral extraction to natural gas. Infrastructure to facilitate the capital-intense industry is extensive, with substantial investment in exploration and pipelines and other transportation methods. This not-so-salient underpinning of the South Texas economy is often lost to the rumble and discourse in the staging and transshipment of merchandise and materials across the international border.

The health of the Mexican economy is pivotal to Laredo's growth and the expansion of commerce via the Port of Laredo. On a national scale the broader Mexican economy demonstrated an overall average annual growth rate of 6 percent from 1932 to 1982. However, during the last two decades of the century Mexico faced new challenges to sustain and enhance economic activity. The collapse of the economy due to a radical devaluation of the peso by roughly 200 percent and the nationalization of the Mexican banking sector in September 1982 marked the beginning of a near-stagnant economy. The 1982 devaluation stunned Laredo and overall South Texas commercial interests and merchants due to a dramatic downturn in the border economy. In the wake of the financial crisis, Laredo's merchandise sales tax receipts in 1983 were down 44 percent.

An exception to the overall economic slowdown was Monterrey, Nuevo León, located 140 miles south of Laredo. Closely allied with the U.S. industrial sector, the metropolis of some 5 million people experienced steady growth. Starting in the 1960s, *grupos industriales*—integrated industrial conglomerates—attracted capital equipment and raw materials from the United States; a large portion was financed, staged, and shipped from Laredo. Over 65 percent of all industrial merchandise entering Mexico came through Laredo. A sample of the emerging Monterrey corporate groups were an alphabet of rising industry: VITRO—glass, CEMEX—cement, IMSA—steel, PROTEXA—petroleum and industrial construction, CYDSA—chemicals and plastics, AFLA—petrochemicals and telecommunication, and VISA—food processing. By the late 1980s, these were among the companies best suited to take advantage of Mexico's proactive steps toward an export-led industrialization policy. To open the once-insular closed economy, the following events occurred: in 1986 Mexico entered the General Agreement on

Trade and Tariffs (GATT); in 1987 the Hacienda (Department of Treasury) began a progressive reduction of tariffs; and in 1988 there was a general liberalization of foreign direct investment laws.

The railroad connections to Laredo in the 1880s remained vital to solidifying a trade center. With the opening of the Pan-American Highway in the late 1930s and expansion of the U.S. interstate system, with the construction of I-35 from Dallas to Austin to San Antonio and to the border at Laredo in the early 1970s, along with the addition of a second multilane international bridge for north-south shipments, Laredo and South Texas experienced steady growth. To augment the highway system and bridge improvements, the freight-forwarding brokerage-warehouse companies began to expand and provide services that allowed consolidation and staging of merchandise into and out of Mexico. Furthermore, several large U.S. freight brokers entered into strategic agreements with Mexican firms. This coincided with the growth of offshore manufacturing globally, better-known in the U.S.-Mexico border region as *maquiladora* or twin plant operations.

The *maquila* system, made possible under the amended U.S. tariff code, allowed for shipments of components and raw materials for partial manufacture and light assembly in Mexico followed by reimportation back to the U.S. parent company for final assembly and distribution. In the case of Laredo, some sixty plants were established in Nuevo Laredo by 1975, while nationwide in Mexico by the early 1990s over three thousand multinational facilities were opened. Following periodic devaluation of the peso, the *maquila* sector, by creating jobs and attracting foreign direct investment (FDI) along the border, remained one of the few bright spots of the sluggish economy. Almost overnight this increased trade and commercial freight crossing reaffirmed the Port of Laredo as the primary port of choice along the 1,952-mile border. However, bolder steps were needed to expand the potential of the region.

In 1990, Mexico, aware of mounting global competition, announced it was willing to open negotiations with the United States and Canada on a free trade agreement—to lower tariffs and increase market access for goods and services. Viewed by many as a politically risky move, industrialists in Mexico as well as government policy makers knew the country needed a new course of action to revive the economy—to enable the economy to grow and attract new FDI.

The result of these actions was the implementation of the North American Free Trade Agreement, or NAFTA, on January 1, 1994. With the stroke of a pen the three-nation open-market accord represented a population of some 425 million, with a combined total GNP of over $6 trillion, and trilateral trade of $1.4 trillion. A devaluation of the peso in December 1994 briefly slowed commercial trade across the border, yet the recovery, unlike previous financial crises, was swift, and apparent by August 1995. In the wake of NAFTA, numerous cities in the region vied to be known as the "NAFTA city," yet none other than the "gateway to Mexico"—Laredo—laid true claim to the title. Laredo is the strategic north-south location with its broad direct access by rail, air, and road to the markets of the Americas. Renowned U.S.-Mexico border economist J. Michael Patrick captured the essence of the agreement and its impact:

> The Texas border region with Mexico is strategically located at the geographical center of the newly formed North American free trade area. The importance of this location derives from the widely held belief that NAFTA will significantly increase the volume of U.S.-Mexican trade over time and will foster greater economic integration between the two countries.

In 1973, two thousand cargo trucks per week moved merchandise across the border at Laredo; by 2005, shortly after the full implementation of NAFTA, the number had ballooned to over nine thousand per day. The growth and commercial dominance of Laredo was facilitated by the annual expansion of logistics facilities and intermodal docks, which today exceed over 60 million square feet of development and represents the investment of over seven hundred of the Fortune 1,000 companies. Merchandise trade via the Port of Laredo totaled over $150 billion in 2006.

For more than a decade in the 1990s and continuing into the turn of the century, Laredo's year-on-year population growth was among the top five fastest growing in the nation. The community is further bolstered by a large international banking sector and is among the most active retail sectors in the region. Thus, from the early days of poling flat-bottom *chalanas* below Water Street across the Rio Grande and the laborious cross-country shipment of freight by cart and mules to the advent of multimodal transportation, bridge, and logistics systems monitored by satellite—Laredo thrives on its modern role as the center for hemispheric international commerce.

Laredo Population, 1755–2005

	Laredo	*Texas*	*U.S.*	*Mexico*
1755	15	1,500	++ 1,270,760	3,600,000
1757	(cuevo) 85	1,846	++ 1,493,625	3,800,000
1767	(visita) 185	2,200	++ 2,048,076	4,000,000
1780	est. 500	cc 3,103	++ 2,780,369	4,200,000
1790	818	3,169	3,929,214	H 4,483,569
1800	est. 800	est. 3,500	5,308,483	H 5,570,000
1810	est. 1,000	est. 3,800	7,239,881	x 6,100,000
1820	(roman) 1,418	B 4,000	9,638,453	6,900,000
1830	(coy) 2,054	B 10,000	12,860,702	7,300,000
1840	1,891	est. 115,000	17,063,353	7,700,000
1850	897	212,592	23,191,876	8,100,000
1860	1,397	604,215	31,443,321	8,500,000
1870	2,615	818,579	38,558,371	x 9,000,000
1880	3,521	1,591,749	50,189,209	10,500,000
1890	11,319	2,235,527	62,979,766	12,000,000
1900	13,429	3,048,710	76,212,168	13,607,259
1910	14,855	3,896,542	92,228,496	est. 14,000,000
1920	22,710	4,663,228	106,021,537	14,334,780
1930	32,618	5,824,715	123,202,624	16,500,000
1940	39,274	6,414,824	132,164,569	19,653,552
1950	51,910	7,677,832	151,325,798	est. 25,000,000
1960	60,678	9,579,677	179,323,175	34,923,129
1970	69,024	11,196,730	203,302,031	48,225,238
1980	91,449	14,229,191	226,543,199	66,846,833
1990	122,899	16,986,510	248,709,873	81,249,645
2000	189,021	20,851,820	281,421,906	97,483,412
2005**	212,000	22,500,000	311,000,000	106,000,000

Sources: Laredo Spanish Archives; U.S. Census; Mexico INEGI; *Handbook of Texas;* S. Green, Census of Laredo; A. V. Tjarts, "Demographic Analysis of Texas, 1777–1793," SWHQ, 1974

x Bland, p. 34 — cc—Croix Census 1777 — **Estimate for 2005

++ U.S. Colonel Period, est. — H—Humboldt, est. — B—Billington

LAREDO BANKING, 1880–2005

Rio Grande National Bank (4146)	Milmo National Bank July 1, 1881– August 25, 1923	The Laredo Bank 1889– February 23, 1892
First State Bank and Trust	First National Bank January 14, 1924– October 5, 1931	Laredo National Bank (5001) June 4, 1895
Merchant State Bank and Trust Company (1094–03) April 7 1917– August 28, 1937	Mexican-American Banking Corporation	South Texas National Bank
Union State Bank (14375)	Tesoro Savings and Loan	Banco Bilbao Visquae
Union National Bank (14375)	International Bank of Commerce	Falcon Bank
Norwest Bank	Commerce Bank	NBC Bank
Wells Fargo Bank	Bank ONE 1999–2003	Bank of America 1994–1997
First American Bank 2003	Texas Community Bank December 6, 2003	Bank of America 2003

Appendix C

English and Spanish Measures Compared

SPANISH	is equivalent to *ENGLISH*
1 foot	11 1/9 inches
1 yard or vara	33 1/6 inches
108 varas	100 yards
1,000 varas	$925\frac{9259}{10000}$ 925 yards, or 2 feet 9 1/3 inches
1,000 varas squared, or one million square varas is one labor	$177\frac{136}{1,000}$ acres or about 117 1/8, equal to about 17,725 2/3 rods
5,000 varas square, is one league	4,629 yards, 1 foot, 10 2/3 inches, or $2\frac{632}{1,000}$ 2 miles 201 rods, 12 feet, 4 1/3 inches
1 league square or twenty-five million square varas is 1 sitio,	$4428\frac{402}{1,000}$

A township of 4 sitios is $17,713\frac{608}{1,000}$ acres, English.

An American Township of six miles square, is 22,040 acres.

To bring Spanish measure into English, deduct $7\frac{41}{100}$ per cent.

To bring English measure into Spanish, add 8 per cent.

4,840 yards make an acre, English; $5,714\frac{285}{1,000}$ varas make an acre, English.

Source: Texas Almanac, 1857

Appendix D

Peso-Dollar Valuation, 1900–2006

Year	*Pesos per dollar*	*Year*	*Pesos per dollar*	*Year*	*Pesos per dollar*	*Year*	*Pesos per dollar*
1900	2.06	1927	2.12	1953	8.65	1980	23.25
1901	2.11	1928	2.08	1954	11.34	1981	26.22
1902	2.39	1929	2.15	1955	12.50	1982	96.48
1903	2.38	1930	2.26	1956	12.50	1983	143.93
1904	1.99	1931	2.65	1957	12.50	1984	192.60
1905	2.02	1932	3.16	1958	12.50	1985	371.70
1906	1.99	1933	3.50	1959	12.50	1986	923.50
1907	2.01	1934	3.60	1960	12.50	1987	2,209.70
1908	2.01	1935	3.60	1961	12.50	1988	2,281.00
1909	2.01	1936	3.60	1962	12.50	1989	2,641.00
1910	2.01	1937	3.60	1963	12.50	1990	2,945.40
1911	2.01	1938	4.52	1964	12.50	1991	3,071.00
1912	2.01	1939	5.19	1965	12.50	1992	3,110.00
1913	2.08	1940	5.40	1966	12.50	1993	3.10
1914	3.30	1941	4.85	1967	12.50	1994	3.25
1915	11.15	1942	4.85	1968	12.50	1995	6.42
1916	23.83	1943	4.85	1969	12.50	1996	7.75
1917	1.91	1944	4.85	1970	12.50	1997	8.25
1918	1.81	1945	4.85	1971	12.50	1998	8.50
1919	1.99	1946	4.85	1972	12.50	1999	8.78
1920	2.01	1947	4.85	1973	12.50	2000	8.97
1921	2.04	1948	5.74	1974	12.50	2001	9.35
1922	2.05	1949	8.01	1975	12.50	2002	9.77
1923	2.06	1950	8.65	1976	19.95	2003	10.86
1924	2.07	1951	8.65	1977	22.73	2004	11.25
1925	2.03	1952	8.65	1978	22.72	2005	11.75
1926	2.07	1953	8.65	1979	22.80	2006	12.50

"THE STREETS OF LAREDO"

The famous cowboy song of the American West tells the story of a young cowboy whose wild living has cost him his life. The song actually derives from an old Irish ballad. Cowboys who tended cattle on long drives through the Midwest were expected to keep the herds pacified by singing, humming, or whistling to them. Many cowboys came from the southern United States, bringing with them familiar folk songs of their British ancestors.

The origin of this tune can be traced through many of the words and phrases used and by its first line, which is a typical opening line for an Irish ballad. The eighteenth-century Irish version of this lament, "The Unfortunate Rake," tells of a young man felled by syphilis who calls for the ladies to carry him. In another version the central character is a young soldier, and in another, a young Englishwoman, and the setting moves from Lock Hospital in Ireland to St. James Infirmary in London. American blacks adapted that story for the famous blues song, "St. James Infirmary Blues."

As I walked out in the streets of Laredo,
As I walked out in Laredo one day,
I spied a young cowboy all wrapped in white linen,
All wrapped in white linen and cold as the clay.

"I can see by your outfit that you are a cowboy,"
These words he did say as I boldly walked by.
"Come sit down beside me and hear my sad story,
I'm shot in the breast, and I know I must die.

"It was once in my saddle I used to go dashing,
Once in my saddle I used to go gay.
It was first to old Rosie's and then to the card house,
Shot in the breast and I'm dying today.

"Get sixteen gamblers to handle my coffin,
Get six jolly cowboys to sing me a song;
Take me to the green valley and lay the sod o'er me,
I'm a young cowboy and know I done wrong.

"Oh, beat the drum slowly, and play the fife lowly,
Play the death march as you carry me along;
Take me to the green valley and lay the sod o'er me,
I'm a young cowboy an' know I done wrong."

SOURCE: REPUBLIC OF THE RÍO GRANDE MUSEUM,
LAREDO, TEXAS

GLOSSARY AND TERMS

acabala:	domestic tax collected by Spanish in Mexico
acequias:	irrigation ditches
aduana:	customs house
aguadoras (or barrileros):	water salesmen
arrieros:	muleteer, cart drivers
audiencia:	audience
bancos:	new channels formed by mending river beds
banqueta:	continuous bench of masonry often near the fireplace wall or along a side wall, also similar feature at base of exterior wall
bisagra:	hinge
bollaster:	corner buttress, round
bordón:	beading on wooden elements such as roof beams
botica:	drug store
bracero:	field hand, from brazos or arms
brasada:	literally, a bed of coals, figuratively, a dry, hot area and frequently used to refer to that area between the Nueces River and the Río Grande; brush country
bronco:	wild, rude, surly
caballada:	mount
caballería:	a measure of land in the shape of a parallelogram (105.75 acres); cavalry
cabildo:	town council
cacique:	powerful landowner who dominated local affairs
cal:	lime
canadá:	a glen or brook between high portions of ground: see *aroylo*
canales:	projecting rain spouts at the upper part of the roof, also called *gárgolas*
carretas:	ox-drawn carts
carrizal:	reed grass, used for thatching
caudillo:	usually a powerful military figure; political leaders

campistas: field hauls
cédula: order, bill, decree
cédula real: a writ of privilege or a grant; proclamation
centralistas: central government
chaparejos: chaps (leather leggings)
charco: pool of water, small lake or shallow pond
charcos: water holes
chimenea: interior cooking hearth
chipichil: local term for lime concrete containing a pea gravel aggregate, also called *tipichil*
chiveras: smugglers
cíudadanos armados: armed citizen militaries
compañías volantes: flying squadrons or highly mobile cavalry force
contrabandistas: smugglers
contraresguardo: customs inspector
cordel: a cord or rope: a distance of five (5) paces
cordero: rack of lamb
criado: a servant
cuaderno: parcel of paper stitched together—for use with official documents
cuadra: a block of houses, stable, block
cura: clergyman or priest

dehesa: pastoral of land held in common; land set aside for grazing stock
derecho de consumo: internal duty
dicho: Mexican proverb

ejidos: a portion of land held in common by community
ejiónes: corbels, wedge-shaped short blocks of wood, often carved, which support the *vigas* or roof beams
el monte grande: a large Texas brush thicket
emigrados: immigrants
empresario: colonial land agent
enganchados: border guerrilla fighters during the Civil War
ensenada: a cove or small bay of water
estancia: mansion, dwelling, landed property

fandega:	2.58 bushels in Mexico
fayuca:	smuggled merchandise
federalistas:	support de-centralized government
frontera:	frontier
fuero:	privilege
galería:	arcade
güero:	red complexioned man
guía:	customs permit to move goods into the interior, guide
hacendado:	owner of a large rural landed estate (hacienda) (hacendero) or ranches, estancias
hacienda:	landed property, either a ranch or farm; an estate or fortune
hectárea:	2.47 acres
horno:	beehive-shaped exterior baking oven
huerta:	vegetable garden
jacal:	a hut, small dwelling of unhewn wood or stucco, stone or mud huts, generally peasant or rural dwellings
juez de campo:	field or range judge
justicia mayor:	chief justice or alcalde (magistrate)
labor:	a "field" of approximately 177 acres
lajas:	flagstones
latías:	small pieces of wood resting on *vigas* to serve as roof covering
latifundio:	large rural ranch or farm; an estate
lazo:	lasso (*la reata* became lariat in cowboy lingo)
leche quemada:	condensed milk candy
licenciado:	generally a title given to a lawyer; a degreed person; a professional
llanos de las mesteñas:	Wild-Horse Plains
lunadas:	wagon ride in the moon light
maíz:	corn or maize
maleza:	small brush thicket
mandida:	Bribe
medios cabildos:	town council
mestizo:	product of racial miscegenation of Indian and Spaniard

monte:	Brush Country of South Texas
mordida:	a bribe
mozo:	servant
mt:	metric ton or 2,205 pounds
onzas de plata:	silver real
norteños:	as used in 1700s, collectively Indian groups of north Texas and the Plains that entered Texas in about the mid 1700s, encroaching on territorial hunting grounds claimed by the Apaches. Most feared of these invaders were the Comanches. In the early 1900s, northerners or North Americans
paisano:	country man
palisado:	hut whose walls are composed of vertically placed wooden members which are usually mudded over
pasaje:	a passageway or road; a fee paid to pass a place; transportation fee
pase:	a written permit to carry or transport goods, a type of passport; see *guía*
paso:	act of passing
patio:	interior courtyard
piloncillo:	brown sugar cones
pochteca:	a cast of Aztec's merchants specialized in trade and commerce
porción:	a lot or section of land, generally a large tract of land
porfirista:	supporters and followers of Porfirio Díaz
propios:	corporate land or lots
ramada:	arbor, generally brush-roofed outside spaces
ranchería:	hut or small cottage; a home site, a small group of huts, see *jacal*
rancho:	a small stock farm or ranch; generally away from organized communities
reata:	lariat
residencia:	official administrative review
regidores:	aldermen
rejiga:	goat skin, used to transport mescal or tequila
rejoneado:	stone bonding pattern which includes a secondary pattern of small, thin stones serving to fill the joints that bond the larger stoners

remudas: spare or corralled animals
resacas: formed channels, formed into lakes

sabana: savannah
savinos: ceiling decking, composed of cypress billets
sexenio: six year presidential term of office
síndico procurador: public attorney
sitio: portion of land, country home; land grant of approximately 4,428 acres
sitio de ganado mayor: a portion of land 5,000 x 5,000 square Mexican varas
sitio de ganado menor: a portion of land 3,333 1/3 x 3,333 1/3 Mexican varas

tablas: thick planks used as ceiling decking
tejanos: Spanish settlers of Texas
tercio: half a load; a mule carries one load (*carga*) comprised of two *tercios*
tienda de raya: "the company store" where industrial workers were obliged to purchase supplies at company prices, thus, driving laborers into debt
tinaja: pool of water trapped in a natural depression above level of river
toalla: towel to cover head and face from sun or cold
tornaguía: legal entry permit
torreón: fortified tower
trastero: free-standing cupboard
tronera: gunport, loophole
tule: reed, used for thatching

vaquero: cowboy or in cowboy lingo "buckaroo"
vara: The Spanish yard: sometime after 1767 the Mexican vara was set in measurement standards as 32.9931 inches; however, this measure of a vara varies from source to source, and from time period to time period; prior to 1750 a Mexican vara (no U.S. equivalent) was described as composing two *medias,* three *tercias* or *pies* (feet of undetermined length), four *cuartas,* six *sesmas,* and thirty-six *pulgada* or inches (also of undetermined length); varying from 32.8 to 35 inches; the Texas legislature fixed it at 33 1/3 inches.

vestimentos:	corn biscuits
vecinos:	neighbors
viga:	roof beam
villa:	a chartered town with certain privileges that distinguish it from a village
zona libre:	free zone

NOTES

CHAPTER 1

1. Paul Horgan, *Great River: The Rio Grande in North American History* (New York: Rinehart and Company, 1954), 21; Carroll L. Riley, *Rio del Norte: People of the Upper Rio Grande* (Salt Lake City: University of Utah Press, 1955), 9–15; Josiah Gregg, *Commerce of the Prairies,* (1844; repr., New York: Citadel Press, 1968), 133–34. See also Michael C. Meyer, *Water in the Hispanic Southwest: A Social and Legal History 1550–1850* (Tucson: University of Arizona Press, 1966), 3–45, and Pat Kelly, *River of Lost Dreams* (Lincoln: University of Nebraska Press, 1986), 1–6.

2. Ulrich B. Philips, *Life and Labor in the Old South* (Boston: Little, Brown, 1929), 62; Omar S. Valerio-Jiménez, "Neglected Citizens and Willing Traders: The Villas del Norte (Tamaulipas) in Mexico's Northern Borderlands, 1749–1846," *Mexican Studies/Estudios Mexicanos* (hereafter *MS/EM*) (Summer 2002): 251–53; Bethel Coupwood, "Notes on the History of La Bahía de Espíritu Santo," *Southwestern Historical Quarterly* (hereafter *SWHQ*) (October 1898): 164; R. L. Duffus, *The Santa Fe Trail* (Albuquerque: University of New Mexico Press, 1958), 5–31; Craig H. Roell, *Remember Goliad! A History of La Bahía* (Austin: Texas State Historical Association [hereafter TSHA], 1994), 8–10; Oakah L. Jones, *Los Paisanos: Spanish Settlers on the Northern Frontier of New Spain* (Norman: University of Oklahoma Press, 1979), 65–78.

3. Timothy K. Perttula, *The Prehistory of Texas* (College Station: Texas A&M University Press, 2004), 149–51; Jaime Montell, *La caída de México-Tenochtitlán* (Mexico City: Editorial Joaquín Mortiz, 2003), 26–28; R. H. Barlow, *The Extent of the Empire of the Culhua Mexica* (Los Angeles: University of California Press, 1949), 8–133; C. Michael Barton et al., eds., *The American Continents: A Multidisciplinary Approach to Human Biogeography* (Tucson: University of Arizona Press, 2004), 91–92; George C. Valliant, *Aztecs of Mexico* (New York: Doubleday, 1962), 104–107; Raúl A. Fernández, *The Mexican-American Border Region* (Notre Dame, Ind.: Notre Dame University Press, 1989), 11–131; David La Vere, *The Texas Indians* (College Station: Texas A&M University Press, 2004), 54–55; Hugh Thomas, *Rivers of Gold* (New York: Random House, 2003), 464. See also Carroll L. Riley and Basil C. Hedrick, eds., *Across the Chichimec Sea* (Carbondale: Southern Illinois Press, 1978), and Brenda R. Lewis, *The Aztecs* (London: Sulton Publishing, 1999); James E. Warren, *Los quemados: An Archeological Testing at the City of Laredo,* Report No. 545 (Georgetown: Texas Antiquities Commission, 1986), 9–12.

4. Charles C. Mann, *1491* (New York: Vintage, 2005), 104.

5. Victor D. Hanson, "Technology and the Wages of Reason: Tenochtitlán, June 24, 1520–August 13, 1521," in *Carnage and Courage* (New York: Anchor Books, 2001), 170–232. The

term *Aztec* is derived from the Nahuatl *Aztlán.* In their time, Moctezuma and his people most likely referred to themselves as Mexicas.

6. William H. Prescott, *History of the Conquest of Mexico* (Philadelphia: J. B. Lippincott, 1843), 1: 149–51.

7. Nancy Hickerson, *The Jumanos: Hunters and Traders on the South Plains* (Austin: University of Texas Press, 1994,) 215–30; La Vere, *Texas Indians,* 28–31, 54–55; Robert S. Weddle, *The French Throne* (College Station: Texas A&M University Press, 1991), 77–78; Michael D. Coe and Rex Koontz, *Mexico: From the Olmecs to the Aztecs,* 5th ed. (London: Thames and Hudson, 2002), 11, 16, 62, 196–201; Victor W. Von Hagen, *The Sun Kingdom of the Aztecs* (New York: World Publishing, 1958), 59; Thomas, *Rivers of Gold,* 108–10; José M. Villalpando and Alejandro Rosas, *Historias de México a través de sus gobernantes* (Mexico City: Planeta, 2003), 16–23.

8. Alejandro Prieto, *Historia, geografía y estadísticas del Estado de Tamaulipas* (Mexico City: Tip. Escalerillas, 1873), 65–70; John R. Swanton, *The Indian Tribes of North America,* Bureau of American Ethnology, Bulletin 145 (Washington, D.C.: Government Printing Office [hereafter GPO], 1952), 309–12, 320–21, 326–27; Jack D. Forbes, *Apache, Navajo, and Spaniard* (Norman: University of Oklahoma Press, 1960), 169–70, 214; Vaillant, *Aztecs of Mexico,* 105. The Karankawan tribes were primarily located along the Gulf of Mexico between Trinity Bay and Aransas Bay, see Robert A. Ricklis, *The Karankawa Indians of Texas* (Austin: University of Texas Press, 1996). Also, with regard to the Indian population of Mexico, in 1900 one-third of the total population of about 12.5 million was of pure Indian stock.

9. Jean Louis Berlandier, *Journey to Mexico during the Years 1826 to 1834* (Austin: TSHA, 1980), 1: 207–11, 246, 249.

10. Gilbert Haven, *Our Next-Door Neighbor: A Winter in Mexico* (New York: Harper and Brothers, 1875), 135.

11. Alvar Núñez Cabeza de Vaca, *The Account: Alvar Núñez Cabeza de Vaca's Relación,* trans. Martín A. Favata and José B. Fernández (Houston: Arte Público, 1993), 71–72; Hubert H. Bancroft, *History of Mexico,* vol. 3 (San Francisco: Bancroft, 1883), 607–609; William Headen, "Southwestern Texas," *Laredo Times,* July 20, 1881; Juan Bautista Chapa, *Texas and the Northeast Mexico, 1630–1690,* ed. William C. Foster (Austin: University of Texas Press, 1997), 7–17; Berlandier, *Journey to Mexico,* 2: 528–31; A. B. Clarke, *Travels in Mexico and California,* ed. Anne M. Perry (College Station: Texas A&M University Press, 1988), 12, 29.

12. U.S. Congress, Senate, Statistical Report on the Sickness and Mortality in the Army of the United States Compiled from January 1839 to January 1855, 34th Cong., 1st sess., Ex. Doc. No. 96, 1856, 360–63; William B. Taylor, *Drinking, Homicide, and Rebellion in Colonial Mexican Villages* (Stanford, Calif.: Stanford University Press, 1979), 28–40. See also Maturín M. Ballou, *Aztec Land* (Boston: Houghton Mifflin, 1890), 118–20.

13. J. Frank Dobie, *The Longhorns* (Boston: Little, Brown, 1941), 289–94; Virgil N. Lott and Mercurio Martínez, *The Kingdom of Zapata* (San Antonio: Naylor, 1953), 156–63.

14. W. W. Newcomb Jr., *The Indians of Texas from Prehistoric to Modern Times* (Austin: University of Texas Press, 1961), 56; Harold E. Driver, *Indians of North America* (Chicago: University of Chicago Press, 1961), 93–100, 162; J. Frank Dobie, *A Vaquero of the Brush Country* (Austin: University of Texas Press, 1981), 191. The oldest indication of farming in the region was discovered in the Ocampo Caves in southwest Tamaulipas, Mexico; gourds, squash, and jerk beans have been dated from about 7000 to 5500 B.C. Corn, or maize, was found in the same caves and was radiocarbon dated from 2772 B.C.

15. As seen in J. Frank Dobie, *Tales of Old-Time Texas* (Boston: Little, Brown, 1928), 94.

16. Herbert E. Bolton, *The Spanish Borderlands* (Albuquerque: University of New Mexico Press, 1996), 35–41; Cabeza de Vaca, *The Account,* 15–90.

17. Bolton, *The Spanish Borderlands,* 36; Carlos E. Castañeda, *Our Catholic Heritage in Texas, 1519–1936* (Austin: Von Boeckmann-Jones, 1936), 1: 39–81; Harbert Davenport and Joseph K. Wells, "The First Europeans in Texas, 1528–1536," *SWHQ* (January 1919): 248–49. See also "Alvar Núñez Cabeza de Vaca: A Preliminary Report on His Wonderings in Texas," *SWHQ* (January 1898): 166–86.

18. C. L. Sonnichsen, *Pass of the North: Four Centuries on the Rio Grande* (El Paso: Texas Western Press, 1968,) 79–87; Cleve Hallenbec, *The Journey of Fray Marcos de Niza* (Dallas: Southern Methodist University Press, 1987), 1–7.

19. Cabeza de Vaca, *The Account,* 72. See also David A. Dary, *The Buffalo Book: The Full Saga of the American Animal* (Athens, Ohio: Swallow Press, 1989); La Vere, *Texas Indians,* 68–70. This description of the buffalo, in a somewhat different translated version, is the same passage used by Bolton, *The Spanish Borderlands,* 34.

20. Adam Smith, *The Wealth of Nations* (London: March 8, 1776; repr., New York: Bantam Dell, 2003), 714, and David Ricardo, *The Principles of Political Economy and Taxation* (London: 1817; repr., New York: Dover Publications, 2004), 122–28. There are numerous early reports of buffalo, or *cíbola;* two of the most interesting were the Declaration of Pedro de Bustamante in 1852, who described the buffalo: "they are humpbacked, shaggy, small-horned, thick set and low of body," and the Accounting of the Expedition of Juan de Oñate in 1601 describing the "monstrous cattle," as seen in Hubert E. Bolton, ed., *Spanish Exploration in the Southwest, 1542–1706* (New York: Barnes and Noble, 1908), 148, 228, 254–55, as well as background data in Dary, *The Buffalo Book,* 7–19.

21. Hallenbec, *The Journey of Fray Marcos de Niza,* 1–95; J. Frank Dobie, *Coronado's Children* (New York: Literary Guild of America, 1931), v-xi, 1–5. The legend dates from A.D. 1150 when seven Spanish bishops were reported to have fled capture by Moor conquerors by sailing westward, in time finding a large island whereupon they landed, burned the ships, and established seven settlements. They named the island Antilia, and with the passage of time the seven cities grew wealthy, known to those who passed down the legend as "The Cities of the Seven Bishops" or "The Seven Cities of Antilia." The discovery, by Columbus, of the West Indies in 1492 further excited the myth.

22. Smith, *Wealth of Nations,* 278–81, 712–15; Kennett Cott, "Mexican Diplomacy and the Chinese Issue, 1876–1910," *Hispanic American Historical Review* (hereafter *HAHR*) (February 1987): 63

23. Mark A. Burkholder and Lyman L. Johnson, *Colonial Latin America* (Oxford: Oxford University Press, 2001), 139–40, 251, 282–84; Gilbert R. Cruz, *Let There Be Towns: Spanish Municipal Origins in the American Southwest, 1610–1810* (College Station: Texas A&M University Press, 1988), 1319; Secretaría General Técnica, *Guía Abreviada: Museo de America* (Madrid: Ministerio de Cultura, 2005).

24. Hanson, *Carnage and Courage,* 201–203; Lott and Martínez, *The Kingdom of Zapata,* 1; Vaillant, *Aztecs,* 105–106; William D. Robinson, *Memoirs of the Mexican Revolution* (London: MacDonald and Son, 1821), 6–15; Thomas, *Rivers of Gold,* 467–69, 474–91. See also Arthur Whitaker, "The Spanish Contribution to American Agriculture," *Agricultural History* (January 1919): 9–10.

25. Hubert H. Bancroft, *History of the North Mexican States and Texas* (San Francisco: History Company, 1886), 609–10, 629; Francis Parkman, *La Salle and the Discovery of the Great West* (1897; Williamstown, Mass.: Corner House Publishers, 1968), 401, 464–69; Lawrence Kinnaird, ed., *The Frontiers of New Spain: Nicolás de Lafora's Description, 1766–1768* (Berkeley, Calif.: Quivira Society, 1958),34; *Texas Almanac of 1857,* 142–45; Jesús F. De la Teja, *San Antonio de Béxar* (Albuquerque: University of New Mexico Press, 1995), 6–7.

26. Bancroft, *History of the North Mexican States and Texas,* 616; François Chevalier,

Land and Society in Colonial Mexico: The Great Hacienda (Berkeley: University of California Press, 1970), 306–14; Herbert E. Bolton, "The Mission as a Frontier Institution in the Spanish-American Colonies," *American Historical Review* (*AHR*) 23 (1917): 42–61; Lawrence F. Hill, *José de Escandón and the Founding of Nuevo Santander* (Columbus: Ohio State University Press, 1926), 25–32; *Texas Almanac of 1857*, 145; Robert S. Weddle, *San Juan Bautista: Gateway to Spanish Texas* (Austin: University of Texas Press, 1968), 114–21, 220–24.

27. José de Escandón, decree, "Sobre las dudas y difficultos, que en la Colonia del Nueva España, han pulzado liqiosos. . . . ," March 20, 27, 1749, Laredo Spanish Archives as seen at The Center for American History, University of Texas, Austin (hereafter Laredo Archives [LA]); I. J. Cox, "The Southwest Boundary of Texas," *Texas State Historical Quarterly* (*SWHQ*) (October 1902): 82; Castañeda, *Our Catholic Heritage,* 3: 120–96; Patricia Osante, *Orígenes del Nuevo Santander, 1748–1772* (Mexico City: UNAM, 1997), 93–120.

28. Clarence L. Ver Steeg, *The Formative Years, 1607–1763* (New York: Hill and Wang, 1964), 279–82.

29. Bolton, *The Spanish Borderlands,* 224–26; Thomas L. Miller, *The Public Lands of Texas, 1519–1970* (Norman: University of Oklahoma Press, 1972), 3–14; John Campbell, *A Concise History of the Spanish America* (London: John Stagg, 1741; repr., Folkestone, England, 1972), 89–134; Duffus, *The Santa Fe Trail,* 19–24.

30. *Fundación de la Colonia del Nuevo Santander,* General Archives, Mexico, vol. 2, 1930, provides an excellent account of settlement of the overall Rio Grande region; Robert D. Wood, *Life in Laredo* (Denton: University of North Texas Press, 2004), 16–17.

31. "Reconosimiento del Seno Mexicano hecho por el Escandón, provincias Internas," as seen in Cruz, *Let There Be Towns,* 84. See also Donald E. Chipman and Harriet D. Joseph, *Explores and Settlers of Spanish Texas* (Austin: University of Texas Press, 2001), 134–48.

32. Herbert E. Bolton, *Texas in the Middle Eighteenth Century* (1915; Austin: University of Texas Press, 1970), 47–60, 294–99; Hill, *José de Escandón,* 89–105, 188; Castañeda, *Our Catholic Heritage,* 3: 160–73; Armando C. Alonzo, *Tejano Legacy: Rancheros and Settlers in South Texas* (Albuquerque: University of New Mexico Press, 1998), 27–29. There are a number of "Doloreses" in South Texas and northern Mexico. The Dolores established on March 5, 1949, was not a villa but a ranch and known as Hacienda Dolores and later Dolores Viejo.

33. Prieto, *Historia, Geografía y Estadística del Estado de Tamaulipas,* 40–41; Cox, "The Southwest Boundary of Texas," *SWHQ,* 86–95; Donald E. Chipman, *Spanish Texas, 1519–1821* (Austin: University of Texas Press, 1992), 168–69; Lott and Martínez, *The Kingdom of Zapata,* 140–41. José Vásquez Borrego and his wife Josefa Imperial's land tract was 329,000 acres, with a large section fronting the Rio Grande in both the current Webb and Zapata counties.

34. Herbert E. Bolton, "Tienda de Cuervo's Ynspección of Laredo, 1757," *SWHQ* (January 1903): 194; Joe R. Moreno Jr. "The Paso de Jacinto Crossing on the Rio Grande, 1746–2006," *Journal of South Texas* (*JST*) (Fall 2006): 152–64; Wood, *Life in Laredo,* 17–18; Weddle, *San Juan Bautista,* 222. See also Ana Maria Alonso, *Thread of Blood: Colonialism, Revolution, and Gender on Mexico's Northern Frontier* (Tucson: University of Arizona Press, 1995); and Guillermo G. Leal, *Laredo 250 Years Ago* (Hidalgo, Mexico: Privately published, 2005), 36–51.

35. A. Bravo y Tudela, *Recuerdos de la Villa de Laredo* (Madrid: Imprenta de la Asociación del Arte de Imprimir, 1873).

36. Bolton, "Tienda de Cuervo's Ynspección of Laredo, 1757," 187–97; *Archivo General de la Nación, Provincias Internas,* Mexico City, vol. 179, 331–32, vol. 180, 181; David B. Edward, *The History of Texas* (Cincinnati: J. A. James, 1836 [1990]), 146–47; Wood, *Life in Laredo,* 18; *Texas Almanac,* 1857, 147–48; Laredo *Morning Times,* August 9, 2007. *Sitio* and *legua* (league) are interchangeable terms. A *sitio de ganado mayor* (large stock) was a plot of land 5,000 x

5,000 (25 million square *varas*) Mexican *varas* in size, or 4,428.4 acres; a *sitio de ganado menor* (small stock) was a plot of land 3,333 1/3 x 3,333 1/3 Mexican *varas* in size, or 1,985.9 acres. One *labor* was 1,000 x 1,000 *varas*, or one million square *varas* (177 acres). Five *sitios*, 22,140 acres, composed one *hacienda*. As a measure of distance, 5,000 *varas* equaled one league. A Mexican *vara* is estimated to be between 32.99 to 33.33 inches, or a *vara*/2.8 feet. The official viceroy-approved effective date of the grant for the Villa de Laredo was August 9, 1756.

37. Bolton, "Tienda de Cuervo's Ynspección of Laredo, 1757," 190–91, 197; Jones, *Los Paisanos*, 70–71.

38. Bolton, *Texas in the Middle Eighteenth Century*, 301.

39. Horgan, *Great River*, 139; Samuel D. McCulluch and James E. Warren, "A Report on Cultural Resources Investigations at Fort McIntosh, Laredo," George West, Texas, Archaeology Consultants, January 2002, 49.

40. Bolton, "Tienda de Cuervo's Ynspección of Laredo," 200; Archivo General de Mexico, "Villa de Laredo," Box 2–22/621, Vol. 56, Number 19, as seen in Texas State Archives, Austin. See also Hill, *José de Escandón*, and Jones, *Los Paisanos: Spanish Settlers on the Northern Frontier of New Spain*.

41. Bolton, "Tienda de Cuervo's Ynspección of Laredo" 197. See also Wood, *Life in Laredo*, 19–20.

42. Chipman, *Spanish Texas*, 187, 192–94, 204–208; Bolton, *Texas in the Middle Eighteenth Century*, 439. Nacogdoches did not become a permanent settlement until April 1779.

43. Chipman, *Spanish Texas*, 195–97; Walter Prescott Webb, *The Great Plains* (New York: Grosset and Dunlap, 1931), 208; Odie B. Faulk, "Ranching in Spanish Texas," *HAHR* 45 (May 1965): 257–66; Sandra L. Myres, "Ranching Frontier: Spanish Institutional Backgrounds of the Plains Cattle Industry," in David J. Weber, ed., *New Spain's Far Northern Frontier* (Dallas: Southern Methodist University Press, 1979), 81–91. See also Terry G. Jordan, *Trails to Texas: Southern Roots of Western Cattle Ranching* (Lincoln: University of Nebraska Press, 1981), and Chevalier's *Land and Society in Colonial Mexico*, 261–314.

44. Dobie, *The Longhorns*, 7; J. B. Wilkinson, *Laredo and the Rio Grande Frontier* (Austin: Jenkins Publishing, 1975), 17; J. Frank Dobie, *The Mustangs* (Boston: Little, Brown, 1952), 100; Jordon, *Trails to Texas*, 152–57; Bolton, *Texas in the Middle Eighteenth Century*, 300–301.

45. Bolton, *Texas in the Middle Eighteenth Century*, 34–35. See also Myers, "Frontier Ranching," 82; Ernest S. Osgood, *The Day of the Cattleman* (Chicago: University of Chicago Press, 1957), 26–27.

46. Castañeda, *Our Catholic Heritage*, 3: 175.

47. Acta de la General Visita al Pueblo de San Agustín de Laredo by Juan Fernando Palacio Governor of Nuevo Santander, and José de Ossorio y Llamas, Laredo, June 1767, translated by J. V. Haggard, November 2, 1936, as seen in the General Land Office of Texas, Austin, Texas (hereafter: General Visita of 1767); Angel S. Brown and Gloria V. Cadena, *San Agustín Parish of Laredo*, vol. 1, *Laredo* (Saltillo: Graficas Canepa, 1989), 1–3. See also Rogelia O. García, *The Bells of St. Augustine* (Laredo: 1963), 10–12; Valerio-Jiménez, "Neglected Citizens and Willing Traders," 252–57. The first resident secular pastor arrived in Laredo in January 1760, yet resided in Dolores and split time between Laredo and Dolores.

48. The French maintained an active inspection of the region well past the inking of the Treaty of Paris 1763, see Pierre-Marie François de Pagès, *Travels Round the World in the Years 1767, 1768, 1769, 1770, 1771* (Dublin: P. Byrne, 1791), 70–90.

49. Luis Navarro García, "The North of New Spain as a Political Problem in the Eighteenth Century." *Estudios Americanos* (1960), 17–31.

50. "Memoria secreta presentada al Rey de España por el Conde de Aranda sobre la inde-

pendencia de las colonias ingleses después de haber firmado el tratado de París de 1783," Folio 33, Cervantes Collection, Biblioteca Nacional (hereafter CCBN), Madrid. See also Colin G. Calloway, *The Scratch of a Pen: 1763 and the Transformation of North America* (New York: Oxford University Press, 2006).

51. Kinnaird, *The Frontiers of New Spain,* 178–81; "The Rubí Recommendation of Texas, April 10, 1768," in *Documents of Texas History,* ed. Ernest Wallace (Austin: Steck, 1963), 22–23; Josefina Zoraida Vázquez and Lorenzo Meyer, *The United States and Mexico* (Chicago: University of Chicago Press, 1985), 12–13; Henry Putney Beers, *Spanish and Mexican Records of the American Southwest* (Tucson: University of Arizona Press, 19798), 96–98; Ver Steeg, *The Formative Years,* 290–306. See also Maury B. Brown, "The Military Defenses of Texas and the Rio Grande Region about 1766" (master's thesis, University of Texas, Austin, August 1924).

52. Dan Stanislawski, "Early Spanish Town Planning in the New World," *Geographical Review* 37 (1947): 101–105; Dora Crouch et al., *Spanish City Planning in North America* (Cambridge, Mass.: MIT Press, 1982), 12–15; Burkholder and Johnson, *Colonial Latin America,* 184–90; Robinson, *Memoirs of the Mexican Revolution,* 8–9; Wood, *Life in Laredo,* 21–24. The Law of the Indies, or *Recopilación de leyes de los Reynos de las Indias* (Madrid: Ivlian de Paredes, 1681), vols. 1 to 9, as seen in Benson Latin American Collection, University of Texas, Austin, was issued in a number of editions between 1573 and 1790 and is an extremely detailed codification of laws and procedures for the community settlement, commercial relations, governance, and judicial procedure in New Spain.

53. General Visita of 1767, 80–85; Wilkinson, *Laredo and the Rio Grande Frontier,* 35–37; Jerry D. Thompson, *Sabers on the Rio Grande* (Austin: Presidial Press, 1974), 25–29; Wood, *Life in Laredo,* 29–30; Kinnaird, *The Frontiers of New Spain,* 34.

54. General Visita of 1767, 100–110.

55. Interview with John Foster by Joe Moreno, Laredo, Texas, May 20, 2004.

56. Stanislawski, "Early Spanish Town Planning," 102–103.

57. General Visita of 1767, 108–12; Rogelia O. García, "A History of the Catholic Church in Laredo" (master's thesis, Texas College of Arts and Industry, Denton, August 1955), 5–10; Bolton, "The Mission as a Frontier Institution," 46; Brown and Cadena, *San Agustin Parish of Laredo,* 1–7. See also Crouch et al., *Spanish City Planning,* 1–15, and Daniel D. Arreola, *Tejano South Texas* (Austin: University of Texas Press, 2002), 68–74. Central plazas were laid out and constructed in over twenty South Texas towns; however, San Antonio and Laredo were the only two regional towns to have more than two plazas. In addition to Laredo's San Agustín Plaza, the town designated six plazas: Market (site of the Laredo City Hall in 1883), Jarvis, and School Block, all three considered public spaces. The private plazas were added after years, and include Bruni (later the site of the public library), St. Peter's Church, and land set aside for the location of the Texas-Mexican Railroad depot.

58. Betty E. Dobkins, *The Spanish Element in Texas Water Law* (Austin: University of Texas Press, 1959), 127.

59. General Visita of 1767, 110–12; LA, Señores Capitanes y Tenientes de Justicias de las Villas de la Cordillera del Margen, October 8 and November 21, 1780; Lyle N. McAllister, "The Reorganization of the Army of New Spain, 1763–1766," *HAHR* 33 (February 1953): 1–32; William C. Foster, *Spanish Expeditions into Texas 1689–1768* (Austin: University of Texas Press, 1995), 177–93. In time, Roma (1765), San Fernando (1791), and Matamoros (1796) would be added to the *cordillera*—referred to only as *las villas de margen;* Luis N. García, "The North of New Spain as a Political Problem in the Eighteenth Century," *Estudios Americanos* (1960): 17–31.

60. Florence J. Scott, *Historical Heritage of the Lower Rio Grande* (Waco: Texian Press, 1966), 71–76; Wilkinson, *Laredo and the Rio Grande Frontier,* 37; Donald D. Brand, "The

Early History of the Range Cattle Industry in North Mexico," *Agriculture History* (July 1961): 134–35. See also Thompson, *Sabers on the Rio Grande,* 25–29.

61. Elizabeth A. H. John, *Storms Brewed in Other Men's World* (Norman: University of Oklahoma Press, 1975), 438.

62. LA, Letter, Don José Ossorio to Señores Capitan, Cabildo y Apoderados de Laredo, April 8, 1768; Miller, *The Public Lands of Texas,* 3–44. The territory between the Nueces River to Corpus Christi to the Rio Grande, often referred to as the "Nueces Strip," was first governed by Spain as Nuevo Santander, 1748–1821, then by the state of Tamaulipas, 1748–1821, and then by Texas after 1836. Claims were not settled until 1848–1850. See also Texas General Land Office, *Guide to Spanish and Mexican Land Grants in South Texas,* 1988.

63. Robert S. Smith, "Sales Taxes in New Spain, 1575–1770," *HAHR* 28 (February 1948): 2–37; David A. Brading, *Miners and Merchants in Bourbon Mexico, 1763–1810* (Cambridge: Cambridge University Press, 1971), 25–27. See also Herbert I. Priestley, *José de Gálvez, Visitor-General of New Spain, 1765–1771* (Berkeley: University of California Press, 1916).

64. LA, Decreto de el Sr. Gobernador de esta Colonia y respecto tobacco de contrabando, Juan Fernando de Palacio, February 19, 1768.

65. Papeles referentes a hacienda, "Impuestos de Entrada," Folio 657, Vol. I, Doc. 12, November 22, 1779; "Sobre el impuesto de pulque," Vol. I, Doc. 14, June 9 1785; and "Pulquerías," Vol. 1, Doc. 28, 1791, as seen in CCBN, Madrid; José Jesús Hernández Palomo, *La renta del pulque en Nueva España, 1663–1810* (Seville: Hispanoamericanos, 1979), 214–21.

66. LA, Governor Vicente González de Santianes, San Carlos, July 5, 1770 to Tomás Sánchez; Sebron Wilcox, "The Spanish Archives of Laredo," *SWHQ* 49 (January 1946): 348–49; Gilberto M. Hinojosa, *A Borderlands Town in Transition, Laredo, 1755–1870* (College Station: Texas A&M University Press, 1983), 10–12. The majority of the excellent analysis by Hinojosa focuses on the dynamic demographic changes within Laredo during the period prior to 1870.

67. Wood, *Life in Laredo,* 31–32; Valerio-Jiménez, "Neglected Citizens and Willing Traders," 256–57; Catherine Bennett, "The History of Education in Laredo, Texas to 1870" (master's thesis, University of Texas, 1939), 46–48.

68. La Vere, *Texas Indians,* 65, 134–46; Brand, "The Early History of the Range Cattle Industry in Northern Mexico," 134–35.

69. Sidney B. Brinkerhoff and Odie B. Faulk, *Lancers for the King* (Phoenix: Arizona Historical Foundation, 1965), 9–25. See also Thomas H. Naylor and Charles W. Polzer, eds. *The Presidio and Militia on the Northern Frontier of New Spain* (Tucson: University of Arizona Press, 1986.)

70. LA, Revilla, March 30, 1783. See also Hinojosa, *Borderlands Town,* 14–18.

71. John, *Storms Brewed in Other Men's Worlds,* 629; Sonnichsen, *Pass of the North,* 79–87; Alfred B. Thomas, *Forgotten Frontiers* (Norman: University of Oklahoma Press, 1932), 5; *Gazatas de Mexico,* May 19, 1784, 85; January 18, 1785, 223.

72. Adán Benavides, "The Fortification of Laredo: The Documentary Evidence for Proposals in 1792 and 1813," *El Campanario* (September 1989): 12; LA, Census Report of Asst. Mayor Miguel Ponce Borrego, January 28, 1789; Wilkinson, *Laredo and the Rio Grande Frontier,* 50–57. See also Naylor and Polzer, eds., *The Presidio and Militia,* vol. 1, *1570–1700.*

73. "Apologia por las Inglesas Insurgentes en la America," ca. 1780, Folio 348, CCBN, Madrid.

74. LA, Sgt. Manuel Dovalina to Mayor José González, June 17, 1790; Kathleen Da Camara, *Laredo on the Rio Grande* (San Antonio: Naylor, 1949), 14; See also Castañeda, *Our Catholic Heritage,* 5: 7–9, and James T. DeShields, *Border Wars in Texas* (Tioga, Tex.: Herald Company, 1912).

75. Benavides, "The Fortification of Laredo," 15–19; Villa de Laredo, February 15, 1792, Provincias Internas, Vol. 55, expediente 2, ff. 131–32, microfilm; Benson Latin American Collection, Austin; Valerio-Jiménez, "Neglected Citizens and Willing Traders," 258; Alcabala Tomo 4, "Leyes, Ordenanzas, Antes Acordados y Otros," February 11, 1792, Mexico Folio 584, as seen in CCBN, Madrid.

76. Conde de Sierra Gorda (Manuel de Escandón) to officials of the villas, December 10, 1794, LA.

77. As seen in David M. Vigness, trans. and ed., "Nuevo Santander in 1795: A Provincial Inspection by Félix Calleja," *SWHQ* (April 1972): 494.

78. LA, Census Report of Lt. Alcalde Miguel Ponce Borrego, Laredo, January 28, 1789; Wood, *Life in Laredo,* 32.

79. LA, as seen in Wilkinson, *Laredo and the Rio Grande Frontier,* 69–70; Dobie, *A Vaquero of the Brush Country,* 15–19; Charles Gibson, *Spain in America* (New York: Harper and Row, 1966), 192–93; Donald D. Brand, "The Early History of the Range Cattle Industry in Northern Mexico," 132–39.

80. Maas, seen in *Postlethwaite's Dictionary of Commerce* (London: ca. 1780), North American Plat III.

81. James E. Warren, *Archeological Investigation of Agustin Catholic Church in Laredo, Texas,* Report No. 217 (George West, Tex.: 1991), 3–33. See also Warren, *San Agustín Catholic Church in Laredo, Texas: An Inventory and Annotated Catalogue of Extant Volumes in the Church Archives,* Report No. 219 (George West, Tex.: 1990).

CHAPTER 2

1. LA, Laredo, August 8, 1825.

2. Webb, *The Great Plains,* 133–37; Jack Jackson, ed., *Texas by Terán* (Austin: University of Texas Press, 2000), 34–35.

3. Andrés Tijerina, *Tejanos and Texas under the Mexican Flag, 1821–1836* (College Station: Texas A&M University Press, 1994), 6.

4. Burkholder and Johnson, *Colonial Latin America,* 304–308; Wilkinson, *Laredo and the Rio Grande Frontier,* 58–59; Castañeda, *Our Catholic Heritage,* 5: 7–9, 118–20. See also Joseph F. Park, "Spanish Indian Policy in Northern Mexico, 1795–1810," *Arizona and the West* (Winter 1962): 325–44.

5. LA, Nemesio Salcedo to Alcalde de la Villa de Laredo, July 30, 1804; Félix D. Almaráz *Tragic Cavalier* (College Station: Texas A&M University Press, 1991), 12–14; James F. Brooks, *Captives and Cousins* (Chapel Hill: University of North Carolina Press, 2002), 32–35, 68–73; Mann, *1491,* 120; Park, "Spanish Indian Policy in Northern Mexico, 1765–1816," 340–44.

6. Webb, *The Great Plains,* 169. See also Dobie, *The Mustangs,* 42–52. Mounted archers predate the Comanches by over two thousand years, as Alexander the Great in 329 B.C. borrowed from the Persians mounted men-at-arms known as Hippotoxotai.

7. Interview with Judge Mercurio Martínez, July 29, 2003, Laredo, Texas, based on a common saying passed on by his father Mercurio Martínez (1879–1966).

8. Webb, *The Great Plains,* 127, 168–70; Edward, *The History of Texas,* 98–99, 108–109.

9. Newcomb, *The Indians of Texas,* 336–37; Castañeda, *Our Catholic Heritage,* 118–20.

10. Ralph A. Smith, "Indians in American-Mexican Relations before the War of 1846," *HAHR* 43 (February 1963): 63–64; Kenneth W. Porter, "The Seminole in Mexico, 1850–1861," *HAHR* 31 (February 1951): 1–36.

11. LA, Laredo, August 8, 1825. See also Frank G. Roe, *The Indian and the Horse* (Norman: University of Oklahoma Press, 1955), 220–22; Ernest Wallace and E. Adamson Hoebel, *The*

Comanches: Lords of the Plains (Norman: University of Oklahoma Press, 1952), 244–45; and T. R. Fehrenbach, *Comanches* (New York: Alfred A. Knopf, 1974).

12. Leslie S. Offutt, *Saltillo, 1770–1810* (Tucson: University of Arizona Press, 2001), 49–50; Robert C. West, *The Mining Community in Northern New Spain: The Parral Mining District* (Berkeley: University of California Press, 1949), 80–87; Burkholder and Johnson, *Colonial Latin America,* 272–75; Odie B. Faulk, "The Presidio: Fortress or Farce?" *Journal of the West* (1969): 22–28.

13. Woodrow Borah, *New Spain's Century of Depression* (Berkeley: University of California Press, 1951), 1–44; Jonathan Kandell, *La Capital: The Biography of Mexico City* (New York: Holt and Company, 1988,) 233–65; El Baron de Humboldt, "Tables, Geog, Politicas del Reino de Nuevo España," 1803, Mexico, Folio 659, CCBN, Madrid.

14. Bancroft, *History of Mexico,* 3: 642–43; Stanley Stein and Barbara Stein, *The Colonial Heritage of Latin America* (New York: Oxford University Press, 1970), 98; Colin M. MacLachlan and Jaime E. Rodriguez, *The Forging of the Cosmic Race: A Reinterpretation of Colonial Mexico* (Berkeley: University of California Press, 1980), 270–74, 283–87; Kandell, *La Capital,* 237–38; Richard L. Garner and Spiro Stefanou, *Economic Growth and Change in Bourbon Mexico* (Gainesville: University Press of Florida, 1993), 17–18. See also Richard J. Salvucci, *Textiles and Capitalism in Mexico* (Princeton, N.J.: Princeton University Press, 1987), 158–63.

15. Domenech, Emmanuel. *Missionary Adventures in Texas and Mexico: A Personal Narrative of Six Years' Sojourn in those Regions* (London: Longman, Brown, Green, Longmans, and Roberts, 1858), 360.

16. Joel R. Poinsett, *Notes on Mexico: Made in the Autumn of 1822* (New York: Praeger, 1969), 137–38.

17. John H. Coatsworth and Alan M. Taylor, eds., *Latin America and the World Economy since 1800* (Cambridge, Mass.: Harvard University Press, 1998), 24–32; James D. Cockcroft, *Mexico's Hope: An Encounter with Politics and History* (New York: Monthly Review Press, 1998), 42–50.

18. Eric Van Young, *The Other Rebellion: Popular Violence, Ideology, and the Mexican Struggle for Independence, 1810–1821* (Stanford, Calif.: Stanford University Press, 2001), 70–77; Valerio-Jiménez, "Neglected Citizens and Willing Traders," 264–65.

19. Robinson, *Memoirs of the Mexican Revolution,* 13–15. Robinson in 1821 noted that Mexico was often a dumping ground "of imperfect products of her agriculture." Furthermore, "to insure Spain the trade in wines and brandies, the Creoles were forbidden to manufacture either; olives were not allowed to be planted; the cultivation of silk-worm was interdicted; and [grape] vines" were uprooted to satisfy the "jealousy of the Cadiz monopolists."

20. Bancroft, *History of Mexico,* 588–89, 642; Burkholder and Johnson, *Colonial Latin America,* 282–85; Jack Jackson, *Los Mesteños: Spanish Ranching in Texas, 1721–1821* (College Station: Texas A&M University Press, 1986), 450–51; Michael C. Meyer and William H. Beezley, eds., *The Oxford History of Mexico* (New York: Oxford University Press, 2000), 281–83; MacLachlan and Rodriguez, *The Forging of the Cosmic Race,* 178–87, 192–95; Kenneth Pomeranz and Steven Topik, *The World That Trade Created* (New York: M. E. Sharpe, 1999), 183–86.

21. George B. Tindall, *America* (New York: W. W. Norton, 1988), 348–49; Jose Maria Tornel y Mendivil, *Relations between Texas, the United States of America, and the Mexican Republic* (Mexico: 1837; trans. Carlos E. Castañeda and reprinted at Washington, D.C.: Documentary Publications, 1971]), 287–316. The purchase of the Louisiana Territory involved two simultaneous transactions, 60 million francs for Louisiana, about $11.25 million, and 20 million francs or $3.74 million to cover French debts owed to American citizens.

22. J. Fred Rippy, "Britain's Role in the Early Relations of the United States and Mexico," *HAHR* (1927): 2–24; Albert K. Weinburg, *Manifest Destiny* (Chicago: Quadrangle Books, 1963); John W. O'Neal, "Texas 1791–1835: A Study in Manifest Destiny" (master's thesis, East Texas State University, 1969); Agustín Cué Cánavos, *Historia social y económica de México, 1521–1854* (Mexico City: Editorial F. Trillas, 1967), 339.

23. Washington, D.C., *National Intelligencer,* July 4, 1803, 1.

24. U.S. Department of Commerce, Bureau of the Census, *Historical Statistics of the United States Colonial Times to 1970,* Washington, D.C.: GPO, 1975, part 1, 428; Horgan, *Great River,* 399–400; Wilkinson, *Laredo and the Rio Grande Frontier,* 76–79; Map, Amerique: Septentrionale, Paris, 1806; Celso Furtado, *Economic Development in Latin America* (Cambridge: University Press, 1970), 19–22; I. J. Cox, "The Southwest Boundary of Texas," *SWHQ* (October 1902): 81–102; Roger G. Kennedy, *Mr. Jefferson's Lost Cause* (New York: Oxford University Press, 2003), 27, 189, 232; Thomas J. Fleming, *The Louisiana Purchase* (New York: John Wiley, 2003), 1–192; Chipman, *Spanish Texas,* 221–29; John Opie, *The Law of the Land* (Lincoln: University of Nebraska Press, 1994), 97. The Louisiana Territory was over 830,000 square miles in size.

25. LA, Aguayo, June 7, 1810; September 14, 1814.

26. Antonio Saenz to Manuel Salcedo, Villa de Salcedo, May 8, 1809, Béxar Archives.

27. Enrique Krauze, *Mexico: Biography of Power* (New York: HarperCollins, 1997), 91–118; MacLachlan and Rodriguez, *The Forging of the Cosmic Race,* 294–314, 334–36; Van Young, *The Other Rebellion,* 111–239.

28. LA, Manuel Yturbe, November 5, 1810.

29. Rogelia O. García, *Dolores, Revilla, and Laredo* (Waco: Texian Press, 1970), 18–19; Julia K. Garrett, *Green Flag over Texas* (New York: Cordova Press, 1939), 41–44, 53, 210; Almaráz, *Tragic Cavalier,* 116; Van Young, *The Other Rebellion,* 141–239; Chipman, *Spanish Texas,* 196–222; Félix D. Almaráz, *Crossroad of Empire: The Church and State in the Rio Grande Frontier of Coahuila and Texas* (San Antonio: Center for Archaeological Research, 1979), 44.

30. LA, Laredo, September 10, 1811.

31. LA, Rio Grande, April 2, 1813; Almaráz, *Tragic Cavalier,* 72–76.

32. LA, April 3, 1813; Harry Henderson, "The Magee-Gutiérrez Expedition," *SWHQ* (July 1951): 43–61; Chipman, *Spanish Texas,* 234–36; Ramiro Sanchez, *Frontier Odyssey: Early Life in Texas Spanish Town* (Austin: Jenkins Publishing, 1981), 64–66; Juan F. Zorrilla, Maribel Miró Flaquer, and Octavio Herrera Pérez, *Tamaulipas: Una historia compartida, 1810–1921* (Ciudad Victoria: Universidad Autónoma de Tamaulipas, 1993), 47–69. See also Henderson Yoakum, *History of Texas, 1685–1846* (New York: Redfield, 1956), part 1, 166–68, and Almaráz, *Tragic Cavalier,* 171–76.

33. Kathryn Garrett, "The First Constitution of Texas, April 17, 1813," *SWHQ* (April 1937): 290–308.

34. LA, Laredo, Census, April 30, 1819; Wilkinson, *Laredo and the Rio Grande Frontier,* 98–99.

35. Van Young, *The Other Rebellion,* 76–81.

36. Isaac J. Cox, "The Louisiana-Texas Frontier," *SWHQ* (July 1913): 1–42; William Manning, "Texas and the Boundary Issue, 1882–1892," *SWHQ* (January 1915): 217–61; Almaráz, *Tragic Cavalier,* 16–18, 41. The Adams-Onís Treaty, signed February 22, 1819, was ratified by Spain on October 24, 1820, and entered into force February 22, 1821. It was terminated on April 14, 1903.

37. LA, Aguago, January 28, 1815 and October 2, 1815.

38. Ibid., April 15, 1815 and February 17, 1816; Bancroft, *History of the North Mexican States and Texas,* 2: 46–53; Tijerina, *Tejanos and Texas,* 21–23; Wilkinson, *Laredo and the Rio Grande*

Frontier, 99; Almaráz, *Tragic Cavalier,* 69; John T. Morse Jr., *John Quincy Adams* (1898 [vol. 15 of American Statesman]; New York: Chelsea House, 1980), 112; Charles F. Adams, ed., *Memoirs of John Quincy Adams* (Philadelphia, 1824–27), 5: 67–69; John D. P. Fuller, *The Movement for the Acquisition of All Mexico* (Baltimore: Johns Hopkins Press, 1936), 13–15. A significant portion of the 1819 accord dealt with the "purchase" of Florida. See also *Annals of Congress,* 1919, 11–2130.

39. For an excellent chronicle of the life and death of Palafox, see Carmen Perry, ed., *The Impossible Dream by the Rio Grande* (San Antonio: St. Mary's University Press, 1971), 1–91. See also Juan A. Padilla, "Texas in 1820," *SWHQ* (July 1919): 53–56.

40. LA, Laredo, January 21, 1819, April 30, 1819, and September 18, 1819.

41. LA, Laredo, Ildefonso Ramón, Census of April 30,1819.

42. Ibid., census reports for the following periods: April 1819; Oct.–Dec. 1820; April 13, 1821.

43. Ibid., June 22, 1822.

44. Krauze, *Mexico,* 124–25.

45. Wilkinson, *Laredo and the Rio Grande Frontier,* 111–12.

46. LA, Laredo, J. G. D., December 10, 1815; LA, Benavides, May 13, 1824; Wilkinson, *Laredo and the Rio Grande Frontier,* 114–15. Formal education efforts to establish a school in the Villa de Laredo date from the royal decree of January 20, 1782, stating, "that no child be left out of such an important task, whatever class he belongs," see LA, Sanchez, March 22, 1783 and January 6, 1785.

47. A Citizen of the United States, *A View of South America and Mexico* (New York: Huntington, 1826), 120–122.

48. Stanley C. Green, *The Mexican Republic: The First Decade, 1823–1832* (Pittsburgh: University of Pittsburgh Press, 1987), 133–39; Robert S. Smith, "Shipping in the Port of Veracruz, 1790–1821," *HAHR* (August 1943): 5–20.

49. LA, Laredo, tobacco: September 7, 1815; July 18, 1815; and February 6, 1822; commercial regulations: December 21, 1821; mules: January 22, 1822; LeRoy Graf, "The Economic History of the Lower Rio Grande Valley, 1820–1875" (Ph.D. thesis, Harvard University, February 1942), 53–54, 286–91. See also Michael Costeloe, "Spain and the Latin American Wars of Independence: The Free Trade Controversy, 1810–1820," *HAHR* 61 (May 1981): 209–15. In addition to the prohibited trade in tobacco, other items banned from import in order to foster Mexican domestic manufactures and production included raw cotton and cotton products, grains, sugar, rice, coffee, shoes, bricks and tiles, carriages, and corn.

50. Padilla, "Texas in 1820," 47–68; Graf, "The Economic History of the Lower Rio Grande Valley," 286–89.

51. Graf, "The Economic History of the Lower Rio Grande Valley," 289, 304.

52. S. G. Reed, *A History of the Texas Railroads* (Houston: St. Clair Publishing, 1941), 4.

53. Gregg, *Commerce of the Prairies,* 231–40, 264–65; Wilkinson, *Laredo and the Rio Grande Frontier,* 113–14; David M. Pletcher, *The Diplomacy of Annexation: Texas, Oregon, and the Mexican War* (Columbia: University of Missouri Press, 1973), 31–33, 43; Frederic Paxson, "England and Mexico, 1824–1825," *SWHQ* (October 1905): 138–41.

54. Stephen F. Austin to James E. B. Austin, March 23, 1822, as seen in Eugene C. Barker, ed., *Annual Report of the American Historical Association,* vol. 2 (Washington, D.C.: GPO, 1928), 487–88; Eugene C. Barker, *The Life of Stephen F. Austin* (Austin: TSHA, 1949), 41; Sebron Wilcox, "Laredo during the Texas Revolution," *SWHQ* (October 1938): 88; Webb, *The Great Plains,* 161; "Description of Texas by Stephen F. Austin," *SWHQ* (October 1924): 113; Gregg Cantrell, *Stephen F. Austin: Empresario of Texas* (New Haven, Conn.: Yale University Press, 1999), 111–12; Vito Alessio Robles, *Coahuila y Texas* (Mexico: 1945), 102–103. Orceneth

Fisher, in *Texas in 1840* [1841], 23, concurred noting: "the country [between the Nueces and Rio Grande] represented as being mostly destitute of water and timber."

55. *Visit to Texas* (New York: Goodrich and Wiley, 1834), 1–264. Other first-person accounts of the era include Edward Stiff, *Texas Emigrant,* 1840; David Edward, *The History of Texas,* 1836; Joseph E. Field, *Three Years in Texas,* 1836, and O. Fisher, *Texas in 1840* [1841]. The Austin Colony ranged from the Gulf of Mexico on the south to the Old San Antonio Road on the north, the Lavaca River on the west, and to the San Jacinto River on the east.

56. Edward, *The History of Texas,* 140–60, and the Mexican Constitution of 1824 can be seen at 322–36. For a list of empresarios and colonization grants, see *Texas Almanac for 1957,* 38–45.

57. "Texas," New York *Statesman,* March 6, 1827, 1; Bancroft, *History of the North Mexican States and Texas,* 2: 73–76; Richard B. Winders, *Crisis in the Southwest: The United States, Mexico, and the Struggle over Texas* (Wilmington, Del.: SR Books, 2002), 7–8; M. V. Henderson, "Minor Empresario Contracts for the Colonization of Texas, 1825–1834," *SWHQ* 32 (1928): 3–13. Among the most significant Mexican nationals who obtained a grant in Texas are: Martin de Leon, Lorenzo de Zavala, Italian-born Mexican general, Vicente Filísola, and Martin Perfecto de Cos, Santa Anna's brother-in-law.

58. Henderson, "Minor Empresario Contracts for the Colonization of Texas, 1825–1834," 3–13.

59. Secretary Van Buren to Col. Butler, October 16, 1829 and Van Buren to Joel R. Poinsett, September 18, 1829, "United States and Mexico," 25th Cong., 2nd sess, House Exec. Doc. No. 351, April 27, 1838, 34–35, 40–53; Robert V. Remini, *The Life of Jackson* (New York: Perennial, 2001), 309. Dissatisfaction with the U.S.-Mexico relations led the Secretary of State to downgrade U.S. representation in Mexico City from "Envoy Extraordinary and Minister Plenipotentiary of the United States" (Poinsett's title) to "Chargé d'Affaires" (Butler's title).

60. "Treaties with Mexico," 22nd Cong., 1st sess., House Doc. No. 225, May 1, 1832; Hunter Miller, ed., *Treaties and Other International Acts of the United States of America* (Washington, D.C.: GPO, 1931), 3: 405–20, 599–640; William R. Manning, *Early Diplomatic Relations between the United States and Mexico* (Baltimore: Johns Hopkins Press, 1916), 277–348. Representing Mexico in the treaty negotiations were Lucas Alaman and Rafael Mangino.

61. "Treaties with Mexico," May 1, 1832, Articles II and III and for a clarification of the stipulation for granting conformity to the principle of "most favored nation," see Secretary of State John Forsyth to Chargé d'Affaires of Mexico Don J. M. de Castillo y Lanzas, Washington, D.C., January 30, 1835, "United States and Mexico," 25th Cong., 2nd sess., House Exec. Doc. No. 351, 701. See also "Inland Trade with Mexico," 26th Cong., 1st sess., House Doc. No. 191, April 17, 1840; and "Treaties and Conventions," 41st Cong., 3rd sess., Senate Ex. Doc. No. 36, 1871, 542–87.

62. Miller, *Treaties and Other International Acts,* 1: 58–59; Vásquez and Meyer, *United States and Mexico,* 26–31; Condy Raguet, *The Principles of Free Trade* (Philadelphia: 1840; repr., New York: Augustus M. Kelly, 1969), 1–439. The first commercial treaty was inked by the United States with France on February 6, 1778. The 1830s was an intense period of U.S. commercial bilateral agreements to include Austria, Turkey, Chile, Russia, Siam, Venezuela, Peru, Greece, Netherlands, Ecuador, and Mexico.

63. LA, Laredo, Census of December 1, 1828.

64. *Visit to Texas,* 264; LA, Laredo census, December 10, 1828; Robert M. Utley, *Lone Star Justice* (New York: Berkeley, 2002), 105.

65. "Explanation to the Public concerning the Affairs of Texas by Citizen Stephen F. Austin," Ethel Z. Rather, ed., *SWHQ* 8 (1905): 234.

66. Barker, *Austin,* 43–97; Arnoldo De León, *The Tejano Community, 1836–1900* (Albuquerque: University of New Mexico Press, 1982), 11; Tijerina, *Tejanos and Texas,* 7, 40–44; Wilkinson, *Laredo and the Rio Grande Frontier,* 133; Eugene C. Barker, "Mexican Colonization Laws," *The New Handbook of Texas,* ed. Ron Tyler et al., vol. 4, 684–85; "Texas, Its Soil, Climate, productions, etc.," *National Intelligencer,* October 14, 1835, 1; Cincinnati *Gazette,* November 1829, and *National Intelligencer* October 21, 1829, as seen in David Woodman Jr., *Guide to Texas Emigrants* (Boston: M. Hawes, 1835). See also Henderson, "Minor Empresario Contracts for Colonization of Texas, 1825–1834," *SWHQ* (April and June 1928).

67. *Visit to Texas,* 262; Wilkinson, *Laredo and the Rio Grande Frontier,* 113–25, 144; Tijerina, *Tejanos and Texas,* 49–50; Haggard J. Villasana, "Epidemic Cholera in Texas, 1833–1834," *SWHQ* (January 1937): 216–30; Joseph E. Field, *Three Years in Texas* (Boston: Justin Jones, 1836), 44.

68. *Visit to Texas,* 198; Wilkinson, *Laredo and the Rio Grande Frontier,* 133.

69. Callcott, *Santa Anna,* 89–107; Krauze, *Mexico,* 135–38; Villalpando and Rosas, *Historia de Mexico,* 153; Randolph B. Campbell, *Gone to Texas* (New York: Oxford University Press, 2003), 125–27; Winders, *Crisis in the Southwest,* 12–13.

70. John H. Jenkins, ed., *The Papers of the Texas Revolution, 1835–1836* (Austin: Presidial Press, 1973), 1: 156.

71. Alwyn Barr, *Texans in Revolt: The Battle for San Antonio, 1835* (Austin: University of Texas Press, 1990).

72. LA, Fernandez to Ramon, May 28, 29,1835; Wilcox, "Laredo during the Texas Revolution," 89; Wilkinson, *Laredo and the Rio Grande Frontier,* 135.

73. LA, Sanchez to Ramon, November 26, 1835; Stephen F. Austin to Edward Burleson, November 15, 1835, in Jenkins, ed. *The Papers of the Texas Revolution,* 1973.

74. Bancroft, *History of the North Mexican States and Texas,* 2: 182–88; Randy Roberts and James S. Olson, *A Line in the Sand* (New York: Free Press, 2001), 51–60; Chargé A. Butler to Hon. John Forsyth, Secretary of State, January 26, 1836, House, "United States and Mexico," 25th Cong., 2nd sess., Exec. Doc. No. 351, 576–78. News of the Texas revolution was widely covered beginning in 1835. The New Orleans *Bee* published numerous "specials" to the paper that were subsequently published in East Coast papers such as New Haven's *Columbia Register,* January 23, 1836.

75. Martín Perfecto de Cos to Santa Anna, December 15, 1835, *The Papers of the Texas Revolution;* Barr, *Texans in Revolt,* 65–66; Wilcox, "Laredo during the Texas Revolution," 93; Vicente Filísola, *Memorias para la historia de la guerra de Tejas* (Mexico City: Impr. Cumplido, 1849), 2: 337; John H. Jenkins and Kenneth Kesselus, *Edward Burleson: Texas Frontier Leader* (Austin: Jenkins Publishing, 1990), 57–94. See also Castañeda, *Our Catholic Heritage,* 6: 286 87, and Wilkinson, *Laredo and the Rio Grande Frontier,* 137 39. Wilkinson notes that in the last five months of 1835, twenty-one civilians from Laredo were killed by Indians and a number were held captive.

76. M. K. Wisehart, *Sam Houston: American Giant* (Washington, D.C.: Robert B. Luce, 1962), 118–58; Campbell, *Gone to Texas,* 139–41.

77. Wilcox, "Laredo during the Texas Revolution," 95–96.

78. Tom Find to Editor, February 20, 1836, *The Papers of the Texas Revolution;* Castañeda, *Our Catholic Heritage,* 6: 287.

79. Letter, William B. Travis to the People of Texas, February 24, 1836, as examined by the author at Texas State Archives, Austin, on February 14, 2005.

80. Wilfrid H. Callcott, *Santa Anna* (Norman: University of Oklahoma Press, 1936), 129–32; Chief Mexican Participants (translated by Carlos E. Castañeda), *The Mexican Side of the Texas Revolution, 1836* (Washington D.C.: Documents Publications, 1971), 97–110; "Texas

Insurrection No. 1," *National Gazette and Literary Register,* April 23, 1836, provides a very good contemporary overview.

81. Letters and document between representatives of the United States and Mexico, March 12, 14, and 15, 1836; April 8 and 20, 1836; June 7 and 21, 1836; July 19, 1936, as seen in "United States and Mexico," 25th Cong., 2nd sess., House Exec. Doc. No. 351, in vol. 12. See also Jonathan W. Jordon, *Lone Star Navy* (Washington, D.C.: Potomac Books, 2006), 80–83.

82. *Document of Major General Sam Houston, Commander in Chief of the Texan Army* (New Orleans: John Cox Printers, circa 1836; repr., Austin: Pemberton Press, 1964).

83. Callcott, *Santa Anna,* 139; Ann F. Crawford ed., *The Eagle: The Autobiography of Santa Anna* (Austin: Pemberton Press, 1969), 54–57; José Enrique de la Peña, *With Santa Anna in Texas: A Personal Narrative of the Revolution,* ed. and trans. Carmen Perry (College Station: Texas A&M University Press, 1975), 132–33; Andrew Jackson Houston, *The San Jacinto Campaign* (N.p.: 1925), 783.

84. J. F. C. Fuller, *Decisive Battles of the U.S.A.* (New York: Harper and Brother, 1942), 144–46; Campbell, *Gone to Texas,* 158; T. R. Fehrenbach, *Lone Star: A History of Texas and the Texans* (New York: Collier, 1968), 233; Callcott, *Santa Anna,* 139–42. Wilcox notes that among the Alamo defenders was Jose Maria Guerrero of Laredo, see also Amelia Williams, "A Critical Study of the Siege of the Alamo and the Personnel of Its Defenders," *SWHQ* (April 1934): 263. The Treaty of Velasco was never ratified by the Mexican Congress.

85. H. M. Gammel, *The Laws of Texas, 1822–1897* (Austin: Gammel, 1898), 1: 1193–94; Bancroft, *History of the North Mexican States and Texas,* 2: 297–98; Margaret S. Henson, *Samuel May Williams: Early Texas Entrepreneur* (College Station: Texas A&M University Press, 1976), 123–24.

86. MG E. Gaines, Western Department HQ, Camp Sabine to Secretary of War, April 28, 1836, *U.S. and Mexico,* 25th Cong., 2nd sess., Exec. Doc. No. 351, 783.

87. Ibid., No. 351, 787. See also Miller, ed., *Treaties and Other International Acts,* 3: 420, Vol. IV, 125–31, 142–43; Robert V. Remini, *Andrew Jackson and the Course of American Democracy 1833–1845* (New York: Harper and Row, 1984), 363–68.

88. David G. Burnet, "Proclamation of the blockade of the port of Matamoros," July 21, 1836, *U.S. and Mexico,* Exec. Doc. 25th Cong., 2nd sess., Doc. No. 351, 603.

89. Utley, *Lone Star Justice,* 38, 603.

CHAPTER 3

1. Joseph M. Nance, *After San Jacinto: The Texas-Mexican Frontier, 1836–1841* (Austin: University of Texas Press), 3–9; Wilcox, "Laredo during the Texas Republic," 98; David Montejano, *Anglos and Mexicans in the Making of Texas, 1836–1986* (Austin: University of Texas Press, 1987), 18; Hinojosa, *Borderlands Town,* 50–51, 54.

2. "Boundary: United States and Mexico," U.S. House of Representatives, 25th Cong., 1st, Doc. No. 42, October 3, 1837, 1–45; E. K. Teulon, "Our National Prospects," *Austin City Gazette,* April 15, 1840, 3; "New Orleans Bulletin," ibid., December 23, 1840, 3.

3. Bancroft, *History of the North Mexican States and Texas,* 332; Fehrenbach, *Lone Star,* 252; Hinojosa, *Borderlands Town,* 48–49; Graf, "The Economic History of the Lower Rio Grande Valley," 57–59; Henson, *Samuel May Williams,* 123–24. As late as 1846, official national maps of Mexico still showed Texas as a state in Mexico.

4. "Deaf" Smith to W. S. Fisher, Secretary of War, March 27, 1837, San Antonio de Béxar, Texas State Library Archives, Austin; Stephen L. Moore, *Savage Frontier* (Plano: Republic of Texas Press, 2002), 232–37. See also *Telegraph and Texas Register,* April 11, 1837. The site of this skirmish was in the area of the Lake Casa Blanca Golf Course.

5. Thomas J. Rush to Sam Houston, July 20, 1836 and July 6, 1836, as seen in *Papers of the Texas Revolution.*

6. Nance, *After San Jacinto,* 5; Webb, *The Great Plains,* 165–66. See also "Annexation of Texas to the United States," U.S. House of Representatives, 25th Cong., 1st sess., Doc. No. 40, October 3, 1837, 1–18.

7. Arnoldo de León, *Mexican Americans in Texas* (Arlington Heights, Ill.: Harlan Davidson, 1993), 38; Dobie, *Longhorns,* 22–29; United States Congress, "Difficulties on the Southwestern Frontier," House Executive Document, 36th Cong., 1st sess., no. 52.

8. Berlandier, *Journey to Mexico,* Vol. I, 169. Sugar produced tremendous profits and sold in different forms, such as 20- to 25-pound loaves called *pilones,* one- to one-and-one-half-pound clock—*panochas,* and as the by-product of sugarcane juice or rum—*chinguirito.*

9. Dobie, *Vaquero of the Brush Country,* 28; Joseph M. Nance, *Attack and Counterattack: The Texas-Mexican Frontier, 1842* (Austin: University of Texas Press, 1964), 513.

10. "The Mexican Traders," *Austin City Gazette,* July 1, 1840, 2. See also *Visit to Texas,* 196–201.

11. United States, Bureau of the Census, *Historical Statistics of the United States, Colonial Times to 1957,* 551, 553; Pletcher, *The Diplomacy of Annexation,* 77, 85; Nance, *After San Jacinto,* 80; Richard J. Salvucci, "Origins and Progress of U.S.-Mexican Trade, 1825–1884," *HAHR* (November 1991): 734–35. [Telegraph and Texas Register (Hou) July 8, 1837.]

12. *London Times,* August 10, 1837; Ephraim D. Adams, *British Interests and Activities in Texas, 1838–1846* (Baltimore: Johns Hopkins Press, 1910), 13–17; Vásquez and Meyer, *United States and Mexico,* 37–38.

13. Michael Costeloe, *Bonds and Bondholders: British Investors and Mexico's Foreign Debt, 1824–1888* (Westport, Conn.: Praeger, 2003), 34–40; Miller, ed. *Treaties and Other International Acts,* 4: 133–43.

14. L. E. Cargous, acting U.S. Consul to John Foster, Secretary of State, March 9, 1839, U.S. Department of State Dispatches from the United States Consul in Veracruz, 1822–1906, Microfilm B 3838, Roll 4; Callcott, *Santa Anna,* 154–60.

15. Asa K. Christian, "The Tariff History of the Republic of Texas" (master's thesis, University of Texas, Austin, June, 1917), 7–15.

16. Ibid., 33; Gammel, *Laws of Texas,* 2: 655; Nancy N. Baker, ed., *The French Legation in Texas* (Austin: TSHA, 1971), 17, 150–206; Ione Cocke, "Texas and the Federal Tariff" (master's thesis, University of Texas, Austin, June 1921), 1–5a. The French were astute observers of the commercial opportunities in Texas (ever mindful of the British influence) and noted the following in a consul dispatch to Paris in mid-1840: "Aside from the culture in tobacco, Texas has . . . an even richer potential for commerce. I refer to the cattle trade. No one in Europe could conceive of their enormous droves of wild cattle which roam the boundless prairies of the west. To count them would be to count the grains of sand on the ocean shore." A. De Saligny, July 17, 1984.

17. Nance, *After San Jacinto,* 78–82; Pletcher, *The Diplomacy of Annexation,* 79–85; Salvucci, "Origins and Progress of U.S.-Mexican Trade," 697–712; T. R. Fehrenbach, *Fire and Blood: A History of Mexico* (New York: Collier, 1973), 386–89; G. K. Teulon, "Recognition by Great Britain," *Austin City Gazette,* December 22, 1840, 2; Graf, "The Economic History of the Lower Rio Grande Valley," 134–36. See also Jason Goodwin, *Greenback* (New York: Henry Holt, 2003), 16–17, and Fehrenbach, *Lone Star,* 247–50, 259; Ephraim D. Adams, *British Interests and Activities in Texas, 1838–1846* (Baltimore: Johns Hopkins Press, 1910), 18–20; J. L. Worley, "The Diplomatic Relations of England and the Republic of Texas," Texas State Historical Association *Quarterly* 9 (July 1905): 1–40.

18. Salvucci, "Origins and Progress of U.S.-Mexican Trade," 699; Peter Temin, *The Jacksonian Economy* (New York: Norton, 1969), 68–91.

19. Edward W. Heusinger, "The Monetary History of the Republic of Texas," *SWHQ* (July 1953): 82–90; Louis Lenz, "Texas Money," *SWHQ* (October 1953): 175–80; Nance, *After San Jacinto,* 79.

20. Costeloe, *Bonds and Bondholders,* 118–19; *London Times,* September 4, 1835. See also Gregg, *Commerce of the Prairies,* 231–35, and William L. Schurz, "Acapulco and the Manila Galleon," *SWHQ* (July 1918): 18–37.

21. "Map of Texas," General Land Office of the Republic, 1839.

22. LA, Matamoros, Filísola to Justice of the Peace Ramon, July 30, 1838; Horgan, *Great River,* 559–69.

23. LA, Resolution, January 5, 1839; J. Smith, "La República de Rio Grande," *American Historical Review* (June 1928): 660–64.

24. Nance, *After San Jacinto,* 253; Lamar Papers, vol. III, 436, and VI, 128; Lott and Martínez, *The Kingdom of Zapata,* 112.

25. LA, Decree, General Antonio Canales, Camargo, November 10, 1839; Harriet Smither, ed. *The Papers of Mirabeau Buonaparte Lamar* (Austin: Von Boeckmann-Jones), vol. 6, *Historical Notes,* May 30, 1947, 97–115; "Our Relations with Great Britain," *Austin City Gazette,* February; David M. Vigness, "Relations of the Republic of Texas and the Republic of the Rio Grande," *SWHQ* (January 1954): 312–21; Jerry D. Thompson, *Laredo: A Pictorial History* (Norfolk: Donning, 1986), 96–103; Lott and Martínez, *The Kingdom of Zapata,* 106–13; Paul N. Spellman, *Forgotten Texas Leader: High McLeod and the Texas Santa Fe Expedition* (College Station: Texas A&M University Press, 1999,) 43–46; Vázquez and Meyer, *United States and Mexico,* 40; LeRoy Graf, "Colonizing Projects in Texas South of the Nueces, 1820–1845," *SWHQ* (April 1947): 431–48; Joel H. Silbey, *Storm over Texas* (New York: Oxford University Press, 2005), 36–38.

26. "From the Louisianian," *Austin City Gazette,* August 13, 1839, 3.

27. Ibid.

28. "Mexico," ibid., February 5, 1840, 3; "Latest News from Mexico," ibid., February 12, 1840; "Spirit of the Mexican Journals in Relation to this Republic," ibid., March 25, 1840, 3; "Our National Prospects," ibid., April 15, 1840; George Fisher to the editor, April 30, 1840, in ibid, May 13, 1840.

29. Lamar, "President's Message," ibid., November 12, 1839, 1–2.

30. *Papers of Mirabeau B. Lamar,* 115–16, 131–32, 137. See also Nance, *After San Jacinto,* 256–67; Wilkinson, *Laredo and the Rio Grande Frontier,* 158–61, 170–74; Bancroft, *History of the North Mexican States and Texas,* 328–32; Milton Lindheim, *The Republic of the Rio Grande* (Waco: W. M. Morrison, 1964), 1–17.

31. *Papers of Mirabeau B. Lamar,* 130; Tyler et al., eds., *Handbook of Texas,* vol. 6, 1142–45. Zapata County was originally a part of Starr and Webb counties. The City of Zapata was originally called Habitación or Carrizo prior to 1858, when it was renamed Bellville, and renamed in 1898 to Zapata.

32. Lott and Martínez, *The Kingdom of Zapata,* 49–50.

33. "Anticipated Invasion by Mexico," *Austin City Gazette,* December 23, 1840, 2.

34. "Santa Fe Expedition," ibid., August 25, 1841. See also Allan R. Purcell, "The History of the Texas Militia, 1835–1903" (Ph.D. diss., University of Texas, Austin, August 1981), 82–85.

35. Nance, *After San Jacinto,* 46–47; Lamar Papers, vol. VI, 116–17; Spellman, *Forgotten Texas Leader,* 7, 52–129.

36. Jenkins and Kesselus, *Edward Burleson,* 290–317.

37. Sam Houston to BG A. Somervell, October 3, 1842, as seen in Sterling B. Hendricks "The Somervell Expedition to the Rio Grande, 1842," *SWHQ* (October 1919): 112–13.

38. Ibid., 127–28; Wilkinson, *Laredo and the Rio Grande Frontier,* 178–79; Sam W. Haynes,

Soldiers of Misfortune: The Somervell and Mier Expeditions (Austin: University of Texas Press, 1990), 48–57.

39. LA, letter, General Jesús Cárdenas to alcalde of Laredo, December 26, 1842; Wilcox, "Laredo during the Texas Republic," 102–103; William A. DePalo Jr., *The Mexican National Army, 1822–1852* (College Station: Texas A&M University Press, 1997), 83–84; Fehrenbach, *Lone Star,* 262; Spellman, *Forgotten Texas Leader,* 113–15, 118–23.

40. Hinojosa, *Borderlands Town,* 53–56.

41. In Silbey, *Storm over Texas,* 25.

42. Miller, ed. "Joint Resolution for Annexing Texas to the United States," *Treaties and Other International Acts,* 4: 689–739; Wilkinson, *Laredo and the Rio Grande Frontier,* 184–91. See also R. Bruce Winder, *Mr. Polk's War* (College Station: Texas A&M University Press, 1977); Justin H. Smith, *The Annexation of Texas* (New York: Baker and Taylor, 1911); John Seigenthaler, *James K. Polk* (New York: Times Book, 2004); and Silbey, *Storm over Texas,* 31, 80–121.

43. William May, *A Review of the Causes and Consequences of the Mexican War* (Boston: Benjamin B. Mussey, 1849), 130–43; U. S. Grant, *Personal Memoirs* (New York: Charles L. Webster, 1885), 85–106.

44. Marcy to Taylor, "Mexican War Correspondence," U.S. House, 30th Cong., 1st sess., Ex. Doc. No. 60, April 28, 1848, 88.

45. President's Message, 29th Cong., 2nd sess., Report No. 70, February 24, 1847; John T. Hughes, *Doniphan's Expedition* (Cincinnati: U. James, 1846; repr., College Station: Texas A&M University Press, 1997), 15.

46. Norman E. Tutorow, *Texas Annexation and the Mexican War* (Palo Alto, Calif.: Chadwick House, 1978), 123–43; Arthur M. Schlesinger Jr., *The Age of Jackson* (New York: Little, Brown, 1945), 427–49.

47. For a biography of Lamar, see A. K. Christian, "Mirabeau Buonaparte Lamar," *SWHQ* (January 1920): 153–70; (April 1920): 231–70; (July 1920): 39–80; (October 1920): 87–139; (January 1921): 195–234; (April 1921): 317–24.

48. John E. Weems, *To Conquer a Peace: The War between the United States and Mexico* (College Station: Texas A&M University Press, 1974), 44.

49. Lamar Papers, vol. IV, pt. 1, 141–44; Christian, "Mirabeau Buonaparte Lamar," *SWHQ* (October 1920): 87–139.

50. Lamar Papers, vol. IV, 22–44, 69–72; Pat Kelley, *River of Lost Dreams* (Lincoln: University of Nebraska Press, 1986), 32–35.

51. José Fernando Ramírez, *The Mexican Republic, 1847,* trans. Dennis E. Berge (El Paso: Texas Western Press, 1975), 12–57.

52. Lamar Papers, vol. IV, pt. 1, 69, 141–45, 159–69; LA, Lamar, order, November 12, 1846. See also Stanley Green, *A Changing of Flags: Mirabeau B. Lamar at Laredo* (Laredo: Border Studies, 1990), 1–28, and J. Fred Rippy, "The Indians of the Southwest in the Diplomacy of the United States and Mexico, 1848–1853," *HAHR* (August 1919): 378–86.

53. Lamar to Taylor, December 24, 1846, Lamar Papers. See also Lamar to Taylor, February 7, 1847, ibid.

54. Wilkinson, *Laredo and the Rio Grande Frontier,* 222–23.

55. Bacilio Benavides, José María González, and José María Ramón to General J. E. Wool, April 10, 1848, Lamar Papers, Box 1909/1–24, Texas State Archives.

56. Lamar to Ramón, Benavides, and González, April 11, 1848, Lamar Papers, ibid.

57. Ibid.

58. Chipman, *Spanish Texas,* 251–54, emphasis added. At http://memory.loc.gov/cgi-bin/ampage?collId=llsl&fileName=009/llsl009.db&recNum=982.

59. George W. Smyth [General Land Office] to H. Bee, February 13, 1849, H. Bee Papers, Box 2Q433.

60. Richard G. del Castillo, *The Treaty of Guadalupe Hidalgo: A Legacy of Conflict* (Norman: University of Oklahoma Press, 1990), 43–86; General Land Office, Austin, Texas, *Guide to Spanish and Mexican Land Grants in South Texas,* 1999; G. W. Paschal, *Digest of the Laws of Texas* (Washington, D.C.: 1870), 732; Charles A. Kupchan, *The End of the American Era* (New York: Vintage, 2002), 171–72; Florence J. Scott, *Royal Land Grants North of the Rio Grande, 1771–1821* (Rio Grande City: La Retama Press, 1969). The treaty was signed on February 2, 1848, and the U.S. Senate ratified it on March 10, 1848, followed by the Mexican Congress on May 30. Furthermore, the Commerce Trade Treaty of 1832 was renewed.

61. John A. Rogers to Lamar, Commandcy at Laredo, February 12, 1847, Lamar Papers, Box 1909/1–24, Texas State Archives, Austin.

62. Lamar Papers, vol. IV, 169–74; Christian, "Mirabeau Buonaparte Lamar," 319–20.

63. J. De Cordova, *Texas: Her Resources and Her Public Men* (Philadelphia: J. B. Lippincott, 1858), 186–87; Zorrilla, Flaquer, and Herrera Pérez, *Tamaulipas,* 192–93. The close friendship between Lamar and Martínez was such that the Martínezes youngest daughter Carlota was named Lamarcita.

64. Lamar Papers, vol. IV(1), 171, 186; Gammel, *Laws of Texas,* 3: 18, 43, 343–47, 760–61, 1012–13; Luke Gounary, *Texas Boundaries: Evolution of the State's Counties* (College Station: Texas A&M University Press, 1995), 53–57; Hinojosa, *Borderlands Town,* 56–58; 7th U.S. Census, Webb County, N.A.; Z. T. Fulmore, *The History and Geography of Texas* (Austin: TSHA, 1915), 283. The Laredo charter was amended on February 9, 1850, to state that no person shall be eligible to any office and not be able to vote of they were not a resident at least six months.

65. "The Texas Frontier: Army Movements," *New York Times,* December 10, 1852, 3; Thomas T. Smith, *The Old Army in Texas* (Austin: TSHA, 2000), 93–94; Wilkinson, *Laredo and the Rio Grande Frontier,* 224–28; Moreno, "The Paso de Jacinto Crossing on the Rio Grande," 152–64.

66. Cass to Lamar, July 23, 1857, Lamar Papers, no. 2522; Christian, "Mirabeau Buonaparte Lamar," 317–24; Senate Documents, No. 194, 47th Cong. 1st sess., 40, 88, 117–25. See also Robert Bromley, "The Nicaraguan Canal Question and the Clayton-Bulwer Treaty," *Nineteenth Century* (January 1901): 100–115, and J. J. Williams, *The Isthmus of Tehuantepec* (New York: D. Appleton), 1852.

67. Richard L. Nostrand, "Mexican Americans circa 1850," *Annals of the Association of American Geographers,* September 1975, 378–90.

68. Florence Scott, *Historical Heritage of the Lower Rio Grande,* 64–68, 145–46; Hinojosa, *Borderlands Town,* 59–63; Thompson, *Sabers on the Rio Grande,* 161; Juan Mora-Torres, *The Making of the Mexican Border: The State, Capitalism, and Society in Nuevo León, 1848–1910* (Austin: University of Texas Press, 2001), 30–36; Wilkinson, *Laredo and the Rio Grande Frontier,* 233; Thompson, *Vaqueros in Blue and Gray* (Austin: Presidial Press, 1977), 59; Scott, *Royal Land Grants,* 26–27.

69. Omar S. Valerio-Jiménez, "Indios Bárbaros" (Ph.D. diss., University of California, 2001), 429–31.

70. Terry G. Jordan, *Immigration to Texas* (Boston: American Press, 1981), 5–27. As a result of aggressive efforts by German overseas colonization societies, by 1850 persons of German birth and parentage, estimated at about nine thousand, outnumbered Mexican Americans in Texas.

71. Hinojosa, *Borderlands Town,* 70–71

72. Fuller, *The Movement for the Acquisition of All Mexico,* 114–20, 153–63.

73. Philip Graham, *The Life and Poems of Mirabeau B. Lamar* (Chapel Hill: University of North Carolina Press, 1938), 76; Tyler et al., eds., *Handbook of Texas,* vol. 1, 458. See also Fredericka Meiners, "Hamilton Prioleau Bee" (master's thesis, Rice University, 1972).

74. Minute Book No. 1, City of Laredo, January 1, 1852, Special Collections, Laredo Public Library; Ronald N. Gray, "Edmund J. Davis: Radical Republican and Reconstruction Governor of Texas" (Ph.D. diss., Texas Tech University, August 1976), 1–10; Tyler et al., eds. *Handbook of Texas,* vol. 2, 526–27.

75. John H. Brown, *Indian Wars and Pioneers of Texas* (Austin: L. E. Daniell, 1880), 720, 676–77, 681; Jerry D. Thompson, *Warm Weather and Bad Whiskey* (El Paso: Texas Western Press, 1991). 11–19; 8th U.S. Census, Webb County, N.A.

76. Minute Book No. 1, January 12, 1852 and February 7, 1852; Rippy, "The Indians of the Southwest in the Diplomacy of the United States and Mexico," 363–96.

77. "Wild Cat and Runaway Negroes," *New York Times,* September 27, 1851, 4; "Further from Texas and Mexico," ibid., September 22, 1853, 1.

78. Philip H. Sheridan, *Personal Memoirs* (New York: Charles L. Webster, 1888), 1, 17–18. See also Grant, *Personal Memoirs,* 69–70.

79. "Citizens of Laredo to the Governor," May 8, 1850, Box 301–19, "Citizens of Laredo to Governor Bell," August 1, 1852, Box 301–19, and "Governor H. Bell to President Millard Fillmore," August 20, 1852, Box 301–18, Governor H. Bell Papers, Texas State Archives, Austin. See also "Message of Governor H. Bell," *Texas State Gazette,* January 15, 1853, and Jerry D. Thompson, *Westward the Texans* (El Paso: Texas Western Press, 1990), 140.

80. Wilkinson, *Laredo and the Rio Grande Frontier,* 238–40; Hinojosa, *Borderlands Town,* 64–7; John S. Ford, *Rip Ford's Texas* (Austin: University of Texas Press, 1963), 162–65, 167; "The Rio Grande Frontier," August 18, 1853, "From Texas," April 3, 1856, and "Southern Texas," *New York Times,* May 22, 1854, 2. See also the Mexican government investigation, *Report of the Committee of Investigation Sent in 1873 by the Mexican Government to the Frontier of Texas,* trans. Baker and Godwin, Printers (New York, 1875).

81. Varios Mexicanos, *Consideraciones sobre la situación política y social de la República Mexicana,* Mexico City, December 1847, in Ramírez, *The Mexican Republic, 1847,* trans. Berge.

82. Bancroft, *History of the North Mexican States and Texas,* 2: 416–19; J. Fred Rippy, "Border Troubles along the Rio Grande, 1848–1860," *SWHQ* (October 1919): 103–104; Mora-Torres, *The Making of the Mexican Border,* 30; Costeloe, *Bonds and Bondholders,* 116–17; Salvucci, "Origins and Progress of U.S.-Mexican Trade," 700–709; Roderic A. Camp, *Politics in Mexico* (New York: Oxford University Press, 1996), 23–32. See also MacLachlan and Rodríguez, *The Forging of the Cosmic Race,* 179–95.

83. Sheridan, *Personal Memoirs,* 18; Thomas T. Smith, *The U.S. Army and the Texas Frontier Economy 1845–1900* (College Station: Texas A&M University Press, 1999), 4–6, 86.

84. Sheridan, *Personal Memoirs,* 27.

85. Smith, *The U.S. Army and the Texas Frontier Economy,* 32, 41, 48–49, 85, 90–92. Overland mail service was contracted to private carriers by the General Post Office. Mail service from Laredo to San Antonio could take as long as ten days. Service from San Antonio to Santa Fe, New Mexico, was scheduled, barring no interruption, to take thirty days. See also "New Mexican Mails," *New York Times,* September 24, 1851, 1.

86. Smith, *The U.S. Army and the Texas Frontier Economy,* 203–13.

87. Assistant Surgeon Glover Perin, "Medical Topography and Diseases of Fort McIntosh," *Statistical Report of the Sickness and Mortality of the Army of the United States,* Senate, 34th Cong., 1st sess., Ex. Doc. No. 96, 360–63.

88. Sheridan, *Personal Memoirs,* 28.

89. Lydia S. Lane, *I Married a Soldier* (Albuquerque: University of New Mexico Press,

1988), 42; Berlandier, *Journey to Mexico,* 1: 271. For a good overview of overland trade and travel along the Río del Norte, see Gregg, *Commerce of the Prairies,* 230–50.

90. Hinojosa, *Borderlands Town,* 69–74; Thompson, *Sabers on the Rio Grande,* 176–78; Emory, *Report of the United States Boundary Survey Made under the Direction of the Secretary of the Interior,* 67; Wilkinson, *Laredo and the Rio Grande Frontier,* 244, 276; LA, Resolutions of June 29, 1850, and June 24, 1854, City Ordinances.

91. "The Rio Grande Frontier," *New York Times,* July 11, 1854, 2. For detailed narratives of hostilities on the Texas frontier, see J. W. Wilbarger, *Indian Depredations in Texas* (Austin: Hutchings Printing House, 1889).

92. U.S. Senate, 32nd Cong., 2nd sess., Ex. Doc. No. 52, 227; ibid., 32nd Cong., 1st sess., Ex. Doc. No. 80, 55–58; Rippy, "Border Troubles along the Rio Grande," 94–98; Mora-Torres, *The Making of the Mexican Border,* 62.

93. U.S. Senate, Committee on Foreign Relations, *Petition of Samuel A. Belden,* 32nd Cong., 1st sess., Ex. Doc. No. 80, June 15, 1852, 80.

94. Rippy, "Border Troubles along the Rio Grande," 95; Del Castillo, *The Treaty of Guadalupe Hidalgo,* 195–96. See also José María Ortiz M. to Anthony Butler, April 14, 1936, House, *United States and Mexico,* 25th Cong., 2nd sess., Doc. No. 351, 590–91.

95. Senate, 44th Cong., 2nd sess., Ex. Doc. 31, claims 131 and 113, 24–25.

96. "Affairs on the Mexican Border," *New York Times,* April 9, 1852, 2; Domenech, *Missionary Adventures in Texas and Mexico,* 327–29; Mora-Torres, *The Making of the Mexican Border,* 22–23, 29, 38.

97. Samuel Bell and James B. Smallwood, *The Zona Libre, 1858–1905: A Problem in American Diplomacy* (El Paso: Texas Western Press, 1982); Zorrilla, Flaquer, and Herrera Pérez, *Tamaulipas,* 196–7; W. H. Chatfield, *The Twin Cities of the Border* (New Orleans: E. Brandao, 1893; repr., 1959), 33.

98. House, Committee on Foreign Relations, *Relations of the United States with Mexico,* 45th Cong., 2nd sess., Report No. 701, April 25, 1878; J. Fred Rippy, *The United States and Mexico, 1821–1924* (New York: Alfred A. Knopf, 1926), 282–95.

99. "The Mexican Frontier," *New York Times,* January 8, 1878, 1; Thompson, *Laredo: A Pictorial History,* 149–52.

100. R. E. Lee to AG, U.S. Army, Washington, D.C., April 11, 1860, as seen in *Troubles on Texas Border,* U.S. House, 36th Cong., 1st sess., Ex. Doc. No. 81, May 5, 1860, 83–84. See also Domenech, *Missionary Adventures in Texas and Mexico,* 117–39, 327–29. See also John H. Jenkins, *Robert E. Lee on the Rio Grande* (Austin: Jenkins Publishing, 1988).

101. Juan N. Cortina, "To the Mexican Inhabitants of the State of Texas," article, November 23, 1859, in John L. Haynes Papers, Box 2J144, American History Center, Austin.

102. Major Heintzelman to Col. R. E. Lee, March 1, 1860, House Ex. Doc. 81, 36th Cong., 1st sess., 13; Chatfield, *Twin Cities,* 23. See also Jerry Thompson and Lawrence T. Jones, *Civil War and Revolution on the Rio Grande Frontier* (Austin: TSHA, 2004).

103. *Message of the President,* U.S. House, Congressional Globe, 36th Cong., 1st sess., December 19, 1859; "The Civil War at Matamoros," *Frank Leslie's Illustrated Newspaper,* April 9, 1864; Utley, *Lone Star Justice,* 107–19. See also Rippy, *The United States and Mexico,* 296–310. The Richardson map of the State of Texas in the 1859 *Texas Almanac* confirming the remoteness of South Texas, labeled Webb County an area of "Wild Horses and Cattle."

104. Governor Sam Houston, April 14, 1860, Austin, Texas, as see in *Troubles on Texas Frontier,* House, 36th Cong., 1st sess., Ex. Doc. No. 81, 95. See also Rippy, "Border Troubles along the Rio Grande," 104–11.

105. Hinojosa, *Borderlands Town,* 74–80; Col. Jos. K. F. Mansfield to U.S. Inspector General, December 13, 1860, as seen in Jerry D. Thompson, ed., *Texas and Mexico on the Eve*

of the Civil War (Albuquerque: University of New Mexico Press, 2001, 143–50. The 1860 Texas Census exceeded 600,000 for the first time: 416,999 "free men" and 184,956 designated as "slave."

106. Quoted in A. F. Muir, "Sam Houston and the Civil War," *Texana* (Fall 1968): 282–83. See also Randolph B. Campbell, *Sam Houston* (New York: HarperCollins, 1993), 158; Wisehart, *Sam Houston: American Giant,* 594–628; and Marquis James, *The Raven: A Biography of Sam Houston* (New York: Blue Ribbon Books, 1919), 408–24.

107. Carl N. Tyson, "Texas Men for War: Cotton for Economy," *Journal of the West* (January 1975): 130–48; Walter L. Buenger, *Secession and the Union in Texas* (Austin: University of Texas Press, 1984), 90–1; Thompson, *Vaqueros in Blue and Gray,* 71–74, 81–83. For Texas "Causes of Secession," see Louis J. Wortham, *A History of Texas* (Ft. Worth: Wortham and Molyneauz, 1924), 4: 391–400.

108. James A. Irby, *Backdoor at Bagdad: The Civil War on the Rio Grande* (El Paso: Texas Western Press, 1977), 18–21. See also "Our Interest in Mexico," *New York Times,* July 11, 1861, 4.

109. Domenech, *Missionary Adventures in Texas and Mexico,* 355–56.

110. John Cheetham, "The Cotton Supply," *London Times,* November 3, 1863, 8; Don Buenaventura Carlos Aribau, "Influencia de la situación de los Estados Unidos, sobre el comercio de esta república con España," ca. 1861, Folio 363, CCBN, Madrid. The *London Times* business section closely tracked world cotton markets, noting: "Increase [of imports] upon 1863, 585,000 bales, or 31 percent. A consumption [for manufacturing] of four days per week, based upon the data of 1860, would require 32,400 bales, and allow as additional export of 2,000 bales weekly over the present year, we have a weekly demand of 46,400, or a total for the year of 2,412,000 bales, to meet which is the estimated import [for 1864] of 2,445,000. In this calculation I have assumed the continuance of the war in America, from which country it is not unreasonable to estimate a supply for 1864 equal to 1863." See also Stephen Yafa, *Big Cotton: How a Humble Fiber Created Fortunes* (New York: Viking, 2005), 163–71.

111. "Cotton," *Galveston Daily News,* June 22, 1865, 2; Clement Eaton, *The Growth of Southern Civilization, 1790–1860* (New York: Harper and Row, 1861), 45, 242; Ron C. Tyler, "Cotton on the Border, 1861–1865," *SWHQ* (April 1970): 456–77; Fredericka Meiners, "The Texas Border Cotton Trade, 1862–1863," *Civil War History* (December 1977): 193–206.

112. BG H. Bee to Major Santos Benavides, November 9, 1863, U.S. War Department, *The War of the Rebellion: A Compilation of the Official Records of the Union and Confederate Armies* (hereafter O.R.) (Washington D.C.: GPO, 1889), vol. 26, pt. 2, 398–99; Robert W. Delaney, "Matamoros, Port of Texas during the Civil War," *SWHQ* (April 1955): 473; Charles W. Ramsdell, "The Texas State Military Board, 1862–1865," *SWHQ* (April 1924): 265; Irby, *Bagdad,* 26–30; James W. Daddysman, *The Matamoros Trade: Confederate Commerce, Diplomacy, and Intrigue* (Newark: University of Delaware Press, 1984), 112–44; Annie Cowling, "The Civil War Trade of the Lower Rio Grande Valley" (master's thesis, University of Texas, Austin, August 1926), 10–13.

113. Santos Benavides to the people of the frontier, Houston *Tri-Weekly Telegraph,* December 18, 1863.

114. William Watson, *The Adventures of a Blockade Runner* (London: Unwin, 1892), 1–27; Bancroft, *History of the North Mexican States and Texas,* 2: 457; Tom Lea, *The King Ranch* (Boston: Little, Brown, 1957), 1: 192; Arthur James Lyon Fremantle, *Three Months in the Southern States: April–June, 1863* (New York: John Bradburn, 1864), 8–9; "Our New Orleans Correspondence—Matters of Texas," *New York Times,* October 19, 1863, 4; Delaney, "Matamoros, Port for Texas during the Civil War," 473–87; *Official Naval Records, War of the Rebellion,* Ser. 1, Vol. 19, 180. See also James Arthur Irby, "Line of the Rio Grande: War and Trade on

the Confederate Frontier, 1861–1865" (Ph.D. diss., University of Georgia, 1969), and "Letters Received by the Office of the Adjutant General (Main Series)," Roll 321, Microcopy No. 689, Washington, D.C., National Archives, 1967. While there was a brisk and regular trade with New Orleans, New York, London, and Cuba, the British used Belize as both a production and staging area for merchandise destined for Texas.

115. O.R., BG Bee to Capt E. Turner, November 11, 1863, vol. 26, pt. II, 405–406; Tyler, "Cotton on the Border, 1861–1865," 461–63.

116. Letter, Col. Santos Benavides to Col. John S. Ford, March 19, 1864, as seen in John H. Keck personal papres.

117. Frank C. Pierce, *A Brief History of the Lower Rio Grande Valley* (Menasha, Wis.: Banta, 1917), 54–8, 137; Jerry D. Thompson, *Mexican Texans in the Union Army* (El Paso: Texas Western Press, 1986), 24; James, Farber, *Texas, C.S.A.* (New York: The Jackson Co., 1947), 203–206; John M. Hart, *Empire and Revolution: The American in Mexico since the Civil War* (Berkeley: University of California Press, 2002), 211–12; John D. Riley, "Battle of Laredo," in "Santos Benavides: His Influence on the Lower Rio Grande, 1823–1891" (Ph.D., diss., Texas Christian University, May 1976), 166–76.

118. O.R., Gen. N. Banks to General, November 7, 1963, vol. 26, pt. 1, 402–404; Daddysman, *The Matamoros Trade,* 127–44; Ron Tyler, *Santiago Vidaurri and the Southern Confederacy* (Austin: TSHA, 1973), 13–156; Tyler, "Cotton on the Border, 1961–1965," 456–77; Ford, *Rip Ford's Texas,* 358–59; Alfred J. Hanna and Kathryn A. Hanna, "Back Door of the Confederacy: The Rio Grande, 1861–1865," in *Napoleon III and Mexico* (Chapel Hill: University of North Carolina Press, 1971), 155–66. See also Isidro Vizcaya Canales, *Los orígenes de la industrialización de Monterrey, 1867–1920* (Monterrey: 1969), xix.

119. O.R., Patricio Milmo to S. Hart, December 5, 1863, vol. 53, 948–49; Delaney, "Matamoros, Port of Texas," 481–5; New Orleans *Time Picayune,* November 12, 30, and December 1, 2, 1864; *New York Times,* February 7, 1983; Tyler, "Cotton on the Border," 463–64. See also Inés Herrera Canales, *El comercio exterior de México, 1821–1875* (Mexico City: El Colegio de México, 1977), 25–39.

120. "Late News from Texas," New Orleans *Times Picayune,* March 18, 1865, 1.

121. Tyler, "Cotton on the Border," 477.

122. International Boundary and Water Commission (IBWC), "Flow of the Rio Grande and Related Data," *Water Bulletin,* no. 70, 2000, 56; Karl F. Keller, "Study of Occurrence of Floods on the Rio Grande at Laredo, Texas for 211-year-period: 1746 through 1956" (El Paso: IBWC, December 1956), 2; Jerry E. Mueller, *Restless River* (El Paso: Texas Western Press, 1975), 93.

CHAPTER 4

1. Eric Foner, *Reconstruction: America's Unfinished Revolution, 1863–1877* (New York: HarperCollins, 2005), 382; Michael Perman, *Emancipation and Reconstruction, 1862–1879* (Arlington Heights, Ill.: Harlan Davidson, 1987), 71–73. See also James A. Baggett, "Origins of Early Texas Republican Leadership," *Journal of Southern History* (August 1974): 441–54, and Allen W. Trelease, "Who Were the Scalawags?" *Journal of Southern History* (November 1963): 445–46.

2. "The Rio Grande Order," *New York Times,* October 22, 1877, 2; Kenneth M. Stampp, *The Era of Reconstruction, 1865–1877* (New York: Vintage, 1967), 83–185, 198; Trelease, "Who Were the Scalawags?" 458; Mark W. Summers, *Railroad, Reconstruction, and the Gospel of Prosperity: Aid under the Radical Republican, 1865–1877* (Princeton, N.J.: Princeton University Press, 1984), 83–84; U.S. Congress, House of Representatives, *Depredations on the Frontiers of Texas,* 43rd Cong., 1st sess., Ex. Doc. No. 257, 13–19.

3. Robert M. Utley, *Frontier Regulars: The United States Army and the Indians, 1866–1891* (New York: Macmillan, 1973), 172; Wilkinson, *Laredo and the Rio Grande Frontier,* 311; quote is in Dobie, *Tales of Old-Time Texas,* 93.

4. O. C. Fisher and J. C. Dykes, *King Fisher: His Life and Times* (Norman: University of Oklahoma Press, 1966), 38, 67.

5. Dobie, *A Vaquero of the Brush Country,* 65–71; Odie Arámbula, "Bad Guys Easy to Find after War," *Laredo Morning Times,* August 7, 2005, C-1.

6. *El Nicaragüense,* August 2, 1856; San Francisco *Chronicle,* November 28 and December 3, 1909, January 23, 1940; Caleb Coker, ed., *The News from Brownsville* (Austin: TSHA, 1992), 102, 195, 206, 307. See also Albert Z. Carr, *The World and William Walker* (New York: Harper and Row, 1963); Minute Book No. 1, City of Laredo, October 18, 1969.

7. Minute Book No. 1, City of Laredo, January 3, 1873.

8. Fisher and Dykes, *King Fisher,* 24.

9. U.S. Congress, House of Representatives, *Depredations on the Frontiers of Texas,* 16–19; Ibid., Committee on Foreign Relations, *Relations of the United States with Mexico,* 45 Cong., 2nd sess., Report No. 701, April 25, 1878, IV–X.

10. Utley, *Frontier Regulars,* 16–174; Fisher and Dykes, *King Fisher,* 38; Dobie, *Vaquero of the Brush Country,* 43–44, 54; Jerry D. Thompson and Lawrence T. Jones, *Civil War and Reconstruction on the Rio Grande Frontier* (Austin: TSHA, 2004), 131.

11. Wilkinson, *Laredo and the Rio Grande Frontier,* 311–25; RG 94, General orders no. 75, Fort McIntosh.

12. U.S. Congress, *Relations of the United States with Mexico,* Report 701, VIII. See also U.S. Congress, House of Representatives, Committee on Military Affairs, *The Texas Border Troubles,* 45th Cong., 2nd sess., Mis. Doc. No. 64, 1–312.

13. Fisher and Dykes, *King Fisher,* 28; See also George Dunham, *Taming the Nueces Strip: The Story of McNelly's Rangers* (Austin: University of Texas Press, 1962).

14. Dobie, *The Longhorns,* 36–37.

15. Message of Governor Richard Coke to the Fourteenth Legislature, January 26, 1874, Texas State Archives; Gammel, *Laws of Texas,* 86–90; Utley, *Lone Star Justice,* 142–47; U.S. Congress, *Relations of the United States with Mexico,* Report 701, VII–VIII. See also "The W . . . Rio Grande Frontier," *New York Times,* October 22, 1877, 2, from which the quote is taken.

16. Thomas Gilgan, U.S. Commercial Agent in Nuevo Laredo to William Hunter, Second Assistant Secretary of State, August 17, 1872, Dispatches from United States Consular Officials in Nuevo Laredo, Mexico, 1871–1906, Roll No. 1, National Archives Microfilm Publications, n.p.

17. Brown, *Indian Wars and Pioneers of Texas,* 613–14; Thompson, *Vaqueros in Blue and Gray,* 8; "From Texas," *New York Times,* April 3, 1856, 2. See also J. L. Haynes, "History of Cameron County," *Evening Ranchero,* July 5, 1876, 1, J. L. Haynes Papers.

18. V. M. Lehmann, *Forgotten Legions: Sheep in the Rio Grande Plains of Texas* (El Paso: Texas Western Press, 1969), 49–53, 79–103; Paul H. Carlson, *Texas Woollybacks* (College Station: Texas A&M University Press, 1982), 62–65; Joseph G. McCoy, *Cattle Trade of the West and Southwest* (Kansas City: Ramsey, Millett and Hudson, 1874), 4–38; Wilkinson, *Laredo and the Rio Grande Frontier,* 327–29; Harry Sinclair Drago, *Great American Cattle Trails* (New York: Dodd, Mead, 1965), 93–94, 101; David Dary, *Entrepreneurs of the Old West* (New York: Alfred A. Knopf, 1989), 210–11; U.S. Congress, *Relations of the United States with Mexico,* Report 701, vii–xiii.

19. Minute Book No. 1 March 16, 1874, July 7, 1874 and December 16, 31, 1873; "The Mexican Frontier: Affairs along the Rio Grande," *New York Times,* January 8, 1878, 1.

20. Minute Book No. 2, June 23, 1878, August 1, 1878, November 30, 1878; "The Rio Grande Border: History of the Present Trouble," *New York Times,* October 22, 1877, 2.

21. See Barbara S. Rozek, *Come to Texas: Enticing Immigrants, 1865–1915* (College Station: Texas A& M University Press, 2003).

22. Minute Book No. 2, June 23, 1878. August 1, 1878, and November 30, 1878. W. H. Prescott's notes and research bibliography written in his hand can be seen in Folio 295, Cervantes Collection, CCBN, Madrid.

23. "A Texas Railway Project," *New York Times,* January 8, 1880, 1; "Laredo: Its Railroad Connections," *Laredo Times,* August 24, 1881, 1. Nuevo Laredo was estimated to also have a population of 5,000 in 1880.

24. *Laredo Times,* July 6, 1881.

25. Ibid., July 13, and August 24, 1881.

26. Ibid., August 24, 1881; Thompson, *Warm Weather and Bad Whiskey,* 51.

27. *Laredo Times,* July 27 and August 3, 1881.

28. Fehrenbach, *Fire and Blood,* 458–9; Fisher and Dykes, *King Fisher,* 41, 46.

29. Lott and Martínez, *The Kingdom of Zapata,* 101; Mora-Torres, *The Making of the Mexican Border,* 52; John M. Hart, *Revolutionary Mexico: The Coming and Process of the Mexican Revolution* (Berkeley: University of California Press, 1987), 6–9, 116–19.

30. Samuel Hays, *The Response to Industrialism 1885–1914* (Chicago: University of Chicago Press, 1957), 116–20.

31. Thompson, *Laredo: A Pictorial History,* 146–47.

32. Quoted in ibid., 147. The use of the term *manufacturing* refers to the New England style of production using water power.

33. Horgan, *Great River,* 713.

34. Lott and Martínez, *The Kingdom of Zapata,* 170–72.

35. Thompson, *Laredo: A Pictorial History,* 148.

36. Brownson Malsch, *Indianola: The Mother of Western Texas* (Austin: Shoal Creek Publishers, 1978), 55–100. Indianola was founded in 1844—and was the hub of Gulf of Mexico trade on the Texas coast—to include an entry port for European immigrants, yet was completely destroyed by a hurricane in August 1886, and with the closing of the U.S. Post Office on October 4, 1887, the town ceased to exist.

37. August Santleben, *A Texas Pioneer: Early Staging and Overland Freighting on the Frontier of Texas and Mexico* (New York: 1910), 108.

38. West, *The Mining Community in Northern New Spain,* 80–88.

39. Wilkinson, *Laredo and the Rio Grande Frontier,* 326. See also Santleben, *A Texas Pioneer,* 106–11.

40. Wilkinson, *Laredo and the Rio Grande Frontier,* 325–6; Lott and Martínez, *The Kingdom of Zapata,* 31; Jackson, *Texas by Terán,* 3.

41. Glenn Porter, *The Rise of Big Business, 1860–1910* (Arlington Heights, Ill.: AHM Publishing, 1973), 7; Ron Chernow, *Titan: The Life of John D. Rockefeller, Sr.* (New York: Vintage, 1998), 211–56.

42. Webb, *The Great Plains,* 279; Hays, *The Response to Industrialism, 1885–1914,* 118.

43. Maury Klein, *The Life and Legend of Jay Gould* (Baltimore: Johns Hopkins University Press, 1986), 296, 249–58; Reed, *A History of the Texas Railroads,* 3–9; Stephen H. Haber, *Industry and Underdevelopment: The Industrialization of Mexico, 1890–1940* (Stanford. Calif.: Stanford University Press, 1989), 15.

44. *Laredo Directory—1889: Description of Laredo, Texas,* reprinted by Central Power and Light, 1966, Special Collections, Laredo Public Library; *Laredo Times,* July 6, 1881, August 24, 1881; Klein, *Jay Gould,* 259, 304; David M. Pletcher, "The Building of the Mexican Railway,"

HAHR 30 (February 1950): 26–62; Graf, "The Economic History of the Lower Rio Grande Valley," 7.

45. Reed, *A History of the Texas Railroads,* 319.

46. Minute Book, May 1, 2, 1872; Klein, *Jay Gould,* 258–59.

47. Austin *Daily State Journal,* October 11, 1872; the quote is from "The Indian Raids in Western Texas," *New York Times,* January 22, 1972, 4.

48. Thomas Gilgan, U.S. Commercial Agent in Nuevo Laredo to William Hunter, Second Assistant Secretary of State, August 17, 1872, Dispatches from United States Consular Officials in Nuevo Laredo, Mexico, 1871–1906, Roll No. 1, National Archives Microfilm Publications; *Texas Frontier Troubles,* 44th Cong., 1st sess., Report 343, 1876; Chuck Parsons and Marianne E. H. Little, *Captain L. H. McNelly: Texas Ranger* (Austin: State House Press, 2001), 162–67, 176.

49. Annual Report of the Texas Mexican Railway Company, October 1, 1891 (articles filed March 13, 1875 as the CC, SD & NG RR Co.), Texas Railroad Commission Papers, Box 2001–025–1, Texas State Archives, Austin; Reed, *A History of the Texas Railroads,* 472–76. See also J. L. Allhands, *Railroads to the Rio* (Salado, Tex.: The Anson Jones Press, 1960), 19, 32.

50. Annual Report of the Texas Mexican Northern Railroad Company, October 1, 1891 (articles filed February 22, 1882), Texas Railroad Commission Papers, Box 2001–025–1, TSA; Laredo Minute Book, November 15, 1880; A. L. Allhands, *Uriah Lott* (San Antonio: Naylor, 1949), 12–22; "Railroads in Mexico," *The Railroad Gazette,* December 31, 1880, 701; Lott [no known relationship to Uriah] and Martínez, *The Kingdom of Zapata,* 11–13. See also Paul S. Taylor, *An American-Mexican Frontier* (Chapel Hill: University of North Carolina Press, 1934, 78–83.

51. Hart, *Empire and Revolution,* 129.

52. "Texas Railroads," *New York Times,* June 2, 1881, from which the Vidaurri quote is taken; "Laredo: Its Railroad Connections," *Laredo Times,* August 24, 1881.

53. "Reciprocity with Mexico," *New York Times,* January 12, 1883, 4; Hart, *Empire and Revolution,* 108–23; Vásquez and Meyer, *United States and Mexico,* 89–90; San Antonio *Express,* March 7, 1876. Secretary of State Frelinghuysen (1881–85) was equally involved with persistent cross-border Indian raids on the U.S.-Canadian border; see Michel Hogue, "Disputing the Medicine Line: The Plains Crees and the Canadian-American Border: 1876–1885," *Montana: The Magazine of Western History* (Winter 2002).

54. Reed, *A History of the Texas Railroads,* 543–58; Klein, *Jay Gould,* 259, 266–71; Rippy, *United States and Mexico,* 312; Chernow, *Titan,* 218, 266.

55. David M. Pletcher, "General William S. Rosecrans and the Mexican Transcontinental Railroad," *Mississippi Valley Historical Review* (March 1952): 657–78, from which the quote is taken; James Baughman, "The Evolution of Rail-Water Systems of Transportation in the Gulf Southwest, 1836–1890," *Journal of Southern History* (August 1968): 357–81.

56. Klein, *Jay Gould,* 270–72; Utley, *Lone Star Justice,* 226–27; Fehrenbach, *Fire and Blood,* 453; Dary, *Entrepreneurs of the Old West,* 192–222, 319–20; Hart, *Empire and Revolution,* 110–12; John S. Spratt, *The Road to Spindletop: Economic Change in Texas, 1875–1901* (Austin: University of Texas, 1955), 34.

57. U.S. Congress, House of Representatives, Committee on Foreign Affairs, *Relations of the United States with Mexico,* 45th Cong., 2nd sess., Report No. 701, April 25, 1878, XI–XIX, XL–XLII; U.S. Army, Office of the Adjutant General, "Compiled papers relating to the Frelinghuysen-Romero Agreement of July 29, 1882," Adjutant Generals Office, National Archives, RG 94, File 663, No. 689, roll 81; "Protocol of Reciprocal Pursuit," *Laredo Times,* October 28, 1882; Mora-Torres, *The Making of the Mexican Border,* 52–57. See also William R. Lewis, "The Hayes Administration and Mexico," *SWHQ* (October 1920): 140–53.

58. New York *Herald,* March 4, 1877, July 17, 1877.

59. John W. Foster to Eleutario Avila, Mexico City, November 26, 1878, in *Papers Related to the Foreign Relations of the United States,* 1879, 791, in Mora-Torres, *The Making of the Mexican Border,* 56. See also John W. Foster, *Diplomatic Memoirs* (London: Constable, 1910), 108–16.

60. Foster, *Diplomatic Memoirs,* 110.

61. U.S. Congress, Senate, *Message of the President,* 36th Cong., 1st sess., December 19, 1859.

62. Robert D. Gregg, *Influence of Border Troubles on Relations between the United States and Mexico* (Baltimore: Johns Hopkins Press, 1937), 547–49; John Coatsworth, "Railroads, Landholdings, and Agrarian Protest in the Early *Porfiriato,*" *HAHR* (February 1974): 65–71; William K. Meyers, "Politics, Vested Right, and Economic Growth in Porfirian Mexico," *HAHR* (August 1977): 401–24. See also George E. Paulsen, "Fraud, Honor, and Trade: The United States–Mexico Dispute over the Claims of La Abra Company, 1875–1902," *Pacific Historical Review* (May 1983): 175–90.

63. Charles W. Hackett, "The Recognition of the Díaz Government by the United States," *SWHQ* (July 1924): 34–55; Hart, *Empire and Revolution,* 109–11, 120–21.

64. "A Texas Railway Project," *New York Times,* January 8, 1880. See also Hart, *Revolutionary Mexico,* 127–28; Annual Report of the International and Great Northern Railroad Company, October 1, 1891, Texas Railroad Commission Papers, Box 2001–025–1, Texas State Archives, Austin; Reed, *A History of the Texas Railroads,* 160; James L. Rock and W. I. Smith, *Southern and Western Texas Guide, 1878* (St. Louis: A. H. Granger, 1878), 217–19. Ironically, the land and tax subsidy was little help to the cash-intensive requirements of the I&GN, who entered receivership in 1878 and reemerged following an affiliation with the Missouri Pacific RR in 1879.

65. Krauze, *Mexico,* 10.

66. "Texas Railroads," *New York Times,* June 2, 1881; Hart, *Empire and Revolution,* 123, 131–66; Chernow, *Titan,* 255–56; Mario Cerutti, Isabel Ortega, and Lydia Palacios, "Empresarios y empresas en el norte de Mexico," *European Review of Latin American and Caribbean Studies* (October 2000): 5–7.

67. "Mexican National," *The Railroad Gazette,* October 22, 1880, 563; "Jay Gould's Latest Purchase," *New York Times,* December 21, 1880, 3; Reed, *A History of the Texas Railroads,* 320–21. The standard gauge of railroads varied from 6 feet to 5 1/2 feet, and finally was set at 4 feet 8 1/2 inches; see Gammel, *Laws of Texas,* vol. 3, February 11, 1854, 1539.

68. Klein, *Jay Gould,* 304, 347.

69. Annette M. Ludeman, *A History of La Salle County* (Quanah, Tex.: Nortex Press, 1975), 8–10.

70. "Railroads in Mexico," *New York Times,* December 24, 1880, 2; "Mexican Railroad Agreement," *The Railroad Gazette,* November 26, 1880, 636; Jean E. Smith, *Grant* (New York: Simon and Schuster, 2001), 618–19.

71. "Jay Gould Coming East," *New York Times,* March 11, 1881, 5; Minute Book No. 2, February 17 and 18, April 1, June 6, July 27, and September 5, 1881.

72. "Heavy Rains Damage Railway Bridge," *Galveston Daily News,* August 22, 1882, and "Laredo: Damage from High Water," August 25, 1882; "The Rio Grande Still on the Rise," September 5, 1882, and "Serious Damage by High Waters," September 6, 1882. General William T. Sherman was no stranger to Texas, having served in the region during Reconstruction, see Sam Houston Dixon, "Sherman's Iron Hand in Dealing with Indians Won Fame in Texas for War Raider of South," *Houston Chronicle,* May 14, 1922, 14.

73. "The Railroad in Mexico," *Laredo Times,* October 19, 1882; "Corpus Christi," *Galveston Daily News,* March 5, 1882; "Laredo," *Galveston Daily News,* March 9 and 20, 1882; Klein, *Jay Gould,* 274–75; "Mexican National RR," *The Chronicle,* January 1898, 85; "Advent of the Mex-

ican Railway," undated manuscript, Railroad File, Box 75, Special Collections, Laredo Public Library; David M. Pletcher, *Rails, Mines and Progress* (Port Washington, N.Y.: Kennikat Press, 1972), 68–9, 151–71, 178–81; Don M. Coerver, *The Porfirian Interregnum: The Presidency of Manuel González of Mexico, 1880–1884* (Ft. Worth: Texas Christian University Press, 1979), 200–210; Lorena M. Parlee, "The Impact of United States Railroad Unions on Organized Labor and Government Policy in Mexico, 1880–1911," *HAHR* 64 (August 1984): 443–75. The Mexican National held controlling ownership of stock in the Texas Mexican Railroad.

74. E. A. Atlee General Bio File, Center for American History, Austin.

75. J. Fred Rippy, "The British Investment 'Boom' of the 1880s in Latin America," *HAHR* 29 (May 1949): 281–86; Hart, *Empire and Revolution,* 123, 129–30, 152; W. B. Devereux, "The Future of Mexican Railroad and Mining Enterprises," *The Railroad Gazette,* October 27, 1882, 660–61; Carleton Beals, *Porfirio Díaz: Dictator of Mexico* (Philadelphia: J. B. Lippincott, 1932), 346: Vázquez and Meyer, *United States and Mexico,* 85; Annual Report of the I&GN, October 21, 1891, Texas Railroad Commission Papers, Texas State Archives. For an excellent first-person account of commercial and investment activities in Mexico during this period, see Thomas R. Crittenden, U.S. Consul-General in Mexico City from 1893 to 1897, in Walter V. Scholes, "Mexico in 1896 as Viewed by an American Consul," *HAHR* 30 (May 1950): 250–57.

76. "Laredo," *Galveston Daily News,* October 21, 1882. See also Salvucci, "Origins and Progress of U.S.-Mexican Trade," 723; Hart, *Revolutionary Mexico,* 133–35, 140–41.

77. Wilkinson, *Laredo and the Rio Grande Frontier,* 364; Menno Vellinga, "The Monterrey Industry and North American Markets: Past and Present Dynamics," *Journal of Borderlands Studies* (*JBS*) (Spring 1995): 45–52.

78. Thompson, *Laredo: A Pictorial History,* 21; *Laredo Lodge No. 547 A.F.&A.M.* [Centennial history 1881–1981], Laredo, December 12, 1981, 22; J. W. Falvella, *A Souvenir Album of Laredo* (Laredo: Falvella, 1917), 7. The site for the first Webb County courthouse was at Flores and Matamoros streets and was purchased for $1,000 in 1880. A bond issue of $40,000 paid for construction.

79. Mario Cerutti, *Burguesia y capitalismo en Monterrey, 1850–1910* (Mexico City: Claves Latinoamericanos, 1983), 20–87; Haber, *Industry and Underdevelopment,* 75; Pletcher, *Rails, Mines, and Progress,* 170; Anita Purcell, ed., *Frontier Mexico, 1875–1894: Letters of William L. Purcell* (San Antonio: Naylor, 1963), 92.

80. *Laredo Times,* July 27, 1881. Milmo also established a bank in Eagle Pass, Texas.

81. "Milmo National Bank Building," ibid., January 18, 1883.

82. *Laredo Directory of 1889,* 1.

83. Egbert L. Viele, "Our Southern Frontier: The East and West Boundary Line between the United States and Mexico," *Frank Leslie's Popular Monthly,* June 1878, 724–34; Sebron S. Wilcox, "The Laredo City Election and Riot of April, 1886," *Southwestern Historical Quarterly* (July 1941): 3–5. See also issues of the *Laredo Times,* 1882–1890; Brown, *Indian Wars and Pioneers of Texas,* 681–82.

84. E. R. Tarver, *Laredo the Gateway between the United States and Mexico: An Illustrated Description of the Future City of the Great Southwest* (Laredo: Daily Times Print, 1889), 5–6.

85. Ella Devine, "History of Electric Utility: Laredo, Texas," unpublished manuscript sponsored by Central Power and Light Company, 1969, 1–3; Willie B. Barry, "History of Water Utility: Laredo Texas," unpublished manuscript sponsored by Central Power and Light Company, 1969, 1–3.

86. Tarver, *Laredo the Gateway,* 1–28. See also *First Annual Report of the Agricultural Bureau of the Department of Agriculture, Insurance, Statistics, and History* (Austin: State Printing Office, 1889), 230–31.

87. "Laredo: The Gate City of Southern Texas," *Frank Leslie's Illustrated Newspaper,* October 4, 1890, 17–20.

88. Ibid.; Tarver, *Laredo the Gateway,* 3; Arthur Foster, map, "The Gateway of the Two Largest Republics in the World" (Laredo: Laredo Improvement Company, February 23, 1889), as seen in Special Collections, Laredo Public Library; "Mexican Street Railways," *Street Railway Gazette* (New York), May 1888, 22; "Laredo, Tex.," *Street Railway Gazette* (New York), April 1890, 193.

89. As seen in *Laredo Directory of 1889.*

90. "Laredo," *Frank Leslie's Illustrated Newspaper,* 17–20; Reed, *A History of the Texas Railroads,* 474.

91. "The Editor of the Waco Day Visits Laredo," *Omaha Daily Bee,* April 12, 1890, 3.

92. Thompson, *Warm Weather and Bad Whiskey,* 43–49.

93. Wilcox, "The Laredo City Election and Riot of April, 1886," 1–6; *Laredo Daily Times,* August 23, 1886; *Galveston Daily News,* April 15, 1886.

94. Thompson, *Laredo: A Pictorial History,* 183–94.

95. Ibid. See also C. L. Sonnichsen, "Boots and Sandals," in *Ten Texas Feuds* (Albuquerque: University of New Mexico, 1957,) 159–66.

96. Thompson, *Warm Weather and Bad Whiskey,* 86–97; San Antonio *Express,* April 8, 9, 11, 13, 18, 1886; *Galveston Daily News,* April 15, 1886; Wilcox, "The Laredo City Election and Riot of April, 1886," 13–15. See also Thompson, *Laredo: A Pictorial History,* 183–94.

97. *Galveston Daily News,* April 6, 1886.

98. Thompson, *Warm Weather and Bad Whiskey,* 100–102; New Orleans *Times Picayune,* April 8, 9, 10, 1886; *New York Times,* April 8, 10, 1886; *Galveston Daily News,* April 8 and 13, 1886; San Antonio *Express,* April 9, 10, 11, 15, 1886; *Austin American Statesman,* April 9, 10, 1886.

99. Wilkinson, *Laredo and the Rio Grande Frontier,* 370–71, from which the Benavides quote is taken; Thompson, *Warm Weather and Bad Whiskey,* 123–44.

CHAPTER 5

1. "Wonderful Growth," *New York Times,* May 29, 1890, 5.

2. "Mexico's Best Customer," ibid., January 2, 1890, 2, and "Special," September 17, 1902, 3. See also Hart, *Empire and Revolution,* 73–154 and Héctor Aguilar Camín and Lorenzo Meyer, *In the Shadow of the Mexican Revolution* (Austin: University of Texas Press, 1993). 1–7.

3. Thompson, *Warm Weather and Bad Whiskey,* 42; *City of Laredo v. Raymond Martin,* Texas Supreme Court Records, TSA; "Mexico's Best Customer," *New York Times,* January 2, 1890, 2.

4. *United States Statutes at Large* (1885), Vol. 23, March 29, 1884, 30–31.

5. Porfirio Díaz and Carlos Pacheco, Secretary of State, Proclamation of Congress, June 6, 1887, as seen in the Laredo Bridge Company Papers, Box 4, Special Collections, Laredo Public Library; Andrew M. Gault, "The Historic Laredo Crossing of the Rio Grande," *American Bridge, Tunnel and Turnpike Association,* December 1953, 40–42.

6. "Laredo Bridge Historical Notes," Laredo Bridge Company Paper; "Swept by a Cyclone," *New York Times,* June 18, 1893, 1.

7. Thomas T. Smith, *The U.S. Army and the Texas Frontier Economy, 1845–1900* (College Station: Texas A&M University Press, 1999), 170.

8. "Laredo: The Gate City of Southern Texas," 17, from which the quote is taken, and "North Laredo Land, Irrigation, and Water Company," *Frank Leslie's Illustrated Newspaper,* October 4, 1890, 20; "Wonderful Growth," May 29, 1880, 5, and "Swept by a Cyclone," *New York Times,* June 18, 1893, 1; "Still Next to Head," *Laredo Weekly Times,* January 12, 1894;

Mora-Torres, *The Making of the Mexican Border,* 126–36, 264–67. See also U.S. Census, Webb County 1890.

9. *Laredo Weekly Times,* January 4, 21, 1894.

10. Arguindegui and McDonell, eds., *Directory of the City of Laredo, 1900* (Laredo: E. Arguindegui [Printers], 1900), 15–16, 62, 79; Invitation, Laredo Casino Association to Max Deutz, August 8, 1894, author's collection.

11. *Laredo Weekly Times,* January 20, 25, 26, 1894.

12. Ibid., January 31, 1894. Full service mail delivery was based on the decennial census, which had as a requirement at least 10,000 inhabitants. The Laredo census in 1890 numbered 11,319.

13. Ibid., February 18, 21, 22, 28, 1894; James W. Westgate, *After the Dinosaurs: A Texas Tropical Paradise Recovered at Lake Casa Blanca* (Austin: Texas Parks and Wildlife Press, 1999), 9–25; Lott and Martínez, *The Kingdom of Zapata,* 231. See also Ralph J. Roske, "The World Impact of the California Gold Rush, 1849–1857," *Arizona and the West* 5 (Autumn 1963): 187–232.

14. "The Late Governor Hunt," *Laredo Weekly Times,* October 31, 1909, "Corpus Christi," *Galveston Daily News,* March 5, 1882, 1. See also "Alexander Cameron Hunt," in *Encyclopedia of Frontier Biography,* ed. Dan L. Thrapp (Spokane: Arthur H. Clark, 1990), 3: 93.

15. Berlandier, *Journey to Mexico,* 1: 262–70.

16. William H. Emory, *Report on the United States and Mexican Boundary Survey, Made under the Direction on the Secretary of the Interior,* House Document, 34th Cong., 1st sess., Exec. Doc. No. 135, Vol. 1, 67–68; U.S. Army, Surgeon General Report, *Statistical Report on the Sickness and Mortality in the Army of the United States from January 1839 to January 1855,* U.S. Senate, 34th Cong., 1st sess., Exec. Doc. No. 96, Washington, D.C., 1856, 360–63; Horgan, *Great River,* 802–804, 895; Roberto R. Calderón, *Mexican Coal Mining Labor in Texas and Coahuila, 1880–1930* (College Station: Texas A&M University Press, 2000), 31; Duane K. Hale, "Prospecting and Mining on the Texas Frontier" (Ph.D. diss., Oklahoma State University, July 1977), 1–23, 25–58. See also A. Joachim McGraw and Jerry Thompson, *Campfires and Coal Dust on the Rio Grande* (Austin: Texas Department of Transportation, February 1998), 7–11.

17. "Coal Discovery in Texas," *New York Times,* September 24, 1881, 5; "Laredo: A Report of Oil," *Galveston Daily News,* March 16, 1881, 175–76; April 27, 1881, 308–11, 316–17; May 20, 1881, 766–80; and in vol. 10, November 29, 1881, 161; December 3, 5, 7, 1881, 168–85.

18. Webb County Deed Records, vol. 9, March 16, 1881, 175–76; April 27, 1881, 308–11, 316–17; May 20, 1881, 766–80; and in vol. 10, November 29, 1881, 161; December 3, 5, 7, 1881, 168–85.

19. George H. Ashley, *The Santo Tomás Cannel Coal Webb County, Texas,* Bulletin 691–1, U.S. Geological Survey, Department of the Interior (Washington, D.C.: GPO, 1918), 251–70 (hereafter Santo Tomás Cannel Coal); B. L. Miller, "Tertiary Coal Fields of the Rio Grande," *Coal Age,* August 23, 1913, 260–63.

20. "Local News," *Laredo Weekly News,* October 12, 1881; "The Snort of the Iron Horse Heard in Laredo—The Texas-Mexican Railroad Completed—Laredo and Corpus Christi Connected by Rail," ibid., September 14, 1881; Webb County Deed Records, vol. 9, April 5, 1881, 208.

21. Calderón, *Mexican Coal Mining,* 34.

22. Ibid., 36; San Antonio *Daily Express,* October 5, 1883. See also "Report of Geologist William DePyee," in Tarver, *Laredo the Gateway,* 25–26.

23. "Laredo," *Galveston Daily News,* May 16, 1882, 1; Webb County Deed Records, vol. 10, March 4, 1882, 360, February 25, 1882, 387–88; May 4, 1882, 449–52.

24. *Galveston Daily News,* April 2, 1882, March 23, 1882, June 22, 1882.

25. Jerry Thompson, "A Brief History of Darwin, Texas," in McGraw and Thompson, *Campfires and Coal Dust on the Rio Grande,* 13–15.

26. Annual Report of the Rio Grande & Eagle Pass Railway Company, June 30, 1892, Texas Railroad Commission Papers, Box 455–43, Texas State Archives, Austin.

27. Calderón, *Mexican Coal Mining,* 36–37; Janet Roy, "The Life and Times of Minera, Texas," *SWHQ* 49 (April 1946): 510–17.

28. "A Train on the Coal Road," *San Antonio Daily Express,* March 23, 1886; "Laredo," *Galveston Daily News,* April 7, 1886.

29. Tarver, *Laredo the Gateway,* 8–9.

30. "Hunt Coal Mining Company," *Laredo Times,* November 2, 1882.

31. "Laredo," *Frank Leslie's Illustrated Newspaper,* October 4, 1890, 20; *Galveston Daily News,* June 11, 1882.

32. Mayor A. Sanchez to Governor Lanham, April 29, 1905, as seen in "Special to the *New York Times,*" *New York Times,* April 30, 1905, and "Twenty-One Killed by Tornado in Texas," ibid. April 30, 1905; Thompson, *Laredo: Pictorial History,* 217–21.

33. Mora-Torres, *The Making of the Mexican Border,* 9–10, 254–65. See also Barbara Hibino, "Cerveceria Cuauhtemoc: A Case Study of Technological and Industrial Development in Mexico," *MS/EM* 8 (Winter 1992): 23–33, and Haber, *Industry and Underdevelopment,* 44–102. American holdings in Mexican railroads grew from $300 million in 1902 to over $650 million by 1912.

34. Calderón, *Mexican Coal Mining,* 4, 38–41, 79–88; Hart, *Empire and Revolution,* 121–24; Roy, "The Life and Times of Minera, Texas," 517.

35. For a detailed analysis for the 1900 and 1910 mining town census in Webb County, see Calderón, *Mexican Coal Mining,* 100–134. See also Thompson, "A Brief History of Darwin, Texas," 17–21.

36. Ashley, *Santo Tomás Cannel Coal,* 269. See also Miller, "Tertiary Coal," 263.

37. J. R. Arlitt, *Llave Coal Lands on the Rio Grande* (Austin: circa 1914), 1–8; San Antonio *Daily Express,* May 2, 1914; Miller, "Tertiary Coal," 262; Tyler et al., eds., "Rio Grande and Eagle Pass Railway," *Handbook of Texas,* 585–86.

38. Peter D. Warwick et al., *Tertiary Coal in South Texas: Anomalous Cannel-Like Coal of Webb County* (Washington, D.C.: U.S. Geological Survey, Report 99–301, April 1999), 5–22; John R. San Filipo, "Some Speculations on Coal-Rank Anomalies of the South Texas Gulf Province," U.S. Geological Survey, Report 99–3001, 40.

39. Scott Cook, *Mexican Brick Culture in Building Texas, 1800s–1980s* (College Station: Texas A&M University Press, 1998), 32–3; John W. Clark Jr. and Ana M. Juarez, *Urban Archaeology: A Culture History of a Mexican-American Barrio in Laredo Webb County, Texas,* No. 31, Austin: State Department of Highways and Public Transportation, December 1986, 70–71.

40. "Laredo," *Frank Leslie's Illustrated Newspaper,* October 4, 1890, 17–20; "Peter Leyendecker, Jr." *Laredo Times,* January 18, 1943, 1.

41. Henry C. Dethloff and Irvin M. May, eds., *Southwestern Agriculture: Pre-Columbian to Modern* (College Station: Texas A&M University Press, 1982), 54–56; Manuel A. Machado, *The North Mexican Cattle Industry, 1910–1975* (College Station: Texas A&M University Press, 1981), 7–20; Lehmann, *Forgotten Legions,* 124–50; "Three Principal Exporters," *Laredo Weekly Times,* March 8, 1914.

42. Da Camara, *Laredo on the Rio Grande,* 35; "Bermuda Onion Culture in Texas," *A&M College Bulletin,* College Station, November 1932, no. 65.

43. W. J. Clay, *Agriculture and Statistical Report, 1905* (Austin: The State Printing Company, 1905), 186–87.

44. "Webb County Farmers," and "Bermuda Onion Association," December 5, 1909, "In Interest of Railroads," and "To Diversify Local Crops," November 21, 1909, *Laredo Weekly Times.*

45. Carlos E. Cuéllar, "The House of Armengol: Doing Business on the Rio Grande Border, 1881–1930" (master's thesis, Laredo State University, December 1990), 53–65.

46. "Laredo the Onion Center," *Laredo Weekly Times,* October 17, 1909.

47. Thompson, *Laredo: A Pictorial History;* U.S. Department of Agriculture, "U.S. Onion Imports," *Year of Agriculture 1926,* 69th Cong., 2nd sess., H. Doc. No. 660, 1927, 930, 1199; Gilberto S. Treviño, *From the Pescadito to the Pentagon* (San Antonio: Lobo Creek Publishers, 2006), 9.

48. "Laredo Board of Trade," November 28, 1909, "Laredo Is Chosen," November 21, 1909, "That New Railroad," November 8, 1909, and "Highway from Laredo South to Mexico City Seems Assured," June 5, 1921, as seen in *Laredo Weekly Times.*

49. "A Friendly Visit," *Laredo Weekly Times,* January 28, 1912.

50. "Summer Excursion Rates," *Laredo Morning Times,* June 13, 1915.

51. "Webb Court House Burns," *Cotulla Record,* October 16, 1906; Stanley Green, *Webb County Court House* (Laredo: The Webb County Heritage Foundation, 1991), 1–12.

52. Hart, *Revolutionary Mexico,* 185. See also "Cutting the Railroads," *New York Times,* April 17, 1911, 2.

53. John Gunther, *Inside Latin America* (New York: Harper, 1941), 63.

54. Stanley R. Ross, *Francisco I. Madero: Apostle of Mexican Democracy* (New York: Columbia University Press, 1955), 20–33; Charles C. Cumberland, "Precursors of the Mexican Revolution," *HAHR* (May 1942): 345–50.

55. *San Antonio Light and Gazette,* November 19, 1910.

56. Michael D. Carman, *United States Customs and the Madero Revolution* (El Paso, Texas Western Press, 1976), 26, 34–36, 50–51; Charles H. Harris and Louis R. Sadler, *Texas Rangers and the Mexican Revolution* (Albuquerque: University of New Mexico Press, 2004), 52–54. See also James A. Sandos, *Rebellion in the Borderlands: Anarchism and the Plan of San Diego, 1904–1923* (Norman: University of Oklahoma Press, 1992).

57. "Airship Coming," *Laredo Times,* February 26, 1911, and "Hundreds See Biplane Fly," ibid. See also San Antonio *Express,* February 27, 28, 1911, March 3, 1911.

58. "Army Airship Breaks Record," *Laredo Times,* March 5, 1911; "Into Hospital Is Aeroplane," March 12, 1911; and "Collier's Laredo Is Making Good," March 26, 1911. See also San Antonio *Express,* March 4, 6, 1911; Barney M. Giles, "Early Military Aviation Activities in Texas," *SWHQ* (October 1950): 143–48; Charles DeForest Chandler and Frank P. Lahm, *How Our Army Grew Wings* (1943; New York: Arno Press, 1979), 185–86. *Collier's Magazine* photographer James Hare took the first aerial photos of Laredo and Nuevo Laredo from a height of 500 feet. These photos were also some of the first ever taken from an airplane.

59. William H. Taft, "Annual Message to Congress," December 7, 1911, U.S. Department of State, *Papers Relating to the Foreign Relations of the United States, 1911* (Washington, D.C.: GPO, 1911); Carman, *United States Customs and the Madero Revolution,* 34–59.

60. "Anarchy All Over Mexico," *New York Times,* May 4, 1911, 2; John S. D. Eisenhower, *Intervention: The United States and the Mexican Revolution, 1913–1917* (New York: W. W. Norton, 1993), 1–11; Ross, *Francisco I. Madero,* 159–65; Hart, *Revolutionary Mexico,* 245.

61. "A Demand for Action," March 1, 1914, and "Seek Only to Enforce Law," *Laredo Weekly Times,* March 19, 1911; Frank Tompkins, *Chasing Villa: The Last Campaign of the U.S. Cavalry* (Silver City, NMex.: High-Lonesome Books, 1996), 1–4.

62. Stacy C. Hinkle, *Wings over the Border: The Army Air Service Armed Patrol of the United States–Mexico Border, 1919–1921* (El Paso: Texas Western Press, 1970), 6–9.

63. "100,000 Militia Are Concentrating for Service on the Mexico Border," *Laredo Weekly Times,* June 25, 1916; Timothy J. Dunn, *The Militarization of the U.S.-Mexico Border* (Austin: CMAS Books, 1996), 8–11.

64. Frederick Palmer, "After Díaz, What?" *New York Times,* February 25, 1909, 6; "Taft and Díaz Meet: Talk of Friendship," ibid., October 17, 1909, 1; Edward Haley, *Revolution and Intervention: The Diplomacy of Taft and Wilson with Mexico, 1910–1917* (Cambridge, Mass.: MIT Press, 1970, 14–15.

65. Hart, *Empire and Revolution,* 262–67; Krauze, *Mexico,* 6, 216, 352; Vázquez and Meyer, *United States and Mexico,* 100; Rippy, *United States and Mexico,* 312; Marvin D. Bernstein, *The Mexican Mining Industry, 1890–1950: A Study of Interaction of Politics, Economics, and Technology* (Albany: State University of New York Press, 1964), 20, 45; "Stop Rifles at Laredo," *New York Times,* April 10, 1911, 3. See also Eileen Nelson, *The General and the Jagua,* (New York: Little, Brown, 2006), 91–135.

66. David Montejano, *Anglos and Mexicans in Making Texas, 1836–1986* (Austin: University of Texas Press, 1986), 107–17; Walter Prescott Webb, *The Texas Rangers* (1935; repr., Austin: University of Texas Press, 1980), 473–85; Tyler et al., eds., "Congreso Mexicanista," *Handbook of Texas,* vol. 2, 267.

67. "Rebel Forces Still Threatening Nuevo Laredo and Retain Ground," *Laredo Weekly Times,* January 4, 1914 and February 8, 1914; "Mexican Rebels Dynamite a Million-Dollar Coal Operation," *Coal Age,* September 13, 1913, 377; Thompson, *Laredo: A Pictorial History,* 273; Eisenhower, *Intervention,* 46–59, 79–82; Wilkinson, *Laredo and the Rio Grande Frontier,* 386–89.

68. B. M. Alexander to S. Bryant, May 6, 1914, Laredo Bridge Company Papers.

69. Larry D. Hill, *Emissaries to a Revolution* (Baton Rouge: Louisiana State University Press, 1973), 63–73, 124; Douglas W. Richmond, *Venustiano Carranza's Nationalist Struggle, 1893–1920* (Lincoln: University of Nebraska Press, 1983), 54–64; Hart, *Empire and Revolution,* 323–28; "Carranza Faction on Guard," *New York Times,* July 1, 1914, 2; Hart, *Revolutionary Mexico,* 268–70.

70. Edward Haley, *Revolution and Intervention: The Diplomacy of Taft and Wilson with Mexico, 1910–1917* (Cambridge, Mass.: MIT Press, 1970), 53–68; Peter V. N. Henderson, *Mexican Exiles in the Borderlands, 1910–1913* (El Paso: Texas Western Press, 1979), 46.

71. Chargé O'Shaughnessy to Secretary Bryan, October 18, 1913, Secretary of State to Chargé O'Shaughnessy, November 24, 1913, and Special Agent Carothers to Bryan, April 23, 1814, U.S. Department of State, *Papers Relating to the Foreign Relations of the United States* (hereafter State, *Papers*) (Washington, D.C.: GPO, 1922), 443, 485, 839.; W. Dirk Raat, *Mexico and the United States* (Athens: University of Georgia Press, 1992), 109–11.

72. *New York Times,* November 21, 1913 and February 22, 1914; Hill, *Emissaries,* 124–28; Hart, *Revolutionary Mexico,* 284–90. See also Charles C. Cumberland, *Mexican Revolution: The Constitutionalist Years* (Austin: University of Texas Press, 1974), 281–88.

73. Secretary Bryan to W. H. Page, January 29, 1914, State, *Papers,* 445; Cline, *United States and Mexico,* 152–3; Hill, *Emissaries,* 130; Hart, *Revolutionary Mexico,* 350–54; Hart, *Empire and Revolution,* 307.

74. Secretary of State to Special Agent Carothers, February 19, 1914, State, *Papers,* 482; *New York Times,* February 19, 1914; Hill, *Emissaries,* 148–55; Cumberland, *Mexican Revolution,* 281–90; Friedrich Katz, *The Life and Times of Pancho Villa* (Stanford, Calif.: Stanford University Press, 1998), 326–30. See also Edgcumb Pinchon, *Viva Villa!* (New York: Grosset and Dunlap, 1933), 259–63.

75. "Proclamation Revoking the Proclamation of March 14, 1912," State, *Papers,* 446–48; Katz, *Pancho Villa,* 328–29.

76. Details of Vergara's activities and his active role in the Webb ranching community are well documented in his efforts to obtain a clear title and patent from the state of Texas for the 113-acre island in the Rio Grande. On August 8, 1910, he applied to the state, but the reviewer in the Texas General Land Office declined his claim on May 20, 1912, noting, "too much doubt as to which side of the river this [the island] is on." See Clemente Vergara Petition, File S4 9791, survey no. 2331, Texas General Land Office, Austin.

77. George W. Smyth to H. Bee, February 13, 1849, H. Bee Papers, Box 2Q433; "Federals Hanged American," February 25, 1914, and "Vergara's Slayers to Be Punished," *New York Times,* February 26, 1914; Harris and Sadler, *The Texas Rangers and Mexican Revolution,* 131, 165–66.

78. "What Has Become of Vergara?" *Laredo Morning Times,* February 22, 1914, "Clemente Vergara Was Hanged," ibid., March 1, 1914; "The Vergara Case," ibid., March 1, 1914; "Criticizing Ferguson," ibid., November 28, 1915; *Dallas News,* March 1, 2, 11, 14, 1914; "Find Vergara Was Hanged," *New York Times,* February 27, 1914, and "Reports Vergara was Shot," ibid., February 28, 1914; Webb, *The Texas Rangers,* 486–95.

79. Katz, *Pancho Villa,* 328–29; Rippy, *United States and Mexico,* 338–39; "Intrigue in Mexico," *The Nation* (July 2, 1914): 5–6; "On the Mexican Border," *New Republic* (October 9, 1915): 256–57; "The Villa Carranza Break," *Literary Digest,* 619–20.

80. "Governor Ferguson Meets First Chief V. Carranza," and "Criticizing Ferguson," *Laredo Weekly Times,* November 28, 1915, 2, 5. Also joining Ferguson, Carranza, and Caballero were Candido Aguilar, governor of Veracruz, and Pablo de la Garza, governor of Nuevo Leon.

81. James E. Ferguson to Lindley M. Garrison, Secretary of War, November 26, 1915, and Ferguson to President Wilson, November 26, 1915, Papers of Governor James E. Ferguson, Box 301–76, Texas State Archives, Austin. See also Benjamin H. Johnson, *Revolution in Texas* (New Haven, Conn.: Yale University Press, 2003), 130–43.

82. "New Three Story Building for LNB," and "Big Movements of Imports from Mexico are Expected," *Laredo Weekly Times,* October 24, 1915; "Opening Up of Big Business," ibid., November 14, 1915; "Transporting of Onions," ibid., November 7, 1915.

83. "The Governor's Visit," *Laredo Weekly Times,* November 28, 1915.

84. "Planning for Celebration," January 25, 1914; "Will Pull Off Sham Battle," January 18, 1914; "Official WBCA Program," February 8,1914; "Many Visitors Have Arrived," February 22, 1914, all from the *Laredo Weekly Times.*

85. Stanley Green, ed., *A History of the Washington Birthday Celebration* (Laredo: Border Studies, 1999). See also Elliott Young, "Deconstructing *La Raza:* Identifying the *Gente Decente* of Laredo, 1904–1911," *SWHQ* (October 1994): 224–59; Elliott Young, "Red Men, Princess Pocahontas, and George Washington: Harmonizing Race Relationships in Laredo at the Turn of the Century," *WHQ* (Spring 1998): 48–85.

86. Haber, *Industry and Underdevelopment,* 122–34.

87. Incorporation Documents, Laredo Chamber of Commerce, March 26, 1915, as seen at the chamber office, Laredo, Texas.

88. "Typhus Leaps Line, Laredo Is Stricken," *New York Times,* December 24, 1915, 4.

89. Hart, *Empire and Revolution,* 329–34; Barbara W. Tuchman, *The Zimmermann Telegram* (New York: Macmillan, 1996); Eisenhower, *Intervention,* 310–12; Frank E. Vandiver, *Black Jack: The Life and Times of John J. Pershing* (College Station: Texas A&M University Press, 1977), 2: 664–68.

90. "Took Possession of Arms and Ammo in Laredo," July 2, 1916, 2, "Laredo as Port of Entry" February 1, 1920, 4, and "Labors Are Permitted to Stay in United States," *Laredo Weekly Times,* January 11, 1920, 3; Douglas W. Richmond, "Mexican Immigration and Border Strat-

egy during the Revolution, 1910–1920," *New Mexico Historical Review* (July 1982): 269–88; Haber, *Industry and Underdevelopment,* 132–49; Fernando González Roa, *The Mexican People and Their Detractors* (New York: Latin American News Association, 1916), 1–88. See also "Mexico," *Special Consular Reports: Emigration to the United States,* House of Representatives, 58th Cong., 2nd sess., Doc. No. 732, 1904, 174–77.

91. "Rio Grande on Big Rampage," *Laredo Times,* September 21, 1919, 2; "Bridge Will Open Tomorrow, Traffic across Rio Grande," ibid., June 25, 1922.

92. "Laredo Census," *Laredo Weekly Times,* August 1, 1921.

93. Burt C. Blanton, *Industrial and Economic Survey of the City of Laredo and Webb County, Texas* (Dallas: N.p, July 1, 1928), 97. See also Wortham, *History of Texas,* 5: 257–59.

94. Blanton, *Industrial and Economic Survey,* 98; Aguilar Camín and Meyer, *In the Shadow of the Mexican Revolution,* 71–73; "City Council Has Granted New Franchise for Bridge," *Laredo Weekly Times,* September 20, 1920. On September 7, 1920, the Laredo City Council approved a twenty-five-year lease to the Laredo Bridge Company effective January 1, 1921, to build a "concrete" structure across the Rio Grande and collect all revenues; in exchange the city would receive $6,000 per year.

95. J. W. Falvella, *A Souvenir Album* (Laredo: 1917), 1–41; February 15, 1920, *Laredo Weekly Times.* In the early 1920s the Rio Grande Buick Company was renamed the Laredo Buick Company under the ownership of Capt. W. W. Ryan and moved to 1305 Farragut Street across from Jarvis Plaza.

96. Falvella, *A Souvenir Album,* 23–24.

97. Ibid., 20, 27; Blanton, *Industrial and Economic Survey,* 102–104; "Hamilton Hotel," *Laredo Weekly Times,* March 30, 1919; "Webb County Cotton Crop Greatest in Its History," ibid., July 25, 1921; "Great Prosperity," ibid., July 20, 1920. See also Cuéllar, "The House of Armengol," 82–94.

98. "Oil Prospecting in Webb County," *Laredo Times,* February 8, 1920, 7; see also "Complete History of Oil and Gas in This Area," *Laredo Times,* November 23, 1937, 10.

99. Henry M. Payne, "Resume of the Twenty-Five Years of Mining," *Mining Congress Journal* (October 1922): 936. The leading annual state producers of oil in 1899 by percentage furnished were Pennsylvania 62 percent, Ohio 23 percent, West Virginia 9.3 percent, Indiana 3 percent, and California 1.5 percent.

100. Alfred Tischendorf, *Great Britain and Mexico in the Era of Porfirio Díaz* (Durham, N.C.: Duke University Press, 1961), 122–24; Hart, *Empire and Revolution,* 154–55. For a review of the early years of the oil industry in the United States, see Porter, *The Rise of Big Business, 1860–1910,* 62–66.

101. Judith W. Linsley, Ellen W. Reinstra, and Jo Ann Stiles, *Giant under the Hill: A History of the Spindletop Oil Discovery* (Austin: TSHA, 2002), 99–127; *Galveston Daily News,* January 21, 1901; Jonathan C. Brown and Alan Knight, eds., *The Mexican Petroleum Industry in the Twentieth Century* (Austin: University of Texas Press, 1992), 1–8; Tyler et al., eds., "Spindletop," *Handbook of Texas,* vol. 6, 29–30; Hart, *Revolution and Empire,* 155–56.

102. Payne, "Resume," 936; Hart, *Revolution and Empire,* 156–63; Calderón, *Mexican Coal Mining,* 55–57; Linda B. Hall, *Oil, Banks, and Politics: The United States and Post Revolutionary Mexico, 1917–1924* (Austin: University of Texas Press, 1995), 1–35, 102; Richmond, *Venustiano Carranza's Nationalist Struggle,* 95–101.

103. Robert G. Cleland, *The Mexican Year Book, 1920–1921* (Los Angeles: Mexican Year Book Publishing, 1922), 309. See also Haber, *Industry and Underdevelopment,* 152.

104. Payne, "Resume," 933–37; Calderón, *Mexican Coal Mining,* 99; Brown and Knight, *Mexican Petroleum Industry,* 9; Hays, *The Response of Industrialism,* 44–58; Henry C. Dethloff, *The United States and the Global Economy since 1845* (Ft. Worth: Harcourt Brace, 1997), 41.

105. Payne, "Resume," 934–37; "Texas March Production Total 10,925,000 bbls," *Houston Chronicle,* April 25, 1922, 12.

106. Thompson, "A Brief History of Darwin, Texas," 31; Calderón, *Mexican Coal Mining,* 99, 215.

107. "They're Off toward Oil Pool in Laredo Section," *Laredo Weekly Times,* February 15, 1920, 3, and "Bor-Tex Is Ready to Spud in Well," ibid., February 29, 1920, 2.

108. "Laredo Almost Encircled by Drilling Operations," *Laredo Weekly Times,* April 18, 1920, 2.

109. Michael F. Black, ed., *Mirando City: A New Town in a New Oil Field* (Laredo: Laredo Publishing, 1972); Diana D. Olien and Roger M. Olien, *Oil in Texas: The Gusher Age, 1895–1945* (Austin: University of Texas Press, 2002), 106–10.

110. "Mirando Gets Another Well," *Laredo Weekly Times,* April 17, 1921, 1; "Excitement Prevails in Laredo as Results of the Mirando Well," ibid., April 24, 1921; "W. O. Killam Is Oil King of South Texas," *Laredo Times,* November 23, 1937, 6; Jennie L. Reed, "Mirando City . . . Where It All Began," *¡Saludos!* (July 11, 1974): 6–10.

111. "Another Monster Gasser," *Laredo Weekly Times,* August 15, 1920; "Oil Struck at Benavides," ibid., July 25, 1921; "Mirando Field Looks Good," ibid., October 2, 1921; Laredo Chamber of Commerce, *The Gateway to Mexico: Laredo South Texas,* Laredo, circa 1926, 12; Tyler et al., eds., "Oliver Winfield Killam," *Handbook of Texas,* vol. 3, 1094; Wortham, *History of Texas,* 5: 259; Blanton, *Industrial and Economic Survey,* 128.

112. "Rio Grande Lyrics," *Laredo Weekly Times,* April 16, 1922, 12.

113. "Land Leases Soaring," *Laredo Morning Times,* April 25, 1920, 3; "Great [Rail] Car Shortage," ibid., March 28, 1920, 9; Manuel A. Machada Jr. "An Industry in Limbo: The Mexican Cattle Industry, 1920–1934," *Agricultural History* (October 1976): 615–25. See also Morris Singer, *Growth, Equality, and the Mexican Experience* (Austin: University of Texas Press, 1969), 102, 116–18.

114. "Laredo Rotary Club Was Organized," *Laredo Morning Times,* March 28, 1920, 7.

115. "Recognition of Mexican Government Being Urged," *Laredo Morning Times,* September 5, 1920; Krauze, *Mexico,* 370–403.

116. Cleland, *Mexican Year Book, 1920–1921,* 218–19.

117. Lott and Martínez, *The Kingdom of Zapata,* 28–29; Blanton, *Industrial and Economic Survey,* 95–96, 131; S. Deane Wasson, "Thousand Mile Loop Plan Is Developed," *Houston Chronicle,* May 14, 1922, 17.

118. "Make Excellent Showing in Both Imports-Exports," *Laredo Times,* September 19, 1924; "Laredo the Gateway to Mexico," ibid., September 8, 1925; Joseph S. Davis, "Economic Factors in Mexico," *American Economic Review* (March 1930): 46–47.

119. "Bankhead Highway Congress," *Laredo Morning Times,* October 16, 1921; "Mexico to Extend Highway," October 9, 1921; "Laredo to Dallas," October 9, 1921; "Experts Say Great Highway through Latin Republics Can Be Built," *New York Times,* October 23, 1927, 13, and Leon A. Dickinson, "Motoring in Mexico," *New York Times,* February 28, 1932, 6; "Mexico Announces Highway Ceremonies," ibid., June 14, 1936, 25; Joseph S. Davis, "Economic Factors in Mexico," *American Economic Review* (March 1930) 40–48. Connecting Laredo to Mexico City by improved highway began on April 28, 1923, when the government granted a concession to ex-senator Guillermo Laveaga for construction of a highway from the capital to Laredo, as seen in "Latin America," *New York Times,* January 1, 1924, 29.

120. "Rolling South of the Rio Grande," *Business Week,* April 4, 1936, 34–35.

121. Ibid.; Victor L. Urquidi, "Technology Transfer between Mexico and the United States," *MS/EM* (Summer 1986): 179–93; Marian D. Irish, "Foreign Policy and the South," *Journal of Politics* (May 1948), 316. See also Douglas C. Bennett and Kenneth E. Sharpe, *Transnational*

Corporation versus the State: The Political Economy of the Mexican Auto Industr, (Durham, N.C.: Duke University Press, 1985).

122. *Laredo, Texas Directory 1935,* Laredo [1935], 2–488.

Chapter 6

1. Interview with Laredo resident Guadalupe Martinez (born 1914), Laredo, April 24, 2005; "297 WPA Projects are Completed in This Area," *Laredo Times,* February 26, 1939, 1; Lott and Martínez, *The Kingdom of Zapata,* 212; Campbell, *Gone to Texas,* 382–95; Haber, *Industry and Underdevelopment,* 168–89; John A. Adams Jr., *Damming the Colorado,* College Station: Texas A&M University Press, 1990, 28–33; Machado, *The North Mexican Cattle Industry, 1910–1975,* 49–66; Haber, *Industry and Underdevelopment,* 150–99; *Laredo City Directory, 1935,* 485–86. The total spent by federal New Deal programs in the sixteen-county South Texas region, which includes Webb County, over 3 1/2 years was $4.6 million. There is no estimate of the number of jobs created or saved. Lott and Martínez note, "The depression following World War I was scarcely felt in the section." Also, with regard to local banking, there were two additional financial institutions in Nuevo Laredo in 1940, Banco Longoria, S.A., and Banco Nacional de México, S.A.

2. "Mayor Albert Martin A Progressive," *Laredo Morning Times,* November 23, 1937, 4.

3. Texas State Highway Commission (WPA), *Texas: A Guide to the Lone Star State,* "Laredo," n.p., 1940, 306–13; "A Splendid Idea," *Laredo Times,* February 28, 1939; see also March 16, 1939 and November 23, 1937; Chester C. Wine, "Laredo Electric Railway Company." Laredo, 1969, 11–13; "Rolling South of the Rio Grande," *Business Week,* April 4, 1936, 34–35; J. W. Williams, *The Big Ranch Country* (Lubbock: Texas Tech University Press, 1999), 258. See also *Bermuda Onion Culture in Texas,* Texas A&M College Bulletin, No. 65, November, 1932, and Lehmann, *Forgotten Legions,* 49–53.

4. Herbert C. Lanks, "The Pan-American Highway," *Scientific Monthly* (October 1939): 324–36; Da Camara, *Laredo on the Rio Grande,* 38, from which the quote is taken; Tyler et al., eds., *Handbook of Texas,* 586; Reed, *A History of the Texas Railroads,* 475: "Port Commission Developing Traffic Facilities," *Laredo Times,* June 30, 1942, 4. The Nuevo Laredo to Panama road was also referred to as the Inter-American Highway.

5. Fernando Piñon, *Patron Democracy* (Mexico City: Contraste, 1985), 100–101; "United Gas Company," *Laredo Times,* February 15, 1949, 5; "Citizens Acclaim Mayor Cluck for Service," ibid., April 21, 1954, 1. UGC obtained gas from the United Pipe Line Company and charged a rate of $1.00 per 900 cubic feet, with a minimum charge of one dollar per month.

6. "Laredo Major Port of Mexican Entry," *Laredo Times,* February 29, 1940; "Laredo Greatest Inland Port in Nation: Has Been since 1755," ibid., August 11, 1941.

7. Texas (WPA), *Texas,* 63, 309, 313; Howard F. Cline, *Mexico: Revolution to Evolution, 1940–1960* (New York: Oxford University Press, 1963), 253–98; Samuel N. Dicken, "Cotton Regions of Mexico," *Economic Geography* (October 1938): 363–71; William T. Chambers, "Lower Rio Grande Valley of Texas," *Economic Geography* (October 1930): 363–73; Haber, *Industry and Underdevelopment,* 171–99.

8. "Work Rapid on Antimony Smelter," *Laredo Times,* October 10, 1930.

9. H. M. Irvin, "Laredo Has Outstanding Plant," *Laredo Times,* September 30, 1934, and "Only One in North, South America," ibid., March 1, 1936.

10. Kurt Block, "China Loses Traditional Rank in Antimony Production," *Far Eastern Survey* (January 17, 1940): 19–20; James J. Parsons, "Recent Industrial Development in Gulf South," *Geographical Review* (January 1950), 67–83; James F. Carlin Jr., "Antimony," n.p., 1999.

11. "Texas Harvest Hats," *Laredo Times,* February 21, 1942, 7; Da Camara, *Laredo on the Rio Grande,* 35, 41; Hall, *Oil, Banks, and Politics,* 174–80; Thomas Lusk, "On the Mexican Highway," *New York Times,* December 8, 1940, 19; CPL, "Laredo Power Station," in CPL File, Special Collections, Laredo Public Library. See also Catherine E. Jayne, *Oil, War, and Anglo-American Relations* (Westport, Conn.: Greenwood Press, 2001). Henequen was grown on plantations in the Yucatán. The plant produces a course fiber when sun dried, and is exported to produce a strong coarse twine for use in wheat binder machines.

12. Lorenzo Meyer, *Mexico and the United States in the Oil Controversy, 1917–1942* (Austin: University of Texas Press, 1972), 173–216; Hart, *Empire and Revolution,* 394–403; Haber, *Industry and Underdevelopment,* 171–99.

13. Vázquez and Meyer, *United States and Mexico,* 155–60; "Mexico Oil," *Laredo Times,* March 20, 1939, 1; Fehrenbach, *Fire and Blood,* 606–609; Krauze, *Mexico,* 503–506. Settlement negotiations included seventeen American and British firms for the over $400 million in property and rights expropriated in 1938.

14. "Mexico Oil Tanker Sunk by Axis Submarine," *Laredo Times,* May 15, 1942, 1; "Laredo to Honor Mexican Ship Heroes," ibid., May 20, 1942, 1; "Another Mexican Tanker Sunk!" ibid., May 22, 1942, 1; Vázquez and Meyer, *United States and Mexico,* 158.

15. Meyer and H. Beezley, eds., *History of Mexico,* 538–41.

16. Leonard Pearson, "Below the Rio Grande," *Laredo Times,* January 6, 1943, 1; Vázquez and Meyer, *United States and Mexico,* 157–60; Henry B. Parkes, *A History of Mexico* (Boston: Houghton Mifflin, 1950), 408. Mexico still celebrates the nationalization of foreign oil companies started by President Lázaro Cárdenas in 1938; see David Luhnow, "Over a Barrel: As Mexico's Oil Giant Struggles, Its Laws Block Foreign Help," *Wall Street Journal,* June 15, 2005, 1.

17. "Visit to Laredo," *Laredo Times,* April 24, 1942, 1; "Much Wheat Going to Mexico," *New York Times,* March 14, 1942, 4.

18. Hart, *Empire and Revolution,* 414–18; Fehrenbach, *Fire and Blood,* 607; Parkes, *A History of Mexico,* 45; Machado, *The North Mexican Cattle Industry,* 61, 68. By December 1943, cattle quotas were capped at 500,000 head. For a snapshot of Mexican domestic production and exports, see "Mexico Last Week: Business and Industrial Development," *Laredo Times,* July 15, 1946, 4 and September 15, 1946.

19. Inspection Trip Logs, Trips of the President, April 13 to April 29 1943, Papers of Franklin D. Roosevelt, Roosevelt Library, Hyde Park, New York.

20. William H. Wallace, "The Bridge Line: A Distinctive Type of Anglo-American Railroad," *Economic Geography* (January 1965): 8, 9, 13; O. Douglas Weeks, "The Texas-Mexican and the Politics of South Texas," *American Political Science Review* (August 1930): 615; Fehrenbach, *Fire and Blood,* 607; W. H. Lawrence, "U.S. and Mexican Presidents Visit an Air Station in Texas," *New York Times,* April 22, 1943, 1, and "Mexican Rail Pact Approved by U.S.," ibid., November 19, 1942, 12. Ulysses S. Grant, James K. Polk, Zachary Taylor, and William H. Harrison had been to Mexico but not during their presidency. President Harry Truman in March 1947 was the first U.S. president to visit Mexico City.

21. Roger Daniels, *Guarding the Golden Door* (New York: Hill and Wang, 2004), 90–91; Paul R. Ehrlich, Loy Bilderback, and Anne H. Ehrlich, *The Golden Door* (New York: Ballantine, 1979), 211–16. See also Wayne D. Rasmussen, *A History of the Emergency Farm Labor Supply Program, 1943–1947* (Washington, D.C.: GPO, 1979), and Barbara A. Driscoll, *The Tracks North: The Railroad Bracero Program of World War II* (Austin: University of Texas Press, 1999). The Bracero Program was first established by executive agreement between the United States and Mexico in July 1942, and was formalized by Congress in 1943. The agreement included pay for transportation and a minimum wage, with an estimated 300,000 bracero

workers in the program in both agriculture and railroad jobs. The program was modified in 1954, and ended in December 1964 when Congress failed to reauthorize its use.

22. Quote is in Vázquez and Meyer, *United States and Mexico,* 162–63; Haber, *Industry and Underdevelopment,* 182–89, 197–99. See also Albert L. Michaels, "The Crisis of Cardenismo," *Journal of Latin American Studies* 2 (1970), and Hart, *Empire and Revolution,* 403–24.

23. For a sample, see "Laredo Business Review," *Laredo Times,* January 6 and 18, 1943; "Weekly Review of Oil Activities around Laredo," ibid., see February 7, 14, 21, 1943.

24. "Laredo Is Project Terminus," *Laredo Times,* July 31, 1946, 2; "$3,415,567.66 Collected by Customs at Laredo," ibid., July 14, 1946, 4.

25. De Camara, *Laredo on the Rio Grande,* 37, charts V and VII; *Laredo Telephone Directory,* Southwestern Bell Telephone Company, Issue No. 27, November 1946, 22–23, 36; "Mexico to Double Traffic Capacity," *Laredo Times,* September 27, 1946, 1; Hart, *Empire and Revolution,* 414–20.

26. "Laredo Streets Thronged for Fete," *Laredo Times,* February 22, 1943, 1, and "Laredo Celebration Stories Appear in 1,400 Newspapers," ibid., February 23, 1943, 1. See also Michael Scully, "Vivas for Jorge Washington," *New York Times,* February 22, 1942, xxi.

27. "For Airplanes When Airport Is Complete," *Laredo Times,* December 23, 1923; Maurer Maurer, *Aviation in the U.S. Army, 1919–1939* (Washington, D.C.: GPO, 1987), 71, 99–106, 161; Charles J. Gross, *American Military Aviation* (College Station: Texas A&M University Press, 2002), 49–94; Kenneth B. Ragsdale, *Wings over the Mexican Border* (Austin: University of Texas Press, 1984), 26–57.

28. "Laredo Gets Airport," *Laredo Times,* May 13, 1942, 1; "Dismantling Airport Starts," ibid, 1939; "Car Crashes into Culvert Post on Highway," ibid., January 20, 1937; Thomas E. Alexander, *The Wings of Change: The Army Air Force Experience in Texas during World War II* (Abilene: McWhinney Foundation Press), 2003, 97–104.

29. Amado F. Cavazos, *Zachry: The Man and His Companies* (San Antonio: Metro Press, 1993), 21. The Webb County project was "Bridge #2, Job 240D, Highway 12A, Webb County, Texas" near Pescadito.

30. "The Master Power of Progress," *Laredo Times,* November 23, 1937.

31. "1940 Project Halted by War Now Reality," ibid., September 18, 1946, 1; Cavazos, *Zachry,* 23, 64–76, 110; Zachry File, Webb County Historical Foundation Archives, Laredo; "Zachry," *Laredo Times,* February 13, 1977; www.zachry.com.

32. Cavazos, *Zachry,* 71–73; "New Airport Deal in Fine Shape," *Laredo Times,* May 14, 1942, 1, and "Laredo Airfield Is Authorized," ibid., May 31, 1942, 1; "All on Bombers to Learn Gunnery," *New York Times,* December 11, 1942, 17; *Laredo: Gateway to Mexico* (Laredo: n.p., circa 1945), as seen in the Special Collections of the Laredo Public Library.

33. Bill Freeman, "Jet Pilots to Be Trained at Laredo Air Base," *San Antonio Evening News,* December 18, 1951; *Laredo: Gateway to Mexico* (Laredo: circa 1943), 2–8.

34. "[A. R.] Sanchez to Head Drive for College," *Laredo Times,* July 17, 1846, 1; "Laredo Votes Junior College," ibid., September 29, 1946, 1. The vote for LJC approval was 616 for and 3 against to levy a tax of twenty cents per $100 valuation.

35. Laredo, *Flame Out,* July 1, 1954, 1–4; Laredo Air Force Base File, Webb County Historical Foundation Archives, Laredo; Hinojosa, *Borderlands Town,* 121–22; Class 57-D, *Jet Wash* (Laredo: LAFB, 1956).

36. Tyler et al., eds., *Handbook of Texas,* vol. 2, 705; "Rio Grande Stops Running at Laredo," *New York Times,* June 6, 1953, 20; "City Seeking Injunction to Assure Supply," *Laredo Times,* April 26, 1954, 1.

37. "Country Club Dam," *Laredo Times,* July 3, 1949, 1; David J. Eaton and John M. Anderson, *The State of the Rio Grande/Río Bravo* (Tucson: University of Arizona Press, 1987), 5–7,

12; Joseph A. Loftus, "2 Presidents Join in Pledge of Amity at Rio Grande Dam," *New York Times,* October 20, 1953, 1; Lott and Martínez, *The Kingdom of Zapata,* 14–21; Eisenhower Memorial Commission, "October 1953 Chronology," at www.eisenhowermemorial.org.

38. "Mexican Peso Devaluation Put in Effect Today," *Laredo Times,* April 19, 1954, 1; "Peso Devaluation Brings Travel Bargains in Mexico," ibid., April 20, 1954; "Construction Work Starts," ibid., April 23, 1954, 1; "Hundreds Pay Tribute to O. W. Killam," ibid., April 28, 1954, 1; City of Laredo, 1950 Tax Roll, Item 7–9, 81, Special Collections, Laredo Public Library. The devaluation of the Mexican peso to 12.50/dollar in April 1954 would prove a significant move; this valuation of the pegged currency remained at 12.50 from 1954 to early 1976; see John A. Adams Jr., *Mexican Banking and Investment in Transition* (Westport, Conn.: Quorum Books, 1997), 161.

39. Mueller, *Restless River,* 90–98.

40. Horgan, *Great River,* 713–14; Wilkinson, *Laredo and the Rio Grande Frontier,* 205–12; Thompson, *Laredo: A Pictorial History,* 148, 258–71.

41. "Toll Reaches 25 in Texas Floods," *New York Times,* June 30, 1954, 16; Mueller, *Restless River,* 91–98; "Record Rise in Rio Due Here," *Laredo Times,* June 28, 1954, 1; "Two Laredos Brace for Worst Flood," ibid., June 29, 1954, 1; "Only One Highway Out of City," June 30, 1954, 1; International Boundary and Water Commission, "Flow of the Rio Grande and Related Data," *IBWC Bulletin* 41 (1954): 102; Interview with General Milton B. Adams, January 15, 2007, Laredo, Texas.

42. Interview with Odie Arámbula, July 26, 2005, Laredo, Texas.

43. Interview with Daniel B. Hastings Jr., August 6, 2005, Laredo, Texas; "Eisenhower Acts for Aid on Flood," *New York Times,* July 2, 1954; "Lake Falcon Being Fed by Flood Water," *Laredo Times,* July 1, 1954; "Bridge Out at Del Rio," ibid., June 29, 1954, 1.

44. Minutes, Special Meeting, June 30, 1954, Laredo Bridge Company Papers, Special Collections, Laredo Public Library.

45. Interview with Lee Knaeble, August 16, 2005, by phone in Sierra Vista, Arizona; he was a member of the Fort Hood Engineer Battalion dispatched to Laredo to install a cross-border pontoon bridge in early July 1954.

46. Minutes, July 1, 1954, Laredo Bridge Company; "Typhoid Follows Rio Grande Flood," *New York Times,* July 5, 1954, 16; "Rio Pontoon Bridge Planned," *Laredo Times,* July 1, 1954, 1; "Rail Bridge Repairs to Start Monday," ibid., July 7, 1954, 1.

47. Charles R. McCord, "The Economy of Laredo," *Texas Business Review* (May 1959): 1–4; TEEX, "An Industrial Inventory of Laredo, Texas," (College Station, TEEX, April 1959), 81–84, 94.

48. Business and Industrial Department Report, Laredo Chamber of Commerce, April 1966; J. C. Martin Jr., R. J. Hammerstrom, and R. H. Waldrop, "The Laredo Story of Sanitation Progress," *The American City* (February 1957): 116–19, 133–36; "Most Urgent Laredo Requirements," *Laredo Times,* April 30, 1954; "Laredo Population," ibid., May 5, 1954. The Laredo population in 1955 was reported to range from 55,385 to 59,268; however, note the official U.S. Census in 1960 was 60,678, up from 51,910 in 1950.

49. McCord, "The Economy of Laredo," 3; TEEX, "An Industrial Inventory of Laredo Texas," 81–85; George W. Grayson, *Prospects for Democracy in Mexico* (New Brunswick, N.J.: Transaction Publishers, 1990), 282–87.

SELECTED BIBLIOGRAPHY

ABBREVIATIONS

AHR	*American Historical Review*
GPO	Government Printing Office
HAHR	*Hispanic American Historical Review*
IBWC	International Boundary Water Commission
JBS	*Journal of Borderlands Studies*
JST	*Journal of South Texas*
MS/EM	*Mexican Studies/Estudios Mexicanos*
SWHQ	*Southwestern Historical Quarterly*
TSHA	Texas State Historical Association
WHQ	*Western Historical Quarterly*

ARCHIVAL AND PRIMARY MATERIAL

Aldrich, Roy Wilkinson, Papers. The Center for American History, University of Texas, Austin.

Archivo General de Mexico. Villa de Laredo, Tomo 56, No. 19. As seen in Texas State Archives, Austin.

Archivo General y Público de la Nación. Documents (1582–1821), 54 vols., and Provincias Internas (1617–1821), 88 vols. University of Texas Archives, Austin.

Atlee, Edwin A. *Description of Laredo, Texas, the Acknowledged International Gateway between the Two Republics. Early History, Manufactories, Progress, Wealth. Population, Climate, and Prospects.* Laredo: Gateway Printing House, 1888.

———. General Bio File, Center for American History, University of Texas, Austin.

Bass, S. B. "Webb County." Unpublished paper, n.d. O. Douglas Weeks Collection, Center for American History, University of Texas, Austin.

Bee, Hamilton Prioleau Papers. Center for American History, University of Texas, Austin.

Béxar Archives. 1717–1836. Manuscript Collection, with calendar. 172-roll microfilm series. Also in Béxar Archives Translations, series 1 (160 vols. To date, covering 1730–89), and series 2 (38 vols., covering 1804–1808). University of Texas Archives, Austin.

Colquitt, O. P. Governor's Papers, Texas States Archives, Austin.

Comptroller's Military Service Records (Texas). Texas State Archives, Austin.

Davis, Edmund J., Papers, Texas State Archives, Austin.

Eberstadt, [Edward], Collection. University of Texas Archives, Austin.

Elliott, Claude, Collection. Texas State Archives, Austin.

Ferguson, James E. Governor's Papers. Texas State Archives, Austin.

General Land Office of Texas, Spanish Archives. Multivolume holdings concerning Spanish-Mexican period land grants. Austin.

———. Guide to Spanish and Mexican Land Grants in South Texas. Austin, 1999.

Grazing Papers ("History of Grazing in Texas"). Spanish ranching in "The Range in Colonial Times," 2 vols. in 3 pts., Historical Records Survey by WPA, 1935. University of Texas Archives, Austin.

Haynes, John L., Papers, Center for American History, University of Texas, Austin.

Lamar, Mirabeau Bonaparte, Papers. Texas State Archives, Austin.

Laredo Archives (City Records, 1749–1836). Manuscript Collection. Center for American History, University of Texas, Austin, and also seen at Special Collections Laredo Public Library.

Laredo Directory—1889: Description of Laredo, Texas. Reprint by Central Power and Light, 1966, Special Collections, Laredo Public Library.

Laredo Vertical Files and Data, Center for American History, University of Texas, Austin.

Martínez Family Papers. Cushing Library, Texas A&M University Archives, College Station.

Matamoros Archives (City Records, 1811–59). Photostats, with calendar. 68 vols. University of Texas Archives, Austin.

Nolan, Philip, Papers. 1797–1808. University of Texas Archives, Austin.

Records of the Cotton Bureau. Record Group 365. Washington, D.C. National Archives.

Register of Imports at the Port of Laredo. District of Brazos Santiago. Confederate Treasury Department. Record Group 365. Washington, D.C. National Archives.

Roosevelt, Franklin D., Papers. Franklin D. Roosevelt Library, Hyde Park, New York.

Traver, E. R., *Laredo: The Gateway between the United States and Mexico. An Illustrated Description of the Future City of the Great Southwest.* Laredo: Daily Times Print, 1889.

Travieso, Vicente Álvarez, Papers. 1771–83. Translation. University of Texas Archives, Austin.

Webb, Walter Prescott, Papers. Center for American History, University of Texas, Austin.

Government Documents

City of Laredo. City Council Minutes and Minute Books. 1864–1920. Office of the City Secretary, Laredo, Texas.

———. Laredo Bridge Company Papers. Special Collections. Laredo Public Library.

———.Tax Roll, 1945–55. Special Collections. Laredo Public Library.

Emory, William H. Record of the United States and Mexico Boundary Survey, Made under the Direction of the Secretary of the Interior. 34 Cong., 1st sess.

Message of Governor Richard Coke to the Fourteenth Legislature, January 26, 1874, Texas State Archives, Austin.

Official Records of the Union and Confederate Navies in the War of the Rebellion. 30 vols., Washington, D.C.: GPO, 1894–1922.

Taft, William H. "Annual Message to Congress." *Papers Relating to the Foreign Relations of the United States,* U.S. State Department, December 7, 1911, Washington, D.C.: GPO, 1911.

Texas Comptroller of Public Accounts. *Bordering the Future: Challenge and Opportunity in the Texas Border Region.* Austin: July 1998.

———. General Land Office. "Guide to Spanish and Mexican Land Grants in South Texas," Austin, 1999.

———. L. L. Foster, Commissioner of Agriculture. *First Annual Report of the Agricultural Bureau of the Department of Agriculture, Insurance, Statistics and History.* Austin: State Printing Office, 1889.

———. State Department of Highways. *Urban Archaeology: A Culture History of a Mexican-American Barrio in Laredo.* John W. Clark and Ana M. Juárez, Report No. 31. Austin: December 1966.

———. *Texas Area Facts.* Austin: 1996.

———. Texas Railroad Commission Papers, Texas State Archives, Austin.

U.S. Congress. *Congressional Globe.* 35th Congress, 1st sess., 1857–58.

U.S. Congress, House of Representatives. *Annexation of Texas to the United States.* 25th Cong., 1st sess., Doc. No. 40, Serial No. 311, October 3, 1837.

———. *Boundaries between Texas and the Territories.* 33rd Cong., 2nd sess., Ex. Doc. 89, March 1855.

———. *Claims for Spoliations Committed by Indians and Mexican.* 36th Cong., 1st sess., Rpt. No. 535, May 18, 1860.

———. Committee on Military Affairs. *The Texas Border Troubles.* 45th Cong. 2nd sess., Mis. Doc. 64, 1878.

———. *Depredations on the Frontiers of Texas.* 42nd Cong., 1st sess., Ex. Doc. 39, December 16, 1872.

———. *Depredations on the Frontiers of Texas.* 43rd Cong., 1st sess., Ex. Doc 257, Serial 1615, 1873.

———. *Difficulties on the Southwestern Frontier.* 36th Cong., 1st sess., Ex. Doc. No. 52, March 29, 1860.

———. *Events Leading Up to World War II,* 78th Cong., 2nd sess., House Doc. No. 541, 1945.

———. *Inland Trade with Mexico.* 26th Cong., 1st sess., Doc. No. 191, April 17, 1840.

———. *Investigation of Mexican Affairs.* 66th Cong. 2nd sess., Serial Nos. 7665–7666.

———. *Kickapoo Indians.* 40th Cong., 2nd sess., Ex. Doc. No. 340, Serial 1346, 1868.

———. *Letter from the Secretary of War in Relation to Depredations on the Texas Frontier.* 42nd Cong., 3rd sess., Doc. No. 13, 1873.

———. *Mexican Affairs.* 39th Cong., 1st sess., Ex. Doc. No. 73, Parts 1 and 2, 1866.

———. *Mexican Affairs.* 39th Cong., 2nd sess., Ex. Doc. No. 76, Serial 1294, 1867.

———. *Mexican Awards.* 45th Cong., 2nd sess., Doc. 27, 1878.

———. *Mexican Border Troubles.* 45th Cong., 1st sess., Ex. Doc. No. 13, Serial 1773, 1877.

———. *Mexican War Correspondence.* 30th Cong., 1st sess., Ex. Doc. No. 60, April 28, 1848.

———. *Military Forces Employed in the Mexican War.* 31st Cong., 1st sess., Ex. Doc. No. 24, January 24, 1850.

———. *Multinational Corporations in Brazil and Mexico: Structural Sources of Economic and Non-Economic Power.* 94th Cong., 1st sess., August 1975.

———. *North American Free Trade Agreement (NAFTA) and Supplemental Agreements to the NAFTA.* 103rd Cong., 1st sess., Serial 103–48, September 14, 15, 21, 23, 1993.

———. *President's Message.* 29th Cong., 2nd sess., Rpt. No. 70, February 24, 1847.

———. *Range and Ranch Cattle Traffic in the Western States and Territories.* Joseph Nimmo Jr. 48th Cong., 2nd sess., Ex. Doc. No. 267, March 2, 1885.

———. *Relations of the United States with Mexico.* Committee of Foreign Affairs. 45th Cong., 2nd sess., Rpt. No. 701, Serial 1824, April 25, 1878.

———. *Tariff of Duties in the Ports of Mexico.* 30th Cong., 2nd sess., Ex. Doc. No. 20 [?50], January 3, 1849.

———. *Texas Border Troubles,* 45th Cong., 2nd sess., Ex. Doc. No. 64, serial 1820, 1878.
———. *Texas Frontier Troubles.* 44th Cong., 1st sess., Rpt. No. 343, Serial 1709, 1876.
———. *Treaties with Mexico.* 22nd Cong., 1st sess., Doc. No. 225, May 1, 1832.
———. *Troubles on the Texas Frontier.* 36th Cong., 1st sess., Ex. Doc. No. 81, May 5, Serial 1056, 1860.
———. *United States and Mexico.* 25th Cong., 2nd sess., Doc. No. 351, July 4, 1838.
U.S. Congress. Senate. *Claims of the State of Texas.* 45th Cong., 2nd sess., Ex. Doc. No. 19, serial 1780, 1878.
———. "Clayton-Bulwer Treaty and Monroe Doctrine," 47th Cong., 1st sess., Ex. Doc. No. 194, pp. 117–25, May 8, 1882.
———. *Equitable Distribution of the Waters of the Rio Grande.* 55th Cong., 2nd sess., Doc. 229, April 7, 1898.
———. *Industrial Relations.* 64th Cong., 1st sess., Doc. No. 415, 1916.
———. *Investigation of Mexican Affairs.* 2 vols. 66th Cong., 2nd sess., Doc. No. 285, 1920.
———. *Message on Hostilities on the Rio Grande.* 36th Cong., 1st sess., Doc. No. 21, 1860.
———. *Message of the President.* 36th Cong., 1st sess., December 19, 1859.
———. *The Mexican Peso Crisis and the Administration's Proposed Loan Guarantee Packaged for Mexico.* 104th Cong., 1st sess., S. Hrg. 104–64, January 31, March 9–10, May 24, and July 14, 1995.
———. *Multinational Corporations in Brazil and Mexico: Structural Sources of Economic and Non-Economic Power.* 94th Cong., 1st sess., August 1975.
———. *Report of the Secretary of State: Regarding the Commercial Regulations of Foreign Nations.* 32nd Cong., 2nd sess., Ex. Doc. No. 52, February 1853.
———. *Revolutions in Mexico.* 62nd Cong., 2nd sess., 1913.
———. *Treaties and Conventions concluded between the United States of America and other Powers since July 4, 1776.* 41st Cong., 3rd sess., Ex. Doc. No. 36, 1871, pp. 542–587.
———. *United States and Mexican Claims.* 44th Cong., 2nd sess., Ex. Doc. No. 31, serial 1720, 1877.
U.S. Department of Commerce. Bureau of the Census. *Historical Statistics of the United States Colonial Times to 1970.* 2 vols. Washington, D.C.: GPO, 1975.
———. Bureau of Manufacturers. *Monthly Circular and Trade Reports.* Washington, D.C. 1899–1910.
U.S. Department of the Interior, Census Office. David T. Day. *Report on Mineral Industries in the United States at the Eleventh Census, 1890.* Washington, D.C.: GPO, 1892.
U.S. Department of State. Dispatches from the United States Consul in Nuevo Laredo, Tamaulipas, Mexico, 1871–1883. General Records of the Department of State, Record Group 59, National Archives.
———. *Papers Relating to the Foreign Relations of the United States, 1865–1881.* Washington, D.C.: GPO, 1922.
———. *Report on the Commercial Relations of the United States with Foreign Nations.* Washington, D.C.: GPO, 1855.
U.S. Department of the Treasury. *First Annual Report of the President's Interagency Task Force on the Economic Development of the Southwest Border.* Washington, D.C.: May 2000.
U.S. Federal Reserve. Dallas Federal Reserve Bank. *The Border Economy.* June 2001.
———. St. Louis Federal Reserve Bank. *NAFTA and the Geography of North American Trade.* Working Paper 2000–17b, St. Louis: November 2000.
U.S. General Accounting Office (GAO). *Border Security.* Report GAO-03–132NI, October 2002.
———. *Free Trade Area of the Americas,* Report GAO-01–1027, September 2001.

———. *U.S.-Mexico Border: Better Planning, Coordination Needed to Handle Growing Commercial Traffic.* Report GAO/NSIAD-00–25.

———. *U.S.-Mexico Border: Despite Some Progress, Environmental Infrastructure Challenges Remain.* Report GAO/NSIAD-00–26, March 2000.

———. *U.S.-Mexico Border: Issues and Challenges Confronting the United States and Mexico* Report GAO/NSIAD-99–190, July 1999.

U.S. Geological Survey, *Floods in Texas of 1940.* Washington, D.C., 1941.

———. *Major Floods in Texas in 1935.* No. 796G, Washington, D.C., 1937.

———. *The Santo Tomas Cannel Coal, Webb County, Texas,* George H. Ashley, Bulletin 691–1, Washington, D.C.: GPO, 1918.

———. *Summary of Surface Waters of Texas, 1898–1937.* No. 580, Washington, D.C., 1939.

———. *Tertiary Coals in South Texas: Anomalous Cannel-Like Coal of Webb County,* Robert D. Warwick, et al., Field Report 15, File 99–301, Washington, D.C.: GPO, April 1999.

War of the Rebellion: A Compilation of the Official Records of the Union and Confederate Armies. 130 vols. Washington, D.C.: GPO, 1880–1901.

Maps and Cartographic Documents

"Carta de las provincias de Tejas," Nuevo Santander, Nuevo Reino de León y Nuevo Estremadura. Mexico City: Servicio Geográfico del Ejercito, Archivos de Planos, 1773.

"Carta ó mapa geográfico de una Gran Parte del Reino de Nuevo España" Archivo General de Indios, Seville, Spain in Archives Division, Texas State Library, 1777.

Foster, Arthur. Map of "The Gateway of the Two Largest Republics in the World." Laredo: Laredo Improvement Company, February 23, 1889, Special Collections, Laredo Public Library.

"Juan de Oliván Rebolledo map of the Northeast Corner of New Spain." Original in Archivo General de Indies, Seville, Spain, and copy in Archives Division, Texas State Library, 1717.

"Laredo Port of Entry—Tamaulipas." U.S. Geological Survey, 1983.

"Laredo West, Texas." U.S. Geological Survey, 1965.

"Map of the Lands Leased by the United States from the City of Laredo, Map No. 26," National Archives, Washington, D.C., 1855.

"Map of the State of Texas." J. De Cordova, Houston, 1849.

"Map of Texas." Austin: General Land Office of the Republic, 1839.

"Map of Texas and the Countries Adjacent," by William H. Emory, Washington, D.C.: Bureau of Topographical Engineers, 1844. Note: The town of Laredo was the only settlement on the map on the north sides of the Rio Grande.

"Map of Texas with Parts of the Adjoining States." Compiled by Stephen F. Austin. Austin: General Land Office, March 13, 1832.? [1937]

"Mapa de Presidio de San Antonio de Béxar por El Capitan Luis Antonio Menchaca." original in Carter Brown Library, Brown University, March 1764.

"Mapa de la Sierra Gorda." Mexico City: Museo Nacional, 1792.

"Plan of San Antonio, 1867." British Library.

"Pueblo de Laredo: Mapas general y chronographico de la nueva colonia de Santander." Compiled by Don Agustín López, London: British Library, 1758.

"Ranches of the Nueces Strip." as seen in Jack Jackson, *Los mesteños,* College Station: Texas A&M University Press, 1986.

"Sketch Map of Productive Portion of Santo Tomas Coal Field, Webb County Texas." *Santo Tomas Cannel Coal,* Bulletin 691–1, Department of the Interior, 1918.

"Texas." By David H. Burr, New York: J.H. Colton and Company, 1834.

Newspapers and Serials

Austin American Statesman
Austin, *City Gazette* (1838–1842)
Austin, *Texas State Gazette* (1853)
Border Business Indicators (TAMIU)
Brownsville, *Rio Grande Sentinel*
Coal Age, 1912–30
Corpus Christi Caller
Cotulla Record
El Nicaragüense
Frank Leslie's Popular Monthly
Galveston Daily News
Houston Chronicle
Houston, *Tri-Weekly Telegraph*
Houston, 1836–45, *Telegraph and Texas Register*
Inlandport Magazine (Laredo Chamber of Commerce)
Laredo Times (to include: *Daily Times, Weekly Times,* and *Morning Times*)
Laredo, *2020* (LDF)
Laredo, *¿Qué Pasa?* [Laredo Air Force Base]
Laredo, *¡Saludos!*
Laredo South Texas Citizen (April 30, 1937)
Laredo, *The Chaparral*
Laredos
London Times
New Haven, Conn., *Columbia Register,* 1836
New Orleans, *Era*
New Orleans, *Times-Picayune*
New York, *The Chronicle*
New York, 1855–1922, *Engineering and Mining Journal*
New York Herald
New York, *Newsweek*
New York, *Statesman*
New York, *Street Railway Gazette*
New York, *Time Magazine*
New York Times
New York, *Wall Street Journal*
New York, *World*
Nuevo Laredo, *El Mañana*
The Railroad Gazette
San Antonio Express
Washington, D.C., *National Intelligencer*
Zapata County News

Books and Articles

3040th Pilot Training Wing. *Jet Wash: Class '57-D.* Laredo: Laredo Air Force Base, November 1956.

Acosta, Teresa P., and Ruthie Winegarten. *Las Tejanas: 300 Years of History.* Austin: University of Texas Press, 2003.

Adams, Charles F., ed. *Memoirs of John Quincy Adams.* Philadelphia, 1824–27.

Adams, Ephraim D. *British Interests and Activities in Texas, 1838–1846.* Baltimore: Johns Hopkins Press, 1910.

Adams, John A., Jr., *Bordering the Future: The Impact of Mexico on the United States.* Westport, Conn.: Praeger, 2006.

———. *Damming the Colorado.* College Station: Texas A&M University Press, 1990.

———. *Mexican Banking and Investment in Transition.* Westport, Conn.: Quorum Books, 1997.

Aguilar Camín, Héctor, and Lorenzo Meyer. *In the Shadow of the Mexican Revolution.* Austin: University of Texas Press, 1993.

Alanso, Ana Maria. *Thread of Blood: Colonialism, Revolution, and Gender on Mexico's Northern Frontiers.* Tucson: University of Arizona Press, 1995.

Alessio Robles, Vito. *Coahuila y Texas en la época colonial.* Mexico City: Editorial Cultura, 1938.

———. *Coahuila y Texas desde la consumación de la independencia . . .* Mexico: 1945.

Alexander, Thomas E. *The Wings of Change: The Army Air Force in Texas during World War II.* Abilene: McWhinney Foundation Press, 2003.

Allhands, James L. *Gringo Builders,* Dallas: Privately printed, 1931.

———. *Railroads to the Rio.* Salado, Tex.: The Anson Jones Press, 1960.

———. *Uriah Lott.* San Antonio: Naylor Company, 1949.

Almaraz, Félix D., Jr. *Crossroads of Empire: The Church and State on the Rio Grande Frontier of Coahuila and Texas.* San Antonio: Center for Archaeological Research, 1979.

———. "Governor Manuel de Salcedo of Hispanic Texas, 1808–1813: A Reappraisal." *Texana* (Spring 1968): 12–31.

———. *Tragic Cavalier: Governor Manuel de Salcedo of Texas, 1808–1813.* Austin: University of Texas Press, 1971.

Almonte, Juan N. "Statistical Report on Texas" (1835). Translated by Carlos E. Castañeda. *SWHQ* (January 1925): 177–222.

Alonzo, Armando C. *Tejano Legacy: Rancheros and Settlers in South Texas.* Albuquerque: University of New Mexico Press, 1998.

Amberson, Mary M., James A. McAllen, and Margaret H. McAllen. *I'd Rather Sleep in Texas: A History of the Lower Rio Grande Valley and the People of the Santa Anita Land Grant.* Austin: TSHA, 2003.

Anderson, Gary C. *The Conquest of Texas: Ethnic Cleansing in the Promised Land, 1820–1825.* Norman: University of Oklahoma Press, 2005.

Anderson, Joan B. "Maquiladoras and Border Industrialization: Impact on Economic Development in Mexico." *JBS* (Fall 1990): 5–9.

Arlitt, J. L. *Llave Coal Land on the Rio Grande.* Austin: n.p., circa 1914.

Arreola, Daniel D. "Plaza Towns of South Texas," *Geographical Review* (January 1992): 56–73.

Arreola, Daniel D., and James R. Curtis. *The Mexican Border Cities.* Tucson: University of Arizona Press, 1993.

Ashcroft, Allan C. *Texas in the Civil War: A Résumé History.* Austin: Texas Civil War Centennial Commission, 1962.

Ashford, Gerald, *Spanish Texas: Yesterday and Today.* Austin: Jenkins, 1971.

Ashley, George H. *The Santo Tomas Cannel Coal, Webb County Texas.* Washington, D.C.: GPO, 1918.

Atkinson, Mary J. *The Texas Indians.* San Antonio: Naylor, 1953.

Baerresen, D. *The Border Industrialization Program of Mexico.* Lexington, Mass.: Heath Lexington Books, 1971.

Baggett, James A. "Origins of Early Texas Republican Party Leadership," *Journal of Southern History* (August 1974): 441–54.

Ballou, Maturin M. *Aztec Land.* Boston: Houghton Mifflin, 1890.

Bancroft, Hubert Howe. *History of the North Mexican States and Texas.* 2 vols. San Francisco: History Company, 1884–90.

———. *History of Mexico.* 3 vols. San Francisco: History Company, 1883.

Bannon, John F. *The Spanish Borderlands Frontier, 1531–1821.* Albuquerque: University of New Mexico Press, 1974.

Barker, Eugene C. "The Finances of the Texas Revolution." *Political Science Quarterly* 19, no. 4 (1904): 612–35.

———. *The Life of Stephen F. Austin.* Austin: TSHA, 1949.

———. *Mexico and Texas, 1821–1835.* New York: Russell and Russell, 1965.

Barker, Eugene C., ed. *The Austin Papers.* 2 vols. Austin: University of Texas Press, 1926.

Barlow, R. H. *The Extent of the Empire of the Culhua Mexica,* Berkeley: University of California Press, 1949.

Barnes, Thomas C., Thomas H. Naylor, and Charles W. Polzer. *Northern New Spain: A Research Guide.* Tucson: University of Arizona Press, 1981.

Barr, Alwyn. *Texans in Revolt: The Battle for San Antonio, 1835.* Austin: University of Texas Press, 1990.

Barry, Tom. *Zapata's Revenge: Free Trade and the Farm Crisis in Mexico.* Boston: South End Press, 1995.

Barry, Willie B. *History of Water Utilities: Laredo Texas.* Laredo: Central Power and Light Company, 1969.

Barton, Henry W. "Five Texas Frontier Companies during the Mexican War." *SWHQ* (July 1962): 17–30.

Baughman, James P. "The Evolution of Rail-Water Systems of Transportation in the Gulf Southwest, 1836–1890." *Journal of Southern History* (August 1968): 357–81.

Beezley, William, and David E. Lorey, eds. *Viva Mexico! Viva la Independencia! Celebrations of September 16.* Wilmington, Del.: SR Books, 2001.

Bell, Samuel E., and James M. Smallwood. *The Zona Libre, 1858–1905: A Problem in American Diplomacy.* El Paso: Texas Western Press, 1982.

Benavides, Adán. "The Fortification of Laredo: The Documentary Evidence for Proposals in 1792 and 1813." *El Campanario* (September 1989): 11–26.

Benedicto, Luis. *Historia de Nuevo Laredo.* Nuevo Laredo: Tamaulipas Talleres Linotipograficos de Impresores de Norte, 1956.

Benson, Nettie Lee, ed. "A Governor's Report on Texas in 1809." *SWHQ* (April 1968): 603–16.

Berlandier, Jean Louis. *The Indians of Texas in 1830.* Edited by John C. Ewers. Washington, D.C.: Smithsonian Institution Press, 1969.

———. *Journey to Mexico during the Years 1826 to 1834.* Translated by Sheila M. Ohlendorf et al. Edited by C. H. Muller et al. 2 vols. Austin: TSHA, 1980.

"Bermuda Onion Culture in Texas." College Station, *A&M College Bulletin,* No. 65, November 1932.

Bernstein, Marvin D. *Foreign Investment in Latin America.* New York: Alfred A. Knopf, 1966.

———. *The Mexican Mining Industry, 1890–1950: A Study of the Interaction of Politics, Economics, and Technology.* Albany: State University of New York Press, 1964.

Bernstein, Peter L. *The Power of Gold: The History of an Obsession.* New York: John Wiley and Sons, 2000.

Betts, Dianne C., and Daniel J. Slottje. *Crisis on the Rio Grande.* Boulder: Westview Press, 1994.

Betty, Gerald. *Comanche Society: Before the Reservation.* College Station: Texas A&M University Press, 2002.

Bilateral Commission on the Future of the United States–Mexican Relations. *The Challenge of Interdependence: Mexico and the United States.* Lanham, Md.: University Press of America, 1989.

Bishop, Morris. *The Odyssey of Cabeza de Vaca.* New York: Century, 1913.

Black, Michael F., ed. *Mirando City: A New Town in a New Oil Field.* Laredo: Laredo Publishing, 1972.

Bollaert, William. "Observations on the Geography of Texas." *Journal of the Royal Geographical Society of London* 20 (1850): 113–35.

Bolton, Herbert Eugene. *Guide to Materials for the United States in the Principal Archives of Mexico.* Publication No. 163. Washington, D.C.: Carnegie Institution, 1913.

———. "The Mission as a Frontier Institution in the Spanish-American Colonies." *AHR* (October 1917): 42–61.

———. *The Spanish Borderlands.* Albuquerque: University of New Mexico Press, 1996.

———. *Texas in the Middle Eighteenth Century.* Austin: University of Texas Press, 1970.

———. "Tienda de Cuervo's Ynspección of Laredo, 1757." *SWHQ* (January 1903): 187–203.

Bolton, Herbert Eugene, ed. *Spanish Exploration in the Southwest, 1542–1706.* New York: Barnes and Noble, 1908.

Bonnell, George W. *Topographical Description of Texas.* Austin: Clark, Wing, and Brown, 1840. Reprint; Waco: Texian Press, 1964.

Borah, Woodrow. *New Spain's Century of Depression.* Berkeley: University of California Press, 1951.

Bracht, Victor. *Texas in 1848.* [*Texas Im Jahre 1848,* Elberfeld, Germany]. Translated by Charles Frank Schmidt. San Antonio: Naylor, 1931.

Brading, David A. *Miners and Merchants in Bourbon Mexico, 1763–1810.* Cambridge: Cambridge University Press, 1971.

Brand, Donald D. "The Early History of the Range Cattle Industry in Northern Mexico." *Agricultural History* (July 1961): 132–38.

Branding, D. A., and Henry E. Cross. "Colonial Silver Mining: Mexico and Peru." *HAHR* (November 1872): 545–79.

Brannon, Jeffery T., W. D. English, and Patricia Kriner. "Commercial Banking on the U.S.-Mexico Border." *JBS* (Spring 1897): 17–33.

Bravo y Tudela, A. *Recuerdos de la Villa de Laredo.* Madrid: Imprenta de la Asociación del Arte de Imprimir, 1873.

Briggs, Charles J., and John R. Van Ness, eds. *Land, Water, and Culture: New Perspectives on Hispanic Land Grants.* Albuquerque: University of New Mexico, 1987.

Briggs, Donald C., and Marvin Alisky. *Historical Dictionary of Mexico.* Metuchen, N.J.: Scarecrow Press, 1981.

Brinckerhoff, Sidney B., and Odie B. Faulk. *Lancers for the King: A Study of the Frontier Military System of Northern New Spain.* Phoenix: Arizona Historical Foundation, 1965.

Brooks, James F. *Captives and Cousins: Slavery, Kinship, and Community in the Southwest Borderlands.* Chapel Hill: University of North Carolina Press, 2002.

Brown, Angel S., and Gloria V. Cadena. *San Agustín Parish of Laredo.* Saltillo: Graficas Canepa, 1989.

Brown, John Henry. *History of Texas from 1685 to 1892.* 2 vols. St. Louis: L. E. Daniell Publishers, 1892.

———. *Indian Wars and Pioneers of Texas.* Austin: L. E. Daniell, 1880. Reprint; Easley, S.C.: Southern Historical Press, 1978.

Bryan, González Vargas y González Baz. *Foreign Investment in Mexico: A Summary of Laws and Regulations Currently in Force.* Juárez: N.p., 1991.

Buenger, Walter L. *Secession and the Union in Texas.* Austin: University of Texas Press, 1984.

Burkholder, Mark A., and Lyman L. Johnson. *Colonial Latin America.* Oxford: Oxford University Press, 2001.

Byfield, Patsy J. *Falcon Dam and the Lost Towns of Zapata.* Austin: Texas Memorial Museum, 1971.

Cabeza de Vaca, Alvar Núñez. *The Account: Alvar Núñez Cabeza de Vaca's Relación.* Translated by Martin A. Favata and José B. Fernández. Houston: Arte Público, 1993.

Calderon, Roberto R. *Mexican Coal Mining Labor in Texas and Coahuila, 1880–1930.* College Station: Texas A&M University Press, 2000.

———. *South Texas Coal Mining: A Community History* : N.p. 1984.

Callahan, James M. *American Foreign Policy in Mexican Relations.* New York: Macmillan, 1932.

Callcott, Wilfrid H. *Santa Anna: The Story of an Enigma Who Once Was Mexico.* Norman: University of Oklahoma Press, 1936.

Calloway, Colin G. *The Scratch of a Pen: 1763 and the Transformation of North America.* New York: Oxford University Press, 2006.

Camp, Roderic Ai. *Politics in Mexico.* New York: Oxford University Press, 1991.

Campbell, John. *A Concise History of the Spanish America.* London: John Stagg, 1741. Reprint; Folkestone, England: Dawsons of Pall Mall, 1972. 89–134.

Campbell, Randolph B. *Gone to Texas.* New York: Oxford University Press, 2003.

Campe, Célebre. *Historia del descubrimiento y conquista de America.* Madrid: Esta. Tipografico, 1845.

Cantrell, Gregg. *Stephen F. Austin: Empresario of Texas.* New Haven, Conn.: Yale University Press, 1999.

Carlson, Paul H. *Texas Woollybacks: The Range Sheep and Goat Industry.* College Station: Texas A&M University Press, 1982.

Carman, Michael D. *United States Customs and the Madero Revolution.* El Paso: Texas Western Press, 1976.

Carr, Albert Z. *The World and William Walker.* New York: Harper and Row, 1963.

Carroll, H. Bailey, ed. "Texas Collection: Governors of Texas 1778–1822." *SWHQ* (April 1963): 593–94.

Caruso, A. Brooke. *The Mexican Spy Company: U.S. Covert Operations in Mexico, 1845–1848.* Jefferson, N.C.: McFarland, 1991.

Casey, Robert J. *The Texas Border.* Indianapolis: Bobbs-Merrill, 1950.

Castañeda, Carlos E. *Our Catholic Heritage in Texas, 1519–1936.* 7 vols. New York: Arno Press, 1936–58.

Castañeda, Jorge G. *Perpetuating Power: How Mexican Presidents Were Chosen.* New York: New Press, 2000.

Cerutti, Mario. *Burguesía y capitalismo en Monterrey, 1850–1910.* Mexico City: Claves Latinoamericanas, 1983.

Cerutti, Mario, Isabel Ortega, and Lylia Palacios. "Empresarios y empresas en el norte de Mexico." *European Review of Latin American and Caribbean Studies* (October 2000).

Chambers, William T. "Lower Rio Grande Valley." *Economic Geography* (October 1930): 364–73.

Chapa, Juan Bautista. *Texas and Northeastern Mexico, 1630–1690.* Edited by William C. Foster. Austin: University of Texas Press, 1997.

Chávez, Thomas E. *Spain and the Independence of the United States.* Albuquerque: University of New Mexico Press, 2002.

Chatfield, W. C. H. *The Twin Cities of the Border and the Country of the Lower Rio Grande.* New Orleans: Brandao, 1893. Reprint 1959.

Cheeseman, Bruce S. *Perfectly Exhausted with Pleasure: The 1881 King-Kennedy Excursion Train to Laredo.* Austin: Book Club of Texas, 1992.

Chernow, Ron. *Titan: The Life of John D. Rockefeller, Sr.* New York: Vintage Books, 1998.

Chevalier, François. *Land and Society in Colonial Mexico: The Great Hacienda.* Berkeley: University of California Press, 1970.

Chief Mexican Participants (translated by Carlos E. Castañeda). *The Mexican Side of the Texas Revolution, 1836.* Washington, D.C.: Documents Publications, 1971.

Chipman, Donald E. *Spanish Texas, 1519–1821.* Austin: University of Texas Press, 1992.

Chipman, Donald E., and Harriett D. Joseph. *Explorers and Settlers of Spanish Texas.* Austin: University of Texas Press, 2001. 134–48.

Christian, Asa K. "Mirabeau Buonaparte Lamar." *SWHQ* (January 1920): 153–70; (April 1920): 231–70; (July 1920): 39–80; (October 1920): 87–139; (January 1921): 195–234; and (April 1921): 317–24.

Cisneros, Jaime E. P. *Los Chapas en Tamaulipas, Coahuila, Nuevo Leon y Texas desde 1650 haste 1990.* Matamoros: N.p., 1999.

Cisneros, José. *Riders of the Border.* El Paso: Texas Western Press, 1971.

A Citizen of the United States. *A View of South America and Mexico.* New York: Huntington, 1826.

Clarke, A. B. Edited by Anne M Perry. *Travels in Mexico and California.* College Station: Texas A&M University Press, 1988.

Clay, W. J. *Agricultural and Statistical Report 1905.* Austin: State Printing Company, 1905.

Cleland, Robert G., ed. *The Mexican Year Book: 1920–21.* Los Angeles: Mexican Year Book Publishing, 1922.

Cline, Howard F. *Mexico: Revolution to Evolution, 1940–1960.* New York: Oxford University Press, 1963.

———. *The United States and Mexico.* Cambridge, Mass.: Harvard University Press, 1969.

Coatsworth, John H. *Growth against Development: The Economic Impact of Railroads in Porfirian Mexico.* De Kalb: Northern Illinois University Press, 1981.

———. "Obstacles to Economic Growth in Nineteenth-Century Mexico." *AHR* 83 (February 1978): 80–100.

———. "Railroads, Landholding and Agrarian Protest in the Early Porfiriato." *HAHR* 54 (February 1974): 48–71.

Cockcroft, James D. *Intellectual Precursors of the Mexican Revolution, 1900–1913.* Austin: University of Texas, 1968.

———. *Mexico's Hope: An Encounter with Politics and History.* New York: Monthly Review Press, 1998.

Coe, Michael, and Rex Koontz. *Mexico: From the Olmecs to the Aztecs,* 5th ed. London: Thames and Hudson, 2002.

Coerver, Don M. *The Porfirian Interregnum: The Presidency of Manuel González of Mexico.* Ft. Worth: Texas Christian University Press, 1979.

Cohen, Barry. "The Texas-Mexican Border, 1858–1867." *Texana* (Summer 1968): 153–58.

Conde, Roberto C. *The First Stages of Modernization in Spanish America.* New York: Harper and Row, 1974.

Cook, Scott. *Mexican Brick Culture in the Building of Texas, 1800s–1980s.* College Station: Texas A&M University Press, 1998.

Cook, Sherburne F., and Woodrow Borah. "The Rate of Population Change in Central Mexico, 1550–1570." *HAHR* 37 (November 1957): 463–70.

Coopwood, Bethel. "Notes on the History of La Bahia del Espíritu Santo." *SWHQ* (October 1898): 164.

Cortes, Carlos E., intro. *The Mexican Experience in Texas.* New York: Arno Press, 1976. Contains translation of Comisión Pesquisidora report of 1875.

Costeloe, Michael P. *Bonds and Bondholders: British Investors and Mexico's Foreign Debt, 1824–1888.* Westport, Conn.: Praeger, 2003.

———. "Spain and the Latin American Wars of Independence: The Free Trade Controversy, 1810–1820." *HAHR* 61 (May 1981): 209–34.

Coulter, E. Merton. "The Movement from Agricultural Reorganization in the Cotton South during the Civil War." *Agricultural History* (January 1927): 3–17.

Cox, I. J. "The Early Settlers of San Fernando." *SWHQ* (July 1901–April 1902): 142–60.

———. "The Southwest Boundary of Texas." *SWHQ* (October 1902): 81–102.

Crimmins, M. L. "An Indian Raid Near Laredo." *Frontier Times,* (August 1932).

Cruz, Gilbert R. *Let There Be Towns: Spanish Municipal Origins in the American Southwest, 1610–1810.* College Station: Texas A&M University Press, 1988.

Cué Cánavos, Agustín. *Historia social y económica de México, 1521–1854.* Mexico City: Editorial F. Trillas, 1967.

Cumberland, Charles C. *Mexican Revolution: The Constitutionalist Years.* Austin: University of Texas Press, 1974.

———. "Precursors of the Mexican Revolution," *HAHR* (May 1942): 345–50.

Curtis, James R. "Central Business Districts of the Two Laredos." *Geographical Review* (January 1993): 54–65.

Dabbs, J. Autry, trans. *Lopez's Report of the Texas Missions in 1785.* Austin: Preliminary Studies of the Texas Catholic Historical Society 3, no. 6 (1940).

Da Camara, Kathleen. *Laredo on the Rio Grande.* San Antonio: Naylor, 1949.

Daddysman, James W. *The Matamoros Trade: Confederate Commerce, Diplomacy, and Intrigue.* Newark: University of Delaware Press, 1984.

Dale, Edward Everett. *The Range Cattle Industry: Ranching on the Great Plains from 1865 to 1925.* Norman: University of Oklahoma Press, 1930. New ed., 1960.

Daniels, Roger. *Guarding the Golden Door.* New York: Hill and Wang, 2004.

Dary, David. *The Buffalo Book: The Full Saga of the American Animal.* Athens, Ohio: Swallow Press, 1989.

———. *Cowboy Culture: A Saga of Five Centuries.* New York: Alfred A. Knopf, 1981.

———. *Entrepreneurs of the Old West.* New York: Alfred A. Knopf, 1989.

Davila, Alberto. "The Impact of the 1982 Peso Devaluation on Maquiladora Profits." *JBS* (Fall 1990): 39–49.

Davis, Joseph S. "Economic Factors in Mexico." *American Economic Review* 20, no. 1 (March 1930) 40–48.

Davis, William C. *Lone Star Rising.* New York: Free Press, 2004.

De Cordova, J. *Texas: Her Resources and Her Public Men.* Philadelphia: J. B. Lippincott 1858. Reprint; Texian Press, 1969.

De la Garza, Lorenzo. *La Antigua Revilla.* Ciudad Victoria: 1944.

De la Garza, Rodolfo G. *Los Laredos: Nuevo Laredo.* 2 vols. N.p., 1989.

De la Teja, Jesús F. "El Camino Real: Lifeline of Colonial Texas." *Gulf Coast Historical Review* (Fall 1992): 64–77.

———. *San Antonio de Béxar.* New Mexico: University of New Mexico Press, 1995.

De León, Arnoldo. *The Tejano Community, 1836–1900.* Albuquerque: University of New Mexico Press, 1982.

DePalo, William A, Jr. *The Mexican National Army, 1822–1852.* College Station: Texas A&M University Press, 1997.

DeShields, James T. *Border Wars of Texas.* Tioga, Tex.: Herald Company, 1912. Reprint Waco: Texian Press, 1976.

Del Castillo, Richard G. *The Treaty of Guadalupe Hidalgo: A Legacy of Conflict.* Norman: University of Oklahoma Press, 1990.

Delaney, Robert W. "Matamoros, Port for Texas during the Civil War." *SWHQ* (April 1955): 473–87.

"Description of Texas by Stephen F. Austin." *SWHQ* (October 1924): 113.

Dethloff, Henry C. *The United States and the Global Economy since 1845.* Ft. Worth: Harcourt Brace, 1997.

Devine, Ella. *History of Electric Utility: Laredo Texas.* Laredo: Central Power & Light Company, 1969.

———. *Laredo Electric Railway Company.* Laredo: Central Power and Light Company, 1969.

Diaz, Bernal. *The Conquest of New Spain.* New York: Penguin, 1963.

Dicken, Samuel N. "Cotton Regions of Mexico." *Economic Geography* (October 1938): 363–71.

Dimmick, Gregg J. *Sea of Mud.* Austin: TSHA, 2004.

Dobie, J. Frank. *Coronado's Children.* New York: Literary Guild of America, 1931.

———. "The First Cattle in Texas and the Southwest Progenitors of the Longhorn," *SWHQ* (January 1939): 171–97.

———. *The Longhorns.* Boston: Little, Brown, 1941.

———. *The Mustangs.* Boston: Little, Brown, 1952.

———. *A Vaquero of the Brush Country.* Dallas: Southwest Press, 1929.

Dobkins, Betty E. *The Spanish Element in Texas Water Law.* Austin: University of Texas Press, 1959.

Documents of Major General Sam Houston, Commander in Chief of the Texas Army. New Orleans: John Cox Printers, n.d. circa 1836. Reprint; Austin: Pemberton Press, 1964.

Domenech, Emmanuel. *Missionary Adventures in Texas and Mexico: A Personal Narrative of Six Years' Sojourn in those Regions.* London: Longman, Brown, Green, Longmans, and Roberts, 1858.

Domínquez, Nadima S., and Isabel R. Perio. *Globalización y competitividad la industria siderúgica en México.* Mexico City: UNAM, 2002.

Downs, Fane, "Governor Antonio Martinez and the Defense of Texas from Foreign Invasion." *Texas Military History* 7, no. 1 (Spring 1968).

Driver, Harold E. *Indians of North America.* Chicago: University of Chicago Press, 1961.

Dueñes, Heliodoro. *Los bancos y la revolución.* Mexico City: Editorial Cultura, 1945.

Duffus, R. L. *The Sante Fe Trail.* Albuquerque: University of New Mexico Press, 1958.

Dunn, William Edward. "Apache Relations in Texas, 1718–1750." Texas State Historical Association *Quarterly* 14, no. 3 (January 1911).

Durham, George, and Clyde Wantland. *Taming the Nueces Strip: The Story of McNelly's Rangers.* Austin: University of Texas Press, 1962.

Dusenberry, William H. *The Mexican Mesta: The Administration of Ranching in Colonial Mexico.* Urbana: University of Illinois Press, 1963.

Eaton, Clement. *The Growth of Southern Civilization, 1790–1860.* New York: Harper and Row, 1961.

Eaton, David J., and John M. Anderson. *The State of the Rio Grande/Río Bravo.* Tucson: University of Arizona Press, 1987.

Edward, David B. *The History of Texas.* Cincinnati: J. A. James, 1836. Reprint; 1990.

Ehrlich, Paul R., Loy Bilderback, and Anne H. Ehrlich. *The Golden Door.* New York: Ballantine Books, 1979.

Eisenhower, John, S.D. *Intervention: The United States and the Mexican Revolution, 1913–1917.* New York: W. W. Norton, 1993.

———. *So Far from God: The U.S. War with Mexico, 1846–1848.* New York: Doubleday, 1989.

Elliott, Claude. "Union Sentiment in Texas, 1861–1865." *SWHQ* (April 1947): 470–73.

Emory, William H. *Report on the United States and Mexican Boundary Survey, Made under the Direction of the Secretary of the Interior.* 2 vols. Washington, D.C.: Cornelius Wendell, 1857.

"The Empire of Mexico," *London Quarterly Review* (April 1864): 195–98.

Enrique, Andres Molina. *Los grandes problemas nacionales,* Mexico City: Ediciones del Instituto Nacional de la Juventud Mexicana, 1909.

Evans, Thomas I. *Bituminous Coal in Texas.* Austin: Bureau of Economic Geology, 1974.

Faber, James. *Texas, CSA.* New York: Jackson, 1947.

Faulk, Odie B. *The Last Years of Spanish Texas, 1778–1821.* The Hague: Mouton, 1964.

———. "Ranching in Spanish Texas." *HAHR* 45 (May 1965): 257–66.

Fehrenbach, T. R. *Comanches: The Destruction of a People.* New York: Alfred A. Knopf, 1974.

———. *Fire and Blood: A History of Mexico.* New York: Collier, 1973.

———. *Lone Star: A History of Texas and the Texans.* New York: Collier, 1968.

———. *Seven Keys to Texas.* El Paso: Texas Western Press, 1983.

Fenn, Elizabeth A. *Pox Americana: The Great Smallpox Epidemic, 1775–1782.* New York: Hill and Wang, 2001.

Fernández, Raúl A. *The Mexican-American Border Region.* Notre Dame, Ind.: University of Notre Dame Press, 1989.

———. *The United States–Mexico Border: A Politico-Economic Profile.* Notre Dame, Ind.: University of Notre Dame Press, 1977.

Ficker, Sandra K. "El Comercio México–Estados Unidos, 1870–1929: Reconstrucción estadística y tendencias generales." *MS/EM* (Winter 2001): 71–107.

Field, Joseph E. *Three Years in Texas.* Boston: Justin Jones, 1836.

Filísola, Vicente. *Memorias para la historia de la guerra de Tejas.* Mexico City: Impr. Cumplido, 1849.

Fisher, O. C., and J. C. Dykes. *King Fisher: His Life and Times.* Norman: University of Oklahoma Press, 1966.

Fisher, Orceneth. *Sketches: Texas in 1840.* 1841. Reprint; Waco: Texian Press, 1964.

Flavella, James W. *Laredo, the Gateway City: Its Many Resources and Advantages Told in Stories and Pictures.* Laredo: Times, 1925.

———. *A Souvenir Album of Laredo, "The Gateway to Mexico": Historical, Pictorial, and Descriptive Stories of Laredo, Webb County, the Military and Other Forces on the Rio Grande Frontier and Mexico.* Laredo: J. W. Flavella, 1917.

Folsom, *C. J. Mexico in 1842.* New York: 1842.

Foner, Eric. *Reconstruction: America's Unfinished Revolution, 1863–1877.* New York: HarperCollins, 2005.

Forbes, Jack D. *Apache, Navaho, and Spaniard.* Norman: University of Nebraska Press, 1960.

Ford, John S. *Rip Ford's Texas.* Edited by Stephen B. Oates. Austin: University of Texas Press, 1963.

Foscue, Edwin J. "Agricultural History of the Lower Rio Grande Valley Regions." *Agricultural History* (July 1934): 124–37.

Foster, John W. *Diplomatic Memoirs.* 2 vols, Boston: Houghton Mifflin, 1909.

Foster, William C. *Spanish Expeditions into Texas, 1689–1768.* Austin: University of Texas Press, 1995.

Francaviglia, Richard V., and Douglas W. Richmond, eds. *Dueling Eagles: Reinterpreting the U.S.-Mexican War, 1846–1848.* Fort Worth: Texas Christian University Press, 2000.

Freeman, James W., ed. *Prose and Poetry of the Live Stock Industry in the United States . . .* Denver, Colo., and Kansas City, Mo.: National Livestock Historical Association, 1905.

Fremantle, Arthur J. L. *Three Months in Southern States: April–June 1863.* New York: John Bradburn, 1864.

"The Friendly Border." *Humble Way,* March–April 1946, 12–17.

Fuller, H. J., ed. *The Laredo Visitors' Guide.* Laredo, October 15, 1935.

Fuller, John D. P. *The Movement for the Acquisition of All Mexico, 1846–1848.* Baltimore: Johns Hopkins Press, 1936.

Fulmore, Z. T. *The History and Geography of Texas.* Austin: TSHA, 1915.

Furtado, Celso. *Economic Development in Latin America.* Cambridge: University Press, 1970.

Gallaway, B. P., ed. *Texas, Dark Corner of the Confederacy: Contemporary Accounts of the Lone Star State in the Civil War.* Lincoln: University of Nebraska Press, 1994.

Gammel, H. P. M. [N]. *The Laws of Texas, 1822–1897.* 10 vols. Austin: Gammel, 1898.

Ganster, Paul, and Eugenio O. Valenciano. *The Mexican-U.S. Border Region and the Free Trade Agreement.* San Diego: Institute for Regional Studies, 1992.

García, Luis Navarro. "The North of New Spain as a Political Problem in the Eighteenth Century." In *New Spain's Northern Frontier: Essays on Spain in the American West, 1540–1821,* edited by David J. Weber. Dallas: Southern Methodist University Press, 1988.

García, Rogelia O. *The Bells of St. Augustine.* Laredo: 1963.

———. *Dolores, Revilla, and Laredo: Three Sister Settlements.* Waco: Texian Press, 1970.

Garner, Paul. *Portfirio Díaz.* London: Longman, 2001.

Garner, Richard L., and Spiro E. Stefanou. *Economic Growth and Change in Bourbon Mexico.* Gainesville: University Press of Florida, 1993.

Garrett, Julia K. *Green Flag over Texas: A Story of the Last Years of Spain in Texas.* New York: Cordova Press, 1939.

———. "The First Constitution of Texas, April 17, 1813." *SWHQ* (April 1937): 290–308.

Garrison, George P. *Texas.* Boston: Houghton Mifflin, 1903.

———. *Western Extension.* New York: Harpers and Brothers, 1906.

Gehlbach, Frederick R. *Mountain Islands and Desert Seas: A Natural History of the U.S.-Mexican Borderlands.* College Station: Texas A&M University Press, 1981.

Gentry, Bruse. "Texas." *Coal Age* (January 16, 1919).

George, Eugene. *Historic Architecture of Texas: The Falcon Reservoir.* Austin: Texas Historical Commission, 1975.

Gerhard, Peter. *The North Frontier of New Spain.* Princeton, N.J.: Princeton University Press, 1982.

Gibson, Charles. *Spain in America.* New York: Harper and Row, 1966.

Gilliland, Maude T. *Horsebackers of the Brush Country: A Story of the Texas Rangers and Mexican Liquor Smugglers.* Brownsville: Springman-King, 1968.

Glaeser, Edward L., et al. "Growth in Cities." *Journal of Political Economy* (December 1992): 1126–52.

Goetzmann, William H. *When the Eagle Screamed: The Romantic Horizon in American Expansionism, 1800–1860.* Norman: University of Oklahoma Press, 1966.

Gouge, William M. *The Fiscal History of Texas.* Philadelphia: Lippincott, Grambo, 1852.

Graf, Leroy P. "Colonizing Projects in Texas South of the Nueces, 1820–1845." *SWHQ* (April 1947): 431–48.

Graham, Don. *Kings of Texas: The 150-Year Saga of an American Ranching Empire.* Hoboken, N.J.: John Wiley, 2003.

Graham, Philip. *The Life and Poems of Mirabeau B. Lamar.* Chapel Hill: University of North Carolina Press, 1938.

Grayson, George W., ed. *Prospects for Democracy in Mexico.* New Brunswick, N.J.: Transaction Publishers, 1990.

Green, Michael R. *Calendar of the Papers of Mirabeau B. Lamar.* Austin: Texas State Archives, 1982.

Green, Stanley C. *Laredo, 1755–1820: An Overview.* Laredo: Border Studies, 1991.

———. *The Mexican Republic: The First Decade, 1823–1832.* Pittsburgh: University of Pittsburgh Press 1987.

———. *An Overview of Rural Webb County.* Laredo: Border Studies, 1992.

Green, Stanley C., ed. *A History of the Washington Birthday Celebration.* Laredo: Border Studies, 1999.

———. *Laredo in 1881.* Laredo: Border Studies, 1990.

Gregg, Robert D. *The Influence of Border Troubles on Relations between the United States and Mexico, 1876–1910.* Baltimore: Johns Hopkins Press, 1937.

Griffin, Charles C. *The United States and the Disruption of the Spanish Empire, 1810–1822: A Study of the Relations of the United States with Spain and with the Rebel Spanish Colonies.* New York: Columbia University Press, 1937.

Grimm, Agnes G. *Llanos mesteños: Mustang Plains.* Waco: Texian Press, 1968.

Guice, C. Norman, ed. "Texas in 1804." *SWHQ* (July 1955): 46–56.

Guice, John D. W. "Cattle Raisers of the Old Southwest: A Reinterpretation." *Western Historical Quarterly* 8, no. 2 (1977): 168–87.

Gulick, C. A., et al., eds. *The Papers of Mirabeau Buonaparte Lamar.* 6 vols. Austin: A. C. Baldwin and Sons, 1921–27.

Guthrie, Keith. *Texas Forgotten Ports.* Austin: Eakin Press, 1988.

Haber, Stephen H. *Industry and Underdevelopment: The Industrialization of Mexico, 1890–1940.* Stanford, Calif.: Stanford University Press, 1989.

Hackett, Charles W. "The Recognition of the Díaz Government by the United States," *SWHQ* (July 1924): 34–55.

Haley, P. Edward. *Revolution and Intervention: The Diplomacy of Taft and Wilson with Mexico, 1910–1917.* Cambridge, Mass.: MIT Press, 1970.

Hall, Linda B., and Don M. Coerver. *Revolution on the Border: The United States and Mexico, 1910–1920.* Albuquerque: University of New Mexico Press, 1988.

Hallenbec, Cleve. *The Journey of Fray Marcos de Niza.* Dallas: Southern Methodist University, 1987.

Hanna, Alfred J., and Kathryn A. Hanna. *Napoleon III and Mexico: American Triumph over Monarchy.* Chapel Hill: University of North Carolina Press, 1971.

Hansen, Niles. *The Border Economy; Regional Development in the Southwest.* Austin: University of Texas Press, 1981.

Hansen, Roger D. *The Politics of Mexican Development.* Baltimore: Johns Hopkins University Press, 1971.

Hanson, Victor D. *Carnage and Culture.* New York: Anchor Books, 2001.

Hardin, Stephen L. *Texian Iliad: A Military History of the Texas Revolution, 1835–1836.* Austin: University of Texas Press, 1994.

Harris, Charles H., and Louis R. Sadler, "The Plan of San Diego and the Mexican–United States War Crisis of 1916: A Reexamination." *HAHR* (August 1979): 381–408.

———. *The Texas Rangers and the Mexican Revolution: The Bloodiest Decade, 1910–1920.* Albuquerque: University of New Mexico Press, 2004.

Hart, John M. *Empire and Revolution: The American in Mexico since the Civil War.* Berkeley: University of California Press, 2002.

———. *Revolutionary Mexico: The Coming and Process of the Mexican Revolution.* Berkeley: University of California Press, 1987.

Hatcher, Mattie Austin. *The Opening of Texas to Foreign Settlement, 1801–1821.* Austin: University of Texas Press, 1927. Reprint; Philadelphia: Porcupine Press, 1976.

———, trans. "Texas in 1820." *SWHQ* 23 (July 1919).

Hathaway, Dale. *Allies across the Border.* Cambridge, Mass.: South End Press, 2000.

Haven, Gilbert. *Our Next-Door Neighbor: A Winter in Mexico.* New York: Harper and Brothers, 1975.

Haynes, Sam W. *Soldiers of Misfortune: The Somervell and Mier Expeditions.* Austin: University of Texas Press, 1990.

Hays, Samuel P. *The Response to Industrialism, 1885–1914.* Chicago: University of Chicago Press, 1957.

Heidler, David S., and Jeanne T. Heidler. *Manifest Destiny.* Westport, Conn.: Greenwood Press, 2003.

Henderson, Dwight F. "The Texas Coal Mining Industry." *SWHQ* (October 1964): 207–19.

Henderson, Harry M. "The Magee-Gutiérrez Expedition." *SWHQ* (October 1945): 43–61.

Hendricks, Sterling B. "The Sommervell Expedition to the Rio Grande, 1842." *SWHQ* (October 1919): 112–40.

Henry, Will. *The Texas Rangers.* New York: Random House, 1957.

Henson, Margaret S. *Samuel May Williams: Early Texas Entrepreneurs.* College Station: Texas A&M University Press, 1976.

Herrera Canales, Inés. *El comercio exterior de México, 1821–1875.* Mexico City: El Colegio de México, 1977.

Hester, Thomas. *Digging South Texas Prehistory: A Guide for Amateur Archaeologist.* San Antonio: Corona Press, 1980.

Hickerson, Nancy P. *The Jumanos: Hunters and Traders on the South Plains.* Austin: University of Texas Press, 1994.

Hill, Larry D. *Emissaries to a Revolution: Woodrow Wilson's Executive Agents in Mexico.* Baton Rouge: Louisiana State University Press, 1973.

Hill, Lawrence F. *José de Escandón and the Founding of Nuevo Santander: A Study of Spanish Colonization.* Columbus: Ohio State University Press, 1926.

Hine, Robert V. *Bartlett's West.* New Haven, Conn.: Yale University Press, 1968.

Hinojosa, Gilberto M. *A Borderland Town in Transition: Laredo, 1755–1870.* College Station: Texas A&M University Press, 1983.

Hoberman, Louisa S. *Mexico's Merchant Elite, 1590–1660: Silver, State, and Society.* Durham, N.C.: Duke University Press, 1991.

Hogan, William R. *The Texas Republic: A Social and Economic History.* Austin: University of Texas Press, 1969.

Holley, Mary A. *Texas.* Austin: 1863, 1935.

Honeyman, Callie K. *History of [the] Water Utility: Laredo, Texas.* Laredo: Central Power and Light Company, 1969.

Horgan, Paul. *Great River: The Rio Grande in North American History.* New York: Rinehart and Company, 1954.

Horsman, Reginald. *Race and Manifest Destiny: The Origins of American Racial Anglo-Saxonism,* Cambridge, Mass.: Harvard University Press, 1981.

House, John W. *French on the Rio Grande.* Oxford: Clarendon Press, 1982.

Houston, Andrew Jackson. *The San Jacinto Campaign.* N.p.: 1925.

———. *Texas Independence.* Houston: Anson Jones Press, 1938.

Irby, James A. *Backdoor at Bagdad: The Civil War on the Rio Grande.* El Paso: Texas Western Press, 1977.

———. *Line on the Rio Grande: War and Trade on the Confederate Frontier.* Athens: University of Georgia Press, 1969.

Irish, Marian D. "Foreign Policy and the South." *Journal of Politics* (May 1948): 306–26.

Ivey, James E., Thomas Medlin, and Jack D. Eaton. *An Initial Archeological Assessment of Areas Proposed for Modifications at Fort McIntosh, Webb County, Texas.* Report No. 32, San Antonio: Center for Archeological Research, 1977.

Jackson, Jack. *Los mesteños: Spanish Ranching in Texas, 1721–1821.* College Station: Texas A&M University Press, 1986.

Jackson, Jack, ed. *Texas by Teran [Manuel de Miery Teran].* Austin: University of Texas Press, 2000.

James, Marquis. *The Raven: A Biography of Sam Houston.* New York: Blue Ribbon Books, 1929.

Jenkins, John H., ed. *The Papers of the Texas Revolution, 1835–1836.* Austin: Presidial Press, 1973.

———. *Robert E. Lee on the Rio Grande.* Austin: Jenkins Publishing, 1988.

Jenkins, John H., and Kenneth Kessler. *Edward Burleson: Texas Frontier Leader.* Austin: Jenkins Publishing, 1990.

Jenkins, John S. *History of the War between the United States and Mexico: From the Commencement of Hostilities to the Ratification of the Treaty of Peace.* New York: Auburn, Derby, and Miller, 1851.

Jennings, N. A. *A Texas Ranger.* New York: Charles Scribner's Sons, 1899.

John, Elizabeth A. H. *Storms Brewed in Other Men's Worlds: The Confrontation of Indians, Spanish, and French in the Southwest, 1540–1795.* College Station: Texas A&M University Press, 1975.

Johnson, Benjamin H. *Revolution in Texas.* New Haven, Conn.: Yale University Press, 2003.

Jonas, Rufus, "Laredo—A Texas Gateway." *Texas Magazine,* April 1919, 79–80.

Jones, Oakah L. *Los Paisanos: Spanish Settlers on the Northern Frontier of New Spain.* Norman: University of Oklahoma Press, 1979.

———. *Santa Anna.* New York: 1968.

Jordan, Terry G. *Immigration to Texas.* Boston: American Press, 1981.

———. *North American Cattle-Ranching Frontiers: Origins, Diffusion, and Differentiation.* Albuquerque: University of New Mexico Press, 1993.

———. *Trails to Texas: Southern Roots of Western Cattle Ranching.* Lincoln: University of Nebraska Press, 1981.

Jordon, John. *Serious Actual Dangers of Foreigners and Foreign Commerce in the Mexican States.* Philadelphia: P. M. Lafourcade, 1826.

Jordon, Jonathan W. *Lone Star Navy.* Washington, D.C.: Potomac Books, 2006.

Katz, Friedrich. *The Life and Times of Pancho Villa.* Stanford, Calif.: Stanford University Press, 1998.

Kearney, Milo, and Anthony Knopp. *Border Cuates: A History of the U.S-Mexican Twin Cities.* Austin: Eakin Press, 1995.

Keeler, Karl F. *Study of Occurrence of Floods on the Rio Grande at Laredo, Texas for the 211-year Period—1746 through 1956.* El Paso: IBWC, December 1956.

Kelley, Pat. *River of Lost Dreams: Navigation on the Rio Grande.* Lincoln: University of Nebraska Press, 1986.

Kennedy, Roger G. *Mr. Jefferson's Lost Cause.* New York: Oxford University Press, 2003.

Kennedy, William. *Texas: The Rise, Progress, and Prospects of the Republic of Texas.* 2 vols. London, 1841. Reprint; Fort Worth: Molyneaux Craftsmen, 1925.

Kessell, John L. *Spain in the Southwest.* Norman: University of Oklahoma Press, 2002.

Kinnaird, Lawrence, ed. *The Frontiers of New Spain: Nicolás de Lafora's Description, 1766–1768.* Berkeley, Calif.: Quivira Society, 1958.

Klein, Alan M. *Baseball on the Border: A Tale of Two Laredos.* Princeton, N.J.: Princeton University Press, 1997.

Klein, Maury. *The Life and Legend of Jay Gould.* Baltimore: Johns Hopkins University Press, 1986.

Knight, Alan. *The Mexican Revolution.* 2 vols. Cambridge: Cambridge University Press, 1986.

Kownslar, Allan O. *The European Texans.* College Station: Texas A&M University Press, 2004.

Kupchan, Charles, A. *The End of the American Era.* New York: Vintage, 2002.

La defensa de Nuevo Laredo. Laredo: 1914.

La Vere, David. *The Texas Indians.* College Station: Texas A&M University Press, 2004.

Lamar, Maribeau B. *The Papers of Maribeau Buonaparte Lamar.* Edited by Charles A. Gulick Jr. and Winnie Allen. 6 vols., Austin: 1924.

Lane, Lydia S. *I Married a Soldier: Old Days in the Old Army.* Albuquerque: University of New Mexico Press, 1964.

Lanks, Herbert C. "The Pan American Highway." *Scientific Monthly* (October 1939): 324–36.

Laredo City Directory, 1961. W. J. Winter Publishing, Dallas, 1961.

Laredo Chamber of Commerce. *The Gateway to Mexico: Laredo South Texas.* Laredo: circa 1926.

Laredo: Gateway to Mexico. Laredo: circa 1943.

Laredo Lodge No. 547A. F. & A. M [Centennial History, 1881–1981]. Laredo: December 12, 1981.

Laredo Telephone Directory. Southwestern Bell Telephone Company, Issue No. 27, November 1946.

Laredo, Texas, Directory 1935. C. H. Jackson Directory Co., San Antonio, 1935.

Lea, Tom. *The King Ranch.* Boston: Little, Brown, 1957.

Leal, Guillermo G. *Laredo 250 Years Ago.* Hidalgo, Mexico: Privately published, 2005.

Lehmann, V. M. *Forgotten Legions: Sheep in the Rio Grande Plains of Texas.* El Paso: Texas Western Press, 1969.

Leiby, John S. *Colonial Bureaucrats and the Mexican Economy.* New York: Peter Lang, 1986.

Lindheim, Milton. *The Republic of the Rio Grande: Texans in Mexico, 1839–40* . Waco: W. M. Morrison, 1964.

Linn, John J. *Reminiscences of Fifty Years in Texas.* New York: 1883.

Linsley, Judith W., Ellen W. Rienstra, and JoAnn Stiles. *Giant under the Hill: A History of the Spindletop Oil Discovery.* Austin: TSHA, 2002.

Looney, Robert E. *Economic Policy Making in Mexico: Factors Underlying the 1982 Crisis.* Durham, N.C.: Duke University Press, 1985.

Lott, Virgil N., and Mercurio Martínez. *The Kingdom of Zapata.* San Antonio: Naylor, 1953.

Lott, Virgil N., and Virginia M. Fenwick. *People and Plots on the Rio Grande.* San Antonio: Naylor, 1957.

Ludeman, Annette M. *La Salle County: South Texas Brush Country.* Quanah, Tex.: Nortex Press, 1975.

Madero, Francisco. *La sucesión presidencial.* San Pedro, Coahuila: El Partido Nacional Democrático, 1908.

Mann, Charles C. *1491: New Revolutions of the Americas before Columbus.* New York: Vintage, 2005.

Manning, William R. *Early Diplomatic Relations between the United States and Mexico.* Baltimore: Johns Hopkins University Press, 1916.

———. "Texas and the Boundary Issue, 1822–1829." *SWHQ* (January 1914): 217–61.

Maril, Robert L. *Patrolling Chaos: The U.S. Border Patrol in Deep South Texas.* Lubbock: Texas Tech University Press, 2004.

Martin, J. C, R. J. Hammerstrom, and R. H. Waldrop, "The Laredo Story of Sanitation Progress." *American City* (February 1957): 116–19, 133–36.

Martínez, Adrian. *Adrian: An Autobiography.* Austin: Morgan Printing, 1986.

Martínez, Vidal E. C. *Compendio de historia de Tamaulipas, 1824–1845.* Cuidad Victoria: Gobierno del Estado de Tamaulipas, 1973.

Mathews, P. L. "The Mexican as a Coal Miner." *Coal Age* (August 1917).

May, William. *A Review of the Causes and Consequences of the Mexican War.* Boston: Benjamin B. Mussey, 1849.

Mazza, Jacqueline. *Don't Disturb the Neighbors: The United States and Democracy in Mexico, 1980–1995.* New York: Routledge, 2001.

McAdams, Sibley M. "Charles Stillman: A Case Study of Entrepreneurship on the Rio Grande, 1861–1865." *SWHQ* (October 1973): 227–40.

McAlister, Lyle N. "The Reorganization of the Army of New Spain, 1763–1766." *HAHR* 33 (February 1953): 1–32.

McBride, G. M. *The Land System of Mexico.* New York: 1923.

McCord, Charles R. "The Economy of Laredo." *Texas Business Review* (May 1959): 1–4. Reprint as seen in Laredo Economic Data vertical file, Center to American History, Austin.

McCulloch, Samuel D., and James E. Warren, "A Report on Cultural Resources Investigations at Fort McIntosh, Laredo Webb County, Texas." George West, Tex.: Archaeology Consultants, January 2002.

Medina, Martin. "Informal Transborder Recycling on the U S.-Mexico Border: The *Cartoneros* of Nuevo Laredo." *JBS* (Fall 2001): 19–40.

Meiners, Fredericka. "The Texas Border Cotton Trade, 1862–1863." *Civil War History* (December 1977): 193–206.

Meyer, Lorenzo. *Mexico and the United States in the Oil Controversy, 1917–1942.* Austin: University of Texas Press, 1972.

Meyer, Michael. *Water in the Hispanic Southwest: A Social and Legal History.* Tucson: University of Arizona Press, 1966.

Meyers, William K. "Politics, Vested Rights, and Economic Growth in Porfirian Mexico." *HAHR* (August 1977): 401–24.

Mier y Terén, Manuel. *Texas by Terán: The Diary Kept by General Manuel de Mier y Terán on His 1828 Inspection of Texas.* Edited by Jack Jackson. Austin: University of Texas Press, 2000.

Miller, B. L. "Tertiary Coal Fields of the Rio Grande." *Coal Age* (August 23, 1913): 260–63.

Miller, Edmund T. *A Financial History of Texas.* Austin: University of Texas Press, 1916.

Miller, Hubert J. *José de Escandón: Colonizer of Nuevo Santander.* Edinburg, Tex.: New Santander Press, 1980.

Miller, Hunter, ed. *Treaties and Other International Acts of the United States of America.* 8 vols. Washington: GPO, 1937.

Miller, Thomas L. *The Public Lands of Texas, 1519–1970.* Norman: University of Oklahoma Press, 1972.

Miller, Tom. *On the Border: Portraits of America's Southwestern Frontier.* Tucson: University of Arizona Press, 1981.

Montejano, David. *Anglos and Mexicans in the Making of Texas, 1836–1986.* Austin: University of Texas Press, 1987.

Montell, Jaime. *La caída de México-Tenochtitlán.* Mexico City: Editorial Joaquín Mortiz, 2003.

Mora-Torres, Juan. *The Making of the Mexican Border: The State, Capitalism, and Society in Nuevo León, 1848–1910.* Austin: University of Texas Press, 2001.

Morfi, Juan Agustín. *Excerpts from the Memorias for the History of the Province of Texas.* Translated and edited by Frederick C. Chabot. San Antonio: Privately published, printed by Naylor, 1932.

———. *The History of Texas, 1673–1779.* Translated and edited by Carlos E. Castañeda. 2 vols. Albuquerque, N.Mex.: Quivira Society, 1935.

Moore, Stephen L. *Eighteen Minutes: The Battle of San Jacinto and the Texas Independence Campaign.* Dallas: Republic of Texas Press, 2004.

———. *Savage Frontier.* Plano: Republic of Texas Press, 2002.

Moorhead, Max L. *The Presidio: Bastion of the Spanish Borderlands.* Norman: University of Oklahoma Press, 1975.

Moreno, Joe R., Jr. "The Paso de Jacinto Crossing on the Rio Grande, 1746–2006." *JST* (Fall 2006): 152–64.

Morrow, William W. *Spanish and Mexican Private Land Grants.* San Francisco: Bancroft-Whitney, 1923.

Muir, Andrew F. "Sam Houston and the Civil War." *Texana* (Fall 1968): 282–87.

Mumford, Lewis. *Sticks and Stones: A Study of American Architecture and Civilization.* New York: Boni and Liveright, 1924.

Muncey, Mary E. "The Two Laredos." *Gulf Messenger,* November 1893, 310–16.

Myres, Sandra L. *The Ranch in Spanish Texas, 1691–1800.* El Paso: Texas Western Press, 1969.

———. "The Spanish Cattle Kingdom in the Province of Texas." *Texana* 4 (1966).

Nance, Joseph M. *After San Jacinto: The Texas-Mexican Frontier, 1836–1841.* Austin: University of Texas Press, 1963.

———. *Attack and Counterattack: The Texas-Mexican Frontier, 1842.* Austin: University of Texas Press, 1964.

———. *Dare-Devils All: The Texan Mier Expedition, 1842–1844.* Austin: Eakin Press, 1998.

Naylor, Thomas H., and Charles W. Polzer. *The Presidio and Militia on the Northern Frontier of New Spain.* Tucson: University of Arizona Press, 1986.

Neal, Charles M. *Valor across the Lone Star.* Austin: TSHA, 2002.

Newcomb, W. W., Jr. *The Indians of Texas from Prehistoric to Modern Times.* Austin: University of Texas Press, 1961.

Nofi, Albert A. *The Alamo and the Texas War for Independence.* New York: Da Capo Press, 1992.

Nostrand, Richard L. "Mexican Americans circa 1850." *Annuals of the Association of American Geographers* (September 1975) 378–90.

Nunn, William C. *Texas under the Carpetbaggers.* Austin: University of Texas Press, 1962.
Nuttall, Zelia, trans. "Royal Ordinances Concerning the Laying Out of New Torons." *HAHR* (November 1921): 743–53.
Offutt, Leslie S. *Saltillo, 1770–1810.* Tucson: University of Arizona Press, 2001.
Olien, Diana D., and Roger M. Olien. *Oil in Texas: The Gusher Age, 1895–1945.* Austin: University of Texas Press, 2002.
Olmsted, Frederick Law. *A Journey through Texas; Or, A Saddle-Trip on the Southwestern Frontier.* New York: Dix, Edwards, 1857. Reprint; Austin: University of Texas Press, 1978.
Opie, John. *The Law of the Land.* Lincoln: University of Nebraska Press, 1994.
Osante, Patricia. *Orígines del Nuevo Santander, 1748–1772.* Mexico City: UNAM, 1997.
Owsley, Frank L. *King Cotton Diplomacy: Foreign Relations of the Confederate States of America.* Chicago: University of Chicago Press, 1966.
Pace, Robert F., and Donald F. Frazier. *Frontier Texas: History of a Borderland to 1880.* Abilene: State House Press, 2004.
Padilla, Juan Antonio. "Texas in 1820: Report on the Barbarous Indians of the Province of Texas." Translated by Mattie Austin Hatcher. *SWHQ* (July 1919): 47–68.
Pagès, Pierre-Marie François. *Travels Round the World in the Years 1767, 1768, 1769, 1770, 1771.* Dublin: P. Byrne, 1791.
Park, Joseph F. "Spanish Indian Policy in Northern Mexico, 1765–1810." *Arizona and the West* (Winter 1962): 325–44.
Parkes, Henry B. *A History of Mexico.* Boston: Houghton Mifflin, 1950.
Parkman, Francis. *La Salle and the Discovery of the Great West.* Williamstown, Mass.: Corner House Publishers, 1968.
Parlee, Lorena M. "The Impact of United States Railroad Unions on Organized Labor and Government Policy in Mexico, 1880–1911." *HAHR* (August 1984): 443–75.
Parsons, Chuck. *John B. Armstrong, Texas Ranger and Pioneer Ranchman.* College Station: Texas A&M University Press, 2007.
Parsons, Chuck, and Marianne E. Hall. *Captain L. H. McNelly, Texas Ranger.* Austin: State House Press, 2001.
Patrick, J. Michael. "A Preliminary Assessment of NAFTA's Impact on the Texas Border Economy." *JBS* (Fall 1996): 23–50
———. "The Price of Security: U.S.-Visit, A Preliminary Impact Assessment." *Inlandport* (Laredo) (January 2004): 8–12.
Patrick, J. Michael, and William Renforth. "The Effects of the Peso Devaluation on Cross-Border Retailing." *JBS* (Spring 1996): 25–41.
Paulsen, George E. "Fraud, Honor, and Trade: The United States–Mexico Dispute over Claim of La Abra Company, 1875–1902." *Pacific Historical Review* (May 1983): 175–10.
Payne, Henry M. "A Resume of Twenty-Five Years in Mining." *Mining Congress Journal* (October 1922): 933–37.
Peavy, John R. *Echos from the Rio Grande.* Brownsville: Springman-King, 1963.
Perman, Michael. *Emancipation and Reconstruction 1862–1879.* Arlington Heights, Ill.: Harlan Davidson, 1987.
Perry, Carmen, ed. *The Impossible Dream by the Rio Grande: A Documented Chronicle of the Establishment and Annihilation of San José de Palafox.* San Antonio: St. Mary's University Press, 1971.
Perttula, Timothy K. *The Prehistory of Texas.* College Station: Texas A&M University Press, 2004.
Pickering, David, and Judy Falls. *Brush Men and Vigilantes: Civil War Dissent in Texas.* College Station: Texas A&M University Press, 2000.

Pierce, Frank C. *A Brief History of the Lower Rio Grande Valley.* Menasha, Wis.: George Banta Publishing, 1917.

Pierce, Gerald S. *Texas under Arms: The Camps, Posts, Forts, and Military Towns of the Republic of Texas, 1836–1846.* Austin: Encino Press, 1969.

Pinchon, Edgcumb. *Viva Villa!* New York: Grosset and Dunlap, 1933.

Piñon, Fernando. *Patron Democracy.* Mexico City: Contraste, 1985.

Pletcher, David M. "The Building of the Mexican Railway." *HAHR* 30 (February 1950): 26–62.

———. *The Diplomacy of Annexation: Texas, Oregon, and the Mexican War.* Columbia: University of Missouri Press, 1973.

———. "General William S. Rosecrans and the Mexican Transcontinental Railroad," *Mississippi Valley Historical Review* (March 1952): 657–78.

———. *Rails, Mines, and Progress: Seven American Promoters in Mexico, 1867–1911.* Port Washington, N.Y: Kennikat Press, 1972.

Poinsett, Joel R. *Notes on Mexico: Made in the Autumn of 1822.* New York: Frederick A. Praeger, 1969.

Pomeranz, Kenneth, and Steven Topik. *The World That Trade Created.* New York: M. E. Sharpe, 1999.

Porter, Glenn. *The Rise of Big Business, 1860–1910.* New York: Crowell, 1973.

Porter, Kenneth W. "The Seminole in Mexico, 1850–1861." *HAHR* 31 (February 1951): 1–36.

Powell, Fred W. *Railroads of Mexico.* Boston: Stratford, 1921.

Poyo, Gerald B., and Gilberto M. Hinojosa. "Spanish Texas and Borderlands Historiography in Transition: Implications for United States History." *Journal of American History* (September 1988): 393–416.

Priestley, Herbert L. *José de Gálvez, Visitor-General of New Spain, 1765–1771.* Berkeley: University of California Press, 1916.

Prieto, Alejandro. *Historia, geografía y estadística del Estado de Tamaulipas.* Mexico City: Tip. Escalerillas, 1873.

Purcell, Anita, ed. *Frontier Mexico, 1875–1894: Letters of William L. Purcell.* San Antonio: Naylor, 1963.

Raat, W. Dirk. *Mexico and the United States: Ambivalent Vistas.* Athens: University of Georgia Press, 199

———. *Revoltosos: Mexico's Rebels in the United States, 1903–1923.* College Station: Texas A&M University Press, 1981.2.

Ragsdale, Kenneth B. *Wings over the Mexican Border.* Austin: University of Texas Press, 1984.

Raguct, Condy. *The Principles of Free Trade.* Philadelphia: Privately published, 1840. Reprint; by Augustus M. Kelley, 1969.

Ramírez, José Fernando. *The Mexican Republic 1847.* Translated by Dennis E. Berge. El Paso: Texas Western Press, 1975.

Ramírez Fentanes. Luis. *Zaragoza.* Mexico City: Editorial Stylo, 1962.

Rankin, Melinda. *Texas in 1850.* Boston: Damrell and Noore, 1850.

Rascoe, Jesse. *Texas Lost Mines.* Fort Davis, Tex.: Frontier Book Company, 1974.

Reed, John. *Insurgent Mexico.* New York: International Publishing, 1969.

Reed, S. G. *A History of the Texas Railroads.* Houston: St. Clair Publishing, 1941.

Rees, Peter W. "Origins of Colonial Transportation in Mexico." *Geographical Review* 65, no. 3 (1975): 323–34.

Reeve, Frank D. "The Apache Indians in Texas." *SWHQ* (October 1946): 189–219.

Reports of Cases Argued and Decided in the Supreme Court of the State of Texas. Vol. 3 (1848),

Austin: State Gazette Office, 1851. Vol. 7 (1851–52), Houston: E. H. Cushing, 1883. Vol. 13 (1854–55), Houston: E. H. Cushing, 1876.

Reséndez, Andrés. *A Land So Strange.* New York: Basic Books, 2007.

———. "National Identity on a Shifting Border: Texas and New Mexico in the Age of Transition, 1821–1848." *Journal of American History* 86 (September 1999): 668–88.

Ricardo, David. *The Principle of Political Economy and Taxation.* London: 1817. Reprint; New York: Dover Publications, 2004.

Richardson, Chad. *Botas, Bolillos, Pochos, and Pelados.* Austin: University of Texas Press, 1999.

Richmond, Douglas W. *Venustiano Carranza's Nationalist Struggle, 1893–1920.* Lincoln: University of Nebraska Press, 1983.

———. "Mexican Immigration and Border Strategy during the Revolution, 1910–1920." *New Mexico Historical Review* (July 1982): 269–88.

Riley, Carroll L. *Río del Norte: People of the Upper Rio Grande.* Salt Lake City: University of Utah Press, 1955.

Riley, Carroll L., and Basil C. Hedrick, eds. *Across the Chichimec Sea.* Carbondale: Southern Illinois Press, 1978.

Rippy, I. Fred. "Border Troubles along the Rio Grande, 1848–1860." SWHR (July 1919): 91–111.

———. "The British Investment 'Boom' of the 1880s in Latin America." *HAHR* 29 (May 1949): 281–86.

———. *British Investments in Latin America, 1822–1949.* Minneapolis: University of Minnesota Press, 1959.

———. "Britain's Role in the Early Relations of the United States and Mexico." *HAHR* (1927): 2–24.

———. "The Indians of the Southwest in the Diplomacy of the United States and Mexico, 1848–1853." *HAHR* (August 1919): 363–96.

———. *The United States and Mexico.* New York: Alfred A. Knopf, 1926.

Roberts, Randy, and James S. Olson. *A Line in the Sand.* New York: Free Press, 2001.

Robertson, Brain. *Wild Horse Desert: The Heritage of South Texas.* Edinburg, Tex.: New Santander Press, 1985.

Robinson, William D. *Memoirs of the Mexican Revolution.* 2 vols. London: Macdonald and Son, 1821.

Rock, James L., and W. I. Smith. *Southern and Western Texas Guide, 1878.* St. Louis: A. H. Granger, 1878.

Roe, Frank G. *The Indian and the Horse.* Norman: University of Oklahoma Press, 1955.

Roell, Craig H. *Remember Goliad! A History of La Bahía.* Austin: TSHA, 1994.

Romero, Matías. *Geographical and Statistical Notes on Mexico.* New York: G. P. Putman, 1898.

———. *Mexico and the United States.* 2 vols. New York: G. P. Putnam, 1898.

———. *Railways in Mexico.* Washington, D.C.: Printed by W. H. Moore, 1882.

Ross, Stanley R. *Francisco I. Madero: Apostle of Mexican Democracy.* New York: Columbia University Press, 1955.

Rouse, John E. *The Criollo: Spanish Cattle in the Americas.* Norman: University of Oklahoma Press, 1977.

Roy, Janet, "The Life and Times of Minera, Texas," *SWHQ* 49 (April 1946): 510–17.

Rozek, Barbara J. *Come to Texas: Enticing Immigrants, 1865–1915.* College Station: Texas A&M University Press, 2003.

Rubel, Arthur J. *Across the Tracks: Mexican-Americans in a Texas City.* Austin: University of Texas Press, 1966.

Ruiz, Ramón E. *The Great Rebellion, Mexico 1905–1924.* New York: W. W. Norton, 1980.
Salinas, Martin. *Indians of the Rio Grande Delta: Their Role in the History of Southern Texas and Northwestern Mexico.* Austin: University of Texas Press, 1990.
Salvucci, Richard J. "The Origins and Progress of U.S-Mexican Trade, 1825–1884: 'Hoc opus, hic labor est." *HAHR* 71 (November 1991): 697–735.
———. *Textiles and Capitalism in Mexico: An Economic History of the Obrajes, 1539–1840.* Princeton, N.J.: Princeton University Press, 1987.
Samponaro, Frank, and Paul J. Underwood. *War Scare on the Rio Grande: Robert Runyon's Photographs of the Border Conflict, 1913–1916.* Austin: TSHA, 1992.
Sánchez, José María. "A Trip to Texas in 1828." Translated by Carlos R. Castañeda. *SWHQ* 29 (April 1926): 249–89.
Sanchez, Mario L., ed. *A Shared Experience: The History, Architecture and Historic Designations of the Lower Rio Grande Heritage Corridor.* Austin: Texas Historical Commission, 1991.
Sánchez Lamego, Miguel A. *The Second Mexican-Texas War, 1841–1843.* Hillsboro, Tex.: Hill Junior College Press, 1972.
Sanchez, Ramiro. *Frontier Odyssey: Early Life in a Texas Spanish Town.* Austin: Jenkins Publishing, 1981.
Sandos, James A. *Rebellion in the Borderlands: Anarchism and the Plan of San Diego, 1904–1923.* Norman: University of Oklahoma Press, 1992.
Santleben, August. *A Texas Pioneer: Early Staging and Overland Freighting Days on the Frontiers of Texas and Mexico.* New York: Neale Publishing, 1910.
Saragoza, Alex M. *The Monterrey Elites and the Mexican State, 1880–1940.* Austin: University of Texas Press, 1988.
Schell, William. "Money as Commodity: Mexico's Conversion to the Gold Standard, 1905." *MS/EM* (Winter 1996): 67–89.
Schmidt, Arthur. *The Social and Economic Effects of the Railroad in Puebla and Veracruz, Mexico, 1867–1911.* New York: Garland, 1987.
Schmitz, E. J. "Geology and Mineral Resources of the Rio Grande Region in Texas and Coahuila." *Transactions of the American Institute of Mining Engineers* (1885): 388–405.
Scholes, Walter V. "Mexico in 1896 as Viewed by an American Consul." *HAHR* 30 (May 1950): 250–57.
Schoonover, Thomas D., ed. *Mexican Lobby: Matías Romero in Washington, 1861–1867.* Lexington: University Press of Kentucky, 1986.
———. *A Mexican View of America in the 1860s: A Foreign Diplomat Describes the Civil War and Reconstruction.* Rutherford, N.J.: Fairleigh Dickinson University Press, 1991.
Scott, Florence J. *Historical Heritage of the Lower Rio Grande.* Waco: Texian Press, 1966.
———. *Royal Land Grants North of the Rio Grande, 1777–1821.* Waco: Texian Press, 1969.
Sepúlveda, César. *La frontera norte: Historia y conflictos, 1762–1975.* Mexico City: Editorial Porrúa, 1976.
Shanks, Ann. *Laredo Reflections.* Laredo: Velia E. Uribe, 1985.
Shaw, J. H. "How Many Bison Originally Populated Western Rangelands?" *Rangelands* 17, no. 5 (1995): 148–50.
Sheridan, P. H. *Personal Memoirs of P. H. Sheridan.* 2 vols. New York: Charles L. Webster, 1888.
Shields, David. *Pemex: Un futuro incierto.* Mexico City: Temas de Hoy, 2003.
Sibley, Marilyn McAdams. "Charles Stillman: A Case Study of Entrepreneurship on the Rio Grande, 1861–1865." *SWHQ* (October 1973): 227–40.
———. *Travelers in Texas, 1761–1860.* Austin: University of Texas Press, 1967.

Silbey, Joel H. *Storm over Texas: The Annexation Controversy and the Road to the Civil War.* New York: Oxford University Press, 2005.

Sloan John W., and Jonathan P. West. "Community Integration and Policies among Elites in Two Border Cities: Los Dos Laredo." *Journal of Interamerican Studies and World Affairs* (November 1976): 451–74.

Smith, Adam. *The Wealth of Nations.* London: March 8, 1776. Reprint; New York: Bantam Dell, 2003.

Smith, Jean B. *Grant.* New York: Simon and Schuster, 2001.

Smith, Justin H. *The Annexation of Texas,* New York: Baker and Taylor, 1911.

———. "La República de Rio Grande." *AHR* (June 1928): 660–75.

———. *The War with Mexico.* 2 vols. New York: Macmillan, 1919.

Smith, Ralph A. "Indians in American-Mexican Relations before the War of 1846." *HAHR* 43 (February 1963): 34–64.

Smith, Robert S. "Sales Taxes in New Spain, 1575–1770." *HAHR* 28 (February 1948): 2–37.

Smith, Thomas T. *The Old Army in Texas.* Austin: TSHA, 2000.

———. *The U.S. Army and the Texas Frontier Economy, 1845–1900.* College Station: Texas A&M University Press, 1999.

Smither, Harriet, ed. *The Papers of Mirabeau Buonaparte Lamar.* Austin: Texas State Library, 1927.

Smithwick, Noah. *The Evolution of a State.* Austin: Gammel, 1900. Reprint; Austin: Steck-Vaughn, 1968.

Sonnichsen, C. L. *I'll Die before I Run: The Story of the Great Feuds of Texas.* New York: Harper, 1951.

———. *Pass of the North: Four Centuries on the Rio Grande.* El Paso: Texas Western Press, 1968.

———. *Ten Texas Fueds.* Albuquerque: University of New Mexico Press, 1957.

Spratt, John S. *The Road to Spindletop: Economic Change in Texas, 1875–1901.* Austin: University of Texas Press, 1955.

Stampp, Kenneth M. *The Era of Reconstruction, 1865–1877.* New York: Vintage Books, 1967.

Stanislawski, Dan. "Early Spanish Town Planning." *Geographical Review* 37 (1947): 101–109.

Steen, Ralph W. *Twentieth-Century Texas.* Austin: Speck, 1942.

Stein, Stanley, and Barbara H. Stein. *The Colonial Heritage of Latin America.* New York: Oxford University Press, 1970.

Stephenson, Anders. *Manifest Destiny: American Expansion and the Empire of Right.* New York: Hill and Wang, 1995.

Stephenson, Nathaniel W. *Texas and the Mexican War.* Toronto: Glasgow, Brook, 1971.

Stern, Alexandra M. "Buildings, Boundaries, and Blood: Medicalization and Nation-Building on the U.S.-Mexico Border, 1910–1930." *HAHR* (February 1999): 41–81.

Stevens, John A. *The Valley of the Rio Grande: Its Topography and Resources.* New York: William C. Bryant & Co., 1864.

Stiff, Edward. *The Texan Emigrant.* Cincinnati: George Conclin, 1840. Reprint; Waco: Texian Press, 1968.

Stillman, Chauncey D. *Charles Stillman, 1810–18 75.* New York: C. D. Stillman, 1956.

Summers, Mark W. *Railroads, Reconstruction, and the Gospel of Prosperity.* Princeton, N.J.: Princeton University Press, 1984.

Swanton, John R. *The Indian Tribes of North America,* Washington, D.C.: GPO, 1952.

Sweet, Alexander E., and John Armoy Knox. *On a Mexican Mustang through Texas: From the Gulf to the Rio Grande.* Hartford, Conn.: S. S. Scranton, 1883.

Tarver, E. R. [Laredo Immigration Society]. *Laredo: The Gateway between the United States and Mexico: An illustrated Description of the Future City of the Great Southwest.* Laredo: Daily Times Print, 1889.

Taylor, Paul S. *An American-Mexican Frontier: Nueces County, Texas.* Chapel Hill: University of North Carolina Press, 1934.

Taylor, Virginia H. *Index to Spanish and Mexican Land Grants in Texas.* Austin: Lone Star Press, 1974.

———. *The Spanish Archives of the General Land Office of Texas.* Austin: Lone Star Press, 1955.

Texas: A Guide to the Lone Star State. Austin: Texas State Highway Commission, 1940.

Texas Almanac for 1857. Galveston: Richardson, 1856.

Texas Almanac. Galveston, 1860.

Texas Highway Commission. *A Plan for Highway Development: Laredo.* Austin, January 1956.

Texas—Laredo—Mexico. Laredo: circa 1931. [Visitors' Guide.]

Texas Scrap Book. Compiled by A. C. Naker, New York: A. S. Barnes, 1875.

Thomas, Alfred B. *Forgotten Frontiers.* Norman: University of Oklahoma Press, 1932.

Thompson, Jerry D. *Juan Cortina and the Texas-Mexico Frontier, 1859–1877.* El Paso: Texas Western Press, 1994.

———. *Laredo: A Pictorial History.* Norfolk: Donning, 1986.

———. *Mexican Texans in the Union Army.* El Paso: Texas Western Press, 1986.

———. *Sabers on the Rio Grande.* Austin: Presidial Press, 1974.

———. *Two Hundred Eighty-Three Days: The Republic of the Rio Grande.* Laredo: Laredo Junior College, 1985.

———. *Vaqueros in Blue and Gray.* Austin: Presidial Press, 1977.

———. *Warm Weather and Bad Whiskey.* El Paso: Texas Western Press, 1991.

———. *Wild and Vivid Land: An Illustrated History of the South Texas Border.* Austin: TSHA, 1997.

Thompson, Jerry D., ed. *Fifty Miles and a Fight: Major Samuel P. Heintzelman's Journal of Texas and the Cortina War.* Austin: TSHA, 1998.

———. *Texas and Mexico on the Eve of the Civil War.* Albuquerque: University of New Mexico Press, 2001.

———. *Westward the Texans.* El Paso: Texas Western Press, 1990.

Thompson, Jerry D., and Lawrence T. Jones. *Civil War and Revolution on the Rio Grande Frontier,* Austin: TSHA, 2004.

Thonhoff, Robert H. "The First Ranch of Texas." West Texas Historical Association *Yearbook* 40 (October 1964).

Tijerina, Andrés. *Tejano Empire: Life on the South Texas Ranches.* College Station: Texas A&M University Press, 1998.

———. *Tejanos and Texas under the Mexican Flag, 1821–1836.* College Station: Texas A&M University Press, 1994.

Tischendorf Alfred. *Great Britain and Mexico in the Era of Porfirio Díaz.* Durham, N.C.: Duke University Press, 1961.

Tjarks, Alicia V. "Comparative Demographic Analysis of Texas, 1777–1793." *SWHQ* (January 1974): 322–34.

Trelease, Allen W. "Who Were the Scalawags?" *Journal of Southern History* (November 1963): 445–68.

Treviño, Gilberto S. *From the Pescadito to the Pentagon.* San Antonio: Lobo Creek Publishers, 2006.

True, C. Allen. "British Loans to the Mexican Government, 1822–1832." *Southwest Social Science Quarterly* (1937): 353–62.

Tuchman, Barbara. *The Zimmermann Telegram.* New York: Viking Press, 1958.

Tyler, Ron C. "Cotton on the Border, 1861–1865." *SWHQ* (April 1970): 456–77.

———. "Santiago Vidaurri and the Confederacy." *Americas* (1969): 66–79.

———. *Santiago Vidaurri and the Southern Confederacy.* Austin: TSHA, 1973.

Tyler, Ron C., et al., eds. *The New Handbook of Texas.* Austin: TSHA, 1996.

Tyson, Carl L. "Texas Men for War: Cotton for Economy." *Journal of the West* (January 1975): 130–48.

Ugarteche, Óscar. *The False Dilemma—Globalization: Opportunity or Threat?* London: Zed Books, 1997.

Utley, Robert M. *Frontier Regulars: The United States Army and the Indians, 1866–1890.* New York: Macmillan, 1973.

Valerio-Jiménez, Omar S. "Neglected Citizens and Willing Traders: The Villas del Norte (Tamaulipas) in Mexico's Northern Borderlands, 1749–1846." *MS/EM* (Summer 2002): 251–96.

Van Young, Eric. *The Other Rebellion: Popular Violence, Ideology, and the Mexican Struggle for Independence, 1810–1821.* Stanford, Calif.: Stanford University Press, 2001.

Vázquez, Josefina Z. "La supuesta República del Rio Grande," *Historia Mexicana* 36, no, 1 (July–September 1986): 49–60.

Vázquez, Josefina Z., and Lorenzo Meyer. *The United States and Mexico.* Chicago: University of Chicago Press, 1985.

Velascos, Jesús A. *Impact of Mexican Oil Policy.* 1983.

Vellinga, Menno. "The Monterrey Industry and North American Market: Past and Present Dynamics." *JBS* (Spring 1995): 45–52.

Ver Steeg, Clarence L. *The Formative Years, 1607–1763.* New York; Hill and Wang, 1964.

Vernon, Raymond. *The Dilemma of Mexico Development.* Cambridge, Mass.: Harvard University Press, 1965.

Viele, Egbert L. "Our Southern Frontier: The East and West Boundary Line between the United States and Mexico." *Frank Leslie's Popular Monthly* (June 1878): 724–34.

Vignes, David M. "Indian Raids on the Lower Rio Grande, 1836–1837." *SWHQ* (July 1955) 14–23

———. *Lone Star Justice.* New York: Berkeley Books, 2002.

———. "Relations of the Republic of Texas and the Republic of the Rio Grande." *SWHQ* (January 1954): 312–21.

———. "La República del Río Bravo." In *Sobretivo de Humanitos* No. 13, 395–407. Monterrey: Universidad Autónoma de Nuevo León, 1972.

———. "A Texas Expedition into Mexico, 1840." *SWHQ* (July 1958): 18–28.

Vignes, David M., ed. "Nuevo Santander in 1795: A Provincial Inspection by Félix Calleja." *SWHQ* (April 1972): 461–506.

Villalpando, José M., and Alejandro Rosas. *Historia de México a través de sus gobernantes.* Mexico City: Planeta, 2003.

A Visit to Texas: Being the Journal of a Traveler through Those Parts Most Interesting to American Settlers. New York: Van Nostrand and Dwight, 1836. Reprint; Austin: Steck, 1952.

Vizcaya Canales, Isidro. *Los orígenes de la industrializatión de Monterrey, 1867–1920.* Monterrey: 1969.

Walbarger, J. M. *Indian Depredations in Texas.* Austin: Hutchings Printing House, 1889.

Wallace, Ernest, ed. *Documents of Texas History.* Austin: Steck, 1963.

Wallace, Ernest, and E. Adamson Hoebel. *The Comanches: Lords of the South Plains.* Norman: University of Oklahoma Press, 1952.
Wallace, William H. "The Bridge Line: A Distinctive Type of Anglo-American Railroad." *Economic Geography* (January 1965): 8–13.
Walsh, Anne, "Laredo 'Grows Out of Its Socks.'" *Info* [Union Pacific Railroad] (Fall 1999): 3–7.
Ward, H. G. *Mexico in 1827.* 2 vols. London: Henry Colburn, 1928.
Ward, Peter M. *Colonias and Public Policy in Texas and Mexico: Urbanization by Stealth.* Austin: University of Texas Press, 1999.
Warner, C. W. "Texas and the Oil Industry." *SWHQ* (July 1946): 1–24.
Warren, Harris Gaylord. *The Sword Was Their Passport: A History of American Filibustering in the Mexican Revolution.* Baton Rouge: Louisiana State University Press, 1943.
Warren, James E. *Archeological Investigations at Agustin Catholic Church in Laredo, Texas.* Report No. 217, George West, Texas, 1991.
———. *Los quemados: Archeological Testing at the City of Laredo.* Report No. 545, Georgetown, Texas Antiquities Commission, 1986.
———. *San Agustin Catholic Church in Laredo, Texas: An Inventory and Annotated Catalogue of Extant Volumes in the Church Archives.* Report No. 219, George West, Texas, 1990.
Washington Birthday Celebration [Laredo]. "Official Program 49th Annual Celebration." Laredo, February 20–24, 1946.
———. "Official Souvenir Program 17th Annual Celebration." Laredo: February 12–23, 1916.
Waters, Carl. *Webb County: Evolution and Change, 1880–2000.* N.p., circa 2002.
Webb County Historical Commission. *Su vida y su espíritu: Webb County Family Histories.* San Antonio: Borderlands Press, 1982.
Webb, Walter Prescott. *The Great Plains.* New York: Grosset and Dunlap, 1931.
———. *The Texas Rangers.* 1935. Reprint; Austin: University of Texas Press, 1980.
Weber, David J. *The Mexican Frontier, 1821–1846.* Albuquerque: University of New Mexico Press 1982.
———. "Mexico's Far Northern Frontier, 1821–1854: Historiography Askew." *Western Historical Quarterly* (July 1976): 279–93.
———. *The Spanish Frontier in North America.* New Haven, Conn.: Yale University Press, 1992.
Weber, David J., ed. *Foreigners in Their Native Land: Historical Roots of the Mexican Americans.* Albuquerque: University of New Mexico Press, 1973.
———. *New Spain's Far Northern Frontier.* Dallas: Southern Methodist University Press, 1979.
Weddle, Robert S. *The French Thorne: Rival Explorers in the Spanish Era, 1682–1762.* College Station: Texas A&M University Press, 1991.
———. *San Juan Bautista: Gateway to Spanish Texas.* Austin: University of Texas Press, 1968.
———. *Spanish Sea: The Gulf of Mexico in American Discovery, 1500–1685.* College Station: Texas A&M University Press, 1985.
———. *Wilderness Manhunt: The Spanish Search for La Salle.* Austin: University of Texas Press, 1973.
Weeks, O. Douglas. "The Texas-Mexican and the Politics of South Texas," *American Political Science Review* 24, no. 3 (August 1930): 606–27.
Weinberg, Albert K. *Manifest Destiny.* Chicago: Quadrangle Books, 1963.

Weintraub, Sidney. *Industrial Strategy and Planning in Mexico and the United States.* Boulder, Colo.: Westview Press, 1986.

Weisman, A. *Frontera: The United States Border with Mexico.* San Diego: Harcourt Press, 1986.

Wellman, Paul I. *The Callaghan, Yesterday and Today.* Encinal, Tex.: Callaghan Land and Pastoral Co., 1949.

———. *The Trampling Herd: The Story of the Cattle Range in America.* 1951. Reprint; New York: Cooper Square Publishers, 1974.

Welsome, Eileen. *The General and the Jaguar.* New York: Little, Brown, 2006.

West, Elizabeth, ed. and trans. "Diary of José Bernardo Gutiérrez de Lara. *AHR* 34 (October 1938–January 1939).

West, Robert C. *The Mining Community in Northern New Spain: The Parral Mining District.* Berkeley: University of California Press, 1949.

Westgate, James W. *After the Dinosaurs: A Texas Tropical Paradise Recovered at Lake Casa Blanca.* Austin: Texas Parks and Wildlife Press, 1999. 9–25.

Whitaker, Arthur P., "The Spanish Contribution to American Agriculture." *Agricultural History* (January 1929): 1–14.

Whitehead, Don. *Border Guard.* New York: Avon, 1964.

Wilbarger, John W. *Indian Depredations in Texas: Reliable Accounts of Battles, Wars, Adventures, Forays, Murders, Massacres, Etc. Etc., Together with Biographical Sketches of Many of the Most Noted Indian Fighters and Frontiersmen of Texas.* Austin: Hutchings, 1889. Reprint; Austin: Pemberton, 1967.

Wilcox, Sebron S. "The Laredo City Election and Riot of April, 1886." *SWHQ* (July 1941): 1–23.

———. "Spanish Archives of Laredo." *SWHQ* 49 (January 1946).

———, and Carmen Perry, eds. *Spanish Archives of Laredo.* San Antonio: St. Mary's University, 2005.

Wilkinson, J. B. *Laredo and the Rio Grande Frontier.* Austin: Jenkins Publishing, 1975.

———. "Laredo during the Texas Republic." *SWHQ* (October 1938): 83–107.

William, J. J. *The Isthmus of Tehuantepec.* New York: D. Appleton, 1852.

Williams, J. W. *The Big Ranch Country.* Lubbock: Texas Tech Press, 1999.

Wilson, Patricia A. "The Global Assembly Industry: Maquiladoras in International Perspective." *JBS* 6 (Fall 1991): 73–105.

Winders, R. Bruce. *Crisis in the Southwest: The United States, Mexico, and the Struggle over Texas.* Wilmington, Del.: SR Books, 2002.

———. *Mr. Polk's Army.* College Station: Texas A&M University Press, 1997.

Winfrey, Dorman H., and James M. Day, eds. *The Indian Papers of Texas and the Southwest, 1825–1916.* 5 vols. Austin: TSHA, 1995.

Winkler, E. W., ed. *Manuscript Letters and Documents of Early Texas, 1821–1845.* Austin: Steck, 1937.

Wisehart, M. K. *Sam Houston: American Giant.* Washington, D.C.: Robert B. Luce, 1962.

Womack, John. *Zapata and the Mexican Revolution.* New York: Vintage, 1968.

Wood, Robert D. *Life in Laredo.* Denton: University of North Texas Press, 2004.

Woodman, David, Jr. *Guide to Texas Emigrants.* Boston: M. Hawes, 1835. Reprint; Waco: Texian Press, 1974.

Woodman, Lyman L. *Cortina: Rogue of the Rio Grande.* San Antonio: Naylor, 1950.

Woodward, Ralph L., Jr. *Here and There in Mexico: Travel Writings of Mary Ashley Townsend.* Tuscaloosa: University of Alabama Press, 2001.

Wooster, Ralph A. "Texas Military Operations against Mexico, 1842–1843." *SWHQ* (April 1964): 465–84.

Worcester, Don. *The Texas Longhorn: Relic of the Past, Asset for the Future.* College Station: Texas A&M University Press, 1994.

Wortham, Louis J. *A History of Texas.* 3 vols. Ft. Worth: Wortham-Molyneaux, 1924.

Wyman, Sherman M., and Ernest J. Gerlach. *Local Economic Development in Texas and Strategies for the South Texas Region.* San Antonio: Center for Economic Development, 1994.

Yafa, Stephen. *Big Cotton: How a Humble Fiber Created Fortunes.* New York: Viking, 2005.

Yoakum, Henderson. *History of Texas, 1685–1846.* New York: Redfield, 1956.

Young, Elliott. "Deconstructing *La Raza:* Identifying the *Gente Decente* of Laredo, 1904–1911." *SWHQ* (October 1994): 224–59.

———. "Red Men, Princess Pocahontas, and George Washington: Harmonizing Race Relationships in Laredo at the Turn of the Century." *WHQ* (Spring 1998): 48–85.

Zorrilla, Juan F., Maribel Miró Flaquer, Octavio Herrera Pérez. *Tamaulipas: Una historia compartida, 1810–1921.* Ciudad Victoria: Universidad Autónoma de Tamaulipas, 1993.

Zorilla, Luis. *Historia de las relaciones entre Mexico y los Estados Unidos de América, 1800–1958.* 2 vols. Mexico City: Editorial Porrúa, 1965.

Zurita, Alonso de. *The Lords of New Spain.* London: Phoenix House, 1963.

Manuscripts, Dissertations, and Typescripts

Adams, John A. "The Jewel of Laredo: Restoration of the Webb County Courthouse." Unpublished manuscript, Laredo, May 2, 1995.

Alonzo, Armando C. "Tejano Rancheros and Changes in Land Tenure, Hidalgo County, Texas, 1848–1900." Ph.D. diss., Indiana University, 1991.

Bennett, Catherine. "The History of Education in Laredo, Texas to 1870." Master's thesis, University of Texas, August 1939.

Blanton, Burt C. "Industrial and Economic Survey of the City of Laredo and Webb County, Texas." Dallas, Texas, report for CP&L, July 1, 1928.

Brown, Harold Owen. "The Building of the Texas-Mexican Railroad." Master's thesis, Texas A&I University, 1937.

Brown, Maury B. "The Military Defense of Texas and the Rio Grande Region, about 1766." Master's thesis, University of Texas, August 1924.

Byfield, Patsy J. "The Building of Falcon Dam and Relocation of Five Communities in Zapata County, Texas." Master's thesis, University of Texas, 1966.

Calderon, Robert R. "Mexican Politics in the American Era, 1846–1900: Laredo, Texas." Ph.D. diss., University of California, Los Angeles, 1993.

———. "The Texas and Coahuila Coal Industries, 1880s to 1920s: A History of Mexican Coal Mining Labor." Master's thesis, University of California, Los Angeles, 1983.

Christian, Asa K. "The Tariff History of the Republic of Texas." Master's thesis, University of Texas, June 1917.

Cocke, Ione. "Texas and the Federal Tariff." Master's thesis, University of Texas, June 1921.

Cowling, Annie. "The Civil War Trade of the Lower Rio Grande Valley." Master's thesis, University of Texas, August 1926.

Crawford, Polly Pearl. "The Beginnings of Spanish Settlement in the Lower Rio Grande Valley." Master's thesis, University of Texas, August 1925.

Crisp, James E. "Anglo-Texas Attitudes toward the Mexican, 1821–1845." Ph.D. diss., Yale University, May 1976.

Cuéllar, Carlos E. "The House of Armengol: Doing Business on the Rio Grande Border, 1881–1939." Master's thesis, Laredo State University, December 1990.

Cuello, José. "Saltillo in the Seventeenth Century: Local Society on the North Mexican Frontier." Ph.D. diss., University of California, 1981.

Da Camara, Kathleen. "The History of the City of Laredo." Master's thesis, Denton, College of Arts and Industries, August 1944.

Davids, Jules. "American Political and Economic Penetration of Mexico, 1877–1920." Ph.D. diss., Georgetown University, April 1947.

Denney, John R. "Santos Benavides: His Influence on the Lower Rio Grande, 1823–1891." Ph.D. diss., Texas Christian University, 1976.

Downs, Fane. "The History of Mexicans in Texas, 1820–1845." Ph.D. diss., Texas Tech University, August 1970.

Dunn, Fabius. "The Administration of Don Antonio Cordero, Governor of Texas, 1805–1808." Ph.D. diss., University of Texas, August 1962.

Gallegos, Juan José. "'Last Drop of My Blood' Col. Antonio Zapata: A Life and Times on Mexico's Rio Grande Frontier, 1797–1840." Master's thesis, University of Houston, December 2005.

Gannett, William B. "The American Invasion of Texas, 1820–1845: Patterns of Conflict between Settlers and Indians." Ph.D. diss., Cornell University, 1984.

García, Rogelia O. "A History of the Catholic Church in Laredo." Master's thesis, Denton, College of Arts and Industries, August 1953.

González, María del Refugio. "The Spanish Folklore of Webb and Zapata Counties." Master's thesis, University of Texas, 1952.

Graf, LeRoy P. "The Economic History of the Lower Rio Grande Valley, 1820–1875." Ph.D. thesis, Harvard University, 1942.

Gray, Ronald N. "Edmund J. Davis: Radical Republican and Reconstruction Governor of Texas." Ph.D. diss., Texas Tech University, August 1976.

Green, Stanley. "The Texas Mexican Railway." Undated manuscript, Special Collections, Laredo Public Library.

Hale, Duane K. "Prospecting and Mining on the Texas Frontier." Ph.D. diss., Oklahoma State University, July 1977.

Harris, Charles H. "A Mexican Latifundio: The Economic Empire of the Sánchez Navarro Family, 1765–1821." Ph.D. diss., University of Texas, 1968.

Hedgepeth, Donald R. "The Plan of San Diego: A Border Conspiracy." Master's thesis, Southwest Texas State College, 1969.

Hinojosa, Gilberto M. "Settlers and Sojourners in the Chaparral: A Demographic Study of a Borderlands Town in Transition, Laredo, 1755–1870," Ph.D. diss., University of Texas, May 1979.

John Armengol Onion Farm. Laredo, n.d.

McArthur, Daniel E. "The Cattle Industry of Texas, 1865–1918." Master's thesis, University of Texas, 1918.

McClung, John B. "Texas Rangers along the Rio Grande, 1910–1919." Ph.D. diss., Texas Christian University, 1981.

McCray, John P. "NAFTA Trade Corridors: U.S.-Mexico Rivers of Trade." San Antonio: Unpublished manuscript, 1996.

Medina, Martín. "Scavenging on the Border: A Study of the Informal Recycling Sector in Laredo, Texas and Nuevo Laredo, Mexico." Ph.D. diss., Yale University, 1997.

Meier, Matthias S. "History of the Tehuantepec Railroad." Ph.D. diss., University of California, 1954.

Moreno, Joe R. "An Indian Ford in Laredo: El Paso de Jacinto, 1746–2005." Unpublished manuscript, Laredo Special Collections, Laredo, May 15, 2005.

Murillo, Hermelinda A. "A History of Webb County." Master's thesis, Southwest Texas State Teachers College, August 1941.

Myres, Sandra Lynn. "The Development of the Ranch as a Frontier Institution in the Spanish Province of Texas, 1691–1800." Ph.D. diss., Texas Christian University, 1967.

O'Neal, John W. "Texas 1791–1835: A Study in Manifest Destiny." Master's thesis, East Texas State University, 1969.

Price, Anne B. "The Diplomacy between the United States and Mexico Growing Out of the Mexican Free Zone, 1858–1905." Master's thesis, University of Texas, August 1923.

Purcell, Allan R. "The History of the Texas Militia, 1835–1903." Ph.D. diss., University of Texas, August 1981.

Rakolta, George. "Robert E. Lee in Texas . . . Revisited." Unpublished manuscript, n.p., March 2003.

Ramírez, Nora F. "The Vaquero and Ranching in the Southwestern United States, 1600–1970." Ph.D. diss., Indiana University, 1978.

Ramos, Raúl. "From Norteño to Tejano: The Roots of Borderlands Ethnicity, Nationalism, and Political Identity in Bexar, 1811–1861." Ph.D. diss., Yale University, 2000.

Ramsdell, Charles William, Jr. "Spanish Goliad." Typescript. University of Texas Archives, Austin.

Rickard, John A. "The Cattle Ranch Industry of the Texas South Plains." Master's thesis, University of Texas, 1927.

Riley, John D. "Santos Benavidas: His Influence on the Lower Rio Grande, 1823–1891." Ph.D. diss., University of Oklahoma.

Rocha, Rodolfo. "The Influence of the Mexican Revolution on the Mexico-Texas Border, 1910–1916." Ph.D. diss., Texas Tech University, May 1981.

Sánchez, Ramiro. "History of Banking along the Rio Grande." Master's thesis, Rutgers University, June 1954.

———. "Memories: A History of the Laredo National Bank." N.p., 1987.

Sandos, James A. "The Mexican Revolution and the United States, 1915–1917: The Impact of Conflict in the Tamaulipas-Texas Frontier upon the Emergence of Revolutionary Government in Mexico." Ph.D. diss., University of California, Berkeley, 1978.

Sjearer, Ernest C. "Border Diplomatic Relations between the United States and Mexico, 1848–1890." Ph.D. diss., University of Texas, 1939.

Tandron, Humberto. "The Commerce of New Spain and the Free Trade Controversy." Master's thesis, University of Texas, 1961.

Terry, Thomas E. "A Survey and Proposed Plan for the Reorganization of the Public Schools of Webb County, Texas." Master's thesis, University of Texas, 1943.

Tijerina, Andrew Anthony. "Tejanos and Texas: The Native Mexicans of Texas, 1820–1850." Ph.D. diss., University of Texas, 1977.

Turner, Oreta. *Border Tensions along the Rio Grande from 1848–1878.* Master's thesis, East Texas Teachers College (Texas A&M Commerce), Commerce.

Valerio-Jiménez, Omar S. "*Indios Bárbaros,* Divorcées, and Flocks of Vampires: Identity and Nation on the Rio Grande, 1749–1894." Ph.D. diss., University of California, Los Angeles, 2001.

Vigness, David M. "The Lower Rio Grande Valley, 1836–1846." Master's thesis, University of Texas, 1948.

———. "Republic of the Rio Grande: An Example of Separation in Northern Mexico." Ph.D. diss., University of Texas, 1951.

Walsh, Natalie. "The Founding of Laredo and St. Augustine Church." Master's thesis, University of Texas, 1935.

Walters, Paul H. "Survey of the History of La Bahía de Espíritu Santo, 1721–1821." Master's thesis, University of Texas, 1944.

Webster, Michael G. "Texan Manifest Destiny and the Mexican Border Conflict, 1865–1880." Ph.D. diss., Indiana University, 1972.

Wilson, Maurine T. "Philip Nolan and His Activities in Texas." Master's thesis, University of Texas, 1932.

Worley, Alicia C. "The Life of John Anthony Valls." Master's thesis, Texas A&I University, 1937.

Wright, Robert E. "Popular and Official Religiosity: A Theoretical Analysis and a Case Study of Laredo–Nuevo Laredo, 1755–1857." Ph.D. diss., Berkeley, Graduate Theological Union, 1992.

Zamora, Emilio. "Mexican Labor Activity in South Texas, 1900–1920." Ph.D. diss., University of Texas, 1983.

INDEX